Managing the Tourist Destination

Also available from Continuum

Urban Tourism – Chris Law
Tourism Marketing – Eric Laws

Managing the Tourist Destination

Frank Howie

continuum
LONDON · NEW YORK

Continuum

The Tower Building	370 Lexington Avenue
11 York Road	New York
London SE1 7NX	NY 10017–6503

It cannot be guaranteed that all the website addresses provided in the text are currently available, due to the very nature of the world wide web. However, all sites were active at the time of their consultation.

British Library Cataloguing-in-Publication Data
A catalogue record for this book is available from the British Library.

ISBN 0–8264–4830–5 (hardback)
    0–8264–4831–3 (paperback)

Typeset by YHT Ltd, London
Printed and bound by Bookcraft (Bath) Ltd, Midsomer Norton, Bath

310849

CONTENTS

PREFACE

This book is intended to be a guide to understanding the nature of tourism destinations and their planning, management and development. It's aimed primarily at students, although it may be useful to others working in tourist destinations – whether in tourism or a related field – and also destination residents. Hopefully, it will assist all to be actively involved with the sustainable development of their village, town, city region or protected area while cultivating and maintaining its 'spirit of place' and welcoming tourists from near and far to enjoy it and enrich it with their presence.

The approach taken is based on ideas evolved over more than a decade of lecturing at Queen Margaret University College, Edinburgh, and draws on my previous work in local government, private consultancy and as a freelance consultant. My thanks go to colleagues whose creative company I've enjoyed and continue to enjoy and to my students who have hopefully gained a little insight from the classes we have shared, much of the time wishing we were out there actually visiting – and studying – the real places.

The nature of the student experience today has strongly influenced the style of the book. I have tried to write it in an approachable manner and have made extensive use of references from both printed and Internet sources. Case studies, exercises and self-assessment questions (SAQs) are provided throughout.

Big thanks to my wife, Mary and to the 'kids', Laura, Jeni, Robbie and Matthew, for their support during the writing of this book. Interesting though 'digital destinations' are, let's pick up from where we left off exploring the spirit of real places.

Frank Howie

THE AUTHOR

Frank Howie is a lecturer at Queen Margaret College Edinburgh. He is a graduate of the University of Edinburgh (BSc Ecological Science and MPhil Urban Design and Regional Planning), the University of British Columbia, Canada (MSc Recreation and Environment) and holds a Diploma from the Institute of Education, London.

His interests – apart from education, of course – include photography, astronomy/space, landscape/nature, hill walking/city strolling, the company of family and good friends and being a tourist.

CHAPTER 1

Destinations and the demands of contemporary tourism

INTRODUCTION

Destination management has a key role in addressing the many and sometimes conflicting issues that arise in contemporary tourism. Destinations present complex challenges for management and development in that they must serve the range of needs of tourists and tourism-related businesses as well as the resident community, local businesses and industries. Moreover, there is rarely a single owner or manager of a destination, and so in contrast to the situation of the manager of a single facility, there is less chance of a coherent set of goals and objectives. As a discipline, or more correctly an amalgam of more established professions, destination management must respond to the reality that a destination is more than the sum of its parts and contribute positively to the synergy that can emerge when these components are functioning together as a harmonious whole.

At the present stage of development of destination management, and of tourism generally, there are certain big issues that demand particular attention. These reflect the changing nature of the tourist and of the emerging role of tourism within society. The tourist of today is a more experienced traveller – therefore more demanding, more informed of his or her rights and less passive in the quest for things to do – than the tourist of a previous generation (Poon, 1993). Today's tourists seek in a destination both activities and experiences that are Rewarding, Enriching, Adventuresome and a Learning experience – the REAL tourism predicted by Read (1980). As such, the tourists addressed in this book are regarded as consumers, certainly, but they are more than that. They are human beings with a far wider range of roles than that of consumption. It seems reasonable to assert that even when on holiday these wider needs and wants remain in operation: 'Leisure/tourism as an encounter (that) occurs between people and space, among people as socialised and embodied subjects, and in contexts in which leisure/tourism is available. [...] Of course, leisure/tourism may not become enjoyment and instead be marked by a frustrated hope or mirage and negative memory. Space is important in each of its aspects (Crouch, 1999:1).

In each of these spaces and contexts that comprise the destination visited, the contemporary tourist has particular interests and expectations. A central role of the destination manager is to respond to these and, wherever possible, integrate them with the equally valid interests and expectations of the other users of these same spaces. Sustainable development is the unifying concept that integrates the environmental, social and economic considerations of contemporary tourism and these form the focus of this chapter.

SUSTAINABLE DEVELOPMENT AND CONTEMPORARY SOCIAL TRENDS

The late 1990s were a period of optimistic anticipation of the new millennium, but also of retrospection. The last few decades in the 'western, liberal, industrial democracies' had witnessed considerable reassessment of contemporary values, prompted only in part by recurring economic recessions. Dramatic political changes – the fall of Communism and the ending of the Cold War have led to a shift of paradigms – a fundamental reassessment of long held values. The most relevant in this context is greatly widened awareness of the environmental impacts of development and social and cultural implications.

This has led to reassessment at the highest levels of government and internationally of certain fundamental assumptions, including the future directions of growth and development, both within and between nations. While this may be dismissed as millennium thinking, there is reason to take the optimistic perspective that significant change is taking place in many sectors in response to a desire for a new world order or, since this has acquired controversial overtones, for a fairer, more ethically and environmentally sensitive pattern for development throughout the world, reducing the vast gulf between standards of living in the developed and the less developed or Third World. The contemporary interest in sustainable development is one major element in this.

A general review of sustainable development is desirable – the term is sometimes criticised as ill defined and vague, arguably by those with a vested interest in maintaining the status quo. Sustainable development as a concept is clearly understood: it is its application to real-world situations and the availability of examples of good practice in a range of circumstances that are less than satisfactory. A general discussion of sustainable development follows. A further section considers the application of these principles to the tourism industry in general and to destinations in particular.

From economic growth to sustainable development

The Rio Conference is the popular name for the United Nations Conference on the Environment and Development (UNCED), held in Rio de Janeiro, Brazil, in 1992. It was attended by most of the world's leaders or their representatives (178 of them, including the UK Prime Minister) and resulted in a commitment to a new approach to economic development. From then on the focus would not simply be economic development regardless of other considerations, but a broader perspective known as sustainable development, which would integrate economic with environmental and social objectives.

> ## Box 1.1 'Agenda 21'
>
> Underlying the Earth Summit agreements is the idea that humanity has reached a turning point. We can continue with present policies which are deepening economic divisions within and between countries which increase poverty, sickness and illiteracy and cause the continuing deterioration of the ecosystem on which life on Earth depends.
>
> Or we can change course. We can act to improve the living standards of those who are in need. We can better manage and protect the ecosystem and bring about a more prosperous future for us all. No nation can achieve this on its own; together we can, in a global partnership for sustainable development.
>
> (Adapted from the introduction to 'Agenda 21')

The foundations of sustainability as a basis for development can be found in earlier writings on conservation and stewardship of natural resources by such as John Muir (1875, 1981), Frank Fraser Darling (1955) and Aldo Leopold (1944). Each discussed humanity's increasing consumption of natural resources and challenged the prevailing notion of the never ending frontier – unlimited availability of material resources – and called for wise, long-term management of the resources on which society depended for both material and social well-being. Similar approaches to the relationship between man and nature can be clearly traced in early religious and philosophical writings in almost every region of the world, but it was only in the late 19th and 20th centuries – effectively since the dawn of the Industrial Era – that the moral or spiritual dimension was considered in the light of humanity's greatly increased potential to change the physical and biological world in the search for economic wealth.

The contemporary perspective on sustainability draws on influential writings of the 1960s and 1970s. A short chronology includes:

1972. *The Limits to Growth: A Report for the Club of Rome* (Meadows *et al.*)
Global issues were addressed and predictions made for the near future, using the most advanced computer technology available at the time. The combination of finite resources, exponential population growth and a rapid but uneven pace of development were considered to be a ticking timebomb. Immediate action was called for.

1974. *World Conservation Strategy.* International Union for Conservation of Nature and Natural Resources (IUCN)
The concept of sustainable development is defined as the key to a desirable future.

1987. *Our Common Future. World Commission on Environment and Development (WCED)*
Sustainable development is affirmed as the solution to current global issues, in the light of growing, scientific evidence of adverse global trends in the environment. A definition was offered:

> Sustainable development is development that meets the needs of the present without compromising the ability of future generations to meet their own needs.

3

1992. United Nations Conference on the Environment and Development (UNCED), Rio de Janeiro, Brazil ('The Earth Summit')

This international conference was attended by the majority of the world's national leaders or their representatives who became signatories to the affirmation that there must be a move from economic development to sustainable development.

Sustainable development

The nature of sustainable development has been the subject of debate for almost a decade and continues. The World Summit on Sustainable Development, dubbed 'Earth Summit 2', was held in Johannesburg in August 2002, attended by more than 100 heads of state and timed to fall ten years after the landmark Earth Summit in Rio de Janeiro. Objectives included a plan to reach a range of goals on poverty eradication and preserving the environment and achieving a political declaration aimed at reinvigorating political commitment to sustainable development (*www.planetark.org*).

The essential characteristics, which together contrast with both the traditional approach to development and to traditional environmentalism are:

- a proactive stance, taking appropriate and precautionary action before an event, rather than remedial action afterwards

- increased ecological and social equity considerations

- continued economic growth – not a steady-state economy.

What is regarded as the first contemporary environmental movement had arisen in the 1960s. Flower power, the swinging 60s, hippies and love and peace are among the images that the 1960s popularly brings to mind. In fact, the idealism and sense of commitment of the time made many lasting contributions to society, notably in terms of wider awareness of serious environmental problems and morally unacceptable inequalities between the rich and poor parts of the world (*www.lib.virginia.edu/exhibits/sixties*).

Arguably, it was the failure of this movement to extend beyond intellectual/ academic circles that led to its demise – although undoubtedly it laid important foundations. Its emphasis on a steady-state level of development as an essential objective had raised major issues. How could the less developed world of poor and disadvantaged people ever reach a satisfactory standard of living if development were to be capped? Who would decide on the level of development of that steady state?

The contemporary stance might be said to acknowledge that societies, like most individuals, are unwilling to give assistance to others to or beyond the point where their own standard of living is reduced; or, expressed differently, they will not stand still to allow the others to catch up – a dismal, but perhaps realistic perspective. In this context, sustainable development embraces continued growth, but acknowledges the inequities of the past that still prevail. It seeks to use that growth to reduce the ethically unacceptable inequalities between and within nations and to address the environmental consequences of unrestricted and scientifically uninformed development. It also works with rather than opposes consumerism and the free market economy, the targets of criticism by the counterculture of the 1960s and 1970s, while a response to the current questioning of 'globalisation' are likely to see a reaffirmation of core values.

While sharing with the 1960s' perspective a condemnation of excessive consumption and waste in the richer world, the prevailing responses to the call for sustainable development are:

- empowerment of the increasingly environmentally and socially aware consumer – to make informed choices

- incentives to industry and business to operate in more environmentally sensitive ways.

Through this approach, it is believed a degree of *self-regulation* will arise, progressively reducing unacceptable imbalances in access to and use of the world's resources. There is, however, a continuing, essential role for governments in the form of proactive *intervention* – for example, by setting the parameters within which the free market can operate and through education. In other words, there is a need for both enticement and enforcement – 'the carrot and the big stick'. Intervention came to be regarded during the 1980s, in both the UK and the USA, as undesirable interference with the free market. The role of government itself was reassessed and much debate centred around establishing what minimum core of government is necessary in societies where the public services were to be progressively privatised. It is part of the perspective of this book that intervention by public authorites continues to be an essential element in the development process.

Key points recommended by the WCED (1987) and accepted by UNCED in 1992 are:

- maintaining ecological diversity

- increasing social equity

- enabling more productivity in developing areas

- increased community/local control

- increased regional self-reliance

- intervention by government

- partnerships (business/government)

- economic viability.

These are general points with relevance to all industries. Tourism is frequently referred to as the world's biggest industry, for example by the World Travel and Tourism Council (*www.wttc.org*), an organisation of travel industry chief executives whose goal is to work with governments to realise the full economic impact of travel and tourism. As such it has a key role to play in international development. No longer is it believed that tourism is a non-extractive industry, with no adverse effects on the environment or cultures of the regions in which it develops. The heavy criticism of the tourism industry in the media in the 1990s frequently exaggerated the realities; however, the actual and potential negative impacts of tourism are more insidious than those of older industries such as coal mining, oil or sand and gravel working and require a greater degree of understanding if appropriate responses are to be applied. The value of the sustainable approach in optimising tourism's development is increasingly recognised and its adoption is essential if, as predicted by WTTC/WEFA (1985), the global tourism industry doubles in economic turnover over the next decade (see Table 1.1).

Table 1.1 *Size of the tourism industry in 1995*

10.9% of world total gross domestic product
10.7% of global workforce – 212 million jobs (1 in every 9 jobs)
11.4% of global capital expenditure
11.1% of total corporate and personal taxes paid
12.6% of total global export earnings

Source: WTTC/WEFA, 1995

Note, however, that interpretation of figures such as these is essential. Many jobs in tourism are related only indirectly to the industry. For example, someone working in a heritage centre, hotel or travel agency is directly working in tourism, while an employee of a restaurant, theatre or taxi service is indirectly employed, since non-tourists such as local residents are also his/her customers.

Exercise

Media coverage of tourism

Using press clippings, news items and/or other media sources, select examples covering tourism's adverse effects on the environment, culture and the economy.

In your opinion, are these fair coverage of actual circumstances? For example, are adequate facts presented? Are details of sources of information given, so readers could follow up the stories?

Select a recent feature article and write an (imaginary) letter to the editor challenging the points raised and giving a 'correct' version of the situation.

Hint

Many newspapers now include archives of previous issues on their websites. Also, many university/college and public libraries frequently hold CD-ROMs of principal newspapers' contents. Examples include:
www.guardian.co.uk
www.thescotsman.co.uk

Sustainability in individual countries

The key points in the international agreements require interpretation to suit the circumstances prevailing in the individual countries that are signatories to the Rio Earth Summit. This is in accord with a watchword from the early days of environmentalism: 'Act local, think global'. *Agenda 21*, an action-oriented set of guidelines for national and local governments which emerged from the 1992 Earth Summit, places a significant role on local authorities and others at the local level to implement action. This should be done without losing or overly diluting the essential spirit or the individual elements of the sustainability agenda, i.e. the environmental, ethical and economic dimensions. While the priority given to each may vary with circumstances, all three must be considered and evaluated in the prevailing national and local development context. Different regions will also require differing timescales to achieve the objectives and even the most affluent nations will be unable to implement many of the radical changes in less than periods of years. For example, global climatic change, caused at least partly by the burning of fossil fuels such as oil, is accepted as a reality – and the longer term implications are agreed as unacceptable. To change the established modern habit of reliance on the private car for most journeys, or to develop alternative forms of energy for industry, may take decades.

CASE STUDY

Sustainable development in one country: the UK experience

Sustainable development is difficult to define. But the goal of sustainable development can guide future policy. We need a hard-headed approach to sustainability based on good science and robust economics. We also need to be sensitive to the intangibles that cannot be reduced to scientific imperatives and the narrow language of economics.

(John Major, British Prime Minister, 1994)

Note the reference to three key aspects of the definition of sustainability:

- good science

- robust economics

- sensitivity to intangibles.

These components of sustainability may be referred to as the *3Es* of sustainable development (Howie, 1996). The scientific, rational component is Ecology or the Environmental sciences; the second component is the Economic dimensions. The third is the Ethical or Equity dimension, addressing social/cultural/'fair play' cosiderations. The three elements are integral components of a framework for development.

The concept of sustainable development can be visualised using a classical architecture metaphor – a pediment supported by three symmetrical columns representing ecological, ethical and economic concerns (see Figure 1.1). But there the architecture analogy ends – the columns are not uniform in stature. In a given development context and time one of the concerns may be prioritised. In a national park, priority might be given to ecological considerations; in a peripheral city housing area suffering from social exclusion priority might be given to economic considerations such as job creation. Importantly, however, due consideration must be given to *each* of the component elements, to justify the term sustainable development.

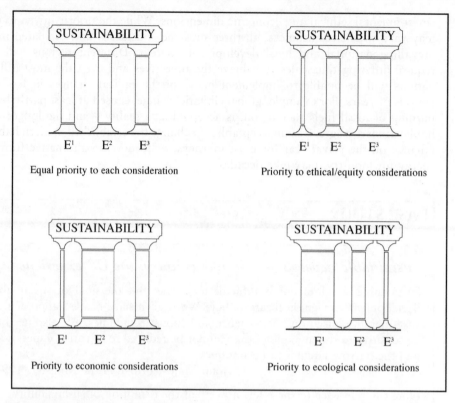

SUSTAINABILITY

E¹   E²   E³

Equal priority to each consideration

SUSTAINABILITY

E¹   E²   E³

Priority to ethical/equity considerations

SUSTAINABILITY

E¹   E²   E³

Priority to economic considerations

SUSTAINABILITY

E¹   E²   E³

Priority to ecological considerations

Figure 1.1 *Sustainable development*

Elkington and Fennell (1998) similarly recognise the three essential elements, referring to them as the 'triple bottom line':

> The triple bottom line agenda requires companies to focus not simply on the economic value they add, but also on the environmental and social value they add – or destroy.

A rationale for sustainable development

Scottish Natural Heritage, the UK Government agency in Scotland charged with the conservation and management of the country's natural resources, asserts that the theory and practice of sustainable development is based on fundamental premises and ethical principles (Scottish Natural Heritage, 1994).

Fundamental premises

1. All human activity is ultimately dependent on the environment – natural resources and processes.

2. The human population is growing rapidly.

3. Resource use per capita is high in developed countries – growing rapidly in developing countries.

4. The high level of human activity is likely to have serious consequences for quality of life and even survival.

5. Our interactions with the environment and its natural processes are complex – it is often difficult to predict the consequences of our activities.

Ethical principles

1. *Intergenerational equity.* Do nothing which puts at risk the natural environment's ability to meet needs, material and non-material, of future generations.

2. *International equity.* Countries should accept responsibility for environmental impacts of their economic activities on other countries; should avoid exporting their environmental problems.

3. *Societal equity.* One sector of society should not exploit natural resources or damage the environment at the expense of another.

4. *Interspecies equity.* Development should respect other life forms: rarely, if ever, is there justification for driving them to extinction for our own purposes.

Arising out of these scientific premises and ethical principles are guidelines for sustainability, although these require changes in the relevant policy, regulatory and planning frameworks.

These guidelines have proved useful and sound; however, in changing political and socio-economic circumstances the emphasis placed on individual elements of them inevitably fluctuates.

Guidelines for sustainable development

Arising out of these principles, guidelines for practical action were prepared by the agency.

Wise use

Non-renewable resources should be used wisely and sparingly, at a rate which does not restrict the options of future generations.

Carrying capacity

Renewable resources should be used within the limits of their capacity for generation.

Environmental quality

The quality of the natural heritage as a whole should be maintained and improved.

Precautionary principle

In situations of great complexity or uncertainty we should act in a precautionary manner.

Shared benefits

There should be an equitable distribution of the costs and benefits (material and non-material) of any development.

In situations of great complexity or uncertainty we should act in a precautionary manner.

These principles and guidelines for sustainable development, as interpreted in the UK, are valuable and practically useful. Inevitably, however, they are challenged. For example, the 'precautionary principle' has been criticised as counter to the entrepreneurial spirit of risk taking which, critics argue, is increasingly necessary in times of uncertainty. They are examined as to their applicability to tourism and destination management later in this chapter.

Doubts about sustainability

Is the contemporary concern with sustainable development just a passing fad? Consider the previous experience of the late 1960s–early 1970s, when the environmental movement flourished, then faded. Are conditions different at the dawn of the 21st century? A wider body of society and business is involved this time. Individuals and businesses increasingly recognise that the environment is not a purely academic concept of little relevance to themselves – it affects their daily lives and long-term prospects for personal and business health. Also today there is increasingly reliable scientific evidence of adverse environmental change, such as global warming, and understanding of the serious implications. A wider audience of new consumers is voting with their wallets for environment respecting products and, more recently, for products which are produced under ethically acceptable conditions.

The crises of the mid- and late 1990s, concerning BSE (bovine spongiform encephalopathy – mad cow disease) and its human form, CJD (Creutzfeldt-Jakob disease), closely followed by the GM (genetically modified) food scare and more recently the foot and mouth epidemic in Britain in 2001, effectively closed down the countryside to tourism, causing severe hardship to rural tourism businesses. Investigations revealed scientific inadequacies in food production and development and suggested the vulnerability of contemporary lifestyles. As some would argue, they emphasise the human race's ultimate dependence on the natural environment, no matter how technologically advanced humanity becomes. However, societies will never (willingly) revert to a non-technological stage; nor, perhaps, will even individuals revert to a less technologically advanced stage. Increasing numbers of people are seeking more 'natural lifestyles' through, for example, the food they eat and their leisure pursuits. This has major implications for the tourism industry where the growth of nature-based and cultural tourism is evident.

TOURISM AND SUSTAINABILITY

Tourism sells physical and human environments. It is a resource-dependent industry using both natural and cultural heritage. For example, annual surveys of the likes/dislikes of tourists to Scotland consistently show 80+% of overseas visitors placing 'scenery' as the top 'like', with 'friendly people' at 70+% (*www.staruk.org.uk; www.scotexchange.net*).

Middleton (1998:10–12) reviewed a Danish study of European holiday motivations conducted in 1995, making the obvious but rarely stated point that:

> Most people do not use words such as environment and sustainable to describe their product expectations and satisfactions. These are technical labels for a particular set of management decisions, not the language of the general public, and not the language of holiday brochures.

He interpreted the responses as meaning that the destination environment is the single dominant underlying motivation, where 'environment' to travelers means the quality experience sought.

Maintaining this resource base through appropriate planning and management is clearly essential but there are obstacles:

- the historical view of tourism as a non-extractive industry

- the assumed benign use of *free resources* by the industry.

'Research has shown that the quality of our environment is one of the main factors which persuade people to holiday in Scotland. It is vital, therefore, in developing our tourism industry we do not kill the goose that lays the golden egg' (Minister's Statement, Tourism and the Scottish Environment Initiative: A Sustainable Response, 1992).

Moving towards a proactive approach

How to make the transition to the proactive approach implicit in a sustainable approach to tourism development is indicated in the Canada Green Plan (Government of Canada, 1990). It identified a sequence of actions:

Integration of ecological, economic and socio-cultural objectives →

This fosters quality environment which, in turn, attracts tourism →

Tourism-generated wealth creation can support environmental conservation/restitution →

Further environmental improvement is economically feasible →

Cycle repeats.

The role of government in setting parameters within which private businesses operate is implicit. In line with the increasingly sophisticated Canadian perspective a more specific definition of sustainable development was proposed:

> ... leading to management of all resources in such a way that we can fulfil economic, social and aesthetic needs while maintaining cultural integrity essential ecological processes, biological diversity and life support systems.
>
> (Tourism Canada, 1990)

Exercise

Sustainable tourism and intervention

Consider the UK government's reluctance to consider intervention – notably during the Thatcher years and the continuing Conservative government to 1997 – and its promotion of the 'voluntary principle', i.e the assertion that a firm or business is best placed to do what is right for itself and should be free to do so unhindered by government intervention.

1. Why might some countries, such as Canada, be more advanced in their response to moving towards sustainable tourism business practice? What factors are involved?

2. What stage do you consider the UK – or another country of your choice – to be at?

3. What do you consider the prospects for moving into the proactive stage of development within a tourist destination of your choice? What mechanisms would you suggest for encouraging this move into the proactive stage?

4. What should the roles and approaches of government be in encouraging sustainable tourism development?

Tourism industry awareness

Initially, businesses and other stakeholders must become aware of environmental and socio-cultural issues and their relevance to their activities. Awareness raising is only significant if it leads to responses from and within the industry. Murphy (1994) suggested that businesses go through several stages of change. In the early to mid-1990s he considered that the pattern within the tourism industry in one country, Canada – arguably one of the countries leading the way – approximated the following:

Early phase (reactive):

- A minority of businesses are in this stage.
- They are considering the implications of a move towards operating in a more sustainable way.

Mid phase (compliance):

- The majority of businesses are at this stage.
- Systems are being established to comply with new regulations.

Third phase (proactive):

- A minority of businesses are in this stage.

- Integration of environmental dimension into corporate strategic planning is considered.

This would appear to be a pragmatic approach to the issues raised by the transition from development to sustainable development. For many industries, and in business generally, the objective is seen as one of moving the consideration of sustainability from the periphery of business concerns to the core, where it cannot be overlooked in times of crisis or regarded as marginal to the mainstream of commerce. Thus a logical location might be within the more familiar and established business context of total quality management (TQM).

The movement of environmental management towards the mainstream in business – generally and within the tourism industry – is reflected in various recent initiatives and publications. In a publication for Edinburgh-based businesses, the city council targeted the busy, working manager. A minimum of basic environmental knowledge is assumed, the outcomes are pragmatic and money-oriented (savings) and the language used is such that the non-specialist can comprehend. For example:

> This guide [was produced] specifically to help the overworked manager realise the commercial benefits of good environmental practice. It applies whether you are offering a service, running a shop or manufacturing a product.
>
> (City of Edinburgh Council, 1999)

The categories of environmental issue within which action can be taken – and savings made – are no different for a tourist attraction than for an electronics manufacturing company, although some of the individual activities will be different (see Table 1.2). In other words, a systematic methodology for assessment is available.

HARD AND SOFT ENVIRONMENTAL ISSUES

Agenda 21, discussed earlier, aimed to translate the broad principles of sustainable development into specifics for action at the local level. The World Travel and Tourism Council (*www.wttc.org*), jointly with the World Tourism Organisation (*www.world-tourism.org*) and the Earth Council (*www.ecouncil.ac.cr*), identified broad actions to achieve sustainable development for the tourism industry, aimed at business operations but also applicable to business operations (WTTC/WTO/ Earth Council in Middleton, 1998).

For the travel and tourism industry it identified the following actions:

- Assessing capacity of the existing regulatory, economic and voluntary framework to bring about sustainable development.

- Assessing the economic, social, cultural and environmental implications of tourism industry operations.

- Training, education and public awareness.

- Planning for sustainable tourism development.

Table 1.2 *Environmental issues for businesses*

	Energy	Water	Waste	Air emissions	Chemical	Other
Tourism						
Bed and breakfast, hotel	Heating, hot-water, lighting	Guest use, catering, laundry, cleaning	Glass and paper, food waste, packaging	Odours and other emissions from kitchens	Cleaning chemicals	Could provide public transport information when bookings are made. Green tourist business scheme
Tourist attraction	Heating, hot water, lighting	Catering, toilet facilities, cleaning	Packaging, food waste, litter		Cleaning chemicals, herbicides and pesticides	Access by public transport. Growing public interest in green tourism
Retail						
Restaurant	Cooking, chilling, heating, hot water, lighting	Food preparation, dish-washing, toilets, cleaning	Solid waste including food scraps, packaging, fats and oils	Odours and other emissions from kitchens	Cleaning chemicals	Demand for organic foods and natural products
Transport						
Transport	Vehicle mileage, driver training	Effluent from vehicle cleaning	Packaging waste, waste from vehicle maintenance	Vehicle emissions	Storing and handling of oil	Route planning, vehicle design, cleaner fuels
Manufacturing						
Electronics	Compressed air, equipment use, heating, lighting	Cleaning systems	Packaging, rework, plastic and metal	Fumes from soldering	Cleaning chemicals	Health and safety/hygiene

Source: City of Edinburgh Council, 1999: 2, Figure 1.3

- Facilitating exchange of information, skills and technology relating to sustainable tourism between developed and developing countries.

- Providing for the participation of all sectors of society.

- Design of new tourism products with sustainability at their core as an integral part of the tourism development process.

- Measuring progress in achieving sustainable development at the local level.

- Partnerships for sustainable development.

Guides to better practice such as these are concerned with hard environmental issues and cost savings. Sustainable development is, however, also concerned with social and cultural issues and the less obvious *intangible attributes* of a destination – atmosphere, image, sense of place, etc. These are merely alluded to in the guidelines above. This is an important point, since sustainable development is frequently confused with environmental management. Clearly, environmental considerations are at the heart of sustainability; but the contemporary perspective, and the strength of the sustainable approach, is that it places environmental considerations firmly within the social and economic mainstream.

The sustainable development approach is not concerned with environmental issues alone.

There have been methodologies for the systematic evaluations of environmental intangibles – such as the beauty of landscapes – from at least the 1960s. Murray (1962) was appointed by the National Trust for Scotland:

> to make a landscape survey of the Highland countries, to delineate areas of outstanding natural beauty, to report on the distinguishing character of these areas, and to assess change. [...] No area was chosen on grounds of accessibility, or for its scientific, social, or historic interest, but all these points are to be held further reasons to commend a selection made on quite another ground. [...] The criterion to cover so wide a range is not complex and exclusive, but simple and universal ... the criterion of beauty itself ... the perfect expression of that ideal form to which everything that is perfect of its kind approaches.

Purist approaches such as this have their place. Certainly, in destination management and tourism generally, it is clear that tourists do give beauty of landscape and townscape as a reason for choice of destination. In the harsh realities of the world of commerce, however, attempts to evaluate the range of values implicit in the contemporary definition of sustainable development – economic, environmental and socio-cultural – generally demand the conversion of each into a common 'currency', since the rationale is their use as aids to decision making by managers. Money tends to be that common currency. The challenge is to devise methodologies that can achieve that conversion, without being open to accusations of 'crass commercialism', that is, *knowing the cost of everything and the value of nothing*.

At the level of destination management these approaches are at an early stage of development, although their value is established in single issue development proposals such as impact assessment of major industrial developments – nuclear power, airport extensions, etc. In increasing numbers of countries, comprehensive impact assessments are incorporated into planning legislation. In the USA, the Environment Protection Agency was established in 1970 and assumed the role of coordinating projects formerly carried out by 15 agencies. Perhaps as a consequence of this, when oil was discovered beneath the floor of the North Sea in the early 1970s, the American company, Occidental, which wanted to construct an oil-handling terminal in the predominantly rural environment of the Orkney Islands, specifically the small island of Flotta, was disposed towards funding the preparation of environmental impact assessments for the proposed development even although British planning legislation did not at that time require it (Howie *et al.*, 1974). The ensuing safeguards – ranging from oil-spill prevention and clean-up procedures to careful design and landscaping of the unavoidably huge oil storage tanks – minimized the impacts on the indigenous farming and fishing industries and on the nature, landscape and heritage-based tourism industry. Increasing numbers of countries are adopting a similar approach, including member states of the European Union.

EVALUATING THE 3ES IN PRACTICE

Science and environmental management

Science – a reflection on values

Science is characterised as being impartial, neutral, objective and rational. It is generally believed to deal in facts. More correctly, it deals in probabilities, offering hypotheses for how things work in given circumstances and offering evidence to support the hypotheses; the evidence being 'guaranteed' to a stated degree of accuracy. Scientific research is geared to improving that level of accuracy – but also to being prepared to reassess or refute the original hypothesis on the basis of new evidence. There is no such thing as absolute scientific proof.

What is regarded as 'science' by the general public is actually 'innovations'. The practically useful applications of science through technology, society, or the market, use that scientific insight to make these possible. Moreover, the use or application of science depends on the values of the users – business, government or society. For example, scientific research progressively reveals understanding of the fundamental particles of nature and their behaviour. Whether that understanding is used to develop (eventually) safe, clean, virtually unlimited energy or weapons of immense destructive power is the value choice of society. Science also offers a perspective on whether we should accept beliefs – perhaps very appealing beliefs – on the basis of inadequate proof. 'I want to believe ...' (Agent Mulder, in the popular science-fiction TV series, *The X-Files*) is not the same as 'I do believe because there is rational, scientific evidence for the existence of ...' (Agent Scully, his colleague):

> Science encourages a healthy scepticism. It is the candle burning in the darkness.
>
> (Sagan, 1996)

CASE STUDY

'Scientism' – a caution

Scientism is the application of scientific conclusions to inapplicable areas; concealing (unintentionally or deliberately) social, economic and/or political implications of an issue.

Example: famine in an (imaginary, but realistic) area 'somewhere in the Third World'

What is the cause of famine in this area? A natural disaster, such as a freak drought? This is possible; local climate and weather statistics are not collected systematically, but the regional data suggest lower than average rainfall. There is clear evidence that crops are failing. There is probably a drought.

Thomas Malthus, an 18th-century philosopher, stated that 'plague, pestilence and war' would always be present as the scourges of mankind ... so there is little that can be done about such natural phenomena.

Could there be another cause? Could the famine be caused by social factors? Further investigation of the wider context shows that traditional farming in the area has been disrupted for some years by loss of the male workforce to jobs in the cities. They have been drawn by the prospects of regular wages and better conditions. Some evidence suggests they have been coerced to leave the countryside to join the labour force for major construction projects designed to boost the national economy through the new focus on tourism. Other evidence suggests that some workers are seeking work on the new cattle ranches supplying meat for a multinational fast-food corporation.

The answer to the question is less clear than previously thought. Ecology is sometimes invoked as providing scientific evidence for problems otherwise caused. However, an example such as this emphasises the value of the sustainability perspective where the 3Es (Howie, 1998) of Ecology, Ethics and Economics are *all* considered in an integrated manner. A science-based approach to this problem is inadequate on its own – it supplements but does not replace social, economic, political and other considerations.

Nevertheless, the scientific contribution is vitally important. The destination manager does not need to be a scientist, but does need to know when to consult with scientific colleagues and should have a basic understanding of the principles of ecology or environmental science:

> A proper understanding of biological, or more specifically, ecological factors can significantly reduce the scale of environmental damage associated with recreational and tourist development. Equally important it can serve to dissuade developers from embarking on schemes whose economic viability is likely to be jeopardised by adverse ecological influences.
>
> (Edington, 1986)

The *premises* just discussed are now illustrated within ecological concepts.

Ecology focuses on the environmental relationships of organisms – including humans, their reactions with one another and the properties of whole assemblages of organisms (communities) occupying the same habitat or place.

Connectivity
All organisms – including humanity – are part of a complex web of mutual interactions (energy – food – is the currency).

Note: Biodiversity is the variety of plant and animal life in an environment (discussed later).

Balance
Animal and plant populations fluctuate in numbers but have evolved to a state

of dynamic balance or equilibrium within their environment over millennia. (Technological man can temporarily(?) escape the restraints that maintain balance.)

Example: *the population problem* – the exponential growth of the human population.

Example: *unsustainable development* – development and management of environments for human use can upset the natural balance, unless adequate ecological understanding is incorporated into management practices.

Homeostasis

When an ecosystem is disturbed by external or internal events, equilibrium is restored through regeneration or succession.

Wildlife tourism is increasingly important in many destination areas – dolphin watching in the Moray Firth of northeast Scotland and photo safaris for lions in Kenya.

If a wildlife population is *excessively* disturbed by tourists – e.g. by selectively shooting prize specimens for trophies or through excessive disturbance by photo safaris which interferes with natural breeding patterns – the population may go into irreversible decline, in the worst case to extinction. If, in the first example, a scientifically determined cull is taken – i.e. a measured percentage only of the population, including females as well as prized males – then the hunting is sustainable and the natural mechanism of homeostasis will maintain the population. In the photo safari example, management that avoids disturbance during the breeding season can also be sustainable, allowing the population to regenerate.

Scarcity

The potential (geometric) rate of increase of plant and animal populations is checked naturally as these populations approach the limit of their available resources of space or food.

In destinations where wildlife tourism is important to the economy, there may be the temptation to raise the likelihood of tourist success in seeing wildlife by artificial feeding. Providing this at specific places would increase both the convenience and the likelihood of viewing the wildlife. Artificial feeding could also help maintain larger populations through severe winters or summer droughts which kill the older and the weaker members of the herd so increasing the absolute numbers of animals. Scientific arguments against this practice are that it artificially raises the wildlife populations while the natural *carrying capacity* of the environment is unchanged. Moreover, if it is stopped, the population will crash through loss of natural feeding behaviour or through winter kill when excessively large numbers of animals compete for scarce winter grazing or prey. (There are further, *ethical* dimensions for discussion elsewhere, in that the authenticity of the tourist experience is impaired, while the wildlife is reduced to the status of begging.)

A restricted season on viewing of wildlife allows recovery of populations disturbed by tourism and other uses. It is comparable to more familiar hunting seasons.

Relationships with physical/biological factors

Organisms have precise relationships with the physical/biological environment – for breeding, shelter and food. Competitive relationships exist in and between species and within the food chain where, for example, plant eaters (herbivores) and meat eaters (carnivores) (e.g. deer and wolves) are mutually dependent. Understanding of population dynamics is important in managing wildlife populations for human use as food or for tourism.

Community structure

The natural community is the total assemblage of species, represented within *populations*, occupying a particular habitat. Different species in a given area have evolved interdependently with other species. Thus management of wildlife for tourism purposes, e.g. red deer (*Cervus elephas*) in Highland Scotland, should recognise that the elimination in the 18th century of the natural predator, the wolf (*Canis lupus*), creates an unstable situation. In its absence the deer will breed to the point where they outstrip their food supply – heathers and moorland grasses of the hills and glens – resulting in winter die-offs. This scientific perspective, in turn, raises ethical arguments as to how the deer should be managed – again emphasising the value of the sustainability perspective and its interrelated consideration of ecological, ethical and economic factors.

Carrying capacity

As discussed in community structure, when a population of, for example, deer (herbivores/plant eaters) is too large to be supported by the available grazing on its range, the *carrying capacity* of that range is said to be exceeded. Overgrazing results in the destruction of the vegetation (it cannot replace itself sufficiently rapidly) possibly leading to erosion of the soil (especially on hillsides) as rain falls on the (now) bare soil and can wash it away. The overall result is impoverishment of the ecosystem and loss of biodiversity.

Ecosystem

The communities and non-living components of the environment function together as the *ecosystem*.

This concept emphasises how management of particular animal species for wildlife tourism purposes – for example, lions in Africa or golden eagles in Highland Scotland – is intimately related to management of the habitat. If the habitat is damaged through mismanagement, then artificial remedies are required – e.g. feeding of wildlife at viewing stations, a less than authentic experience for the tourist.

Biodiversity

Biodiversity is a measure of the richness and diversity of life (plant and animal) in a given area. Frequently, although not necessarily, it is high biodiversity landscapes that are perceived as beautiful by tourists. For example, a mature pine forest – such as the majestic and poignant remnants of the ancient Caledonian Forest found at Rothiemurchus in Strathspey, Scotland – is far richer in biodiversity than a commercial forestry plantation of Sitka spruce which is largely a monoculture of exotic (non-native) trees, all of the same age.

> *Gaia – the Earth as self-regulating organism*
> Biological populations in a particular habitat plus the chemical and physical influences on them generally result in a dynamic balance. This *homeostasis* is illustrated in undisturbed wilderness areas in various parts of the world (although these are declining in area) and is colloquially referred to as the *balance of nature*.
>
> It has been suggested (Lovelock, 1982) that the earth itself demonstrates this balance prompting the speculation that the planet itself is a self-regulating organism – an organism in the sense that it responds to any threat against it in such a way as to maximise the chances for survival of life on the planet – the *Gaia Hypothesis*.

Basic ecological premises

Tourism and recreational pursuits and potential ecological impacts

Any tourist activity will result in some ecological impact within a destination area. The management question is how to react to this when scientific measurement makes clear the extent of the problem. Tourist use of the car contributes to air pollution. At the global level it contributes (alongside industrial pollution) to global warming. Within the confines of cities it contributes – again, alongside more than a century's legacy of industrial pollution – to the blackening and erosion of historic buildings and it contributes significantly to the incidence of asthma. Transport is a major issue in destination management, in both urban and rural areas. (Chapter 6 examines this in some detail.)

In rural areas, the impacts of tourism are arguably more obvious and more diverse. Some potential effects in rural areas are the following.

Rural activities

Hiking, rambling, mountaineering
Litter; disturbance of cliff nesting and moorland birds; erosion.

Erosion problems are increasingly tackled by professional (and volunteer) teams trained in mountain path building and restoration. They construct and repair hard-wearing, sensitively designed footpaths in popular rural areas (*www.path-craft.com*).

Mountain biking
Litter and erosion, notably where cyclists have to use paths designed for walkers.

Horse riding and pony trekking
Competition with native herbivores → overgrazing in remote areas → erosion.

Hunting and fishing
If there is a selective focus on prey species such as deer, notably where natural predators have been exterminated to increase numbers, overgrazing of the range is a probable ecological consequence. Example: overpopulation of red deer (*Cervus elephas*) in Highland Scotland through elimination of the wolf (in the 18th century).

If alien (non-native species have been introduced to an area to diversify hunting opportunities, the imported species may compete successfully with the native species leading to its elimination in some cases.

Boating
Noise; shore erosion from wave action (powerboats); damage to lake/seabed habitats by anchor drag.

Off-road vehicles (4-wheel drives), trailbikes (motor) and snowmobiles
Soil compaction → increased water run-off → soil erosion. Noise, mechanical disturbance → out-movement of wildlife; breeding disturbance; animal burrows collapse.

'Going for a drive'
While apparently innocuous, pleasure driving can lead to major congestion and hold-ups on rural roads and within popular villages. Certain rural destinations gain a reputation as places to be avoided at certain times of year. The car is the most popular means of access to the countryside, raising related issues of inadequate public transport provision in rural areas. Many former bus routes in rural areas are – in a political context of deregulation (where competitor private bus companies may operate) and privatisation of public transport – 'uneconomic', when subject to narrow economic analysis. The social (and environmental) benefits of local services should not be undervalued, however (e.g. providing services on 'uneconomic routes'). Systematically measured impacts of pleasure driving would include local erosion from off-road parking and increased air pollution through traffic jams in honey-pot areas.

Touring drivers towing caravans are a frequent subject of criticism, although caravanning is at least confined to specific areas where its impact has been largely visual. Sites are increasingly well managed and designed since the grading of sites was introduced, generally with tree screening and other ameliorating techniques of landscaping.

Reducing the ecological damage caused by tourism

Waste disposal
Inadequate waste disposal and sewage treatment at tourism facilities and campsites can encourage troublesome or dangerous species to gather at dumps or outflows. In North American national parks, e.g. Jasper National Park in Alberta, Canada (*www.parkscanada.pch.gc.ca/jasper/*), on wilderness trails campers are required to take all their rubbish away, and when overnight camping all camp food must be suspended on simple pulleys (provided, discretely at campsites), that remove it to the treetops out of reach of bears. Compulsory 'back-country' permits linked to trail quotas provide opportunities for informing hikers of visitor management as well as of wildlife management. Comprehensive interpretive programmes further persuade visitors of the neccessity of such limitations on their freedom in the interests of conservation objectives.

Observing wildlife
Attracting animals to viewing stations by the use of baits has already been criticised in this volume as undesirable interference with behaviour patterns and, potentially,

with population dynamics. There are other ways for the manager to bring the wildlife to the tourist.

A wildlife reserve of the Royal Society for the Protection of Birds (*www.rspb.org.uk*) at Loch Garten, near Boat of Garten on the northern fringe of the Cairngorm Mountains has given several generations of visitors an intimate experience of the rare osprey or fish eagle (*Pandion haliaetus*), shot to extinction by the late 19th century by sportsmen. There were reported sightings in the early 1950s and after scientific consideration of the chances of successful reestablishment the Loch Garten area was made a statutory bird sanctuary and the Royal Society for the Protection of Birds organised a viewing station for public use, providing powerful binoculars and telescopes. In the nesting seasons between 1959 and 1964 some 106,000 people saw the eyrie (Darling and Boyd, 1964) and since then the general public's interest in wildlife has grown steadily, reflected in increasing tourist numbers.

The Cairngorms case study (Chapter 10) addresses further the role of wildife, outdoors and nature-based tourism in this destination area. In a predominantly rural region apparently moderate visitor numbers and the related economic impact are significant. Similar reintroductions of species driven to extinction in earlier, less enlightened times have taken place in other regions and countries, based on scientific arguements but also with an awareness of the potential benefits arising through tourism. In the Parc National des Cévennes (*www.parcsnationaux-fr.com/ cevennes*) in southeast France the griffon vulture was introduced in the 1990s with comparable economic boosts to the established wildlife and landscape-oriented tourism in the destination area. The new Seabird Centre (*www.seabird.org*) at North Berwick, East Lothian, opened in 2000, uses state-of-the-art video technology to bring live images of nesting seabirds on the 350-feet high basalt Bass Rock Island to tourists. This is making a significant economic contribution to the town, a still popular seaside destination, although like other 'cold water destinations' in need of an upgrading of its 'product'.

Souvenir trade

Collecting plants and animals for processing as souvenirs has pushed certain species to the brink of extinction. Examples of souvenirs that are increasingly discouraged or prohibited are ivory, coral, skins, plumage, etc. Arguably the tourist who is interested in wildlife could readily be dissuaded from purchasing certain souvenirs when informed of the true scientific implications of the purchase. On a strictly scientific basis, quite apart from possible ethical arguments, a harvest of animal products for souvenir and other purposes could be sustainable in certain circumstances and might be encouraged for economic reasons such as the creation of local employment, so providing a lifeline to otherwise threatened human settlements. Hunting by local communities has been a part of traditional life in, for example, parts of Greenland and a 'harvest' of even such now endangered species as the polar bear has been sustainable. This is rarely so with 'sport hunting' where the satisfaction of the tourist (and so the likelihood of return visits) is often dependent on securing a trophy even when populations of the animals are below a sustainable level (*www.ngo.grida.no/wwfap/polarbears/hunting.html*).

Scientifically, there might be a necessity for culling certain species in a given area – for example, roe deer in certain UK forests and red deer on Highland mountain estates where there are no natural predators. It would be for the tourists/sportsmen themselves and entrepreneurs in the destination area to consider whether there were ethical arguments against turning the ecologically necessary cull into a commercial tourist activity (see the Cairngorms case study in Chapter 10). The historic fur trade in northern Canada – based on land mammals or sea creatures such as the seal – and the fishing industry in the UK where grey seals are killed for allegedly reducing fish stocks are frequently criticised in the media for cruel practices. Scientific argument is frequently used by both sides to support or condemn the practices.

Economic arguments are also used to support the needs of local communities whose livelihoods have long depended on the natural harvests of their area; so too are ethical arguments – in this case to support the local communities' rights to continue their traditional ways of life. It has to be considered, however, whether a lifestyle is still 'traditional' if the harpoon of olden times has been replaced by a modern weapon capable of culling a far higher percentage of the wildlife population than was ever possible before, so upsetting the delicate population dynamics.

Zoning

Zoning is a normal element of planning practice in national parks where management is adequate to enforce it. Broadly, it establishes a core zone (an area prioritising nature conservation) and recognises an existing community zone where the tourist accommodation and other services are located and where the indigenous local community resides, perhaps in one sizeable settlement such as in Banff in Alberta, Canada, or a string of villages such as in the Cairngorms National Park to be established in 2003. A buffer zone of mixed uses will separate these zones (see the Cairngorms case study in Chapter 10).

SAQ

Is any management approach that makes the opportunities for tourists to see wildlife more likely, more easy or more frequent a questionable example of 'Disneyfication'/'McDonaldisation'/'stage management'? Or is it an acceptable means of attracting a wider public, beyond the existing minority of committed enthusiasts, who may not be bringing sufficient income into a given rural destination area? In an increasingly urban and mechanised society, does the approach not also serve the valuable function of allowing children and inexperienced adults to come into contact with the natural world, in a managed way, perhaps opening to them opportunities and, significantly, building their confidence for more natural, subsequent visits? Even if these non-special interest tourists do not become 'wildlife tourists' they may become part of the 'constituency of support' for wildlife and conservation issues generally (see the Cairngorms case study in Chapter 10).

CASE STUDY

Predator control

Example: the red grouse (*Lagopus lagopus scoticus*) in Scotland

In natural conditions, predator and prey are generally in a dynamic balance and mutually dependent. Predation is only one of several mortality factors – remove it and other factors increase in compensatory manner. For example, in the absence of predators – as where eliminated by human action – the prey population will increase in numbers to the point where starvation occurs due to overgrazing of their habitat and disease kills off the weakened animals (see Figure 1.2).

The ethical dimension in sustainable tourism

An earlier section reviewed the 'scientific' aspect of sustainable development and management. What is the significance to tourism and destination management of the second 'E' of the sustainable approach, the 'Ethical' or Equity dimension? Reference was made to the ethical principles influencing the actions of the government agency, Scottish Natural Heritage (Scottish Natural Heritage, 1993) (*www.snh.org.uk*). Mention was also made of the prevalence of values and beliefs that run counter to the scientific perspective. Whereas the western, industrial, liberal democracies place great emphasis on science, the application of science depends on the *values* of the users – whether business, government or society. Values affect the beliefs of individuals and the collective beliefs of societies. Thus, religious beliefs, superstitions and belief in UFOs are widely – and very dearly – held by very many people, despite the lack of rational, scientific evidence to support these beliefs.

The role of ethics in a scientific-technological society

Ethics assists society and individuals in making difficult choices. At a day-to-day level, ethics can be used to address such 'intangibles' as whether nature or wildlife have 'rights' in the face of the advance of tourism or other developments. Equally it can be used to consider whether local communities in tourism destinations have the 'right' to modify or even halt tourism development in what they regard as their locality. Ethics also addresses the issues of tourist rights – to health and safety, to 'a good deal' and perhaps they also have a right to quality experiences that are Rewarding, Enriching, Adventuresome and a Learning experience – REAL tourism (Read, 1980) – so long as local communities are not culturally, environmentally or economically impoverished by the process. Ethical considerations can also address whether businesses should be permitted to ignore certain environmentally desirable actions, or impractically strict regulations, if so doing would threaten their survival or cause job losses.

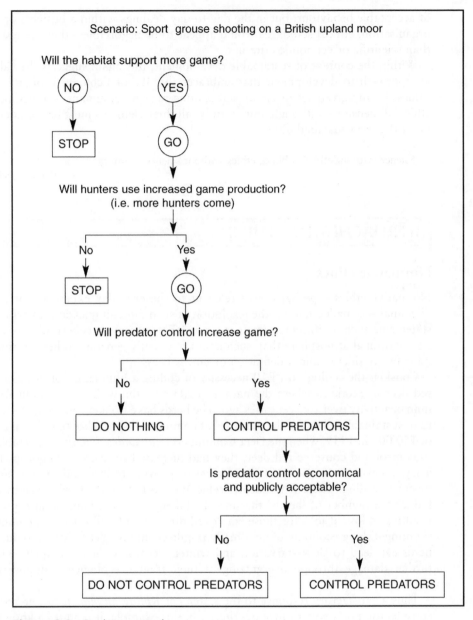

Figure 1.2 *Predator control*
Source: Adapted from Connolly, 1980 in Edington, 1980

ETHICS AND VALUES

Ethics deals in such issues as rights, justice, respect, even 'goodness'. It deals in values, but the question may be asked, 'Whose values?', for there are no absolutes in ethics. 'Codes', such as the United Nations Charter of Human Rights (*www.un.org/overview/rights.html*) may approximate to such universal standards of acceptable behaviour, but in the day-to-day dealings within a business or other organisation, ethical standards would appear to be negotiable – they are less *hard* than scientific or economic criteria.

Within the context of sustainable development, this again suggests the value of an approach to development that embraces the 3Es of Ecology, Economics and Ethics. In any given set of circumstances one may be dominant – sometimes the ethical dimension – although, importantly, all three elements must be considered to merit the term sustainability:

> Science without ethics is blind; ethics without science is empty.
>
> (Sagan, 1996)

APPROACHES TO ETHICS

Normative ethics

Normative ethics – perhaps most relevant to the everyday experience of ethical dilemmas – is inadequate for the resolution of such difficult questions as arise from statements such as *Killing animals is wrong*. The statement is best addressed in a less emotional atmosphere than such issues frequently generate; other information must be considered and a definition of *norms* is essential.

Consider the ecological ('E1') necessity of culling a population of, for example, red deer in Scotland where the natural predator – the wolf – was eliminated by human activity over two centuries ago. The herds have been encouraged to increase to unsustainable levels for the purposes of commercial sport shooting. From a total of 150,000 in 1959, when the Deer Commission (*www.dcs.gov.uk*) was established to control and conserve red deer, they had increased to nearly 400,000 in 1999. They outstrip the capacity of their range to provide fodder and require supplementary feeding. There is frequently reluctance to reduce the herds since this will reduce the number of 'heads' that may be taken by paying hunters, also possibly resulting in loss of jobs for those employed directly and indirectly in the hunting–shooting–fishing economy of an already fragile economy. Yet failure to reduce the herds can lead to slow starvation and winter die-offs for many animals; also to further damage through overgrazing of their fragile, ecologically impoverished habitat.

Thus a satisfactory response to the statement *Killing animals is wrong* requires consideration of a wider range of criteria. In this example, it requires a knowledge of ecology and population dynamics; also of rural economics, quite apart fom the initial 'simple' ethical aspect.

A further example centres on the assertion that *only local people are entitled to voice opinions on local development proposals*.

Consider a community in a remote rural area. The local opinion appears to be that the real development need in their area is tourism based on the traditional culture and resources of the area. They point out that previous attempts to develop skiing in the area have failed to provide sustainable employment due to the uncertainty of the climate and the perception of local young adults that skiing-based tourism does not provide real jobs, only part-time and seasonal work. Much dissatisfaction has been created by this approach, no matter how well meaning the original intention.

Closer examination of the situation reveals that the community members arguing for this new approach are incomers – recently settled in the area, well educated and financially independent or earning a living through telecommuting. There is some ill feeling towards the incomers because they are blamed for an increase in housing prices in the area and because some have been elected onto the local community council and other voluntary organisations in the area. The local authority is committed to involving the public in local decision-making but recognises that the community is deeply divided.

SAQ

Should only those people who show enough commitment to take an active part in local affairs be entitled to vote on proposals for local developments? In some cases an early decision must be taken as failure to prove local support. Delays to allow the 'uncommited' to participate may result in the available development funds being allocated to another more coherent community.

ETHICAL THEORIES

Awareness of the long history of ethics can assist in debate and provide a degree of gravitas to sometimes stormy, argumentative situations. This is also useful in the presence of sceptical 'rationalists' who might ask 'Where is the evidence for your claims?' or 'pragmatists' who might ask 'Just how much will that cost?' Reference to established cases can raise the status of the ethical arguments.

Teleological approaches

Teleological approaches to ethical dilemmas address the ends or outcomes of actions. They are 'consequentialist' in that they focus on the actual balance of *good* and *bad* consequences of an action. They are forward looking, considering how best to maximise good results on a long-term basis in the future. One example is *utilitarianism*.

Utilitarianism

Jeremy Bentham (1748–1832), a British philosopher, is associated with utilitarianism. He asserted that an action itself is neither good nor bad – it is only the *consequences* of the action that can be assessed. This involves weighing up the bads and the goods (costs and benefits) that an action produces: good outcomes are said to have utility; bad outcomes, disutility. The goal is the greatest good (or happiness) for the greatest number of people.

An application of this theory is in the context of 'global warming'. There is a strongly supported – and contested – contemporary ethical argument that 'we,' the present generations, should not leave a legacy of a build-up of greenhouse gases, which contribute to global warming, to a future generation to clean up. Ethically, this seems 'obviously right' but it can be challenged. It could be asserted that by adopting a policy of cutting back on the emission of these gases we would suffer a certain amount of inconvenience – 'disutility' – due to the costs incurred. We could further conclude that a future generation that inherits a world suffering the consequences of many decades of global warming will have such technological advantages that it will experience less disutility than we would in cleaning up the damage caused by our actions. This would also be consistent with the *techno-centrist* arm of environmentalist ideology, whose extreme proponents would argue that consumers and the free market should be entirely free of restraints since future technology will always find a way to overcome any environmental limits.

But such teleological arguments are not consistent with sustainability criteria which can be interpreted as ruling out policy programmes that impose substantial risk and emphasising above all that we provide for flexibility so that future generations can adapt to unforeseeable events (Howarth and Monahan, 1992 in Turner *et al.*, 1994). Providing this flexibility is characteristic of the sustainability approach and was discussed previously as the intergenerational equity criterion (Scottish Natural Heritage, 1993). This is criticised, however, by supporters of the opposite arm to technocentrism in environmentalist ideology, extreme ecocentrism or *deep ecology*. According to this perspective, economic systems must be transformed into minimum resource-take systems, necessitating reduced economic activity and population levels (Turner *et al.*, 1994). The Institute for Deep Ecology (*www.deep-ecology.org*) defines its objective: 'It promotes ecological values and actions through experiential workshops that transform old modes of thinking, honor spirit, and support bold actions'.

SAQ

What forms of tourism might be compatible with a 'deep ecology' perspective which would place severe constraints on any development that would diminish present or future environmental quality, insisting the humanity must live within 'natural limits'? What types of destination might be favoured?

SAQ

Mass tourism provides the greatest good for the greatest number of people. It is wrong to criticise it because of alleged negative impacts. Do you agree?

Deontological approaches

Deontic principles are concerned with duties, rather than the consequences of actions. Certain actions are right or wrong in themselves. For example, correct or positive duties include telling the truth or doing your duty (whatever the consequences); negative duties include not being deliberately unkind and cruel, not deliberately killing.

Deontological approaches present a major criticism of utilitarianism in that evaluating the costs and benefits of an action is irrelevant if the action itself is wrong (or right). However, a criticism of this approach is exemplified in implied rightness of 'always tell the truth' – regardless of the consequences, even where the consequences could be disastrous. *Formalism*, associated with Immanuel Kant (1724–1804) a German philosopher, is an example of a non-consequentialist theory and addresses dilemmas such as this. According to Kant, the motives behind an action are what should be focused on – the 'categorical imperative'. Thus an action which is condemned as morally wrong may not be wrong if the person performing it does so as an act of good will or duty and not, for example, out of self-interest. This view emphasises the freedom of the individual (to choose right from wrong).

ETHICAL DILEMMAS IN TOURISM

Exercise

Ethical tourism?

As a developer with a conscience I believe that the indigenous people living in this remote region must be removed from what my critics call 'their ancestral lands'. While I am accused of acting purely to further my big game hunting tourism business, I argue that these people will be better off accepting my financial incentives to leave the land and establish themselves in homes and jobs in the city where they will have the benefits of education and modern health services that they are clearly in need of in their present primitive circumstances.

Do you agree? Do you disagree?
   Give arguments for and against the views of this would-be tourism entrepreneur, relating them where possible to ethical theories.

CASE STUDY

Applications of ethical theories: conservation vs preservation – Gifford Pinchot and John Muir (early 20th century): The 'right use' of the forest resource in US national parks

This 'classic' case study is regarded as symbolising two major competing environmental 'world views'.
   The utilitarian tradition was invoked by Pinchot – a leader of the '*conservationist*' movement. He argued that natural forest exploitation for the greatest (material) good for the greatest number of people should take place wherever the resources were available. It was wrong to do otherwise – conservation is the 'wise use' of resources. His view was in line with the 'progressive' tradition in US politics of the time, as forests had been generally

regarded as an enemy to be subdued, ever since the European colonisation of North America had begun in the late 15th century:

> The object of our forest policy is not to preserve the forests because they are beautiful ... or because they are refuges for the wild creatures of the wilderness ... but ... the making of prosperous homes.
>
> (Pinchot)

John Muir was a leader of the *preservationist* movement and founder of the Sierra Club (see Chapter 8). He argued that preservation of wilderness for spiritual and aesthetic values of human beings and the intrinsic rights of the land itself should prevail:

> The clearest way into the Universe is through a forest wilderness. [...] Climb the mountains and get their glad tidings.
>
> *(Muir)*

While John Muir lost the argument for the general principle, he succeeded in having Yosemite established as the second US national park and went on to become known as the founding father of the international national park movement and an inspiration to the later environmental movement (John Muir Trust, *www.jmt.org*).

SAQ 1

Discuss the pros and cons of Muir's and Pinchot's arguments. How does Pinchot's use of the term 'conservation' relate to contemporary associations of the word?

SAQ 2

Golden eagles are only important because tourists enjoy seeing them.

Do you agree? Is this the only reason why eagles (or any other endangered species) should be protected?

SAQ 3

One way to protect endangered species is to privatise them. Only unowned species are threatened. Property rights would ensure that people have an incentive to protect them.

Do you agree? (The 'tragedy of the commons' – Garrett Hardin, *www.die-off.com/page95.htm*).

SAQ 4

To avoid an ecotourism business going under, management decides to permit more tourists to enter an area than they believe the ecological carrying capacity can sustain – the carefully worked out 'LACs' (limits to acceptable change) would be exceeded – 'but for one year only ...'. The company reasons that since its business makes an important contribution to conservation and to employment of local people in the area, this is justifiable.

> Do you agree? Give arguments for and against the company's proposed action.

ENVIRONMENTAL ECONOMICS

Does economics provide the real-world realism to temper the 'rarified' scientific imperatives and the 'sentimental' ethical aspirations that destination management and development is frequently confronted with? 'It's the economy, stupid' is a statement attributed to a former US president when asked what the voters are really concerned about at election time. It is a widely held view; but consider this assertion:

> Economic analysis can measure the intensity with which we hold our beliefs; but it cannot evaluate these beliefs on their merits. Yet such evaluation is essential to political decision making.

From this standpoint, economics is one element of the sustainable development approach, often dominant in 'real-world' controversies, but arguably – in certain circumstances – it should be secondary.

Cost-benefit analysis is widely used as an approach to evaluating alternative strategies. For comparison purposes the costs and benefits of each strategy are generally expressed in the common currency of economics, but realistically how can all the tangible and intangible values essential to the quality of a destination or the quality of the tourist experience be converted to economic terms? Methods for the comparison of environmental qualities, such as beauty in various scenic areas, were discussed previously, but no attempt was made to place an economic value on these. However, in an increasingly market-oriented world that may be required. For example, a destination manager in a city may have to produce strong arguments as to whether a popular city view should be preserved – or not – in the context of a development proposal for an 'essential' new multi-storey office block or a new shopping development which will block that view.

A rural destination manager may be faced with the dilemma of choosing between refurbishing and upgrading an existing visitor and heritage centre or ski complex or a complete redevelopment (see Chapter 10).

The existing facility – for example a mountain-top visitor/interpretive centre may have been constructed on the mountain at a time when that was considered appropriate – it offered the best views. With the passage of time – and change in attitudes towards conservation and wilderness values and the nature of the tourist experience – there may be strong demands to relocate the facility, but at considerable expense.

It is relatively simple to put a monetary value on the extra sales that might be generated by a new shopping mall and the additional jobs that might be generated. It is more difficult – and certainly less common – to be required to place an economic value on the loss – or gain – in quality of the view or of the visitor experience that would result from the development.

Complications arise from the fact that the institutions of private property and the prevailing economic system in western societies have evolved together so that efficient use is made of things that are *owned*. This may be attributed to Adam Smith, the 18th-century economist, who suggested that the 'invisible hand' of competitive markets would guide resources into uses where they will produce the things that people, as consumers, want most and will buy and use as they see fit. Resources which are not owned will therefore not be used efficiently; neither will there be an incentive to provide them. From this perspective, many of the environmental problems faced at the dawn of the 21st century are a consequence of both public *and* private ownership. However, key resources of the contemporary tourism industry which contribute to the quality of the tourist experience of destinations – the beauty, image and ambience of a restored historical town, the clean waters of an unpolluted lake, the clean air of a city – are *not* owned and thus when threatened by development proposals present a difficult challenge to those who wish to protect them. These resources have been referred to as 'free goods' or more prosaically, 'Gifts of God' and, being free, are – allegedly – not valued as they otherwise would be. A dramatic, non-tourist example of the use and mis-use of free goods is the decline of certain seafish stocks where governments are belatedly imposing fishing limits on fishermen accustomed to taking as much as they can catch, secure in the knowledge that there is demand. Examples such as these have been referred to as the 'tragedy of the commons' (Garrett Hardin, *www.dieoff.com/page95.htm*).

Private ownership of all resources would not resolve all difficulties, even if it were feasible. Neither is public ownership the solution to all such problems. Many of the resources that make up 'the environment' are not suitable for private ownership since they lack the 'excludability' attribute – it is not practical to exclude people from them or prevent people using them; moreover such practice might also be socially or politically unacceptable.

Exercise

Subsidising uneconomic farming practices

It is no longer considered politically appropriate to subsidise uneconomic forms of agriculture such as upland sheep farming. This is causing severe hardship in many parts of the UK and other EU countries where this form of agriculture is traditional.

Arguably, upland agriculture is part of the tourist experience sought by many visitors to the countryside. This is on account of its contribution to many 'cultural landscapes' which are considered to be highly attractive on account of the picturesque evidence of the landscape management efforts of many generations of hill farmers – the dry-stone dykes and distinctive vegetation patterns of parts of many popular destinations such as the Scottish Highlands and the Borders, the English Lake District and the Yorkshire Dales and the Cévennes Mountains of Southeast France.

Prepare an argument for the continuation of subsidies, or other forms of support, to hill agriculture, outlining the priorities in Britain or another country (where hill farming is practised) of your choice.

Moreover, *economies of scale* apply to the use of many natural resources. Many users 'consume' environmental resources such as beaches and the sea, open space such as mountain and hill areas and these tourists and recreationists are exercising their basic rights to air and water and, increasingly, to land through 'access' legislation. In the process they interfere with other users, sometimes reducing the convenience and the opportunities for alternative use or the enjoyment of others.

Likewise, there are many road users. While the roads are generally owned by a local authority, and are more correctly regarded as public goods, there are analogies. Users – motorists, bus passengers, cyclists, pedestrians, lorry drivers and others – generally do not pay to use the roads (with notable exceptions such as motorways in certain countries and proposals for road pricing in certain cities) but they are indirectly paying for them through taxation. Despite mounting congestion in many cities the aggrieved individual motorist, for example, has little incentive to stop using the road. The general reaction is: 'Why should I, rather than some other driver?' As a result, road congestion continues to grow. The traditional reaction has been to construct more roads, but as physical space runs out in many cities, and as public attitudes towards the role of the private car change, other solutions are sought. A powerful argument powering the search for alternative transport strategies in cities, notably, is rising awareness of the true cost of increasing car use. For example, individual motoring is heavily subsidised by non-car-owning taxpayers many of whom are no longer prepared to tolerate the reduction in scale and quality of public bus services resulting from past prioritising of the needs of the motorist.

Road pricing may be a part-solution. A number of British cities are giving it a trial. It requires cordons to be set up around the city centre and motorists charged a once-a-day fee when they cross the cordon. The schemes are generally enforced by automatic cameras which record the vehicle's registration number and these are connected to a computer system which deducts a fee from the motorist's pre-paid account.

How should free or public goods be evaluated and managed?

Public goods may be defined as resources or commodities from which potential users cannot be excluded. The inevitable mutual interference between users is one example of an *externality*. Externalities arise where the activities of one person affect the welfares or production functions of other people who have no direct control over that activity. General principles for the management of free or public goods must take this into account. Access to public goods cannot be restricted, by definition, so the real decision is with supply – how much to make available. (Within national parks and protected areas where restrictions on access are possible management can, in practice, impose a degree of restriction – both overt and covert – on users.)

If the 'good' occurs *entirely* naturally, e.g. a natural and difficult route which has been created by the passage of migrating wildlife through a wilderness area to what is, to the tourist determined enough to risk the journey, a spectacular viewpoint, then there is no management decision to be made. If a route to the viewpoint had to be created at some trouble and expense, then no single individual is likely to find it worth providing, since he could not enforce a charge for its use and so recover his costs of construction. A *social* decision would have to be made about whether to provide the good and if so, on what scale and of what character. Such decisions are central to the theory of public goods (Dorfman and Dorfman, 1972).

A systematic approach to evaluating options – 'willingness to pay'

To illustrate further, consider a town with three neighbourhoods of equal population. Traffic passing through the town has increased considerably since a theme park was created nearby by the local council. The townspeople welcome the theme park since it celebrates their local heritage and employs a number of local people, but they are concerned about the noise and danger created by the increased traffic.

The 'public good' in question is a bypass that would divert the traffic bound for the theme park around the outskirts of the town. None of the neighbourhoods is willing to pay for the bypass on its own and the local council is unable to meet all the costs, but the residents of each would accept a small rise in their local taxes to cover the expense. Whether the bypass is built, and if so how effective it should be, and the design standards (since this is an area of high amenity) depends on:

- its actual costs

- its perceived value to each of the communities.

Figure 1.3 illustrates this. The effectiveness of the bypass, as measured by the percentage of through traffic removed from the town is plotted horizontally; the costs in pounds sterling or euros to the individual tax payers are plotted vertically. The line P is the *marginal cost curve*. The cheapest bypass would be constructed along the route easiest to construct, of low cost materials and would be narrow, uneven and contorted; in consequence it would be likely to achieve only a small reduction in through traffic since no one would want to drive along it. It would cost 40 ecu per annum per taxpayer. A better bypass would reduce through traffic by 20% and would cost 115 ecu per annum per taxpayer. The most expensive option would cost 220 ecu per annum per taxpayer but because of its quality and efficiency would be likely to achieve an almost 50% reduction in through traffic.

Extrapolating the figures produces curves A, B and C, the willingness to pay curves for each neighbourhood since there are equal numbers of individual taxpayers in each. Curve A shows how much a taxpayer would be willing to pay for traffic reduction in the neighbourhood. If only 10% of traffic were being removed the willingness to pay would be 120 ecu per year to have an additional 1% removed and so on. If neighbourhood A were able to buy traffic reduction itself, curve A would be its demand curve for through traffic removal. But it cannot, since the bypass (the means of through traffic removal) is a public good and the services cannot be delivered to it alone, without providing the same amount to neighbourhoods B and C.

The aggregate curve A + B + C is the vertical sum of the three willingness to pay curves, the aggregate willingness on the part of all the residents of the community – the consumers who must pay for additional improvements. The point where P crosses this curve has special importance. It is the level of traffic removal where the cost of an additional percentage is just equal to the amount that all the beneficiaries taken together are willing to pay for an increase. If less were removed, they would be prepared to pay for an increase; if more, they would not be prepared to pay for

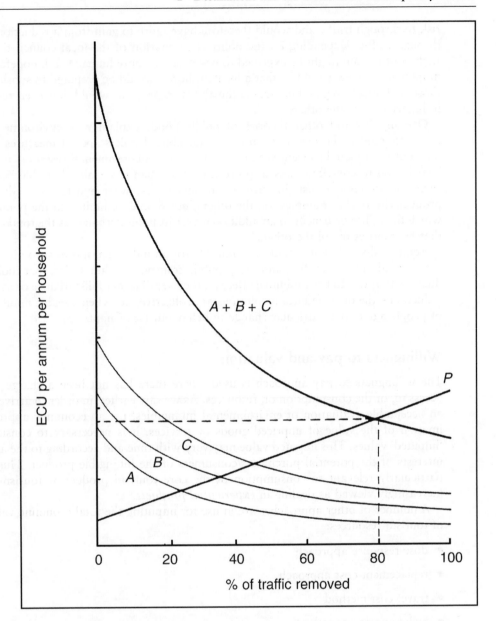

Figure 1.3 *Optimal provision of a public good*
Source: Adapted from Dorfman and Dorfman, 1972

any further reduction in traffic. In this example, they would be prepared to pay towards a bypass that would remove 80% of their through traffic.

This example illustrates the basics of the theory of public goods: the appropriate level to provide is the one for which the vertical sum of beneficiaries' willingness to pay curves crosses the marginal curve. Other issues are, of course, present in real-world situations. The *distribution* of cost among the beneficiaries is one example and might take into account ability to pay (which is not the same thing as willingness to pay). For example, older people or children might be considered more at risk to through traffic and would therefore have more to gain from a reduction in through traffic. Depending on the political persuasion of the local council those with most to gain might be expected to pay more. A more humane and, hopefully, more realistic view would be that a local authority would be prepared to subsidise those with much to gain but lacking the ability to pay; this would, however, result in higher tax for the others.

Overall, this and other theories of public goods explain why environmental resources tend to be overused, misused and abused unless special measures are taken. An individual's incentives induce him to use environmental resources more heavily and to contribute less to protecting them than is socially desirable. Since each user imposes a cost (in terms of inconvenience, wear and tear or reduced productivity of the resources) on the others, use should be limited to the point at which the utility or benefit to an additional user just counterbalances the total cost that he imposes on all the others.

Additionally, while it would be admirable for an individual motorist to give up the car and take up cycling and using public transport within a city, that individual's action would have minimal effect on the overall level of disturbance or smog reduction – the only significant solutions are collective, i.e. when sizeable numbers of people agree to a particular change in behaviour (see Chapter 5).

Willingness to pay and valuation

The willingness to pay approach is used where there has not been a charge for access to, or the consumption of, resources. As we saw earlier, in order to arrive at an acceptable evaluation of environmental intangibles, i.e. an economic approximation of the value of unpriced goods or services, it is neccessary to consider 'imputed' values. This imputed value may vary with time and according to the age/interests of the potential purchasers/consumers of the intangible product. This is particularly relevant to consumption of the core tourism product as tourism is increasingly viewed as dealing in *experiential products*.

A number of other approaches are in use for imputing the total economic value of tourism resources:

- dose-response approach
- replacement cost approach
- travel cost method
- hedonic pricing method
- expressed preference methods
- contingent valuation method.

These methods and their applications are discussed in detail in specialist texts on environmental economics (for example, Turner *et al.*, 1994).

What does the destination manager need to know?

Destination management is arguably not a 'subject' in its own right but a multi-disciplinary field whose managers need a working knowledge of a wide range of 'older' established professional fields and disciplines. The following is a 'primer' on environmental economics – basic, essential information on one specific subject area within this wide field.

What are the basic principles of economics in a destination/place perspective?

- All economic decisions have environmental consequences – and vice versa.

- Human well-being is an economic effect.

- Economics can complement ethical considerations, often criticised as 'woolly'/ lacking in hard facts.

- Economics is not just about 'money' – but money is a convenient measuring rod of what people want/don't want concerning the environment.

The environment – what are its basic functions/roles in this context?

- It supplies resources, spaces, etc.

- It assimilates waste products – although waste never totally 'disappears'; pollution will have consequences, however indirect or small.

- It provides people with natural services, e.g. aesthetic enjoyment, spiritual uplift, recreation.

Note: Some but not all of these functions have accepted market prices. This results in market failure with regard to *free goods* or 'intangible assets' such as clean air, 'safety', fine views, a sense of freedom, etc. How can a *value* be put on these clearly *valuable* assets? The *value* of these attributes of places/destinations is missing from traditional approaches to cost-benefit assessment yet often they are the key 'sought after' tourist objectives. An 'indirect' valuation has to be put on them, for example through questions such as 'How much would we be prepared to pay not to lose this public good?' (e.g. a park in a city which could be sold for a very high sum to a developer who wishes to turn it into a carpark). Another approach is to interview tourists as to how important to their choice of a destination is the presence of public parks and/or a townscape of beautiful old buildings. These could be demolished to make way for more 'economic' tower blocks. At issue are material tangible attributes, and the 'intangible assets' of (some) destinations such as a 'sense of security' and 'friendly local people'.

Are there 'limits to growth' (or development)?

A 'big question'! Basically 'bigger is not always better' is an easy way out. For example, would a particular destination – let's say a historic city – be 'better' if it were bigger? There is such a thing as an 'optimum' size – deciding what that is is more difficult! It may be influenced by factors such as 'walkability' and 'friendliness' and a sense of 'everything within reach'. Contrariwise, with size comes the 'buzz of city life' and the wide variety of activities that are on offer within a larger city.

Here are some key historical perspectives (*www.encyclopedia.com.html/section/ economics_MatthusRicard.andMill.asp*).

Absolute limits prevail (Malthus, 1798)

A stationary state (of misery) is inevitably achieved as human populations grow until they are checked by 'war, pestilence and plague'.

Malthus was writing before modern medicine and other technical advances we take for granted today were invented. Clearly war (in its various forms) remains a major concern, however.

Relative limits prevail (Ricardo, 1817)

Rising costs are incurred as the best, or the most accessible, resources are used up. At a certain level the cost is so high that further exploitation is unprofitable and stops until market conditions change.

Ricardo could scarcely have imagined today's huge rate of growth of cities – and other places/destinations – often accelerated by tourism development. The 'best locations' are already taken up – we must be more creative in using what is left and in conserving the best of what is already developed.

Social limits prevail (Marx, late 19th century)

The unfair distribution of wealth in society leads inevitably to social unrest. Social 'exclusion' is today's term for the same concern – now more positively renamed 'social inclusion'. This is a very contemporary objective. In an affluent destination/place, it is considered unethical – and wasteful – if some of the citizens are excluded from sharing in and contributing to the growth of a place.

Sustainable development implies there are constraints on sheer size increase, but 'growth' is definable and achievable in other ways. Improved technology enables more to be done with less and with less wastage. This is more productive, producing more wealth. By contrast, the 'deep ecology' model of the economy is committed to a steady-state (*www.deep-ecology.org*). Critics argue (perhaps through insufficient study of it) that it postulates an ideal state beyond which there is no reason to go ... a rather negative alternative to a more mainstream belief in the 'inevitability of progress'. The common ground shared with mainstream views is that all human activity has side effects and these 'externalities' must be taken into account to avoid an imbalance in the use of resources.

What are external costs?

These are frequently omitted from conventional calculations of the costs and/or benefits of development proposals. Examples include:

- health damage
- mortality increases
- less pleasurable leisure experiences.

Clearly these are undesirable! Avoiding them costs money. They are outcomes we haven't planned for or anticipated in our calculations and plans. For example, many people would argue that there are too many restrictions on driving. Some will have memories (or good imaginations) of 'the early days of motoring' when there were far fewer cars on the road and few restrictions. Unfortunately, cars do pollute the atmosphere, do take up road space, do cause serious accidents – but because they are inherently desirable (due to powerful advertising?) too many people want to own and drive one. Those without access to a car are the losers – and even in an affluent city (like Edinburgh) that is more or less half of all households. However, they and car owners share some of the externalities – air pollution, for example. Reduced bus services is another, resulting from reduced demand, although in this case it is only the non-car owners who suffer.

Such externalities have been referred to as forms of 'economic pollution'. Who should pay for the remedial action – the victim? Or should the approach be 'polluter pays'?

What are private costs and social costs?

These are two aspects of production and consumption and are related to 'externalities' discussed earlier. 'Private costs' are incurred directly by, for example, the developer/owner in the construction of a new hotel or visitor attraction. 'Social costs' are experienced by those who do not use or benefit directly from these developments. For example, arguably there is increasing traffic in city centres driven by additional tourists who have been attracted to the city by the new attractions and hotels. 'Social' costs are the inconveniences or 'prices' paid by all residents of the destination in terms of the inconvenience caused by more tourists – queues in shops and on the roads and, in the longer term, the loss of local amenities – and even the costs of medical treatment for illnesses that arise due to increased tourist traffic. Social costs have been largely ignored in many assessments of development alternatives.

What is meant by 'resources' in this context?

Resources are the building blocks of development. For example, through a process of appropriate development, natural or cultural resources are converted into attractions for the use of tourists and others.

Resources are of two types:

- renewable

- non-renewable.

Renewable resources
Generally, biological (and living cultural resources), e.g. landscape, wildlife, fisheries, forests. Conservation-based management maintains sustainable levels of use which can, theoretically, 'last forever'.

Non-renewable resources
Only finite quantities are available. Examples include mineral reserves such as oil, gas, coal, etc. Once these reserves are 'worked out' they are gone forever. Generally, 'optimal rates of depletion' are identified and pursued to the inevitable point of depletion (absolute or economic) by which time – it is assumed – technology and/or human ingenuity will have replaced the need for them with acceptable alternatives. More relevant to tourism are irreplaceable/non-renewable cultural resources such as original works of art, archaeological remains and traditional lifestyles. These would not be 'worked out' to depletion. These *resources* should be 'developed' as protected heritage *attractions*. Art and archaeological works can be

displayed and interpreted in appropriate secure locations/galleries. Traditional lifestyles are more complex! Can they continue to be 'authentic' if the social and economic reasons for their existence have disappeared? At best, they can be continued as actual but subsidised part-time/seasonal livelihoods while 'performance' for tourists provides the additional essential income.

Access to resources

Open access
With *open access* to resources there is no apparent ownership. Examples include extractive industries:

- sea fisheries

- stock grazing and timber harvesting on wild land but which may also be suitable for certain increasingly desired types of nature-based tourism.

No individual or company holds back on rapid, extractive uses of such resources. Why should it, in a free market? A competitor would simply take over. It may even choose to ignore restraints on the enterprise that are ecologically or socially necessary or desirable. This is a further example of the 'tragedy of the commons'. The results are:

- adverse socio-cultural and/or environmental impacts

- loss of markets, damage to resources, etc.

- deterioration of the (potential) destination.

Only the introduction of regulations by government, effectively enforced, can avoid deterioration and ultimate depletion/extinction of species or create a level playing field where a sustainable harvest can be maintained.

THE POLITICAL DIMENSION

Are certain political set-ups more environmentally friendly than others? Consider:

- free market economies (capitalist)

- planned economies (from Communism to various degrees of state Socialism)

- mixed economies (as in the UK).

Each of these 'models' attempts in its own way to influence supply and demand using a variety of means:

- command and control regulations on production and consumption

- market-based incentives (both 'carrots' and 'sticks')

- behavioural/social changes in producers and consumers, e.g. new tourists (Poon, 1993), REAL tourism (Reid, 1980).

How much is social evolution; how much is due to subtle 'influence' by 'unseen hands' such as the media, government and 'big business'?

Exercise

Politics and environmental conditions

Consider the environmental pros and cons of various political ideologies. Examine the environmental conditions now apparent in a central or eastern European country of your choice. Poland, for example, had, until recently, a 'grey' image as a (former) Soviet satellite subjected to a lack of political freedom and heavy, polluting industrialisation. Since the decline of the 'Soviet Empire' and the reemergence of these countries Poland's image has 'greened' as 'explorer/allocentric' tourists have discovered its many natural and cultural attractions.

Hint

Using a search engine (e.g. *www.Yahoo.com*) find and examine relevant websites on these countries/emerging destinations. Alternatively, visit local travel agents who deal with these coutries. What tourism 'products' are being offered, what organic images are being projected and what induced images are being created?

REGULATION OF RESOURCE USE

Legal means

This is generally conducted through the issuing of orders or laws by governments governing the extraction of resources.

Examples of regulatory tools (historic and current) – standards, orders and laws (not specifically for tourism industry purposes) are as follows:

- Environmental Impact Assessment (introduced in the USA in early 1970s)
- The Environmental Protection Act, 1990
- BS7750 (British Standard for Environmental Systems, 1991)
- BS5750 (British Standard on Quality)
- Best practicable means (BPM)
- BPEO – best practicable environmental option (EU)
- Best available technology not entailing excessive costs (BATNEEC)
- Best available control technology (BACT) (USA)
- CEMAS, the Community Eco-Management and Audit Scheme (EU, 1993 and 1995) (see Figure 1.4).

Figure 1.4 *CEMAS – Community Eco-Management and Audit Scheme*

The EU Eco-Management and Audit Scheme (EMAS) is a management tool for companies and other organisations to evaluate, report and improve their environmental performance. The scheme has been available for participation by companies since 1995 (Council Regulation (EEC) No 1836/93 of 29 June 1993) and was originally restricted to companies in industrial sectors.

Since 2001 EMAS has been open to all economic sectors, including public and private services (Regulation (EC) No 761/2001 of the European Parliament and of the Council of 19 March 2001). In addition, EMAS was strengthened by the integration of EN/ISO 14001 as the environmental management system required by EMAS; by adopting an attractive EMAS logo to signal EMAS registration to the outside world; and by considering more strongly indirect effects such as those related to financial services or administrative and planning decisions.

Participation is voluntary and extends to public or private organisations operating in the European Union and the European Economic Area (EEA) – Iceland, Liechtenstein and Norway. An increasing number of candidate countries are also implementing the scheme in preparation for their accession to the EU.

Source: Adapted from *www.europa.eu.int/comm/environment/emas*

Economic incentives approach

Resource developers are 'encouraged' to adopt particular ways of operating:

- a pollution tax *not* to pollute
- grants/soft loans to develop in a certain, specified (sustainable) way
- a tourism tax (imposed on tourism businesses)
- standards to achieve, with cash incentives, e.g. ISO standards; 'green' awards.

Exercise

Use of a tourism tax within a given destination

In what sectors of the industry could tourism tax be imposed on: accommodation? Transport? Or tourism activities that directly 'use' environmental resources? How much could or should be charged? How much are people willing to pay?

INDICATORS FOR SUSTAINABILITY AND AUDITS

Indicators

Indicators are in widespread use as guides for decision makers in a range of fields, e.g. gross national product (GNP) and net trade balance at the national level.

Economic indicators are particularly well established. Indicators in other fields include: cholesterol levels (human health); population growth rate and literacy levels.

Historically, one of the earliest instances of an environmental indicator was the use of caged canaries in coalmines to detect poisonous gases. The birds would show signs of distress or die before levels of gas were high enough to injure or kill the miners.

Indicators for the sustainable management of tourism

(Adapted and summarised from International Institute for Sustainable Development, Canada, 1993; *www.iisd.org/measure/faqindicator.htm*.)

Governments and businesses make decisions that affect the business of tourism and the destinations in which tourism operates. Decisions are often made with inadequate awareness of their effect on the environment or on the residents of destinations and of the consequences of negative environmental and social impacts on the economic well-being of tourism businesses.

Information on these impacts is increasingly available as the scale of tourism's negative as well as positive consequences is recognised. However, the information is frequently in such a form that the typical tourism or destination manager is ill-equipped to understand it or simply cannot or will not spare the time to study it.

To enable the tourism industry to become a knowledgeable participant in the planning of the use of the environment and a knowledgeable manager of its own impacts there is a need for readily comprehensible information in forms appropriate to the tourism manager (IISD, 1993).

For the busy and non-specialist destination manager, practical and useful indicators would focus on and measure these factors relevant to the destination. Most indicators have focused on biological and physical measures of environmental quality or health, while indicators of social and cultural stresses are less well developed. Other indicators are essential to permit destination planners and managers to minimise the risk of inadvertent damage to the industry and its own resource base of natural and cultural resources. They would be applicable at the different scales and levels at which tourism operates, i.e. local, city-wide, regional, national and international levels, and in each of the destination types addressed in this book.

Types of indicator

(Based on what the manager needs to know.)

Warning indicators

These alert decision makers to potential areas of concern and the need to anticipate and prevent problems.

SAQ

The caged canary was the early coal industry's indicator. Is there an equally convenient tourism industry equivalent or is the tourism industry too complex?

Measures of pressure or stresses
These would measure key external factors of concern, e.g. competitor destinations, changing tourist tastes, international tensions.

SAQ

Are these already available to the tourism industry? What are they? Give some examples.

Measures of the state of the resource base
What has changed/what is changing?

- Current use levels of facilities and neighbourhoods within the destination.

- Current levels of air, coastal and beach pollution. (What standards are used in the Blue Flag award for EU beaches? *www.blueflag.org*)

Impacts and their consequences
Beach closures due to marine pollution; hillpath closure due to erosion (the 'pressure of feet' of too many walkers in too few places); loss of wildlife in areas of overintensive wildlife viewing.

Measures of management effort/action (by others)
Levels of pollution regulation; amount spent to control waste; establishment of protected areas; existence of sustainable tourism plans.

Measures of management impact
What has destination management actually done and achieved? How effective are recent interventions to improve sustainability?

Audit of organisations

Environmental, social and other criteria

Organisations themselves can and should be subject to audit and assessment. The destination management 'organisation' is likely to be but one part of a larger organisation, such as a tourist board, or a local authority department, such as planning, and it may be difficult to 'isolate' the destination management contributions.

Appropriate criteria of measurement and ratings of these would be developed to suit the nature of the organisation (see Table 1.3).

Table 1.3 *Criteria for measurement and ratings*

Scales would range from 'well above average' to 'well below average':
- Disclosure – openness to questioning beyond statutory minimum requirements
- Gender issues – e.g. percentage of women in senior positions
- Ethnic policy – e.g. percentage of non-whites in senior positions
- Community – e.g. community service by seconded staff, charitable donations
- Environmental impact – effect of company's activities on the environment
- Environmental action – significant initiatives taken by company to reduce impacts
- Dealings with certain 'blacklisted' organisations or countries (e.g. because of poor employment conditions of porters/tour guides/hotel workers)
- Respect for (non-human) life – e.g. baited or tethered wildlife for viewing; animal testing of products
- Respect for people – employment of locals as guides, translators, hotel staff etc., with training opportunities
- Politics – financial contributions to specific political parties
- Military connections/support – destination/tourism facilities constructed by 'forced' labour, military equipment or services used.

Source: Adapted from Adams *et al.*, 1991

Types of audit

- Compliance audit – assessment of compliance with environmental and other relevant regulations.

- Site audit – spot check of sites known to be actual or potential environmental or other relevant hazards.

- Activity audit – assessment of activities that cross business boundaries.

- Corporate audit – assessment of entire business.

- Associate audit – assessment of subsidiary, agent or supplier companies.

- Issues audit – assessment of company's activities on a specific environmental problem such as rainforest loss.

- Acquisitional or transactional audit – assessment of environmental and other costs of disposing of subsidiary companies.

- Health and safety audit – assessment of health and safety issues in relation to particular plants or processes.

- Life cycle analysis – assessment of environmental and other impact of product or service throughout its lifetime.

Bibliography

Adams, R., Carruthers, J. and Hamil, S. (1991) *Changing Corporate Values: A Guide to Social and Environmental Policy and Practice in Britain's Top Companies*. New Consumer/Kogan Page. London.

City of Edinburgh Council (1999) *Edinburgh Business Environmental Guide*. CEC. Edinburgh.

Commission of the European Communities (1992) *Towards Sustainability – A European Programme of Policy and Action in Relation to the Environment and Sustainable Development: Com (92) 23 Final*. CEC. Brussels.

Darling, F.F. (1955) *West Highland Survey: An Essay in Human Ecology*. HMSO. London.

Darling, F.F. and Boyd, J.M. (1964) *The Highlands and Islands*. Collins New Naturalist. London.

Dorfman, R. and Dorfman, N.S. (1972) *Economics of the Environment: Selected Readings*. W.W. Norton & Company. New York.

Edington, J. (1986) *Ecology, Recreation and Tourism*. Cambridge University Press. Cambridge.

Elkington, J. and Fennell, S. (1998) *The CEO Agenda: Can Business Leaders Satisfy the Triple Bottom Line?* Sustainability/UN. New York.

Goldsmith, F.B. *Ecological Effects of Visitors and the Restoration of Damaged Areas*.

Government of Canada (1990) *Canada Green Plan*. Tourism Canada. Ottawa.

Harrison, C.M. (19) *Lowland Heathland: The Case for Amenity Land Management*.

Howie, F. *et al.* (1974) The Flotta Orkney Environmental Protection Scheme. *Petroleum Review*.

Howie, F. (1996) Skills, Understanding and Knowledge for Sustainable Tourism. In G. Richards (ed.) *Tourism in Central and Eastern Europe: Educating for Quality*. ATLAS (European Society for Tourism and Leisure Education)/Tilburg University Press. Tilburg.

International Union for Conservation and Nature, United Nations Environment Programme, World Wildlife Fund (1980) *The World Conservation Strategy: Living Resource Conservation for Sustainable Development*.

International Union for Conservation of Nature and Natural Resources (1974) *World Conservation Strategy*. IUCN.

Johnson, S. (1993) *The Earth Summit*. Kluwer Law International. London.

Leopold, A. (1944) *A Sand County Almanac*. Oxford University Press. New York.

Lovelock, J. (1988) *Gaia: A New Look at Life on Earth*. Oxford Paperbacks. Oxford.

Meadows, D.H., Meadows, D.L., Randers, J. and Behrens, W.W. (1972) *The Limits to Growth: A Report for the Club of Rome*. Potomac Associates. New York.

Middleton, V.T.C. (1998) *Sustainable Tourism: a Marketing Perspective*. Butterworth-Heinemann. Oxford.

Miller, G.R. and Watson, A. *Heather Moorland in Northern Britain*.

Muir, J. (1981) *Our National Parks*. University of Wisconsin Press. Madison.

Murphy, P.E. (1994) Tourism and Sustainable Development. In *Global Tourism*. Butterworth-Heinemann. London.

Murray, W.H. (1962) *Highland Landscape: A Survey Commissioned by the National Trust for Scotland*. NTS. Edinburgh.

Pearce, D.W. and Turner, R.K. (1990) *Economics of Natural Resources and the Environment*. Harvester Wheatsheaf. Hemel Hempstead.

Poon, A. (1993) *Tourism, Technology and Competitive Strategies*. Cabi Publishing. Oxford.

Scottish Natural Heritage (1993) *Sustainable Development and the Natural Heritage*. SNH. Edinburgh.

Scottish Tourist Board (1992) *Tourism and the Scottish Environment*. STB. Edinburgh.

Scottish Tourist Board (1998) *Tourism in Scotland*. STB. Edinburgh.

UK Government (1992) *This Common Inheritance: The Second Year Report on the UK's Environmental Strategy*. Cmnd 2068. HMSO. London.

UK Government (1994) *The UK Strategy*. Cm 2426. HMSO. London.

UNESCO (1972) *World Heritage Sites*.

United Nations (1993) *The Earth Summit: the United Nations Conference on Environment and Development* (UNCED). Graham & Trotman. London.

Warren, A. and Goldsmith, F.B. (eds) *Conservation in Perspective*. John Wiley & Sons. Chichester.

World Commission on Environment and Development (1987a) *Our Common Future*. United Nations. New York.

World Commission on Environment and Development (1987b) *Our Common Inheritance*. Oxford University Press. Oxford.

CHAPTER 2

Principles and theories

INTRODUCTION

This chapter gives a broad overview of key ideas that are useful to the practical destination manager in understanding the tourist and of the processes of change within destinations. They give a theoretical underpinning to the destination case studies presented in this book and emphasise the transferability of good practice – with appropriate adaptation and interpretation – to other destinations. Out of these comparative studies of various destinations, assisted by the rapid and inter-active exchange of knowledge that use of the world wide web permits, general guidelines can emerge for the planning and management of specific destinations for the benefit of tourists, tourism businesses, their residents and the spirit of place.

UNDERSTANDING THE TOURIST

The class system

In the UK an established method of stratifying people into socially structured divisions is the use of the so-called Registrar General's classification (*www.soc.-surrey.ac.uk/sru/SRU9.html*). According to the nature of the occupation of the 'head of the household', an individual or family is assigned to a particular social class – A, B, C, C1, C2 ... F, representing those in the highest status 'professional/managerial' jobs, through managers, to non-manual, to manual, to retired people or pensioners on the lowest incomes. This is taken as indicating a range of other shared characteristics – house type, newspapers read, TV programmes watched, types of food eaten, recreation and types of holiday destinations chosen. In effect it elaborates the more familiar 'class system' where people belong to the 'upper', 'middle' and 'lower' classes within each of which they share a common culture of interests, lifestyles and values. In contemporary society one weakness is the fact that in many households there are two 'heads of household' and class 'barriers' are arguably less distinct than they were.

Exercise

Class factors

Why is it predominantly people in the ABC1 socio-economic groups who take 'special interest' holidays and who are members of conservation/heritage organisations such as the National Trust? Are poorer people and others with 'non-professional' jobs not interested?

Income is certainly a factor in destination and holiday choice. So are factors such as level of education, amount of disposable income, family and social commitments, amount of leisure time, peer group pressure, 'keeping up with the neighbours', fashion and trend setters such as media and music personalities and royal patronage. These have influenced the rise and (sometimes) the subsequent fall of destinations. For example, St Tropez (*www.nova.fr/saint-tropez*) on the French Riviera has evolved from 'a little village gathered around a port founded by the ancient Greeks to [...] an enduring and in some ways rather wonderful fantasy' (Baillie *et al.*, 1986). In the 19th century it was a small fishing port; then Paul Matisse and other artists arrived creating a bohemian atmosphere, distinctly different from the respectability of nearby Cannes or Nice. In 1956 the filmmaker Roger Vadim arrived to film Brigitte Bardot in *Et Dieu Créa la Femme* (*And God Created Woman*) and 'the cult took off, the 1960s took place, and the resort is now big money mainstream' (Baillie *et al.*, 1986). Aviemore in the Scottish Central Highlands, which aspired to the status of glamorous ski resort in the 1960s, subsequently declined to its present uncertain future (see Chapter 10).

Lifestyle classifications

Lifestyle classifications have acquired a certain popularity. They combine a number of social characteristics and arguably giving a better indication of how leisure time is spent. Examples of categories, expressed as acronyms, include:

YUPpies – Young, Upwardly mobile Professionals

DINKYs – Double Income, No Kids Yet

WOOPies – Well-Off Older People.

These and other social classifications give reasonable indications of the lifestyle of modern people in the 'western industrial liberal democracies'. Within specific areas of modern life, attempts have been made better to understand the motivations and consequent choices of the consumer – tourism is no exception.

TOURIST TYPES

Typologies and motivation

Development models of destinations clearly suggest the significance of understanding the nature of the tourist and tourist motivations. Differing types of tourist generate differing impacts on a destination or on a place in the early stages of becoming a destination – a 'pre-destination'. By understanding this the destination manager can take – or more likely, attempt to encourage – appropriate directions of development to encourage positive growth and avoid a subsequent decline, as predicted by destination life cycle theory, discussed later in this chapter. Ideally, a sustainable level of tourism development would be attained, where a destination can maintain a desired type of tourism for an indefinite period of time.

The idea that distinct types of tourist can be identified and described – a 'tourist typology' – is founded largely on an understanding of tourist motivation, i.e. what an individual tourist desires and hopes to find within a given destination and is therefore prepared to purchase a holiday package – of an appropriate style – to satisfy these motivations.

Tourist motivations

Tourists' motivations play a major role in destination choice and are responsible, in the aggregate, for the observed destination life cycle; notably the desire to 'move on' when a destination becomes, as some regard it, 'too popular' or, as others see it, 'deteriorating in quality'. They move on to 'new' destinations, in turn initiating the tourist destination life cycle in these 'new' areas. It is the *allocentric* tourist who initiates this quest for new destinations, being more adventurous and demanding authentic experiences in contrast to the *psychocentric* tourist who seeks the reassurance of familiar and unchallenging destinations (Plog, 1972). The safe haven of the 'environmental bubble' protects them from overexposure to 'foreigners' and their strange ways. A knowledge of tourist motivation is valuable when identifying and planning for the 'type' of tourist that the destination aims to attract – notably in its mature stage.

TOURISM, LEISURE AND HUMAN NEEDS

What prompts one person to pack the basic minimum of necessities and go by public transport to a remote part of a country where a place to eat and sleep is not guaranteed, while another chooses a package that guarantees transport, regular and familiar meals, accommodation, entertainment as well as a glimpse of a far-away place?

Why do some people visit art galleries and museums when they visit a capital city while others frequent strip clubs and bars? Why do some people do both?

Many factors are at work. People have different personalities – the genetic inheritance from their parents. Environmental factors play a major role. Advertising – television, magazines, the world wide web etc. – are highly influential and people spend their personal and working lives in different social and economic circumstances. Their working lives are constrained by the dictates of employment, by their social lives and by family, friends and neighbours. On holiday, however, they are 'away from it all' and free to 'be all they can be'. Yet it is clear that 'even' as tourists, people can be placed in distinct categories that tend to reflect their underlying personalities. One individual may display a range of apparently contradictory behaviours. He/She may have a high income, yet eat simply and live modestly and take holidays that are low cost while physically demanding. The psychological explanation would point to a unifying explanation or motive – perhaps he/she is simply saving money for a major purchase or to give to a charity. In this instance there is an intervening variable, a factor which explains the connection between the environmental stimuli and the behavioural responses. In holiday choices, the motivation might be a desire to travel far and gain a deep experience of another culture, minimising the barriers that a 'guaranteed' package might set up. Motivation cannot be observed – it can only be deduced from what is observed (Bernstein *et al.*, 1997: 337–8).

Motivation varies over time. Thus the habitual package holiday tourist may become health conscious as a result of a doctor's warning over his/her bad diet and take up small group walking holidays. In the real-world, however, motivations do not occur in isolation. At any one time several different motivations may be present, although one may be dominant.

On holiday and within the chosen destination, the archetypal tourists feel 'free to be all they can be'. They are temporarily free of the dictates of the workplace (though developments such as mobile telephones interfere with this freedom for increasing numbers of people; however, basic underlying *social influences* on behaviour continue. 'Norms' are learned, socially based rules that prescribe what people should and should not do in various situations (Bernstein *et al.*, 1997: 596). They are culturally influenced, one example being the characteristically British habit of forming orderly queues for various services, rather than a disorderly 'everyone for themselves' crowd. A practical example concerns litter. Tourists comment on the varying prevalence of litter in different places. It is a significant detraction from the beauty of many areas, from the summit of Ben Nevis, Scotland's highest mountain (*www.travelscotland.co.uk/features/ben_nevis.htm*) to the streets of London or Barcelona. Whether British cities are more littered than Spanish cities is unclear, but Edinburgh has recently introduced a 'rapid response service' for litter removal outwith the normal times of litter and refuse collection. Even this is challenged by the urban plague of 'pavement mottling' – caused by the indiscriminate dropping of chewing gum.

Norms are 'descriptive' and 'injunctive'. Descriptive norms are based on what seems to be normal practice, the way most people behave. If it is common for locals to drop litter, others – tourists – will tend to do likewise. 'Injunctive' norms are based on more specific information on what is acceptable or unacceptable behaviour. In an experiment, Rino *et al.* (1993 in Bernstein *et al.*, 1997) had a collaborator drop litter within a specific area and, on other occasions, pick it up and bin it. Thirty percent of people in the area who saw him drop litter then littered the area themselves; only 5% of people in the area seeing him pick up litter dropped litter themselves. If the street scene conveys the message that lots of people drop litter, the injunctive norm communicated to at least 30% of the people is that it is acceptable to do so. Seeing someone (not an 'official' refuse collector) picking up litter and placing it in a litter bin, communicates that it is *not* acceptable to litter.

Norms thus convey what is acceptable social behaviour for a given time and place. The reverse is deindividualisation – sometimes attributed to certain types of holiday maker. 'Lager louts' – notably British youths on holiday in certain Spanish 'sun-sand-sea' destinations in the 1980s – attained a degree of notoriety for their unruly behaviour. Being away from the home environment and known social norms and fuelled by readily available cheap alcohol, it became easy to be 'one of the herd' (see Chapter 8).

Maslow's pyramid of human needs

Maslow (1943) defined a 'hierarchy' of human needs (see Figure 2.1). He suggested five classes of needs or motives, from 'highest' to 'most basic':

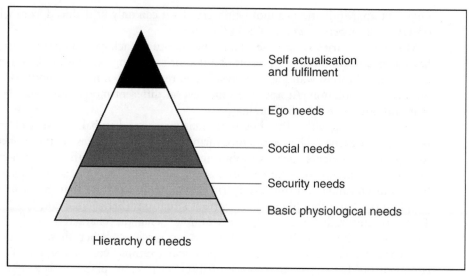

Figure 2.1 *Maslow's hierarchy of human needs*

- self-actualisation (maximising your own potential)
- esteem (e.g. the respect of others)
- social (e.g. belongingness and love)
- safety (e.g. nurture and money)
- physiological (e.g. food and drink, shelter).

Generally, the lower level needs must be satisfied at least partially before a person can be motivated by higher level goals. Maslow asserted that it was natural for an individual to want to progress from the most basic to the highest levels of satisfaction and achieve his/her human potential. The barriers – and the opportunities – were created by society; for instance, education *can* be a hindrance. But it can also promote personal growth.

All these factors influence the choice of destination selected by individual tourists. An extreme-adventure tourist might forego all lower needs to achieve self-actualisation, taking into a remote wilderness only survival rations and equipment to climb a remote mountain or to photograph rare wildlife. The context might well be, however, that in this person's personal and professional life the lower level needs are satisfied by a secure income, loving family and friends – this is the foundation for achievement of that highest goal.

APPLICATION OF PSYCHOLOGICAL THEORY TO DESTINATION MANAGEMENT

People are individuals, although social and other pressures overtly or covertly act on them, resulting in modified behaviour. As discussed earlier, 'social classes' – or more usefully here, tourist 'types' – can be identified. They may be criticised as over-generalisations, but they do contribute to more effective marketing of tourism products, to an understanding of the behaviours and expectations of tourists and, consequently, the impacts of tourism within destinations. The differences, as noted in Chapter 1, are conveyed in the rather elitist: 'I'm an explorer, you are an independent traveller, while *they* are .... tourists'.

Technically all three are 'tourists' – but different motivations are implied, each group has different expectations from a destination and there is an implication that the 'tourists' are inferior to the others.

Various researchers have been concerned specifically with understanding the tourist. As previously noted, Plog (1972) identified two basic types – the *allocentric* and the *psychocentric*, with mid-centrics sharing certain characteristics of each and constituting the largest group. The allocentrics are motivated to seek out destinations where they will experience culture, landscape and lifestyles that contrast with their experiences back home. It is the very 'differences' of the destination from their home place that is the main draw. By contrast, psychocentrics seek in their chosen destinations most if not all of the familiar comforts and assurances of their lives back home – but with certain essential differences or added values such as the absence of work and 'guaranteed sunshine'.

Other researchers made comparable observations. Drifter, explorer, individual mass tourist and organised mass tourist were described by Cohen (1972). The terms are largely self-explanatory, defining groupings within what is actually a continuum of interactions between the desire for new experiences and the need for security and reminders of home, both of which are required by all tourists, albeit in differing proportions. One 'type' was the focus of a best-selling novel of the 1970s, *The Drifters* (Michener, 1971) which perhaps captured the Zeitgeist of that decade. It portrayed a hedonistic search for self-fulfilment, starting in Spain, and moving through Morocco to Goa.

Cohen grouped these types into two categories. Drifters and explorers are 'non-institutionalised' tourists while the two types of mass tourists are 'institutionalised'. These groupings aided him in his primary objective of understanding the impacts of tourism on destinations. The former accept the places they seek as they are – that is their attraction; the institutionalised tourists require considerable change in their destinations to reduce the 'difference' between there and home to a tolerable level.

There is a contemporary tendency to attribute the adverse impacts of tourism to the institutionalised tourists and the mass tourism industry that supplies their needs. The drifters and explorers are not 'blameless' – it is they who 'kickstart' the process of tourist development within a place by the very fact of 'discovering' it and telling others about it. Then the 'others' respond to these travellers' tales of an 'undiscovered' and undeveloped 'paradise' by visiting these places in ever increasing numbers, at which point local people respond by beginning to provide 'improved' facilities. The drifters and explorers move on, repelled by the changes, endlessly seeking new places, which in turn succumb to the lure of development (Figure 2.2, page 57).

Smith (1977) identified comparable categories of tourist – explorer; elite; off-beat; unusual; incipient mass; mass; charter tourist – ranging from very limited numbers of people who accept fully the local norms of a destination area, to the massive numbers who demand 'western' amenities. His interests were in the cultural impacts of tourism on destinations.

Mention has been made of the increasingly prevalent criticism of mass tourism in its various forms, although each characterised by high degrees of standardisation and high numbers of tourists. 'REAL' tourism was a term coined by Read (1980) for his prediction of some time around the year 2000 when, he asserted, most tourism will be of the type characterised by being REAL, an acronym for Rewarding, Enriching, Adventuresome and a Learning experience.

Green tourism, ecotourism, responsible tourism, alternative tourism, good tourism, soft tourism: these and others are terms that imply an interest on the part of the tourist in the natural environment and/or the social-cultural aspects of a destination and its residents as well as the desire to avoid adverse impacts on that destination. Each could be said to be an example of Read's REAL tourism: each shares his key elements of the 'new' tourist experience, although each has a particular subject focus. A broader context for these contemporary forms of tourism is provided in Poon's (1993) term 'new tourism' or 'post-Fordist' tourism (Sharpley, 1994; Urry, 1990).

The motivations implicit in these forms of tourism imply different approaches to destination development. It is unfair – with the benefits of hindsight – to condemn the 'mistakes' of the early phases of mass tourism development that have been resulted in, for example the 'concrete costas' of Mediterranean Spain or the 'commoditisation' of cultural traditions in countries as far apart as Scotland and Hawaii.

Today there is greater understanding of the needs of tourists and their expectations of tourist destinations than in the early phase of development of the tourism industry. This understanding also permits greater awareness of the pattern of development within destinations and allows more informed planning and management to take place. The 'mistakes' of early mass tourism have also demonstrated the reality that tourism *does* consume scarce resources, *does* cause pollution and other forms of environmental deterioration and *can* disrupt 'traditional' ways of life. Consequently, contemporary tourism must be effectively planned, developed and managed in contrast to the earlier 'laissez-faire' approach based on a perspective on tourism as somehow different from other industries in being entirely benign.

Destination development in the early phase of modern mass tourism had been largely geared towards the demands of the allocentric tourist. By the 1980s, with increasing recognition of various forms of 'special interest' tourism and their potential economic benefits, awareness of the deteriorating environmental quality and relationships between tourists and residents in many destinations, attention began to focus on these types of tourist who, being more allocentric in their motivations, might avoid the problems of mass tourism. With the passage of several generations since mass tourism began in the immediate post-World War II period, the 1950s, more and more people were losing their 'fear' of the unfamiliar and were beginning to question the overdevelopment of many mass tourism destinations. What had been 'paradise' for their parents and grandparents was no longer so attractive to this generation, except for a brief period in their late teens to early 20s when sun, sand, sea and ... sex held their undiluted appeal.

Box 2.1 *Contemporary t-shirt art*

'Been there. Done that. Bought the t-shirt. There must be more to life ...'

'Don't Californicate Oregon'

'Welcome to Xxxxx. Enjoy it, then leave it – as you found it'

On a world scale 'mass tourism' remains overwhelmingly the dominant form of tourism, but the most dynamic growth is in the less institutionalised, special interest, REAL tourism that offers more individuality to the tourist. This is broadly in line with other trends in consumerism, emphasising tourism's nature as an integral part of contemporary society. In the late 20th and early 21st centuries – at least in those parts of the world that can afford it, i.e. the western, industrialised, liberal democracies – certain consumer and lifestyle characteristics are clear. In an era of 'post scarcity' (Bookchin, 1986), when for the majority of the population the 'basic' necessities of life are relatively secure, attention turns to the higher levels of aspiration. Health, exercise, wholesome food, clean environment and more fulfilling leisure become popular issues. The trend is pioneered by the 'shakers and movers', popularised by the media and entertainment industries and filters down to the rest of society.

'Special interest tourism' embraces all the forms of tourism that focus on, or 'use', specific natural and/or cultural resources, while the special interest tourist is alleged to have certain specific characteristics (Weiler and Hall, 1993). The foundation is sustainable development – awareness that tourism is not exempt from the contemporary approach to development generally. Poon (1993) has placed tourism firmly within this global context. Mass tourism was the 'correct' form for the tourism of the 1950s to the 1980s; 'new tourism' is the form of tourism that is most appropriate to the contemporary social, economic and environmental context.

UNDERSTANDING PROCESSES WITHIN DESTINATIONS

Destinations are places where tourism has developed spontaneously or has been actively encouraged. That passive or active process is influenced by the prevailing social, cultural, environmental, economic and political contexts within the place in which it develops, as well as by the purposeful drives of the businesses and other agencies that wish to develop tourism for their own specific commercial or other reasons. Also, it is fundamental to the concept of the tourist destination that tourism is generally not the sole industry or economic activity of the area identified as a destination; tourism must be integrated into the general development pattern. In some destinations tourism may be – or be intended to become – the dominant industry; in which case particularly careful planning and management of it are essential to general economy (see Chapter 3).

In this context it is clear that the management, planning and development of tourism destinations is more complex than that of a single business or enterprise. There are far more 'interested parties' or stakeholders, a wider range of objectives to be met – some of which may well be in conflict with each other – and different timescales to be harmonised. There may well also be no single 'manager' with the overall power or responsibility to direct the overall process in the desired direction. The 'destination manager' is a professional employed in an increasing number of destinations, but the 'powers' that go with the job are largely ones of influence and persuasion rather than authority.

MODELS OF DESTINATION PROCESSES

Models are widely used in many fields:

- to simplify a complex subject

- to identify the main aspects

- to aid communication

- to aid understanding

- to reveal linkages between actions and outcomes.

Models are simplifications of reality, constructed after study of representative real-world circumstances and are valuable in making predictions about change if certain conditions are altered. By altering these conditions and observing or predicting the results, the 'optimum' approach to management or development from a range of alternatives might be selected. They may be tangible, such as plastic or cardboard scale models of buildings or neighbourhoods, constructed to help understanding of how, for example, new road layouts or other developments will affect pedestrian movement or obstruct views. In more complex circumstances, they will be theoretical models – conceptual frameworks – relying on mathematics, while computers are increasingly able to transform these numerical outcomes into virtual realities for the less technically minded. Models are used widely in the scientific, social, political, business and other fields. In destination management they may be used to predict the outcomes of policy change such as favouring planning for sustainable development rather than for maximum growth; or in the context of 'best value', to indicate the most acceptable choice between limited opportunities (see Chapter 5).

The concept of a destination life cycle can be traced to an article published in 1939 in the *Scottish Geographical Magazine* by E.W. Gilbert (O'Hare and Barrett, 1997). The tourist area life cycle (TALC) and Butler's model of resort development (Butler, 1980) are derived from the product life cycle concept in marketing (see Figure 2.2). It is a useful model concerned with the hypothetical evolution of a tourist area. Numbers of tourists – or the income generated from tourism – replaces numbers of products sold. The model is based on knowledge of the development of a range of established tourist destinations that predate the contemporary period where there is increasingly a foundation on planning and sustainable development. In the absence of these contemporary considerations a destination evolves through identifiable stages (Butler, 1980).

Visits to a place by adventurous, independent travellers (allocentrics) in small numbers characterises the 'exploration' stage. These tourists are drawn by the absence of 'tourism development' and by the 'pristine' environment and character of the place. The 'involvement' stage sees local communities deciding whether positively to encourage tourism through provision of the facilities they assume to be desired by tourists, in conjunction with the local authorities. Appropriate tourism organisations may be set up.

The 'development' stage sees growth and consolidation of the local tourism industry while the decision-making power may move out of local hands, potentially resulting in over-institutionalization. Psychocentric tourists become the majority of

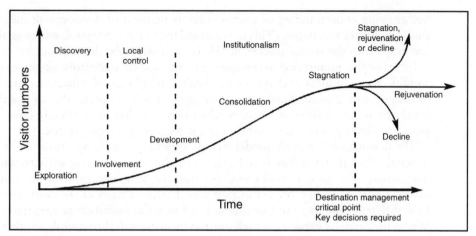

Figure 2.2 *Destination life cycle model (Adapted from Butler, 1980)*

visitors, while the allocentrics move on in search of new, 'undeveloped' places.

'Stagnation' marks the beginning of decline. The destination has failed to retain a fashionable status and environmental quality may be declining through failure to invest. Social and economic problems may arise through loss of income.

'Decline' is the consequence of inadequate or inappropriate attempts to stem the decline. Tourists are favouring new or revitalised resorts and the market is primarily day trips. It is a time of (belated) introspection, of asking, 'What went wrong/what can be done?'.

'Rejuvenation' is the outcome of successful strategies arising from the period of introspection and of drawing inspiration and lessons from comparable destinations. Limitations on development are inevitably imposed by the built environment since tourism has frequently been built into the way of life of the destination. Successful strategies may be based on repositioning; rejuvenation; new markets; or even on 'non-tourism' futures where the existing infrastructure lends itself to, for example, a focus on the retirement population: hotels are converted to retirement homes, some shops and leisure provision adjust to service the needs of the elderly.

The destination life cycle model thus allows understanding of how a place which has no identity as a tourist destination – a town or region or country which has existed exclusively for the benefit of its residents and or workers – is 'discovered' by a specific type of tourist, in sufficient numbers for the entrepreneurs in that area to take notice and begin to serve their needs. Beyond this, the resort may evolve towards – or be deliberately directed towards – a desired pattern of development. It is an objective of destination management to identify the nature of this desired 'maturity' stage of development of a destination and manage the future pattern of development towards this objective. In the absence of such 'intervention' the tourist area life cycle model predicts the inevitability of decline. In the more general 'product life cycle' model from which the destination life cycle model is derived, such decline is generally accepted as the norm. Thus when a washing powder, 'Sudso', has had an appropriate period of successful sales it will be allowed to decline – it can be readily replaced by 'New Wonder Sudso'. Clearly, in a destination – a real place where the livelihoods, lives, hopes, aspirations and businesses of the residents are at stake – acceptance of such decline is unacceptable morally, quite apart from the economic consequences. Destinations *have* gone into decline, but growing understanding of tourism and its patterns of development mean that this is no longer inevitable. (This is examined further in Chapter 8, where analogies are made with the circumstances in '3S' or 'sun-sand-sea' destinations.)

Increasingly, monitoring techniques and the use of indicators of the environmental, socio-cultural and economic 'health' of places (destinations) are being developed and applied. These '*proactive*' approaches are preferable to *re*active or 'after the event' studies of impacts when deterioration may already have taken place to a level where a destination cannot recover its former status.

The destination life cycle model has an appealing simplicity, however, it overlooks the fact that tourism is unlikely to be the sole economic activity within a destination. The model works well for 'resorts' where tourism is the principal activity, but less so in more complex places. Different parts of the destination will have different tolerances to tourism and will respond positively or negatively to it. Where the carrying capacity is high tourism business will thrive while another area, under the same tourism pressure, will decline – either in terms of its physical character, or in terms of increasing 'friction' between tourists and local residents (see Doxey's Irritation Index, page 59). In other parts of the destination, small local shops will give way to tourist boutiques or other up-market shops, increasing cash turnover in the local area, but depriving residents of the convenience of the neighbourhood 'papershop' or 'corner store'. In other words, environmental, social and economic impacts – positive and negative, at different levels of intensity – influence the 'progress' of the destination through the life cycle (see the discussions on St Mary's Street, Old Town in Chapter 6, and Yosemite National Park in Chapter 10).

Different types of tourism may be viable within different parts of the destination, particularly above a certain minimum size. While a village is unlikely to attract and sustain a wide range of different types of tourist activity, a city or, with care, a resort could.

Exercise

The destination life cycle

Consider a village or small town, preferably one you know reasonably well. What stage of the destination life cycle is it at? What is your evidence for this? What are the barriers (if any) to further development of the destination? Consider environmental, socio-cultural and economic implications.

Miossec's tourism development model

Miossec's model (Miossec, 1977) examines interactions of the four key elements within a 'resort' in different phases of tourism's development – the destination itself and its characteristics, the role of transport, tourist behaviour patterns and attitudes of the decision makers and residents of the destination.

In the early phases of development, the area scarcely merits the term destination – only occasional visitors are present and residents and decision makers hold no particular attitudes toward them.

Once an area is 'discovered', either passively or through deliberate marketing as an outcome of policy decisions, a 'pioneer' resort may be distinguished. Attitudes towards tourism change, both positively and negatively. A hierarchy or specialisms of services may arise within the evolving destination, perhaps within different centres, which may be complementary to, or in competition with, each other according to the success of planning or other forms of intervention by the local authority or other agency. An ideal would be a clearly defined hierarchy of inter-connected centres, acting together as a unified destination area with a strong image.

In this phase it is the new character of the place that is attractive to the majority of tourists, not the original, so certain types of tourist, the allocentrics, begin to 'move on'. The development of the destination's facilities over time, the behaviour of tourists and the host community's attitudes follow a pattern of change as development takes place. The 'final' phase would ideally be the development pattern arrived at through conscious decision making reflecting the desires of all stakeholders. Miossec's model is notable in this respect. Local authorities, for example, may see tourism development as primarily a means to an end, for example generating income to fund social or environmental objectives within the area, while private developers will be pursuing their own economic objectives. The sometimes conflicting nature of these objectives has led in recent years to an increasing desire for 'public-private partnerships' (PPPs) for action and develop-ment in an effort to derive more complementarity between objectives.

Other models have been developed, taking ever more sophisticated approaches to the study of destination development. What is clear is that tourism development causes change – social, cultural, environmental and economic – within places as they evolve to meet the needs of tourists. These changes will be regarded as positive or negative according to the perception of different stakeholders. Thus increasing numbers of tourists within a historic city centre can raise the turnover of local tourism and tourism-related businesses. This economic benefit has to be evaluated against decreasing amenity of the area as perceived by local residents, caused by increasing traffic, loss of local shops providing for daily needs and other change.

An understanding of the changing *attitudes* towards tourism held by residents of a destination as it progresses through the stages in the life cycle is provided by Doxey's Irritation Index or the 'Irridex'.

Doxey's Irritation Index

The stages in the destination life cycle are the result of interacting social, environ-mental, economic and political changes taking place in the local area and in the wider context. Doxey's Irritation Index is concerned with the social relationships between tourists and locals (the 'host community') as the tourism industry evolves. Tourist–host relationships can be characterised as typically going through four phases:

NEW DESTINATION

Euphoria
↓
Apathy
↓
Annoyance
↓
Antagonism

DECLINING DESTINATION

In the *Euphoria* stage, visitors to the destination are few in number and are allocentrics, being drawn to the place primarily because it is 'undeveloped' for tourism purposes. They make little if any environmental or social impact while the limited amount of economic income they bring is generally welcomed and their presence adds some interest to the local day-to-day life of the place. This welcoming atmosphere is enjoyed by the tourists who naturally speak well of the place when they return home. Perhaps unsurprisingly, their friends, acquaintances and others are therefore encouraged to visit this new, unspoiled destination.

As visitors increase in number they are increasingly taken for granted – the *Apathy* phase. Informal hospitality gives way to formalised contracts between tourists and the residents offering services. The need for planning new opportunities is recognised, primarily in terms of marketing.

As the emerging industry grows within the destination some residents begin to question whether it is an unquestioned 'good thing'. They criticise the various negative effects of tourism – the *Annoyance* phase. Policy makers such as the local authority may be unwilling to intervene in the growth of an economically successful industry – indeed they may develop further infrastructure to support this growth – and so there is continuing, unimpeded growth of tourism to saturation point. In the final phase – *Antagonism* – irritation is no longer covert, it is openly expressed. Any problems – such as overcrowding or late-night noise and disturbance – are blamed on the tourists (see Table 2.1).

Table 2.1 *Doxey's Irritation Index – antagonism (overheard remarks)*

'The locals just rip us off'

'The tourists treat us like we had no right to be here'

'This used to be a real neighbourhood. Now my local grocers has closed and been replaced by a tourist souvenir shop. The same thing is happening with the newsagents, the bakers, the...'

'I can't park my car by my door – the tourists leave their cars in our residents' permit zone and the traffic wardens don't book them'

'They're pedestrianising our main street just so that tourists can wander around, but now I can't drive to work. What's more important?'

'We can't even get into our own city centre to celebrate New Year – now you need a ticket and the tourists have been given most of them'

In the annoyance phase the remaining allocentric tourists who were drawn to the 'undeveloped/unknown' destination are deciding never to return; psychocentric tourists drawn by the increasingly developed tourist infrastructure arrive in increasing numbers. Visitor numbers overall increase, drawn by the increased marketing. This counteracts the decline in the reputation of the destination, but only temporarily.

The Irridex is a further useful 'tool' in gaining an understanding of the changing overall status of a tourist destination and in drawing attention to the need for appropriate management and planning if the changes predicted are to be avoided.

A criticism is that Doxey assumes a homogeneous community – one in which everyone thinks alike. In reality there is no single set of attitudes towards tourism shared by the whole community. It is likely, therefore, that there will be generation differences where old folk strongly dislike change to the established ways of life, whereas their children and grandchildren may have longed for the types of change that tourism brings in its wake.

Tradespeople and others working but not living in a specific area may be regarded as part of 'the community'. Residents may regret the loss of local services whereas the traders welcome the opportunity to 'go up-market' selling expensive consumer goods rather than day-to-day basics. There will also be the age-old divisions that separate or unite people in communities – income levels, education levels, religious affiliations, political leanings and whether long-term resident or incomer. Other factors may also be relevant; for example in a study of residents' attitudes to tourism in the Old Town of Edinburgh it was noted that those with some connection with the tourism industry, for example a member of the family or a friend employed in tourism, were significantly more supportive of tourism-induced changes in the neighbourhood than those with no such connections (Lopez, 1997).

How these disparate groups within a given community choose to use their power to influence tourism development depends further on the extent to which they participate in decision-influencing forums. Increasing opportunities for such participation are available as local authorities decentralise certain functions and actively seek local opinion, but inevitably some people will feel *alienated* from the process: 'No one listens to what I say, anyway'; or are simply *apathetic*: 'I can't be bothered'. Others will consider that the listening process is mere tokenism. Arnstein (1969) described stages or levels of participation in the decision-making process available to citizens (or stakeholders) in response to development proposals by councils, private developers or other 'decision makers' (see Figure 2.3). This was a pioneering effort in the progressive movement towards greater empowerment of citizens/consumers, continued today in the context of sustainable development and 'social' inclusion. The resulting balance of power between the groups will influence the overall response to tourism in a destination (see Chapter 5).

The theoretical perspectives offered by the destination life cycle model and the ladder of participation are valuable. However, it is the *responses* to the process of change that are important. At the various stages, there is interaction between the social, cultural, economic and environmental factors. These require measurement, analysis and evaluation. Then appropriate policy making can take place in the attempt to make the destination sustainable – in the broadest sense – for residents, local businesses and tourists. In other words, the objective is to enable tourism to become integrated into the *place*, where it is only one among many functions.

IMPACT ANALYSIS AND AUDIT

Several theoretical approaches are available to permit this deeper understanding of what is actually taking place in a destination at each stage in its evolution. *Impact analysis* addresses the social, cultural, environmental and economic consequences of development as components of a comprehensive assessment of change – an *audit*

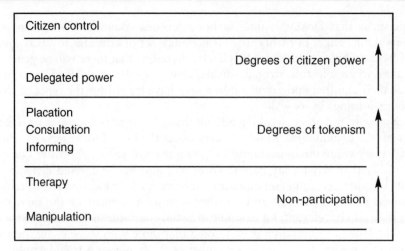

Figure 2.3 *The ladder of participation*
Source: Arnstein, 1969

– which can then be evaluated as a basis for policy decisions and action. Increasing awareness of the impacts of tourism is leading to these 'after the event', reactive approaches being supported, or replaced, by *proactive monitoring* of change 'as it happens'. Response to the signals from the environment, in the form of policy decisions and subsequent planning and management, can then be made on a more informed basis. *Limits of acceptable change* (LACs) are increasingly used to aid in defining sustainable types and levels of development for a destination as a whole and for neighbourhoods within it. These measures allow acceptable change to take place up to social, environmental and economic levels agreed by all stakeholders. An example might be a limit to the growth of a major or mega event within a city (see the discussion of Edinburgh's Hogmanay in Chapter 6).

Impact assessment

Since modern tourism's birth in the immediate post-war period, the *pioneer stage* of its development has drawn to a close. What was once considered a non-extractive, non-polluting industry with unlimited growth potential is now recognised as sharing common features with other major industries. It *is* resource dependent, *is* capable of adverse as well as beneficial effects and consequently requires appropriate planning, development and management. Rather than offering unlimited development opportunities, the objective is the *optimum* level of development and appropriate type of tourism for a given place at a given time.

At the end of this pioneer stage in the evolution of tourism, there is, arguably, ample evidence of the need to reexamine the industry that has evolved – its many benefits, but also its costs (see Figure 2.4). It is argued that it is necessary to 'manage the breakdown, and create the breakthrough' (Robertson, 1976). This breakthrough would be to sustainable tourism. Failure to reassess the world's biggest industry could result in a backlash against tourism development – host communities could say 'no more tourists'; tourists could decide to go elsewhere. This would be a tragedy for those whose livelihood depends on tourism and a denial of the joys of travel and hospitality that are at the heart of the experience of tourism.

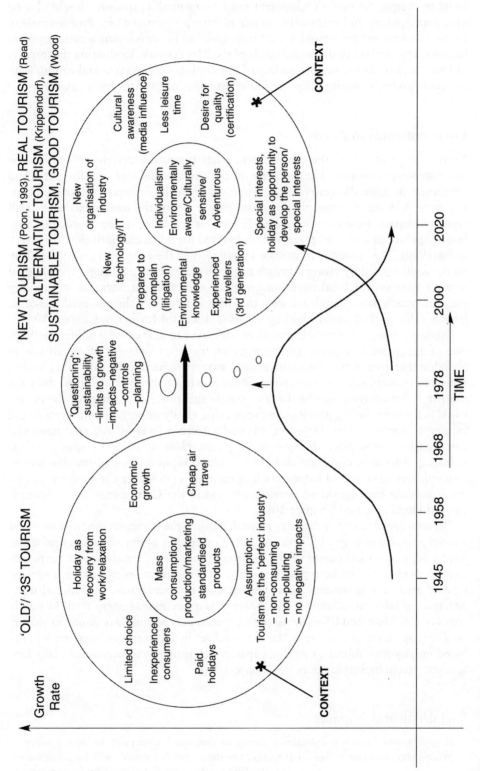

Figure 2.4 *A reexamination of the tourism life cycle*
Source: Adapted (in part) from Poon, 1993

In its next stage tourism development must be profitable; tourism should also be just, participatory and sustainable (*www.tourismconcern.org.uk*). Professionals in tourism and related fields hold a great responsibility for developing a better tourism industry appropriate to the wider needs of the 21st century. Evaluating the impacts of tourism aids further understanding of the destination life cycle and can indicate the appropriate 'maturity stage' or optimum levels of tourism for a destination.

Environmental impacts

There is a point where the environment itself physically deteriorates under the sheer pressure of visitors. The 'pressure of feet' can actually wear out footpaths and vegetation in natural/country areas. More subtle is the indirect impact of visitor numbers. A dramatic example illustrates this and also the interrelatedness of all types of impact. In a cave system in France, at Lascaux, in the Dordogne, pre-historic paintings had been preserved undetected for millennia until their discovery in the 1930s. The subsequent increase in humidity in the caves and growth of algae on the walls caused by visitors' breath began to destroy the paintings. The physical impacts were on the local environment inside the cave – an increase in humidity etc. – but much more significant were the cultural impacts – the potential loss of an irreplaceable part of human heritage. This is discussed further in Chapter 10.

Excessive numbers of people in a given location can also cause wildlife – perhaps one of the most important components of the attractiveness of an area – to abandon that area or the disturbance may cause reproductive disorders that lead to a decline in numbers. In many parts of the world, if the animals go so does the tourism – and tourism may be the only significant source of income for the people living in the area. Skiing developments can bring vitally important employment and income to remote areas. However, beyond a certain level of use, environmental deterioration takes place. Snow-covered pistes, clear of snow by spring, reveal damaged vegetation cover which in turn leads to rapid erosion of the thin mountain soil. Rare species and habitats of international significance can be destroyed by overextending existing skiing developments as in the Cairngorms of the Scottish Central Highlands (see Chapter 10).

The concept of *carrying capacity* helps determine the optimum intensity of use of a given area, for example for tourism. Based on studies of impacts and criticised as imprecise, it is an indication of the maximum number of tourists, of a particular 'type', engaged in specific types of activity, that should be permitted in a specific type of area at a given time. It is widely used in countryside recreational management, notably in national parks where it is a key management tool. In fragile zones of Canadian and US national parks, 'wilderness permits' are issued to visitors on a strictly rationed basis up to the user level set by the carrying capacity. Initially based on physical impacts, carrying capacity determinations increasingly take into account psychological impacts (see Chapter 10).

Social/cultural impacts

> If your travel brochure indicates a dance of the vestal virgins at 10.00 am every Wednesday, you can be sure that neither the dance nor the virgins will be authentic.
> (Anon., 1990; *www.ethicalconsumer.org/online.htm*)

Does it matter? How authentic is the 'bagpipes, tartan and heather' image of Scotland? If tourists are willing to pay for it, why worry? Do cuddly, furry donkeys or plastic castanets give a true representation of Spain? Can tourism not help maintain an *authentic* vestige of former ways of life and generate income in declining or under-developed regions? The lure of jobs in tourism may actually lead to the destruction of stable, 'traditional' employment. Superficial impact assessments are inadequate – short-term benefits from tourism may fail to produce a stable, sustainable industry (see Tables 2.2 and 2.3).

Table 2.2 *Negative socio-cultural impacts of tourism*

Envy – of the conspicuous apparent wealth of tourists

Displacement – of local/traditional employment patterns; young people are drawn to the higher earning, though possibly less stable, tourism industry

Demonstration effect – residents adopt aspects of the behaviour and fashions of tourists and aspire to owning the same luxury consumer goods: cameras, personal stereos etc.

Staged authenticity (MacCannell, 1976) – local culture is adjusted to suit tourist tastes and schedules

Widening of the 'generation gap' – young people become increasingly estranged from the elders as they adopt tourist norms and abandon traditional values and customs

Crime – from pick pocketing to international terrorism

Table 2.3 *Positive socio-cultural impacts of tourism*

New opportunities for employment – local jobs directly in tourism, e.g. in hotels; indirectly in transport and local shops as demand for services is increased

New leisure opportunities – e.g. provision of leisure facilities otherwise uneconomic for local (only) use

Wider perspectives – local people can 'see' their own culture in context of others

Emancipation of women – as by progressively influencing, by the power of example, what is acceptable women's work, behaviour etc.

Economic impact

Generally, tourism development has brought economic benefits to destination areas. But there is increasing demand to examine the situation more closely – how much money leaves the area in interest charges; how many new jobs are going to local people; how many non-menial jobs have been created for locals; how long will the new industry last?

Psychological impact

In wilderness areas some users/visitors/tourists feel that if they meet half a dozen people on a day's hike the place is overcrowded – for them, the 'wilderness experience' is lost. During the May Bank Holiday, 1987, Venice exceeded its carrying capacity. In five hours, 630 tourist coaches brought in 36,000 tourists, while ferries brought 30,000 more from the nearby beach resorts. The crowding was terrifying for many – a psychological impact – while the physical impacts on the city were also measurable (*www.tourismconcern.org.uk*). Again, the carrying capacities – psychological and environmental – were exceeded. Similar problems were experienced in Edinburgh in 1997, where the traditional New Year celebrations had been developed into a major international event, 'Edinburgh's Hogmanay'. The traditional event '... has shaken off its maudlin, self-parodying image and received a new lease of life' (Davidson and Maitland, 1997). However, serious injuries through overcrowding in a confined area were only narrowly avoided when inadequately determined carrying capacities were exceeded. Lessons were learned and the Festival has gone on to become 'Britain's biggest street party of free musical concerts and fireworks. Another impact is that every hotel and guesthouse in the capital is now fully-booked at a time of year when the tourism trade used to be relatively quiet' (Davidson and Maitland, 1997: 85) (see Chapter 6).

CASE STUDY

Socio-cultural impacts of tourism: indigenous language 1

Does tourism invigorate or destroy 'minority languages'?

Prentice and Hudson (1993) examined the generally held view that the 'living' presence of a local language may be an additional attraction to a destination, heightening the local sense of distinctiveness. They concluded that the presence of tourism may contribute to the decline of that language as local young people increasingly copy the ways of the 'outsider' in their desire to be 'modern' ('demonstration effect'). This is more pronounced when the cultural difference between the tourist and the local population is greater. They cautioned, however, against ascribing too much to 'the influence of linguistic competence in the Welsh language in determining residents' perceptions of tourism impacts' in the locality studied. They argue that it is only one among many influences. 'Welsh speakers are not more anti-tourism than others.' However, being Welsh speaking is strongly associated with less strong support for the view that tourism is essential to the economy of the area and with strong support for the view that tourists need to be made more aware of the importance of language to Welsh culture. Welsh speakers are less endeared to tourism than others, as they consider that tourism alters the Welsh lifestyle.

Exercise

Should road signposts be bilingual?: indigenous language 2

Bilingual signposts in Highland Scotland
Should bilingual signposts be the norm throughout the region or should this be standard practice only where more than a certain percentage of the population is bilingual? Alternatively, should there be bilingual signing only where Gaelic is the *first* language, with English as a *second* language (virtually nowhere in Scotland)?

Why confine bilingual signs to only the Gaeltacht, i.e. the Gaelic-speaking parts of the country? Why not within the whole of Scotland? Notably, why should signs not be bilingual in Edinburgh, the capital – since a capital has 'special obligations' to the rest of the country?

Which form of Gaelic should be used? There is more than one form. This may be too extreme ... How far back in history should we go to discover what is 'authentic'? Should established 'English' place names in the Gaelic-speaking areas be returned to the 'original, pre-Union of the Crowns' titles? For example Scotland would become 'Alba'.

Relevant considerations from a destination management perspective

Safety
Road signs would necessarily contain more wording – slower response times would result.

Authenticity
Would a result of bilingual signs be increased tourist appeal due to the enhanced sense of a 'foreign country'? Or would the result be antagonism, through increased confusion?

Does the situation in Corsica offer clues? In parts of the island where separatist/nationalist sentiments are strong, defacing of signs in French only is common – French place names and information are replaced with the Corse-language equivalent

What recommendation would you – as a destination manager or hired consultant – offer?

CASE STUDY

Tourist art and tourist tat: Canadian Innuit ('Eskimo') traditional soapstone carving

This is a successful example of (re)development of a dying traditional handicraft:

- It uses local materials ('part of the landscape'); minimal transport costs.

- There is sustainably managed production and sale of carvings to tourists.

- Only local people are employed.

- Control of all aspects is in the hands of the host community.

In many localities 'traditional crafts' have responded to increased demand by simplifying traditional designs for speed in manufacture to satisfy demand:

- Belief that the tourists would not know the difference.

- Leads to downgrading of craftsmanship.

- Loss of traditional values associated with the artefacts.

CASE STUDY

Tourist art and tourist tat: the Dalarna Horse, Sweden

This is a successful example of (re)development of dying traditional handicrafts, based originally on the production of toys for children. Characteristics of manufacture include:

- The main product, the Dalarna Horse, is nationally respected as one image of traditional Sweden.

- There is carefully managed production and sale of carvings to tourists.

- Use of local materials.

- Local control by the host community.

Questions of authenticity and sustainability are raised by this apparently insignificant craft industry. Is Sweden more confident of its national identity than Scotland is? Arguably, modern Scotland is obscured by the stereotype of 'bagpipes-tartan-haggis'. By contrast, 'Sweden' brings to mind not only the image of the Dalarna Horse, but also Swedish steel, Swedish Volvo, Swedish Hasselblad, Swedish IKEA ... i.e. 'Swedish Modern' as well as 'traditional Dalarna'.

CASE STUDY

Tourist art and tourist tat: Caledonian evenings, Scotland

These are arranged for the benefit of tourists and held in many hotels, pubs and other 'tourist venues':

- The well-known 'stereotype image' is heavily projected – 'bagpipes, tartan and haggis'.

- Bears only a superficial relationship to (one) region of Scotland and to 'Highland traditions and culture'.

- A source of embarrassment/irritation to many Scots.

- A questionable relationship to the contemporary 'Scotland the Brand' debate – where a more contemporary image of Scotland is of a modern European destination and business/enterprise/technology centre.

Tourist tat is arguably produced in greater quantities in Scotland than in any other tourist destination.

(Tourism Consultant, *pers.com*)

DEFINING A COUNTRY IMAGE

Scotland the Brand

A strong positive image for your country, to meet the needs of tourism, exporters and those seeking inward investment will heighten the prosperity of Scotland. [...] The world leaps with examples of strong country brands, from the modernness of America through partying Ireland to stylish Spain and brash Australia. [...] Scotland is known for its traditional qualities of integrity, tenacity and spirit, yet the more modern values remain hidden. Our inventiveness and innovation is not seen; images of our mountains and lochs totally overshadow those of a modern economic infrastructure.
[...]
A group of teenagers who looked for a Scotland in which they wanted to live, a Scotland with progressive images, a Scotland which was hip and wild and great and sexy, a Scotland where tartan stood for style rather than tradition.
[...]
The superb imagery from the Scottish Tourist Board – superb, that is, if you are a middle-aged couple to whom dark mountains and mystic lochs appeal; but hardly the most alluring image for an inward investor.
(J. Spence, Chief Executive of Lloyds TSB Scotland, *The Scotsman*, 26 January 2000)

The Tat Gallery (*www.thetatgallery.com*) takes a light-hearted but also critical perspective on the questions raised by tourism's relationship to national/regional identities, local crafts and traditions and sustainable livelihoods in rural/remote areas (see Figure 2.5).

From the prospectus
The Tat Gallery was featured in the *Edinburgh Evening News* and on Scottish Television when it was set up by Frank Howie in 1990 in the Department of Tourism and Hospitality Management at Queen Margaret University College, Edinburgh. It has since 'migrated' to the world wide web, although a small collection of cultural treasures remain at QMUC to complement the 'virtual' museum.

A laugh or a lament...?
What you see here is a sample from our collection of tourist souvenirs – souvenirs which share something in common. That 'something' is ... the absence of the apparently illusive quality that arises out of the combination of quality, taste and authenticity.

Yes, the collection is biased – the founder stuck his neck out and offered a tongue-in-cheek version of what constitutes quality, taste and authenticity. But while the phrase 'tourism tat' is light hearted – and hopefully our museum gives you a laugh – there is a deeper concern....

Tourist or traveller?
Tourism is a major industry and an important aspect of our quality of life. It contributes greatly to the national income of many countries – notably Scotland – and the right to be a tourist ourselves is something we all hold dear. There is also a subtler message. Tourism affects the way we think about ourselves as citizens of our own city and country, whether Edinburgh and Scotland or any country where tourism is important.

For example, how many of you are happy to call yourselves 'tourists' when on holiday? Do you prefer the terms 'traveller' or 'visitor'? Why? Is 'the tourist' now 'someone else'/the 'other'; someone noisy, nosey and brash, who goes to 'non-you' places?
    '*I am an explorer; you are an independent traveller; they are tourists...*'
The Tat Gallery is a light-hearted forerunner of a potential, more serious project – the development of a centre which reflects the history and development of tourism in a country, in this case Scotland.

Photographs of tourism souvenirs – 'tat' and quality; the worst and the best – are welcome. (A brief descriptive and/or critical commentary should also be included.)
                    The Curator, Gallery of Tourist Tat, *www.thetatgallery.com*

A few of the precious artefacts and atrocities contained within our little collection are illustrated here. Contributions are welcome!
On display are:

- *The classic Scottish tartan dolly*
  Crafted (not) in Scotland, made (not) of local materials from sustainable sources, (not) something to be proud of
- *The Bavarian-style tankard*
  Made in Japan, in the Bavarian style, but sold as a souvenir of London
- *The Dalarna Horse*
  A souvenir of Sweden that genuinely reflects an aspect of the local heritage of Central Sweden, Dalarna. It *is* made of local materials, employs local people, sells at low cost and is complementary to strong images of 'Swedish modern'

Figure 2.5 *The Tat Gallery (www.thetatgallery.com) prospectus*

Exercise

Character or caricature?

Are you happy with the 'image' of your country, city or region that the tourism industry or 'the media' project abroad? Too often we hear the call: 'We want tourism, but not the tourists...'.

That's impossible – we cannot have the economic and environmental benefits that a well-managed tourism industry can bring without the visitors themselves. And these visitors deserve – and increasingly demand – a quality tourism product.

Projecting a better image of our country is one important step along the way of developing a better and mutually beneficial relationship between the residents and the visitors. Souvenirs should reflect that image.

Identify existing souvenirs (or icons) of your country/region and comment on them from the perspective of representativeness of your country both as a 'living, working place' and as a tourist destination. Give your arguments as to why at least one is a bad example and one a good.

Bibliography

Arnstein, S.R. (1969) A ladder of citizen participation. *Journal of the American Planning Association*, 35 (4), 216–24.

Baillie, K., Salmon, T. and Sanger, A. (1986) *The Rough Guide to France*. Routledge and Kegan Paul. London and New York.

Bernstein, D.A. *et al.* (1997) *Psychology* (4th edn). Houghton Mifflin. Boston and New York.

Bookchin, M. (1986) *Post-Scarcity Anarchism*. Black Rose Books.

Burton, R. (1995) *Travel Geography* (2nd edn). Pitman. London.

Butler, R.W. (1980) The concept of a tourism area cycle of evolution: implications for resources. *Canadian Geographer*, 24 (1), 5–12.

Cohen, (1972) Towards a sociology of international tourism. *Social Research*, 39 (1), 164–82.

Davidson, R. and Maitland, R. (1997) *Tourism Destinations*. Hodder & Stoughton. London.

Doxey, G. (1975) A causation theory of visitor-resident irritants, methodology and research. *Conference Proceedings*. Travel Research Association. San Diego.

Lopez, E. (1998) *Attitudes towards Tourism in the Old Town of Edinburgh*. Unpublished honours dissertation. Queen Margaret University College. Edinburgh.

MacCannell, D. (1976) *The Tourist: A New Theory of the Leisure Class*. Schoken. New York.

Maslow, A.H. (1943) A theory of human motivation. *Psychological Review*, 50 (4), 370–96.

Maslow, A.H. (1968) *Toward a Psychology of Being*. D. Van Nostrand. New York.

Michener, James A. (1971) *The Drifters*. Corgi Books. London.

Miossec, J.M. (1977) Un modèle de l'espace touristique. *L'Espace Geographique*, 6 (1), 41–8.

O'Hare, G. and Barrett, H. (1997) The destination life cycle: international tourism in Peru. *Scottish Geographical Magazine*, 113 (2), 42–7.

Pearce, D. (1989) *Tourist Development* (2nd edn). Longman. London.

Plog, S.C. (1972) Why destination areas rise and fall in popularity. *Cornell HRA Quarterly*, November, 13–16.

Prentice, R. and Hudson, J. (1993) Assessing the linguistic dimension in the perception of tourism impacts by residents of a tourist destination: a case study of Porthmadog, Gwynedd. *Tourism Management*, August, 298–304.

Read (1980) in B. Weiler and C.M. Hall (1993) *Special Interest Tourism*. John Wiley & Sons. Chichester.

Rino, *et al.* (1993) in D.A. Bernstein, *et al.* (1997) *Psychology* (4th edn), Houghton Mifflin. Boston and New York.

Robertson, J. (1983) *The Sane Alternative: a Choice of Futures* (3rd edn). Intermediate Technology Development Group of North America.

Smith, V. and Brent, M. (eds) (2001) *Hosts and Guests Revisited: Tourism Issues of the 21st Century*. Cognizant Communications Corp. New York.

Urry, J. (1990) *The Tourist Gaze: Leisure and Travel in Contemporary Societies*. Sage. London.

Weiler, B. and Hall, C.M. (1993) *Special Interest Tourism*. John Wiley & Sons. Chichester.

CHAPTER 3

The nature of tourism destinations

INTRODUCTION

Destinations are places of interest to tourists. A place that is not visited by tourists is, by this simple definition, not a tourist destination; however, through marketing it could attract the attention of potential tourists. Given certain attributes, it could hold the attention of those attracted enough to visit and, with appropriate understanding of the needs of these tourists and a commitment to develop its resources to supply these needs, that place could then become a tourist destination. How long it remained successful would depend on whether it was managed in a sustainable manner.

From that simple account of destination development it is clear that simply encouraging people (tourists) to visit a given place is, in itself, insufficient to create a destination. This need not be an adverse comment on the place itself. That village, town, region or country may well continue to provide the necessities and the pleasures of everyday life for its residents and trade for its business. However, without appropriate tourist-oriented development the place will not become a *tourist destination*. There are several essential actions:

1. Convert resources with potential into attractions.

2. Provide an appropriate range of tourist accommodation.

3. Provide appropriate transport to, from and within the destination.

4. Ensure the successful integration of the tourist-related developments into the changing activity patterns of the place on a long-term, sustainable basis.

Aspects 1 to 3 comprise the traditional approach. It is in response to the growing importance of tourism and awareness of its potential adverse as well as beneficial effects that aspect 4 is generally considered essential today.

This is a central point addressed in this book. A given place – town, city, village, region, country – has, with few exceptions, evolved or been designed and developed to suit its inhabitants, rather than its visitors. How can that pattern of development be modified to continue to satisfy the legitimate needs of the residents, while also catering for the sometimes similar but often different needs of the tourists it may wish to attract?

COMMON CHARACTERISTICS OF DESTINATIONS

Gunn (1988) suggested that all destinations share certain common characteristics and that recognition of this would facilitate their design and development. He referred to the work of Mathieson and Wall (1987) who listed key characteristics of destinations as:

- natural environmental features and processes
- economic structure and economic development
- social structure and organisation
- political organisation
- level of tourist development.

Gunn (1988) discussed a basic anatomy of destinations and identified the major components within his 'destination concept'. This is based on the known behaviour patterns of the tourist. The tourist begins the trip from home and moves towards the chosen destination along 'circulation corridors' using various modes of transport – water, land or air. The corridors lead to 'termini', generally in or adjacent to the host community or 'service community' where attractions and services may be located. The points at which the tourist leaves the corridor and enters the destination are the 'gateways' – significant because 'first impressions' are formed there. The tourist experiences the attractions and services of the destination – perhaps dispersed throughout it or located in 'attraction clusters' – moving between them along 'linkage corridors'. Finally, the tourist leaves the destination via the gateway (or another one), travelling along circulation corridors to other destinations or to return home, taking images and memories of the total experience.

All types of destination – by definition – have these basic elements (although their scale and significance will show individual variations) and each element of its 'anatomy' offers design and development opportunities. Gunn noted also that within the destination residents and tourist share certain characteristics and elements of the destination while others are used exclusively by one group or the other. For example a 'corridor' can be modified for its primary user group – for residents the emphasis in road design might be on time efficiency – quick travel times; tourists, however, might prefer that same road to be redesigned for pedestrian use and a generally slower pace that would permit street traders, wide pavements, busking musicians, window shopping and generally enhanced 'interest value'.

Conflicts can arise where the use made of the various elements of a destination by tourists and by the local community are different or are more intensive than the feature or system can tolerate – as it may have been designed solely with residents in mind. As noted, a popular street is one example; an example of 'system strain' could be a bus service designed for residents but now, or at least at certain times of year, also heavily used by tourists. Again, an opportunity for good design and management to reconcile the perspectives of residents and tourists. Should the interests of residents be given priority over the expectations of tourists? To the resident, the 'destination' is where they live – it is their home and where they stay, they have a vested interest in it, it is '*here*'. The tourist perspective is that the destination is *'there'*, they are temporary visitors to it and they have little vested interest in it beyond the duration of their visit. If they do not enjoy it they can move on and never return (see Figure 3.1).

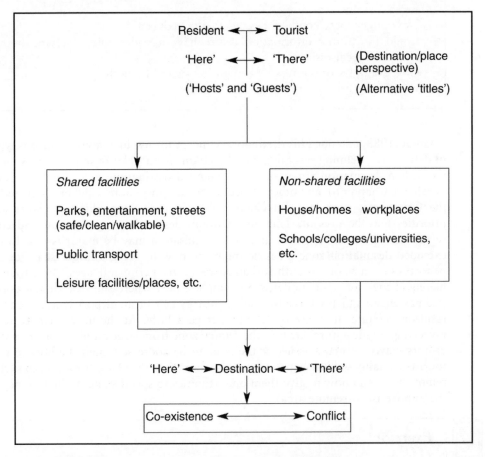

Figure 3.1 *Perspectives of residents and guests in a destination*

Destination management is increasingly focused on bringing these two perspectives closer together, through design of the shared environment of the various stakeholders and through fostering increasing awareness of the mutual interests of both tourists and residents as major stakeholders in the experience and shared use of a real place which is both 'destination' and 'home' *and* 'here' and 'there'.

Exercise

Residents and tourists 1

How integrated are the attractions and services of a city/town you know?

Do they provide for each of the user groups – residential community, business community, tourists? Or are they focused on a particular group?

Are 'tourist developments' largely 'cosmetic', with little use, benefit or contribution to the quality of life of residents and businesses outside the 'tourist 'season'?

What 'conflicts' arise where use is shared by tourists and locals? What are these shared uses?

How might these conflicts be removed or reduced?

Could the tourist information centre have a wider role – serving both tourists and local residents?

Give examples of services that might be shared by both.

Could civic pride be revitalised by tourism?

Gunn (1988) extended his destination concept for use in analysing various types of destination, defining several 'zones' based on spatial relationships – for example the 'urban destination zone' and the 'extended destination zone' (such as Edinburgh, see Chapter 6); and others based on his 'urban-remote scale' (as discussed in the Cairngorms case study in Chapter 10). In each zone, different issues and priorities may be present. Thus in an urban destination regeneration and conservation, visitor management and pedestrianisation may be major issues. In the extended destination zone an issue might be how to bring a larger share of the benefits of tourism out from the urban centre to the 'peripheral' area where tourists merely change transport nodes, for example a port where ships berth and goods and passengers quickly leave to visit the nearby city or an airport where the local residents tolerate the noise of aircraft but gain little. At the urban-remote scale protecting fragile natural areas in the remote zone from large numbers of short-stay visitors may be a major issue; or the issue to be addressed might be how to give tourists a quality wildlife experience in the short time they have for a visit to such a remote area (and how to give them opportunities to spend some of their money in the impoverished remote area).

Exercise

Residents and tourists 2

In a city with which you are familiar, consider the following:

- Are policing, street cleansing, road maintenance, medical services and other services designed for residents equally suitable for tourists?

- Parking. Does meter parking and resident-only parking cater adequately for tourists?

- Are there conflicts between the two?

Destination zones

Gunn's destination zones are useful in clarifying 'flashpoints' where impacts may occur and consequently, where there are likely to be opportunities for improvement through good destination management and design. A number of key points must be considered:

- Destination zones are not uniformly developed.

- There are no definite boundaries between zones.

- The zones may not be permanent (as through changes in international currency rates, political change, changing tastes and fashions, deterioration of services and attractions, etc.).

- There may simply be an intrinsic lack of resources.

The harsh reality is that some places simply do not have what it takes to be a successful destination. Generally, however, a key in successful destination development is the realisation that 'resources' are not 'attractions'. A given place may have an abundance of 'raw resources' such as beautiful scenery, historic towns, fascinating cultural remains. However, if these resources are inaccessible due to lack of adequate transport, an absence of hotels or other accommodation or perhaps political instability and a perceived lack of security, then some form of appropriate development will be required (see Figure 3.2). If the attractions created are to have long-term viability and to be welcomed by the local community then only sustainable development is acceptable.

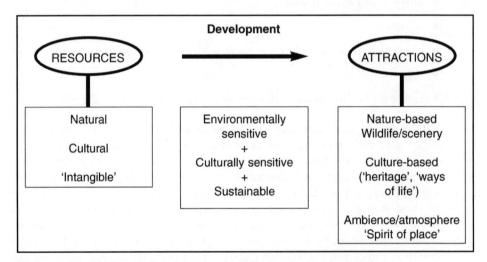

Figure 3.2 *Relationship between resources, development and attractions*

Such complexity is the norm in the 'real world'. The contemporary approach to development is through 'joined-up thinking' and generally a cooperative partnership approach.

A typology of destinations

While destinations share a common, basic anatomy, no two places are the same. This is obviously true, but modern processes of mass production, comparatively cheap and efficient transport and, perhaps, a convergence of lifestyles (at least throughout the western, industrialised liberal democracies) have tended to generate a certain 'sameness', notably in cities where the central business districts, the outer ring of high-rise apartments, the department stores, the general street scene and the motorways can confuse and disappoint the traveller. This originates in standardised building materials having long ago replaced the locally available, distinctive natural materials and in a standardisation in the functions of many cities – 'traditional', regionally based industries have succumbed to the conforming pressures of globalisation. This overall trend is likely to continue and may be a contributing factor to the quest for more individuality in the choice of destinations expressed by the new tourist (Poon, 1993). Indeed Urry (1994: 236) draws attention to the cultural change of 'resistance through localization'. This has manifested itself partly through the increasing 'importance of local vernacular building architectures (and local building materials) and widespread rejection of the international modernist style'.

Various responses to these challenges are illustrated through the case studies in this book. While not rejecting the fact that all destinations share broadly comparable key elements or ignoring the adage that no two places are alike, for the practical purposes of addressing a representative range of destinations the following broad categories of destination type are used in this book:

- cities, notably historic, cultural, tourist cities

- villages and small towns

- resorts

- protected areas, notably rural areas with extensive nature-based attractions

- regions

- countries (although countries per se are not addressed in detail).

In each, key characteristics are described and evaluated. The development processes and their outcomes are reviewed and general principles established. The applicability of the 'lessons' – the examples of good and bad practice – to other comparable destinations is discussed. Thus a detailed examination of tourism in a village in central Scotland may, on the surface, appear to have little to offer destination managers in its counterpart in, say, Poland. However, while the natural resources, social norms, cultural contexts, historical background and political realities may differ, by moving from the specifics of detail to general guidelines and common topics and themes, for example transport; public participation; heritage, sustainable development, etc., important pointers for destination development and management can be established.

RESOURCES AND ATTRACTIONS OF DESTINATIONS

The perspective taken in this book makes an emphatic distinction between resources and attractions. 'Resources' are the precious 'raw ingredients' of a place and to a great extent determine what it may become – and from the perspective of the residents of the (potential) destination they may be entirely satisfactory as they are. Alternatively the residents may even be oblivious of these resources – they are merely the 'ordinary things', taken for granted as the backdrop to their daily lives (Howie, 2000). The increasingly important 'spirit of place' or *genius loci* of a destination is dependent on both the 'obvious' attractions of a place and the intangible characteristics that make it distinctive.

Resources require some form of development in order to have 'utility'. According to Wilkinson (1994: 42):

> [r]esources are attributes of the natural world that are no more than 'neutral stuff' until a combination of increased knowledge, expanding technology, and changing individual and societal objectives results in their presence being perceived, their capacity to satisfy human wants and needs being recognized, and the means to utilize them being devised.

Thus a natural forest has a range of possible 'uses'. It may be developed as a commercial stand of timber where the primary function is the supply of wood for construction purposes etc. Alternatively, it may be developed for recreational purposes as a tourist attraction – selective felling may be necessary to provide sunlit glades and paths and the extra light will encourage an increase in biodiversity – a richer range of plants resulting in a more attractive forest. Increasing tourist use may suggest the need for campsites, log cabins, a visitor centre etc. The forest might be purposefully developed for multifunctional or mixed use. For example, forestry operations could exist alongside various tourism and recreation uses – informal walking, picnicking, orienteering, wildlife photography, hunting etc. Sophisticated 'eco-management' will encourage a sustainable forest.

An ancient cathedral might also be developed for 'multiple use'. It was originally constructed for religious purposes; perhaps in the early 21st century that single use cannot justify its expensive repair and maintenance. Tourism may provide an additional – ideally complementary – use and source of income. Again development and management will be essential to permit the original function to continue undisturbed – that is part of the attraction – but also to increase the understanding and enjoyment of the visitors. In both examples the 'development' will at least partially be in terms of facilities for visitor management.

CASE STUDY

Resource development – Yosemite Valley, California

John Muir was born in Dunbar, near Edinburgh, Scotland, in 1838. He emigrated as a child with his family to the USA, later to become a founding father of the American National Park system, a model for the rest of the world, and of the international conservation movement (*www.sierraclub.org/ john_muir_exhibit/*).

An early example of conflict in resource evaluation centres on whether the Hetch Hetchy Valley should be dammed to provide water or maintained in its wilderness condition as a recreational and ecological area. Water was much needed for the growing city of San Francisco, then only recently devastated by the major earthquake of 1908 and therefore viewed sympathetically by the rest of the country. John Muir argued for preservation of the area and for finding a water supply elsewhere.

While Muir rarely used the word 'tourism', he certainly encouraged his readers, through his regular writings in the press and his books, to get out and enjoy nature, at a time when the prevailing view was that wild country, notably forests, should be exploited for the greater good of society. He also wanted his readers to enjoy these places 'indirectly' through his writings rather than physically visit them, perhaps an early example of understanding of carrying capacity.

This was a classic example of 'conservation' versus 'preservation' equally relevant to many current 21st-century circumstances. Conservation was directed by the prevailing philosophy of utilitarianism – actions should be carried out so as to achieve the greatest good for the greatest number of people. While John Muir was certainly sympathetic to this, he argued that in certain special places, such as Yosemite, there were intangible resources which should be preserved for the spiritual or non-material benefit of mankind. Thus 'preservation' should be the dominant philosophy in that context.

His thinking predated certain of the key perspectives of the contemporary 'green' movement, which demonstrates a spectrum of values from 'deep ecology' to 'environmental management' (O'Riordon, 1976).

More recently McCannell (1990: 116) sees Yosemite as an area of such beauty and power that it commands its own sanctity and may well be 'immune to the ravages of civilization'. Elsewhere nature can be seen to have fared less well in the 'battle' with society. The National Park system, created by John Muir, has been used to compensate for the destruction of nature for our own social needs and this is 'symptomatic' of society's 'guilt' (p.115). A new battle may be just emerging: that of 'nature vs. corporate society' (p. 117) with the expansion of tourism within Yosemite to such an extent that commercial operations have taken over. The destination manager must be aware of these conflicts if an appropriate and sustainable solution is to be achieved. As Henry and Jackson (1996: 27) state:

> Without development of this potential for critical reflection, the tourist industry and tourism policy is in danger of reproducing the errors of the decades of growth, with serious and cumulative consequences.

It must also be considered that, in certain locations, it will be inappropriate to develop tourism. There may be no possibility for it to exist satisfactorily alongside existing social, cultural or economic activities; or there are simply not the resources for successful tourism development.

In addition to the attractions that may be developed from the available physical and cultural resources, a further category must be considered. These are the *intangible elements* that contribute to the attractiveness of the destination and the visitor experience and are essential to the distinctiveness of the destination – its spirit of place or *genius loci*. These may result from the successful integration of the attractions' interplay of resources and contribute to the good (or bad) experiences and memories that the tourist takes home and shares with others. Thus the built environment includes 'heritage' features such as castles and monuments, tourist and leisure buildings such as visitor centres, museums and swimming pools, but also 'ordinary' houses, factories, office blocks and civic buildings that contribute to the general 'townscape' resulting from the 'organic' or planned layout and street pattern. Local festivals, fairs, traditions, artistic works and crafts are also part of the reality of places. More subtle and more challenging to develop and manage are the elements that help create a positive image held by a place. These are intangible, but no less 'real' attributes such as a sense of friendliness, security, 'walkability', excitement, 'youthfulness', dynamism, age and history are uplift and inspiration.

> Amsterdam's attractions, for example, range from high culture such as the art of the Rijksmuseum and music in the Concertgebouw to a tolerant, liberal and youthful counterculture [...] the hospitality and perceived warmth and friendliness of the host community affect both image and attractiveness of the destination and the satisfaction tourists gain from their visit. A place's image is fundamental, since tourists do not visit places of which they have never heard, or which they find unattractive. Image can affect both numbers and types of visitor.
>
> (Davidson and Maitland, 1997: 21)

Box 3.1 *Walkability*

Edinburgh risks falling behind other cities in the race to attract visitors and their money because of the lack of space for pedestrians who have to vie with traffic. [...] A report co-authored by the Chief Constable and the Director of City Development said measures improving pavements, cycle provision and reducing speed could generate extra spending. Changes to the Royal Mile would be worth an estimated £26 million in extra trade. [...]

Improvements to pedestrian conditions in competitor cities is an obvious threat to the city economy. Twenty years ago, Barcelona was perceived as a stopping point en route to Majorca. Now, however, after extensive improvements it is one of the top destinations in Europe.

Currently, Dublin, and Berlin are undergoing major city centre redevelopments and it is predicted that this will attract significant increases in visitor numbers to these cities. Against this background this is an opportune time to consider public realm improvements in Edinburgh city centre.

(*Edinburgh Evening News, 1999*)

Components of a destination

Within a destination, the sum total of what is relevant to the tourist – which is not always the same as the totality of attributes of the place as perceived by its residents – has been described as the *total tourism product* (Middleton, 1994), referring to the combination of 'resources' or the initial attraction the destination has for visitors and 'services', provided to make possible or enhance the visit. Attractions are a key element. Swarbrooke (1995) defines four categories of attraction:

1. features in the natural environment

2. man-made buildings, structures and sights designed for a purpose other than attracting visitors or tourists, which, with the passage of time, have become attractive, e.g. cathedrals

3. man-made buildings, structures and sights purpose designed to attract visitors and tourists, e.g. theme parks

4. special events.

Certain 'non-tangible' aspects of destinations deserve specific note. Page (1995), referring to the work of Jensen-Verbeke (1986), includes these in his 'elements of tourism' as features of the 'leisure setting' (see Table 3.1).

This is a useful and comprehensive illustration of the diversity of the tourism product, showing the roles of two sectors of the industry – attractions and accommodation. The approach also gives appropriate recognition to the essential 'intangible' elements which contribute to the atmosphere of destinations, for example 'friendliness' and 'ambience'. As Doxey (1975) notes, the 'irritation' stage in the development of a destination occurs when the essential goodwill between tourist and resident deteriorates, hastening the overall decline stage in the destination life cycle (see Chapter 2). While these elements are 'intangible', they can be purposely encouraged by destination managers and others through training and awareness schemes that target residents and tourism staff. 'Awareness raising' could, for example, explain the benefits for residents that tourism generates in a place, countering the bad publicity that it sometimes receives.

While tourists increasingly identify specific activities or interests as the reason for their choice of destination, in general their experience involves a 'bundle of products' (Jensen-Verbeke, 1986). Thus a visitor to a city may express his/her interest in a destination as an arts festival, but he/she is likely also to 'consume' several other products.

Attractions in the destination

Gunn (1998: 37) described attractions as the fundamental reason for the tourist visit:

> Without developed attractions tourism as we know it could not exist; there would be little need for transportation, facilities, services, and information systems.

Cultural, sport and entertainment attractions

Cultural, sports and entertainment facilities are obvious tangible attractions. This may suggest that whereas 'activity places' are owned by 'someone' and clearly require management, the 'leisure setting' is merely a passive framework within which the attractions and activities operate. In practice, the 'leisure setting' is just as requiring of management and development and this may be part of the problem of some contemporary destinations – deterioration of the public spaces and the general 'fabric'. There is a failure to recognise or acknowledge that the 'free goods' that constitute the wider environment are not 'free' – ownership is just not apparent in the term 'public property'. Nevertheless, resource management and appropriate planning and environmental design are essential. It may, in fact, be these 'free' or public goods which primarily create the essential 'spirit of place' that draws the tourist to the destination in the first place; or it may be its 'ordinary' details and idiosyncrasies which are everyday objects to the residents but an expression of the 'difference' that is so attractive to many tourists.

Hughes and Benn (1994, in Richards and Bonink, 1994: 179) state on this subject that there 'needs to be a recognition that culture is much more than museums and monuments, and includes a wide range of activities formerly denigrated as 'mass' or 'popular' culture'. Such reflection raises the question: Is tourism separate from culture or part of it? Tourism can be seen also as comprising signs,

Table 3.1 *Elements of tourism*

PRIMARY ELEMENTS
   Activity place   *Leisure setting*

     Cultural facilities   *Physical characteristics*
     Concert halls   Ancient monuments and statues
     Cinemas   Ecclesiastical buildings
     Exhibitions   Harbours
     Museums and art galleries   Historical street pattern
     Theatres   Interesting buildings
                             Parks and green areas
     Sports facilities   Water, canals and river fronts
     Indoor and outdoor

                             Socio-cultural features
     Amusement facilities   Folklore
     Bingo halls   Friendliness
     Casinos   Language
     Festivities   Liveliness and ambience of the place
     Night clubs   Local customs and costumes
     Organised events   Security

SECONDARY ELEMENTS
Hotel and catering facilities
Markets
Shopping facilities

ADDITIONAL ELEMENTS
Accessibility and parking facilities
Tourist facilities: information offices, signposts, guides, maps and leaflets

Source: Adapted from Page, 1995, based on Jensen-Verbeke, 1986

images, texts and discourse (Urry, 1994). The new tourist may be more 'reflexive' and aware of these elements and his/her part in this. They may seek out 'touristy' things to see and do as these things have now passed into the 'ordinary' at established tourist resorts (Howie, 2000) (see Figure 3.3).

The interaction between local residents and visitors is an essential element in the 'spirit of place' which tourists appreciate. With resident cooperation visitors can experience the 'real' spirit of place. Recent initiatives from the City of Edinburgh Council can be seen as trying to bridge this gap. The Council has started to encourage the residents of Leith to act as voluntary tour guides (Deal, 2000). In addition to this, it is promoting active citizen adoption of the monuments and statues which abound in the city. These can be seen as examples of including residents more actively in the tourism system.

Shopping

In certain destinations a 'secondary' element may be the primary attraction – shopping, for example. In the Edinburgh case study (Chapter 6) the challenges

Storks nesting on roofs – central Poland, northern Spain etc.

Traditional costumes – in remoter regions comparatively untouched by tourism or other 'western/industrial' developments

Street markets

Cycle and walkways through the urban area

Public rights of way

Traditional building styles ('vernacular' architecture)

Red-light districts

Local 'boozers' – pubs frequented by locals

City and town monuments

Disused industrial monuments – the Finneston Crane, Glasgow; disused gas towers, Granton, Edinburgh

Local teams' football/rugby matches

Idiosyncrasies – little details and evidence of the human touch

Figure 3.3 *'Ordinary things' – ordinary to a resident, exceptional to a visitor*

posed by this major aspect of destination attractiveness are addressed, notably in the context of how the cherished traditional images of certain places can adapt to the demands of the contemporary retail industry as in shop frontages etc. Out of town retail parks are widely considered serious rivals to the traditional centre of town areas, although others argue they are merely a passing phase. Shopping malls are a further contemporary retail style, frequently in response to severe climates, as in Edmonton, Canada (*www.westedmontonmall.com*), which boasts the world's largest shopping mall. Edinburgh's (1999) plans for a mall underneath the world famous Princes Street – still controversial and awaiting planning permission – aim to permit expansion of existing shops, arguably essential if they are to compete with out-of-town retail parks. A major consideration is, however, avoidance of construction of buildings above ground level as that would be an unacceptable visual intrusion on the striking views from Princes Street to the castle and the historic Old Town.

Edinburgh shop front improvement scheme (grants etc.)
The more pleasant the urban environment is for walking and socialising combined with a sense of security, the more time is spent on shopping. The English Historic Towns Forum of 1992 (*www.ehtf.org.uk/default.asp; www.historic-towns.org/*) on retailing and tourism found that street entertainment, attractive shop fronts and cleanliness are significant factors – three quarters of tourists combined shopping with visiting attractions and purchased not only the expected souvenirs and snacks but also clothing. Trading and licensing laws in the UK are an impediment to some aspects of shopping growth, although there is some movement towards the '24-hour city' as local bylaws are liberalised.

Pavement tables and chairs, so potent a symbol of 'continental' living, have for long been banned in many British cities, although are now increasingly permitted –

Photograph 3.1: *Street life, Edinburgh, Royal Mile*

with clearly demonstrable success. The evolution or the purposeful development of 'quarters' associated with 'street life' may be a side effect (as discussed in the Edinburgh case study in Chapter 6).

In a context of globalisation and look-alike high streets, the 'unique shopping experience' becomes increasingly attractive. Less obvious elements become necessary – public 'conveniences' i.e. toilets perhaps with attendants or automatic 'superloos'. East Lothian Council prides itself on the cleanliness of its public toilets and informal surveys note that many visitors comment on the pleasant environment they found when visiting these toilets, contributing favourably to the overall impression of a destination ('*Loo of the Year Award*' (*www.loo.co.uk*)).

Street signposting

Street signposting may seem a mundane consideration but is increasingly recognised for its significant informational and interpretive roles.

The development of tourist-attractive shopping areas may lead to conflict with the needs of residents. Development of the new commercial/financial district in west central Edinburgh from 1997 on led to an increase in local property values. Some local traders sold their businesses willingly to incoming entrepreneurs aiming at the new clientele. Other shops serving local needs, particularly those run on the basis of 'hobby businesses' or 'retirement businesses' – less bound by the traditional 'rules' of the marketplace and with no desire to 'take the money and run' – have seen a decline in custom. Souvenir shops have their place in this new context, but competition can lead to a proliferation of tourist 'tat' shops or 'bargain stores' taking advantage of short-term leases (*www.thetatgallery.com*).

World-class examples of shopping streets/quarters include London – Oxford Street, Madrid – Puerto del Sol, Barcelona – Las Ramblas and Edinburgh – Princes Street and George Street.

Purposely 'up-market' shopping complexes are a frequent element of 'waterfront developments'. *The Scotsman* (22 April 2000) commenting on developments accompanying the final berthing of the former Royal Yacht, *Britannia*, on Edinburgh's Waterfront at Leith, suggested that the recently named 'Ocean Terminal' 'owes more to Miami than to Muirhouse', an ironic comment on the development of luxurious shopping facilities in the shadow of an area of severe multiple deprivation. Commenting on London's Docklands, Page (1995: 98–110) noted the vital role of public transport in bringing the consumers to the traditionally separated dockland areas. In Edinburgh, there is criticism that tourists 'leapfrog' Leith and its local shops and attractions, heading straight for the new attractions, bringing little direct economic benefit to the area. One response to this is to encourage these tourists to venture into the traditional parts of the area. However, without significant development of what is, in places, a run-down area of high unemployment, there are issues of tourist safety if tourists wander out of the 'safe' areas – as illustrated by the mugging of the American tourist in both the novel and the film *Trainspotting* (Welsh, 1994).

Howie (2000) has described these and other controversial aspects of tourism as 'grey area tourism':

'Grey-area' tourism refers to contemporary, controversial topics in tourism development, including 'moral panics' frequently highlighted by the media, such as sex tourism and begging. Issues raised include: moral acceptability; threats/challenges/ shocks to the 'assumed' status quo; the location of possible developments with a particular focus on the local community, as opposed to strategic perspectives.

Despite these cautions, tourism, on balance, plays a major role in the successful development of former industrial waterfronts that otherwise would have fallen into dereliction as their traditional roles disappeared in the world of the global economy. International examples include Fisherman's Wharf in San Francisco and the waterfronts of Halifax and Vancouver in Canada.

New developments such as Freeport Shopping and Leisure Centre (*www.west-lothian.net/HeraldAndPost/Herald_News_1999/21_Oct_99/Freeport.htm*) have sought to blend shopping with the themes of the industrial past of West Lothian. Compare this with the redevelopment of Liverpool's Albert Dock, where the former storage warehouses have been redeveloped into a vibrant shopping and leisure resource. In this way heritage can be used as a 'cultural device for managing as well as "stage managing" economic change' as McCrone *et al.* state (1994: 30).

How directly do the residents of a tourist destination benefit from increased shopping facilities? Intense debate on the issue of the proposed Edinburgh Princes Street underground mall flourished in the local press for many months after the plan was proposed. Earlier research focusing on Edinburgh's Old Town by Parlett *et al.* (1995) concluded that many residents undertook their shopping needs outside the area due to the lack of shopping facilities – caused in part by the expanding nature of local tourism businesses. This may suit those who are mobile, but unless tourism development brings with it a more equitable distribution of wealth then those worse off will remain unconvinced of its benefits.

Transport and the destination

Jensen-Verbeke's 'elements of tourism' model excludes the transport sector of the tourism industry. Transport is fundamental to tourism, as contemporarily defined: 'The activities of persons travelling to and staying in places outside their usual environment for not more than one consecutive year for leisure, business and other purposes' (WTO and UNSTAT, 1994).

The opportunity to see or ride distinctive or historical forms of transport may be an attractive element of a holiday, but transport is rarely the raison d'être of a visit to a destination; it is a means to an end. Transport to and within a destination, in a range of modes, is, however, essential to its success. Murphy and Keller (1990) suggest that tourist visitation is affected as much by the means of transport and route used as the image of a place and its attractions. They conclude from research on tourism travel patterns on Vancouver Island, British Columbia, that travel patterns were subject to 'distance decay'. This concept is familiar to geographers whereby places off the main routes are not visited or the tourists fail to recollect the places they had passed through due to the overriding compulsion to continue on a set route. Murphy and Keller found that a fast-moving highway had contributed to the failure of the tourists to recollect several places they had travelled through and this was exacerbated by the lack of place promotion – both en route and prior to travelling.

Conversely, Butler (1996) sets forth the analysis that remote places such as the northern isles of Scotland achieve a form of equilibrium with regards to tourism traffic. On the one hand, remote communities and lifestyles are sensitive to increases in tourism whereby lack of a robust infrastructure may exacerbate impacts. On the other, the distance, expense and time consumption involved in getting to these islands means that the islands are relieved, for the most part, from mass tourism exceeding carrying capacity. Economically, the islands gain the benefits of access to the mainland because of a ferry service subsidised to a large extent by tourism traffic.

In rural areas there is disquiet over the cost of petrol which is significantly dearer than in the vicinity of urban areas. Because of the increased distances necessary to travel to work and leisure activities rural communities are at a double disadvantage. Deregulation of public transport introduced to place a more commercial focus on services exacerbates this situation by placing the threat of removal or reduction on unprofitable routes (Innes, 1998).

Tourism could subsidise transport services to these remote communities, but first transport must be improved and integrated so that it can be promoted as part of the tourism product. This realisation is emerging. There are now inter-modal transport tickets, reduced entry to visitor attractions with public transport ticket and collaboration over greater geographical networks, for example the southeast of Scotland travel network (East Lothian Transport Strategy, 2000). Reinstatement of disused railway lines, such as proposals for the 'Waverley Line' railway once again to link the Scottish Borders with Edinburgh, could do much to revive areas with ailing economies.

Getting to a destination is one aspect of concern to the tourist; movement *within it* is another. From a destination management perspective, the movement of tourists within a destination must also be compatible with the transport (and other) requirements of the local residential and business communities and this raises significant challenges. While tourists and locals can certainly share much, such as use of public transport and parking provision, there are also potential conflicts (see Figure 3.4).

Rush hour – residents going to and from work – by car (traffic jams); by public transport ('standing room only')

Parking – residents 'normal' places taken by tourists

Public transport – ticketing systems assume familiarity (e.g. 'correct fare payment required')

Information – place names unfamiliar, signs often assume local knowledge

Restrictions on private car use may be resented by tourists

Absence of restrictions on private car use may disappoint certain tourists familiar with pedestrian-friendly cities

---

Figure 3.4 *Tourist-resident 'flashpoints'*

Elements of transport network

The elements of a transport network are the *links*, i.e. roads, and the *nodes*, i.e. termini or interchanges. Important aspects are the volumes of traffic on each route; also the connectivity of the network as measured by the number of links between destinations. Network *accessibility* is measured by network density, the total area of the network divided by the total unit length of the network.

The car – a special case?

The car is only a means of transport. *Or is it?* For many it is a lifestyle statement, an expression of individual liberty. This was a sentiment expressed by Margaret Thatcher, UK Prime Minister from 1979 to 1990, when she referred to the Falklands War which took place during her time in office by saying: '*It is exciting to have a real crisis on your hands, when you have spent half your political life dealing with humdrum issues like the environment*'.

Transport satisfies the need for spatial interaction between places, a central criterion of tourism. In this context, transport would ideally be centred on offering optimum choices to all for travel to, within and from it. For the last 30 years or so, in most western, industrial democracies, the primary means of achieving this has been considered to be the private car. In the same period, the popularity of the car for travel to the destination has increased dramatically within Britain (see Table 3.2).

Table 3.2 *Mode of travel to holiday, 1951–81*

Year	Car	Rail	Bus or coach
1951	28%	48%	24%
1961	49%	28%	23%
1971	63%	10%	17%
1981	72%	12%	12%

Source: ETB annual reports

This general pattern continued over the following two decades. A similar picture emerges from figures for travel to specific destinations, thus for Edinburgh, 54% of all journeys to the city are by private car (1% by hire car) and to Scotland as a whole the figures are 64% and 2% respectively.

While the private car has grown in popularity, and this growth has been generally encouraged, alternatives to its use have been deliberately phased out or have simply declined in popularity. From the contemporary perspective of sustainable development, where the growing problems associated with this approach are clear, great challenges must be met by transport planners – in collaboration with other professionals such as destination managers. These problems lie in each aspect of sustainability, i.e. across the 3Es (Howie, 1996) of environment, equity and economics. Vehicles – notably in cities – make a significant contribution to atmospheric pollution, now measurably related to certain illnesses, such as asthma, to damage to the fabric of buildings and, most pertinently, to 'heritage' buildings.

Transport costs

A 'true' or 'total' measure of the cost of transport requires consideration not only of 'private costs' borne by the user or operator of the system and comprising fixed costs (overheads) and variable costs (running costs), but also a measure of 'social costs', the 'invisible' costs to the community. It is the combination of physical elements and cost structures of a system that determine the suitability of different modes for different types of journey. From a sustainability perspective high dependency on the private car is unacceptable in cities, as measured by scientific, social equity and economic indicators:

> Since 1970 the amount of car travel per head of population has nearly doubled. By 1997 people were travelling, on average, over 6,500 miles per year by car. [...] traffic is forecast to increase by more than a third over the next twenty years. This will mean more traffic jams, longer rush hours, greater costs to business, and more damage to the environment and our health. [...] Individuals can do their bit, for example by making one less journey a week or occasionally leaving the car at home and walking, cycling or using public transport instead.
>
> (Department of the Environment, Transport and the Regions, 1998: 20)

Urban transport

A study (2000) centred in Edinburgh identified that the modal share of all motorised trips was bus – 41%, train – 4% (i.e. public transport 45%), while private cars were used for 55% of all trips. In terms of the total (motorised) journey distances the proportions were, respectively: 26% bus, 9% train, total public transport 35% and total private car 65% (*www.ebs.hw.ac.uk/EDC/facts-and-figures95/transport.html*, 2000, 28 May). Car availability had also increased steadily and in 1991 over 74% of households had one car. In 1991 the total number of cars was 127,525 while in 1981 the figure was 93,960 cars.

Total road lengths in the city was 12 km of trunk roads, 199 kms of A or principal roads, 165 km of other classified roads (i.e. B and C roads) and 1,098 km of unclassified roads. There were only 470 km of cycle routes (including off-road routes and shared cycle/pedestrian paths). In Central Edinburgh's controlled parking area there were 3,635 on-street and 3,880 off-street parking spaces, 2,130 on-street residential spaces, 10,700 off-street private spaces (non-residential), making a total of 20,345 spaces.

CASE STUDY

The private car and its suitability for tourist transportation within a city – a sustainability audit

In 1952 the great London 'pea-souper' fog caused 4,000 deaths. In its wake, the Clean Air Act was introduced in 1956, permitting smokeless fuel only in UK cities. By the 1990s, the Department of Health (UK) attributed to man-made air pollution:

- several thousand premature deaths p.a.

- 20,000 hospital admissions p.a.

- various illnesses, reduced activity and distress.

Ninety per cent of that pollution comes from vehicles. The 'social costs' must be considered.

A CHALLENGE IN DESTINATION MANAGEMENT

Why is making the change from car dependency so difficult?

- 'We cannot ban cars from our city centres overnight [...] it will take a sea change in our views on traffic before real change can be affected.'
  (Dr W. MacNee, Edinburgh University,
  Department of Respiratory Medicine, 1999)

- 'Seventy five per cent of drivers in Oxford said that a total ban of traffic from the city centre would be preferable to the existing daily congestion. This percentage was even higher – 84% – amongst those who did not own a car [...] Since drivers do not trust others to cut down on car use, they are unwilling to do so themselves.'
  (Environmental Transport Association, 2000)

- 'The car is a symbol of individual liberty and freedom.'
  (Margaret Thatcher, UK Prime Minister, 1979–1990)

- Asthma is the only treatable condition in the western world which is on the increase. It affects one adult in ten and one child in seven. Incidence of severe asthma doubled in Scotland between 1981 to 1993 – 9000 p.a. In UK, 5 million working days p.a. (£450 million cost) and 2 million school days are lost through asthma. Air pollution is one alleged cause of the increase, along with cigarette smoke, genetic factors, diet and home environment.

Taking a sustainable development perspective on this clearly complex challenge in destination management, a social equity or ethical perspective would emphasise that in many cities car use is by no means universal – even in affluent cities such as Edinburgh (*www.ebs.hw.ac.uk/EdWeb/*) ownership rates are just over 50% and considerably less elsewhere. The elderly and poorer households are dependent on (much reduced) public transport.

Economically, while 'easy payment schemes' are widely available for car purchase and technological advances will increase engine efficiency, fuel prices will continue to rise and inevitably there will be increasing demands for motorists to pay the real cost of the damage caused. Schemes such as 'road pricing (direct charges on cars entering certain areas such as city centres), increasing parking charges and various forms of 'car-free' zones will encourage the search for a wider range of transport options. Some countries are more 'advanced' than others in making the transition to a more sustainable approach to transport, although in each case the move towards the car as 'one option' rather than as the 'dominant option' has not been without conflict. As many commentators have noted, the private car is not merely a means of transport – for many it is an expression of personal liberty and success, while the vested interests of the automobile industry also 'contribute' to slow progress in the transition. Significantly, the costs of heavy reliance on the private car incur 'social costs' which are shared by non-user.

Challenging the domination of the car/civilising the city

Particularly in urban destinations, tourists increasingly value opportunities to explore at a leisurely pace. Attributes such as 'walkability', 'cycle-friendly' and 'traffic-free' areas feature in promotional brochures.

Examples of cities that have made the transition to more integrated transport systems include Barcelona, where 'reclaiming the streets' has encouraged a return to traditional, social use of (now) quiet streets and public squares.

In some countries, the climate may seem a barrier to such objectives, but evidence from northern, maritime climate countries such as Scotland has shown that people – tourists and residents alike – are keen to drink, eat and generally socialise out of doors, as long as simple precautions are taken to moderate the unexpected shower or drop in temperature. The real barriers have often been political and business inertia and the prevailing 'moral climate' which frowned on such open displays of al fresco socialising. The role of destination managers (whose role necessarily links them with many 'separate' professional areas) in 'encouraging' such culture change is significant.

Amsterdam and Copenhagen are other northern European countries where 'going Italian' has proved popular. Even in winter, the pleasures of 'people-watching' over a glass of wine or a coffee in a now car-free street can continue from within easily moveable glass/plastic enclosures.

In any destination, the broad aims – supported necessarily by policies – are likely to include developing the local economy, reducing poverty and disadvantage and promoting a healthy and sustainable environment. A transport system, within which the car has a role in serving but not dominating, is crucial to achieving these. In many urban destinations a sustainable transport system is urgent; in rural areas, greatly reduced bus and train services are likely to require longer term approaches, while rising fuel costs exacerbate the problems (see Figure 3.5). (These issues are discussed further in the Edinburgh case study in Chapter 6, and the Culross case study in Chapter 7.)

Choice of transport modes

Planning for more compact cities

Lower polluting vehicles (e.g. electric trams/buses)

Carpools/shared vehicles

Higher tolls for cars carrying only one person

Consideration of disadvantaged groups – the elderly, children, poorer families

Traffic-free zones

20 mph/30km-per-hour zones and streets

Cycleways/walking routes

Simplified ticketing on public transport

Better, more tourist-friendly directional signs

City car-share schemes

Figure 3.5 *Examples of new thinking in transport within destinations*

Exercise

Transport in destinations

What other examples can you suggest of more sustainable people-friendly transport in destinations? What obstacles prevent these being introduced in a destination with which you are familiar?

URBAN DESTINATIONS

All destinations share key common features, as discussed earlier in this chapter. However, certain issues and themes are particular to urban destinations – while others are more relevant to rural destinations, hence the separate discussion later in this chapter.

Urban destinations

'Urban tourism is tourism that takes place in towns and cities where historic heritage is not the main attraction, even though pre-industrial revolution buildings are present' (Burton, 1995). From this perspective, urban tourism is not just the tourist activities that occur in cities, but activities which with few changes could take place in other spatial settings. Significantly, urban tourism is a form of tourism but also 'an integral, traditional and proper part of urban life. If this is so then a profitable line of enquiry would acknowledge that different sorts of cities nurture different sorts of tourism' (Ashworth, 1990: 50).

Urban tourism can thus include:

- sightseeing
- visiting cultural attractions such as art galleries, concerts, museums, heritage centres etc.
- shopping
- eating out
- business tourism, e.g. conferences.

Activities are usually based on man-made attractions. This includes 'parks' (even though these are partly 'natural'), often shared with the local residents who regard them not as 'tourist facilities' but as 'leisure' or 'recreational' facilities. Tourists – as opposed to 'day visitors' – also make use of the accommodation provided within the destination.

Development and growth of urban tourism

Urban tourism has received increasing attention since the mid-1980s in many industrial countries and has generally grown rapidly. This attention has often been as an outcome of the established industries being no longer economically competitive in the new context of 'globalisation', whereby many traditional 'heavy industry' products and raw materials – such as ships, cars, steel, coal – can be made or mined more cheaply in less developed countries. As a consequence, the nature of the labour force has to change. In many cities that change is towards growth in the service industries, i.e. industries which provide services rather than manufactured products – banking, insurance, education . . . and tourism. Tourism is attractive in that it *appears* to require less investment than other service industries, since its 'products' are the existing attributes of that place. But tourists also need 'purpose-built' services such as accommodation; also – less obviously – they need appropriate development of the existing resources of the place for their purposes; and they need a trained – or retrained – workforce to provide the essential customer services: a redundant manufacturing-industry worker cannot become a successful tourism/hospitality worker overnight.

The need for integrated management of the emergent 'destination', where tourism is integrated with the existing physical, economic and social characteristics of the place, has been a latterday realisation. This delayed response to change has led to less success with tourism than the initial promise. The second reason for the focus on tourism in many urban areas is the fact that tourism can contribute directly to the essential urban redevelopment process itself. Tourism 'demands' quality environments: tourists are unlikely to comment favourably to friends and acquaintances – potential tourists – about a destination with extensive areas of dereliction and industrial wasteland. Land clearance and rehabilitation are essential prerequisites for aspiring destinations but expensive. A further positive attribute of tourism as a significant component of urban regeneration is that it is perceived as a 'good companion' for such desirable other incomers as 'hi-tec'/new technology industries – the 'sunrise industries' replacing the old 'smokestack/sunset' industries. Urban tourism is generally-oriented towards the arts and culture and high environmental standards and these are attributes sought by the executives and highly skilled employees of the new industries – a hoped-for chain reaction leading to a new service/technology economic future for many cities.

Contexts within which tourism plays its part in urban destinations include 'waterfront developments' (see the Edinburgh case study in Chapter 6) and garden festivals as held in Glasgow and other cities. On balance, tourism has played a major role in the successful development of former industrial waterfronts that otherwise would have fallen into dereliction as their traditional roles disappeared in the world of the global economy. International examples include Fisherman's Wharf in San Francisco, the waterfronts of Halifax and Vancouver in Canada and London's Docklands. The restoration and conversion of warehouses and other industrial buildings into flats and apartments, restaurants or heritage centres is generally welcomed, although this can mask the adverse side of 'deindustrialisation' and the concomitant dislocation and dispersal of former working-class/blue-collar communities unable to afford increasing house rents or rates, forced to move out of the area to find employment. Whether tourism employment can fully compensate is still an open question in many areas. Planning constraints on development of buildings of conservation value may be a further issue, although change of use can often be compatible with preservation of the townscape, if not the social make-up of an area.

Garden festivals have played a substantial role in 'kickstarting' redevelopment of cities although these are temporary events and cannot be the only element in the redevelopment of a city. The Glasgow Garden Festival of 1988 played a significant role in a chain of events that led to a new, dynamic image of the city, a transition from one of 'no mean city' to European City of Culture, 1990. The sustainability of this bright prospect is still in question, however, as the city continues to have major problems with housing and healthcare. This illustrates basic characteristics of the tourism product. It is largely inflexible in that it cannot respond quickly to changes in demand as influenced by social change or more fickle fashion.

Conversely, in this respect the tourist's 'selective perception' (Middleton, 1988) will largely determine what function a destination's 'bundle' of resources can perform in fulfilling 'push' or 'pull' attractiveness, for example the push factors of the traveller's physiological or psychological needs; or the 'pull' factors of the destination's unique social, cultural or landscape features and resources (see Riley and Van Doren, 1998). With proper marketing, research and planning a destination should be more aware of the 'push' needs of its potential visitors and the unique 'pull' attributes it holds so that it can maximise the 'sales' of its 'product' to as many consumers as possible or as seen to be appropriate, promoting different aspects to different market 'segments'.

Urban tourism and historic-cultural tourist cities a special case?

Large cities are arguably the most important type of tourist destination (Law, 1993). Many a small town also tries 'to float its own little bit of bait upon the sea of tourist consumerism' (Boniface, 1993). The implication that 'a little bit of bait' has little chance of success may be challenged. Undoubtedly there are many examples of failure to regenerate a sound economy through the alleged catalysing effect of tourism after more than a decade of 'economic development initiatives', but it is 'little bits of bait' that may be the sought-after attractions of an increasing number of contemporary tourists. Ashworth (1990) specifically concerned with the tourist-historic city, cautions that it is value judgements that often determine the courses of action determining *whose* local heritage – whose little bits of bait – is favoured in development decisions.

Special obligations often prevail in a historic–cultural tourist city, the more so if it is a capital city. The controversies surrounding the location of major new developments are often centred on the tension between the locally perceived 'costs' of major events and the strategic gains to the city.

Evaluating the resources in a city or town

Evaluating the resources in a city is an important prerequisite to decision making on how development should proceed or whether it should even go ahead. The resources are both physical and intangible. Thus, a mid-19th century redundant grain warehouse is tangible – it is 'bricks and mortar'. It can be conserved as a fine example of industrial architecture and a contributor to the local spirit of place and/ or developed as a visitor centre commemorating and interpreting that former trade for visitors. But consider the resident community of the area. They are no longer employed in the trades that made that building necessary. In one sense, they are a liability – the younger members may be unemployed and a nuisance to tourists (and locals). In another sense, they may be an asset – the older members may be actively involved in the local history society and sharing 'living history' with tourists as informal guides. In practice, it is a small percentage who pursue these contrasting roles; the majority will be living their ordinary lives oblivious to or perhaps hostile to the tourism industry that has replaced their 'real' livelihoods, while others will have left the area.

Other less controversial, intangible assets include views and historical or other associations, many of which can be indirectly assessed in terms of their value, for example via the number of tourists interviewed in opinion surveys who mention them as positive factors in their choice of destination.

Tangible and intangible assets contribute to the ambience of a place and the enjoyment of daily life within it. They also contribute to the perception of that place as a tourist destination and to the spirit of place associated with it. For example, are city parks a residents' amenity or a part of the reason for a tourist choosing to visit a particular city or town? In many cities and towns, trees which were planted by visionary planners and designers in the mid- and late 19th century have now reached maturity or old age and require decisive management decisions. Some may have become unsafe and require felling; whether they are replaced with new trees is a decision with both immediate and longer term financial implications, since such biological features require ongoing management.

Views or 'vacationscapes' (Gunn, 1988) may also be regarded as 'intangible assets' of a place, undoubtedly contributing to the enjoyment of it. It may, however, be necessary to establish a semblance of tangibility by indirectly putting a financial value on them. For example, the tangible benefits of, say, a new hotel will be diminished if it is built on a site where it will obscure or spoil that cherished view. As for the evaluation of urban trees, the contingent valuation methodologies establish what 'users' are (theoretically) willing to pay *not* to lose the view. This can then be compared with the financial benefits the hotel would generate in a cost-benefit analysis. The issue of values is the linchpin around which these decisions are made. As Getz (1994: 448) relates in his analysis of the overall costs and benefits to the community of hosting event tourism:

> *Who* benefits and *who* pays the costs is often more important than determining and measuring the actual costs and benefits. [...] The tourism industry gains, but the community is forced or encouraged to change.

Whose values are being prioritised when decisions such as these are made? The community? The government? Business interests? Fostering a sense of ownership of a new development is desirable. It is likely to contribute to the hospitality that the tourist gets when he/she visits the community. These issues should be debated and efforts made to involve the local community.

Exercise

City parks as tourist attractions

City parks are clearly popular, but their management is increasingly beyond the financial resources of their 'traditional' managers – leisure and amenity or parks departments.

From a destination management perspective present a case – environmental, social and economic – for their 'recognition' as tourist attractions and so for their management and upkeep from 'tourism budgets'.

Suggest developments that 'traditional' city parks might require for increased tourism use. How would these differ from the amenities traditionally provided for residents' use of parks and would there be any conflict of interests between tourists and local residents?

Local festivals are a further example of assets that are ambiguous in their 'ownership'. As traditional, age-old celebrations they are part of the history of a place. As long as they are enjoyed by local communities alone they are not part of the tourism product. As they are 'discovered' by allocentric tourists venturing off the beaten track they may be subsequently 'adopted' by the local authorities which will invest money in them and market them to make them more accessible and, perhaps, 'more interesting' to tourists. Hughes (1999: 121–3) analysed the contemporary approach to city management using the example of the Edinburgh Hogmanay Festival as a move towards increasing 'entrepreneurialism' within local government. This has evolved in response to 'global economic rationalisation' which has forced many local authorities to develop a more market-based approach rather than focusing on the traditional areas such as economic development, e.g. offering tax incentives to companies to locate in their area, providing land etc. Eisinger (1988, in Hall and Jenkins, 1995: 37) comments on this form of local government as the 'entrepreneurial state'.

As Edinburgh's Lord Provost stated of the Hogmanay Festival:

> We hope to attract people from overseas to come to the city at this time of year, but also to involve our own people.
>
> (Hutchison, 1994 in Hughes, 1999: 127)

Exercise

The impacts of Hogmanay

Consider the impacts of the Edinburgh Hogmanay celebrations on tourists and on local people. Is it a successful example of the use of cultural and other city resources for the benefit of both tourists and the local community (*www.edinburghshogmanay.org*)?

ACCOMMODATION IN THE DESTINATION

A basic requirement in a destination is tourist accommodation – preferably a range of accommodation types appropriate to the place. A full range would include budget through to luxury accommodation but this might not be necessary in all destinations, depending on their target markets for tourism. The integration of accommodation into the wider life of the place is a further consideration. Heeley (1986) noted that planning authorities in Britain have been concerned with 'product and place, but not promotion and price'; in other words what is desirable from social and environmental perspectives may not always be economically viable. The destination management perspective must address all these considerations and may face difficult choices. Thus for the core of a historic city the need for a new hotel might ideally be met by sensitive redevelopment of an existing, but redundant commercial premises – the external appearance would be retained, while the interior would be adapted to contemporary expectations, although taking care to conserve 'period' features such as ceiling cornices, fireplaces and the general proportions of rooms.

However, market analysis may reveal that the deficiency lies in the supply of budget accommodation, notably for young, independent travellers and/or families or for business tourism accommodation, incorporating conference suites and full computer facilities and internet connections in each bedroom.

In addition, the use of the internet for promotion should be considered, as its potential has already been recognised in the hospitality industry (Buhalis, 1994). Moreover, the introduction of the internet will improve communication both internally and externally – using it as a means of internal marketing to foster enhanced communication and responsiveness.

Increasingly, technology is a key differentiation in the hospitality industry (Reid and Sandler, 1992) and this may be combined in the guest history database to create loyal relationships (Warren, 1999). This forms part of the enhanced product at the 'online hotel' and could be achieved using guest history technology (Gilpin, 1996; Warren, 1999) to customise the service to suit a particular guest based on information gained from previous stays or research. For example: pre-registering from prior information; provision of guests' favourite snacks and drinks; personal greeting from front desk; and provision of favourite newspapers, theatre tickets, etc.

Related to the stage of a town or city on the destination life cycle the accommodation stock may be plentiful but has failed to adapt to changing demands. In the traditional coastal resort of Dunbar, near Edinburgh, years of inattention to the changing tourism market resulted from full use of the traditional hotels and guest houses by the large labour force employed on the construction of a nearby nuclear power station. Quite apart from the impact of this development on the destination image, the hotels became run down and 'unfashionable'.

On the Isle of Man (*www.gov.im*), which had long been geared to 'traditional British' seaside holidays, fine terraces of hotels and guest houses in towns such as Port Errin began to lose their regular customers, who were opting for package holidays to Mediterranean beach resorts. The 'offshore island/tax haven' status is nowadays more significant economically than tourism and the legacy of once fine hotels and guest houses is increasingly run down. Revitalisation would require considerable investment to match modern requirements. Recent attempts to regenerate the destination include a campaign that attempted to capitalise on its 'traditional' image and the nostalgia held by many former visitors. A recent focus is on heritage-based tourism, notably the significant 'Viking' associations of the island and a major heritage centre has been constructed at Peel.

Comparable changes are taking place in 'new'/emerging destinations in central and eastern Europe. The city of Poznan (*www.cs.put.poznan.pl/poznan/*), like other cities in Poland, is keen to attract western tourists – both leisure and business. Leisure tourism had been heavily geared to subsidised holidays for workers within the country or in other former Soviet bloc countries, in state-run hotels and a range of smaller hostels and other communal facilities associated with specific workplaces. A strong commitment to 'social tourism', where taking a holiday is regarded as a right for all regardless of income, physical or metal handicap or family circumstances, was and is a commendable ideal, but it resulted in a degree of uniformity and blandness in much of the accommodation stock – unappealing to the average western tourist. Considerable moves are underway to renovate existing quality hotels and to attract the western hotel chains to establish new hotels offering the 'expected' high standards to both leisure and business tourists.

The 'new tourist', the 'green tourist' and other contemporary tourist types may preferentially seek out bed-and-breakfasts or smaller guesthouses, not as cheap options but in the expectation that there they will tap into local knowledge and gainer a deeper insight into the 'real place' that is the destination. For this market, the changes required in accommodation are less structural than cultural and educational. Destination-oriented organisations such as local enterprise companies and tourist boards offer training programmes under such names as 'Welcome Host' (Scotland) to staff across the range of accommodation types who recognise the contemporary tourist's wider demands for tourism that is REAL – 'Rewarding, Enriching, Adventuresome and a Learning Experience' (Read, 1980).

BUSINESS TOURISM

In many destinations business tourism is a significant element. From this perspective the 'attractiveness' of a place will include the intrinsic qualities that draw leisure tourists, but also specific other elements. These include conference facilities, offices or corporate headquarters, corporate entertainment opportunities and specific hotel or other accommodation for delegates and/or business travellers (perhaps incorporating the latest information technology facilities). Where conference centres are required, adaptations of existing buildings may be possible, otherwise new-build will be necessary, requiring site clearance possibly resulting in controversy over the threatened loss of 'heritage' buildings and/or disturbance to residents. If encouragement of business tourism is an objective within the destination's overall development plans the local authority and other public/quasi-public organisations in the destination will be supportive in resolving conflicting objectives. The rise of 'technology parks' and other business development areas in peripheral areas of cities, in response to lack of sites or high property and land values in the centres, is one approach to resolution of problems. Good access to airports and other transport nodes and to the city centre will generally be essential: despite the increasing use of the internet in business, 'face-to-face' contact remains important. The comparative 'freedom' for building design innovation outwith the centres of historic/'heritage' city centres permits innovative design. New corporate architecture in Edinburgh's new financial district (see Chapter 6) has been criticised as bland.

SAQ

Why are modern buildings so bland?

> The enclave of major players who have built headquarters around Xxxx Road in recent years may be business competitors, but are largely united in their patronage of mediocrity. The added value and positive publicity an internationally recognised building can generate have eluded institutions which have the resources to create architecture of epoch-defining quality. [...] How refreshing it is to go out to the west of the city and see a clutch of new buildings. Masterminded by a celebrated architect, Xxxx Park has buildings by some of the younger luminaries of British architecture fit for today. [...] One of those has recently completed a new headquarters building on one of the Park's most

important sites. Fortunately, it is a sufficiently strong visual bastion [...] This is a corporate headquarters fit for today. It is a shame so many others are stuck in the 1980s.

(Cameron, 2000: 15)

Exercise

New building design

Consider the forces that influence new building design within a historic city or town centre familiar to you. As destination manager for such a location you are required to present your case to the multidisciplinary committee set up to consider possible designs. Outline your case for the innovative design of a new conference centre, rather than a building that borrows from the predominant Victorian or other historic character of most buildings in the area.
(These issues are discussed further in Chapter 5.)

The Edinburgh case study (in Chapter 6) illustrates the potential conflicts between local residents and small businesses in the context of development of a new commercial zone within the city; this in turn results in the 'migration' of existing offices from the city's Georgian 'New Town' and a temporary phase of uncertainty. The implications for destination managers in the development of new attractions and activities within the destination are considerable, addressing such controversial issues as traffic generation and parking, but also the positive opportunities for 'breathing new life' into sometimes 'run-down' areas.

The process of decision making on where new developments go is complex, addressing economic, social and environmental issues. Whereas private sector developers will identify possible sites according to criteria focused on their enterprises and generally centring on profitability, public sector development will include the wider issues and the final choice will be seen as politically sensitive. Again, the input of the destination manager will be as only one member of the decision-making 'team' and his/her choice will reflect the stakeholders he/she prioritises.

THE RESIDENT COMMUNITIES OF A DESTINATION

Murphy (1988) wrote: 'It is the citizen who must live with the cumulative outcome of such [tourist] developments and needs to have greater input into how his community is packaged and sold as a tourist product'. Concern for the resident communities within actual or potential tourism destinations has rightly moved to centre stage in consideration of tourism planning and development. This – along with the contemporary concern for sustainable development – has arisen from awareness of the adverse effects of tourism development in many areas during the early stages of the emergence of mass tourism in the early 1960s, when tourism was perceived as an entirely innocuous and benign industry, non-polluting, making use only of the 'free resources' of a pleasant environment and generally welcomed by residents.

At this stage in the development of tourism a more critical perspective is generally taken of tourism's 'obligations' towards resident communities. This is undoubtedly right, notably since the early phase of tourism development was based on the assumption that tourism can only be 'a good thing' for the residents. However, it is suggested here that a rather less obsequious view be taken of 'the community'. While tourism certainly may cause inconvenience – and at times major disruptions – to the residents and businesses of a destination, there is a case to be made that the resident community has reciprocal obligations to a tourism industry that is also making significant contributions to the economy and quality of life within that destination in the form of employment opportunities and a range of amenities enjoyed by tourists and residents alike. Thus even in a major city certain sport, leisure and cultural facilities would be beyond the resources of the residents alone without their use by tourists and thus the income derived from tourism.

It is necessary, moreover, to be clear in defining 'the community' in a given destination. Quite rightly, there has in recent years been a move away from the 'master planner' elitist approach to development and genuine attempts are made to inform and involve all the *stakeholders*, rather than only the *shareholders*. This more inclusive perspective would also counter the view of some that the pendulum has swung too far towards 'community' which has become almost a 'godword' – a non-debatable 'good thing'.

The useful 'Irridex' developed by Doxey (1975) (see Chapter 5) is in fact only a generalisation about community reaction to tourism development. There is no single community view towards tourism development within a destination. It is likely that 'young people' will have different attitudes from those of 'older people', that 'incomers' will have a reaction different from that of long-term residents, that the local business community will have a different reaction from that of the local residential community to specific tourism developments and, perhaps, towards tourism development generally in 'their' neighbourhood, village, town, city, region or country. It is possible through a comprehensive survey process of discussion, questionnaires, focus groups etc. – and in the near future, through electronic referenda using local, interactive television, which will at least offer the *theoretical* possibility of 100% participation rates – to gauge the overall attitude towards tourism development in a destination. But elected representatives have a duty to consider all the relevant factors and to listen to the advice of their technical advisors and unpopular decisions will sometimes have to be taken with little more than public statements to all the stakeholders to soften the blow to the 'anti-groups'.

IMAGE AND THE TOURIST DESTINATION

Imagination and reality

Images of destinations are in the 'mind's eye' whether these places have been visited or not. 'London' may conjure up images of Buckingham Palace and guardsmen in ceremonial uniforms or 'sex and drugs and rock and roll'. 'Edinburgh' may bring to mind 'bagpipes and tartan and haggis' or festivals and culture or *Trainspotting* 'low life' and the music/club scene. 'San Francisco' may evoke an image of the Golden Gate Bridge shrouded in fog or the sound of cable cars clanking their way up steep sunlit, city streets. These contrasting images are created both passively, through informal conversations with friends or through television and films using the setting as a location, and actively through the promotional campaigns of tourist organisations.

Images are made up of real, tangible things and also qualities like atmosphere and ambience. These elements – the 'real' and the 'intangible' – form the *genius loci* or spirit of place of that destination. It is how close the actual experience of the destination lives up to this mental image that determines whether we are pleased or disappointed with our choice. Destination management and development has a critical responsibility for maintaining and enhancing the elements that contribute to the place's image.

The spirit of place

But as you get to know Europe slowly, tasting the wines, cheeses and characters of the different countries you begin to realize that the most important determinant of any culture is, after all – the spirit of place. Just as one particular vineyard will always give you a special wine with discernible characteristics so a Spain, an Italy, a Greece will always give you the same type of culture – will express itself through the human being just as it does through its wild flowers. We tend to see 'culture' as a sort of historic pattern dictated by the human will, but for me this is no longer absolutely true. [...] so long as people keep getting born Greek or French or Italian their culture-productions will bear the unmistakable signature of the place. [...] And this, of course, is the target of the travel-writer; his task is to isolate the germ in the people which is expressed in their landscape. (Durrell, 1969: 156)

DESTINATION CHOICE AND THE INFLUENCE OF THE TRAVEL WRITER

The development of tourism has been dominated by an assumption that *escape* from the everyday or the commonplace is what the tourist wants – something special must be created or the tourists will not come. As already discussed, however, Plog (1972), Cohen (1979) and Smith (1977) each identified groups who sought the 'ordinary' in their travels – Plog's 'allocentric' who is happy to board with local residents; Cohen's 'experiential' traveller who looks for meaning in the lives of others; Smith's 'explorer' who desires to interact with his hosts and accepts local norms. In the 1970s these groups were the oddities. Today many popular guidebooks explain how to meet the 'real locals' (e.g. the *Rough Guide* or *Lonely Planet* series). Such 'independent travellers' have been considered marginal to the business of tourism, while today, companies target them as one of the fastest growing sectors of the industry.

Poon (1993) argues that best practice in tourism at any given time should be seen in the context of the prevailing paradigm – 'the ideal pattern or style of productive organisation or best technological "common sense" that prevails at the time' (Perez, 1983 in Poon, 1993). Mass production – in tourism as in car manufacturing –

was 'common sense' from the 1930s to the 1980s. Best practice may now lie in this context of 'new tourism' where the motivations of previous minorities contribute strongly to a new mainstream.

The frequent use of such terms as 'unusual places' and 'local facilities' in the language of independent travel should be seen in this context. It is a perspective on 'the other' i.e. places not the visitor's own. It should influence destination managers but may be misinterpreted – what to the destination manager and the residents is 'commonplace' (and therefore 'ordinary' and 'less important') may be significant to the spirit of place or *genius loci* sought by a growing number of experienced travellers, tired of purpose-built tourist facilities and manufactured experiences.

Donegan (1997) criticises what travel writing has become – 'pointlessly dangerous scrapes ... of derring do adventurers' and 'haughty essays on the strange habits of the natives'. He asserts readers have grown tired of such self-indulgence, noting the high popularity of Bill Bryson who claims: 'I am just a tourist who writes books. I am one of us, a person who is slightly out of his element, lost and worried'. His product is 'the travel book which is extraordinary only in its ordinariness'. Norman Lewis (1997), the veteran travel writer, expresses a similar sentiment: 'In my travels I look for the ordinary things that make up the lives of ordinary people'.

The implication here is that there is a growing common ground between certain 'everyday' elements of the quality of life of host communities and the sought-after experiences of a growing number of 'new tourists'. This is not to preclude destination management improving on the status quo. A significant outcome of the Earth Summit (WCED, 1992) was the replacement of a former environmentalist objective of the 'steady-state' with a commitment to growth within a framework of sustainability – local communities and local authorities (and by implication destination managers) have a key role in the implementation of desired change under 'Agenda 21'. The envisaged integration of the highly localised and the strategic approaches is essential: neither party should dominate since neither is infallible (Shoard, 1999).

IMAGE THEORY

As already discussed, before a tourist actually visits a destination, he/she will already have a mental image of it. The image may be a negative one, based on prejudiced (or honest) accounts, or a highly attractive one, based perhaps on only partially true stereotypes. Either way their decision on whether to visit that place some day – or not – will be influenced by this 'organic' image.

Image types

An 'organic' image is created largely through informal or passive consideration of a place – conversations with friends or family or half-remembered magazine articles or television programmes over a lifetime. More purposefully created images of destinations – 'induced' images – are the result of advertising, in, for example, tourist brochures designed to promote one destination over its rivals. Wahab and Pigrim (1997) further develop destination image theory, identifying sub-stages: 'overt induced 1'; 'overt induced 2'; 'covert induced 1'; 'covert induced 2' and 'autonomous'.

CASE STUDY

Induced images – the Canadian Rockies

In the 1870s, the expansion of Canada was focused on enticing the western province of British Columbia to join the Canadian Federation. This it did, in return for the construction of the Canadian Pacific Railway. The enormous cost of construction was met by the small, if well-developed, tourism industry, through the foresight of the general manager of the CPR, William Cornelius Van Horne. He developed a philosophy of capitalising the scenery made accessible by the railroad: 'If we can't export the scenery, we'll import the tourists'.

The CPR's advertising 'delineated the view of Canada, both at home and around the world. Its view of Canada as a place of scenic wonders and cultural diversity prevails even to this day' (Hart, 1983:7).

While tourism was in fact a small part of the company's main business, freight traffic (although its hotels were significant earners), this is a vivid indicator of the wider implications of tourism, here serving to create a positive image of Canada, influencing immigration, trade and international political relations and helping to influence national unity, a major Canadian concern.

Gunn (1997: 29) explained the process of destination image formation and subsequent tourist experience with reference to earlier psychological theory (Bruner, 1951) – a sequence consisting of: 'Hypothesis, Input and Check' (see Figure 3.6). When considering a destination the potential tourists imagine themselves in that destination and consider their likely experience.

Hypothesis stage

In the 'hypothesis' stage, only if the imagined experience is positive will they consider visiting that destination.

The images tourists or potential tourists have of specific destinations have thus arisen through a range of 'inputs'. Evaluation of these images is dependent on the social context of the potential tourist – education levels, occupation and stage in the life cycle – and the cultural context. For example, landscapes which are valued for tourism may once have been regarded as 'terrible', yet now are considered 'beautiful' or 'awe inspiring' etc. Examples include images of the Alps in the 18th century, and Wordsworth's image of the Lake District.

While the cultural attitudes towards a given place change with time, the individual holder of the 'hypothesis' (the prospective tourist) shows resistance to change if the organic image held is a pleasant one. For example, there is a proposal to relocate the Edinburgh Military Tattoo from its famous and spectacular location on the Castle esplanade to a new location in Princes Street Gardens or even a site outwith the city's central area. The relocation is based on impact considerations – the considerable disturbance to local residents caused by the erection and dismantling of the necessary scaffolding for seating and by the noise of the ceremonial military activities themselves. Based on the powerful image of the established site

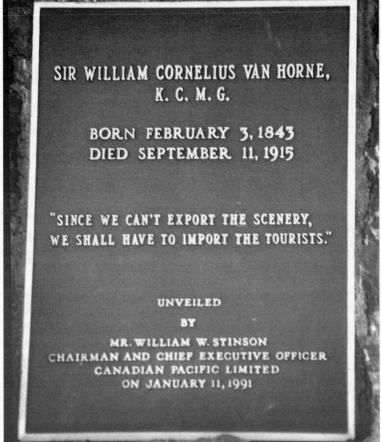

SIR WILLIAM CORNELIUS VAN HORNE,
K. C. M. G.

BORN FEBRUARY 3, 1843
DIED SEPTEMBER 11, 1915

"SINCE WE CAN'T EXPORT THE SCENERY,
WE SHALL HAVE TO IMPORT THE TOURISTS."

UNVEILED
BY
MR. WILLIAM W. STINSON
CHAIRMAN AND CHIEF EXECUTIVE OFFICER
CANADIAN PACIFIC LIMITED
ON JANUARY 11, 1991

Photographs 3.2a and b   *'If we can't export the scenery, we'll import the tourists' – Van Home statue in Banff National Park*

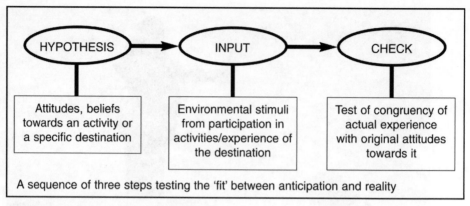

Figure 3.6 *Travel image psychology*
Source: Adapted from Gunn, 1997

there is strong resistance to change. However, attitudes may change with the 'maturity' of the opponents – age and experience may bring a sense of sympathy for the residents and a willingness to compromise – as by accepting relocation to a still beautiful but different site.

Input: experiencing a destination/viewing an attraction

This is a multisensory/complex reaction, in contrast to the hypothesis stage of viewing a photograph of the destination as in a promotional brochure – a single sensory (visual) experience.

The five familiar senses are involved – vision, hearing, touch, taste and smell – and there are also important interrelationships of the senses, giving rise to kinaesthetic, vestibular and chemical sensations. Together these form the totality of sensory experience.

Multisensory tourist experiences
- Hill walking/mountain climbing can include exertion/pain/adrenalin 'highs'/exhilaration.

- A sea view includes the smell of the salt water, the feel of the breeze, sounds of lapping waves, bird calls, etc.

- A historic reenactment or landscape interpretation can be affected by political or historical awareness e.g. of the Highland clearances in 18th-century Scotland or the forced resettlement of French Canadians in 18th-century Nova Scotia (*http://explore.gov.ns.ca/links.htm*) and the consequences for the landscapes as perceived in the early 21st century.

In destination area design and management, the *visual* sense cannot be considered alone. This is an established cardinal principle in the design of interpretive facilities within a destination if not yet for the actual destination as a whole.

Check stage

In this stage, input is checked against expectation. 'A heavy responsibility falls on the roles of designers and developers to create attractions that will exceed all expectations' (Gunn, 1997). An alternative, or perhaps complementary, approach is to avoid creation of a situation where a state-of-the-art audio-visual presentation may induce a reaction greater than that produced by the reality. The 'check' will reveal the disappointment of the tourist when expectation outperforms reality (as discussed in Chapter 4).

Box 3.2 *Expectation versus reality*

Crossing the English-Scottish border was until recently an anti-climax as no indication of the actual border was given and there are no visible differences in the landscape character on either side of the border. Construction of a simple but dramatic 'monument' has been effective – a large boulder of local stone with the countries' names on either side and nearby a stainless steel interpretive panel.

Crossing the 'continental divide' in the USA was written about by the author John Steinbeck (1961) who described his disappointment that this is only a line on a map, rather than the yawning chasm that he imagined:

> I remember as a child reading or hearing the words, 'The Great Divide' and being stunned by the glorious sound, a proper sound for the granite backbone of the continent. I saw in my mind escarpments rising into the clouds, a kind of natural Great Wall of China. [...] Were it not for a painted sign I never would have known when I crossed it. [...] The place wasn't impressive enough to carry such a stupendous fact like that.

The city of Glasgow mounted a successful campaign in the 1980s to change its image from one of a declining industrial city to a 'postmodern' city founded on culture, the arts and its 'friendliness'. It succeeded in this, spectacularly winning the accolade of European City of Culture in 1990 as a worthy successor to its catchy promotional slogan, 'Glasgow's Miles Better'.

The city continues to build on this success, attracting new industry and constructing buildings of high architectural acclaim, yet in terms of health and housing it continues to have serious problems. While these negative aspects are generally beyond the gaze of the 'average tourist', the more adventurous 'new tourist' will not miss them when he/she performs the 'check'.

Exercise

The role of the destination manager

How much of a role can/should destination management have in addressing the wider 'realities' of a place beyond the proud image it successfully projects to the tourist?

Should the destination manager be directly involved in these social and environmental issues, perhaps arguing for the preferential location of new (tourism) developments in 'difficult' areas so that 'social exclusion' may be tackled directly through job creation? (see the discussion of Wester Hailes in Chapter 6).

> Alternatively, should the destination manager avoid the risks of tourism development in difficult areas and concentrate on developments in established tourist areas where success is 'guaranteed', so that the benefits from the wealth generated by tourism and other modern industries will 'trickle down' to the needy areas of the destination?

Destination image and tourism policy

A further consideration is the political context of destination images. Hall and Jenkins (1995: 74–6) offer a powerful critique in their analysis of 'Power, place and the heritage of Monterey' where tourism:

> redefines social and political realities. [. . .] Destinations may therefore become caught in a tourist gaze from which they cannot readily escape. [. . .] Different tourist landscapes [. . .] whether they are historic or commercial, can be read as distinct cultural texts, a kind of outdoor museum which displays the artifacts of a community and society. [. . .] The rich and complex history of [a place] is almost completely absent in the 'official' historic tours and residences available for public viewing.

Factors influencing the spirit of place

Architecture and urban design

Gunn (1997) asserts the importance of design in destinations and tourism development generally:

> All tourism takes place on land; and yet how little attention is paid to how that land is protected, planned, developed and managed for tourism – that land through which all visitors flow. What do we as travellers see, smell, feel, and hear as we travel, and are designers and developers sufficiently sensitive to our interests and reactions?

Lynch (1984) emphasises that a city itself is a designed product: 'We may at times enjoy a city, but only as a fact of nature – just there, like a mountain or the sea. But, of course, we are mistaken; cities are created objects, and at times in history they were managed and experienced as if they were works of art. However misshapen, a city is an intended landscape'. He argues that part of the failure to take a comprehensive perspective is that: 'There seems to be a universal division in the field, between those engaged in social, economic and locational policy at urban level and those concerned with physical form at the project level'. This is a gap the emerging profession of destination management might bridge.

A postmodern perspective would however suggest that comprehensive city design – even if desirable – could not be wholly successful because:

> For each citizen the city is a unique and private reality: and the novelists, planners or sociologists (whose aims have more in common than each is often willing to admit) finds himself dealing with an impossibly intricate tessellation of personal routes, spoors and histories within the labyrinth of the city. A good working definition of metropolitan life would centre on its intrinsic illegibility: most people are hidden most of the time, their appearances are brief and controlled, their movements secret, the outlines of their lives obscure.
>
> (Raban, 1975)

This perspective questions whether there can be a true community viewpoint in the 'soft city' – 'Perhaps no more is possible than a temporary agreement on certain elements of the individual constructs of personal reality to suit current aims and needs in the context of the less controllable city itself and the mega-objectives which "the planners", from their "rational" perspective on the "common good", wish to foist upon the city and its inhabitants.'

Urry (1990) goes further, questioning authenticy itself: 'Authenticity does not reside in reality, but in interpreted representations of reality'. A 'democratic' vision for a designed city appears impossible. Perhaps significantly the most notable examples of such are associated with authoritarian regimes – for example Haussmann's Paris – though mellowing with the passage of time obscures these origins. It is at the smaller scale of individual buildings or neighbourhoods that design finds a place. The destination manager does not need to be an architect, neither do the tourists who undoubtedly respond favourably to a destination with a strong sense of place enhanced by interesting buildings, people-friendly open spaces and streets and distinctive neighbourhoods. It is an awareness of, and sensitivity to, these qualities that the destination manager must cultivate.

Architectural styles help define neighbourhoods within urban destinations. Ward (1985), commenting on the exuberant styles of former 'railway hotels' that occupy prominent sites in many European cities, describes the 'design philosophy' of the 19th-century railway barons as, 'any style as long as it's impressive'. Thus the Balmoral Hotel in Edinburgh (formerly the North British) is 'an unlikely blend of Dutch Baroque and French Second Empire plus some Renaissance detail for good measure' (see the Edinburgh case study in Chapter 6).

Destination interpretation – a visitor service

A more interpretive, less formal approach to understanding the design elements of the urban destination can be taken. For example, a church may appear to, and may even have been designed to, 'loom like a reproachful conscience above the dome of the Bank' (Ward, 1985). Such symbolism was well understood by the God-fearing merchants of the 18th and 19th centuries. They founded charitable and educational works such as orphanages – often significant architectural works themselves – perhaps to ease their conscience, troubled by their financial successes, a distinctly Scottish contradiction. Interpretation of the urban environment, revealing new perspectives such as this, is an important visitor service capable of enhancing the tourist experience of a destination. It is also a powerful tool in the destination manager's approach to visitor management. Conveying the reasons why, for example, certain visitor 'restrictions' may be necessary is more likely to be successful than simply stating, 'Do not do this'.

Urban design attempts to integrate the individual buildings, spaces, streets and other elements into a coherent and pleasing whole. Increasingly, such design-led approaches are backed by policy statements and development guidelines within a local plan (see Chapter 5).

A working knowledge of the 'language' of architecture and urban design can help identify styles and put into context, new, possibly intrusive elements proposed for existing neighbourhoods – a strong persuasive tool in arguments. Thus, Princes Street in Edinburgh was an important element of the original 18th-century design for the New Town. The street is no longer Georgian – yet neither is it 'modern' – it is a mix of mainly Victorian and modern blocks. Some consider the street to be less distinguished than it was, but generally pleasing and with exceptional vistas. They argue that the juxtaposition of different styles of building is visually stimulating. Others claim that the street has declined greatly due to a failure to retain the integrity of the original design.

Photograph 3.3a *Contrasting architectural styles/same retail company*

Photograph 3.3b *Contrasting architectural styles/same retail company*

Exercise

A monument or a mess?

Such controversy is nothing new. One of Edinburgh's most familiar landmarks, the Scott Monument, has been a focus of differing opinions since its completion in 1846. Consider these and form your own conclusions. Consider the likely differing opinions on a building or part of a streetscape in a destination with which you are familiar.

> I am sorry to report the Scott Monument a failure. It is like the spire of a church taken off and stuck in the ground.
>
> (Charles Dickens)

> It is ... the central and supreme object in the architecture of our present Edinburgh ... the finest which has yet been raised anywhere on Earth to the memory of a man of letters.
>
> (*The Scotsman*)

The designer, George Meikle, was an 'obscure man'. (Prejudice – he was a carpenter and self-trained architect – or a fitting comment on his building?)

An 'official view':

A striking romantic 200ft tall Gothic shrine (1836–1846) standing in defiance of its neoclassical setting: like an implant of the wild Old Town into the classical discipline of the New. [...] Influences from Melrose Abbey and the continent, it has the proportions of a mediaeval space rocket.

(McKean, 1992)

There is no single 'correct' view in design matters – but design matters! This emphasises the need for the destination manager to be a good communicator and negotiator.

(*Job advertisement – Edinburgh City Centre Manager*)

Exercise

Building design

Why should new buildings copy the old? Why not make bold contrasts or harmonies between the old and the new?

Is there a 'standard' building style that would please everyone?

Are there certain heights and proportions of buildings that are 'human in scale' and 'therefore' pleasing? (See the discussion of the *Scandic Crown Plaza Hotel* in Chapter 6.)

RURAL DESTINATIONS – PERCEPTIONS OF THE COUNTRYSIDE AND THE PLACE OF TOURISM AND RECREATION

Rural change

In the UK and many other industrial, developed countries at the beginning of the 21st century a number of key issues characterise the context in which rural tourism and the appropriate development of rural destinations must be considered. These issues and their consequences are responses to 'globalisation' – the increasing mutual dependence (although frequently imbalanced) between nation states – and to the dominance of the 'market economy' which challenges prevailing political perspectives where support for certain 'uneconomic' practices was commonplace on social and environmental grounds (as discussed in Chapter 5).

A number of key changes can be observed:

- 'Traditional' countryside industries, predominantly those founded on natural resources, are in decline.

- Job losses are increasing, resulting in a declining local tax base with repercussions on local services.

- Community change – significant structural change – is taking place. Generally the rural population is aging as young people migrate to urban areas to find work and perhaps excitement; in others cultural and social change is occurring as newcomers settle in villages to 'escape' the pressure and high costs of urban living.

- Intra-industry conflict can occur – e.g. in the tourism context, between walkers/climbers and deer stalkers.

- Inter-industry conflict can occur – e.g. where increasing tourist numbers results in trespass or damage to farmers' crops or disturbance of livestock; also where 'super-quarries' are developed, sometimes damaging the potential for tourism.

At the same time:

- Industries are developing out of what were only secondary activities – with potential to integrate with and support declining core industries or to replace them – including tourism, recreation and conservation.

- New communication and information technology is emerging, potentially creating new patterns of work that will enable high productivity from workers able to live and work in the countryside.

The rural crisis

Together these consititute the 'rural crisis'. The 'solution' is considered to lie, broadly speaking, in 'rural diversification'. Tourism is frequently considered to be the key. In many places it can be *part* of the solution but there are examples of failure. It is not only a question of financial support to enable those affected to make the transition to a more diversified rural economy; attitudes – and temperaments – may need to change to enable a farmer who may have very little experience of dealing with people to become a 'host' to tourists. Training will almost certainly be necessary – in a range of business skills. The farmer's partner and family will also need to be committed to the markedly different lifestyle.

The changes taking place in rural areas are economic, environmental and social. They cannot be considered in isolation from each other and only a sustainable approach to development is appropriate. The economic crisis facing many farmers is dramatic and high profile and the resulting social changes are clear. Suicide rates in rural areas are increasing and are highest among farmers. Other social indicators confirm a similar serious situation. The traditional image of the countryside – probably always little more than a 'townie's' fantasy – is changing. The 'urban–rural divide', symbolised by the contrasting images of the 'mean streets of the city' and the 'cottage with roses round the door', is not the cosy simplification it used to be.

The end of the 'urban–rural divide' may be occurring – the real or imagined geographical and cultural boundaries between town and country. The expansion of towns, formerly inhibited by green belts and other planning controls is once again on the national agenda alongside calls for new settlements. Problems of unemployment and structural change are common to both. Industrial techniques of manufacturing are increasingly applied to agriculture. Town–country is more of a continuum than two opposites. The idea of the urban areas being the 'core' and rural areas the 'periphery' – remote and dependent on rural economic activity – is less valid (Page, 1995).

The general decline of rural activities may, in many areas, make tourism of secondary concern (see the discussion on political differences towards tourism in Chapter 5). Characteristics of decline include the closure of local services – buses, primary schools, post offices, village shops. Revitalisation based on tourism, or including tourism as part of a diversified strategy, can make an area attractive for incomers. Some of those who settle may have children making it possible to keep open or reopen schools as the school role rises. They may also bring in 'new ideas' and money for local investment. A 'chain reaction' may take place. The area acquires a new attractive image and non-traditional industries may locate in the area, drawn by the lure of a pleasant environment and the financial incentives that may be offered by government and local authorities. These are industries based on new communication technologies such as e-commerce, 'dotcom' businesses and 'call centres' which are nomadic, i.e. not tied to a particular place in which to do business, through use of the internet. Conservation may also be seen as an 'industry' in the sense that it helps create a product – a sustainable countryside – and employs people, sometimes more than in the 'traditional' rural industries (Scottish Natural Heritage, 1997). Conversely, the success of regeneration of an area through tourism can make it attractive for incomers/ 'white settlers' which pushes up house prices – putting them beyond the reach of young local people.

Characteristics of rural areas

Lane (1994: 7–21) suggested three main characteristics of rural areas:

1. population density/settlement size
2. activities
3. social structures.

Sharpley (1997: 15) describes the common perception of rural social structures. They tend to be 'traditional' with a strong sense of community, economies are simple, the focus is local rather than cosmopolitan and there is a slower, less materialistic way of life. Others have commented critically that rural politics are conservative – there is a hierarchy, where everyone knows their place and is, allegedly, content with it. This might be criticised as a nostalgic or 'old-fashioned' view, but to many rural tourists this is actually a positive thing. 'Old fashioned' is used in an admiring way, reflecting the tourist's sense of nostalgia for a way of life which is just beyond living memory (and so cannot be subjected to a 'reality check').

The decline of rural industries, the loss of rural services and the migration to the cities has resulted in a less romantic situation. Ironically – but fortuitously – it is the poorer areas, those that have not proven suitable for intensive agriculture, that are most attractive to the tourist. This is clearly an opportunity for business and entrepreneurship. From a wider perspective it is also an opportunity for tackling the socio-economic and environmental problems that result from decline of the traditional activities of the countryside. Ironically, the very success of rural tourism can carry risks. For example, the revitalisation of an area – its emergence as a destination – can also increase the attractiveness of an area.

'Rurality' is the quality most rural tourists seek. It is a combination of the identifiable characteristics of rural areas *plus* the cultural meaning attached to them. The countryside is thus an antithesis to modern, urban life and the objective 'truth' is less important. For destination management this poses a dilemma. Can it deliver what the tourist wants while generating the wealth and services that the local communities want? And how can 'authenticity', an essential attribute of contemporary tourism experiences, be assured in the changing environment of the contemporary countryside?

Defining rural tourism and rural destinations

What is rural tourism? It has a long history. Until the Industrial Era, when increasingly rapid transport became available, travellers had to pass through the countryside in order to reach their actual destinations – cities and towns – for trade etc. Uncultivated countryside was not generally considered attractive. Local accommodation such as coaching inns provided for these travellers. In the post-war years rapid change took place – migration to the cities, withdrawal of agricultural subsidies and subsequently an increase in leisure time and the rise of modern tourism. In the 1960s the boom in package holidays resulted in over 50% of European Union residents taking their main holiday by the sea and almost 30% taking a second or subsequent holiday there (Davidson, 1992: 5). By the 1980s environmental decline in many coastal resorts coupled with changing tourist tastes led to other types of destination rising in popularity. Rural tourism was favoured by those attracted by its associations – no over-crowding, a clean environment and opportunities for healthy activities rather than 'just lying on the beach'. Heritage and cultural associations contributed further to the increasing popularity while overall social change prioritising healthy lifestyles and activity was a contributory factor.

At its simplest rural tourism could be described as 'tourism that takes place in rural areas' and this was an accepted understanding within the European Community. Keane *et al.* (1992 in Page and Getz, 1997) has criticised this as leading to confusion between the various terms used to describe tourism in rural areas, some forms of which only incidentally take place there. The description is too simplistic to be useful here – common sense would suggest that a development such as a theme park, say, Disneyland Paris, is not 'rural tourism' even though located in a rural area. Also it is necessary to consider that 'rural' has different meanings in different countries. However, certain core 'values' are generally implicit in the term, values that are also associated with sustainable approaches to development and 'responsible' tourism. These values would include a degree of local management of facilities and the participation of local people in the development of the industry. Rural tourism would have its basis in the natural and cultural resources of the area, although 'outside investment' could be involved. Terms such as 'rurality' and even 'rusticity' help describe this narrower interpretation of the term since they imply further intangible qualities, although Robinson (1990) suggests that the value of 'rusticity' is in helping define rural through associated problems, rather than virtues. Thus problems in rural areas include 'depopulation and deprivation [. . .]; a reliance on primary activities; and conflicts between local needs and legislation emanating from urban-based legislators'. Collins English Dictionary (2000) places 'rustic' in the context of 'simple, unsophisticated rustic pleasures'.

Despite the availability of more sophisticated definitions of countryside, for some purposes largely spatial definitions are used. The Organisation for Economic Co-operation and Development (OECD, 1993) offers:

Rural areas comprise the people, land and other resources, in the open country and small settlements outside the immediate economic influence of major urban settlements. Rural is a territorial or spatial concept; it is not restricted to any particular use of land, degree of economic health, or economic sector.

This would include some 90% of the land of OECD countries and embrace a diverse range of landforms, land uses, social structures and cultures. The Scottish Rural Partnership Fund (1999) uses a definition that defines rural as:

1. Local areas which have a population density of less than 100 persons per square kilometre, all of whose area is regarded as rural except for settlements with a population of more than 10,000;

2. Post code sectors which have a population density of less than 100 persons per square kilometre lying within the areas of all other Scottish local authorities.

The numerical preciseness is related to the need to identify clearly areas that would qualify for consideration for development funds from this national agency. Other countries use different figures although sharing the desire for definitions relating population density and settlement size without the 'complications' that less definable characteristics bring. Other national criteria for 'rural' include:

Australia – population clusters of fewer than 1,000 people

Austria – parishes of fewer than 5,000 people

Canada – places of fewer than 1,000 people or under 400 per square mile

France – towns of fewer than 2,000 people in houses which are contiguous or less than 200 metres apart

Norway – agglomerations of fewer than 200 people.

(Lane, 1994)

Sharpley (1997) refers to the English Tourist Board's (1998) use of a figure of fewer than 10,000 inhabitants as defining rural towns and villages, noting that there is no 'official' UK figure for 'rural' settlements. This figure is also used by Italy and Spain, while in Ireland the figure is a very different 100 inhabitants (Hoggart *et al.*, 1995: 22).

Figures alone are generally an inadequate indicator of rural areas (Sharpley, 1997), particularly from a tourism perspective. Tourists are predominantly urban dwellers, since that is where some 90% of the population of the UK live and other industrial developed countries have comparable high figures. They seek contrast with their home environment. Rural areas are therefore attractive since however much the figures vary between countries, they have far lower population densities than towns and cities. Rural activities offer a further contrast – agriculture and forestry (albeit with some exceptions) are intrinsically attractive to the urban eye, unaware of the economic uncertainties that may lie behind the image. Other legitimate rural activities are locally unattractive but are generally seen as anomalies in an otherwise rustic scene. For example, in central Scotland, in a national scenic area, quarrying takes place and there are recurring applications for planning permission to undertake gold mining, while quarrying takes place in the English Lake District National Park.

'Man made the city, but God made the country' runs an old saying. Other evidence of the 'hand of man' in an otherwise 'natural' landscape is generally welcomed as part of the scene. Vernacular architecture and 'heritage buildings' whether grand and stately or small and homely are generally welcomed as complements to the rural scene (as discussed in the Culross case study in Chapter 7).

Vernacular architecture refers to buildings which have a regional style which is clear even to the untrained eye. They seem native to a particular place. The distinctiveness is an attractive 'opposite' to the uniformity of much contemporary urban development. These 'traditional' buildings acquire their distinctive character from the appearance of being hand crafted, and constructed with materials that somehow reflect the countryside itself. This *is* often the case – generally they were built before standardised building materials were the norm and when transport limitations dictated that local materials be used wherever possible. Thus in the northeast of Scotland – old Aberdeenshire – many older buildings are made of granite giving rise to the epithet 'Aberdeen, the granite city' (*www.granite-city. com*). In Britain as a whole the building materials can be related to the two main divisions of the country – the uplands and the lowlands. Much of Scotland and the north and west of the English Midlands are 'stone country', from the hard rocks of the Atlantic coastline to the eastern boundary of sandstone that extends from Dorset to Yorkshire. Elsewhere brick was the normal building material. The variety of stone and of brick (itself made from softer stones of differing colours and textures) and the distinctive building styles contribute to the diversity of the country. This is common to most long settled countries.

In the increasingly urbanised countryside of many countries vernacular architecture is overwhelmed by the spread of suburban uniformity and, more recently, by apparently less harmful 'infill' developments in existing villages and small towns and by the 'big shed' architecture of out of town superstores. In this context the diversity and charm of traditional buildings becomes that much more sought after and destination management has an obligation to recognise and value them.

An important distinction is made between arable/pastoral/farmed or otherwise 'humanised' countryside and 'wilderness' or wild countryside. Countryside which is apparently untouched by human activities is protected in most countries on account of the scientific value of its natural resources and/or its scenic beauty. (see Chapter 5). In fact, in Britain, perhaps less than 1% of the total land area meets a strict definition of wilderness, that is land which is unchanged by human activity (*www.fs.fed.us/outernet/htnf/wildact.htm*). Even that is confined to the summits of the highest mountains. Indeed, on a world scale true wilderness is declining steadily and the great majority is in remote or otherwise inhospitable country, although it is now of increasing interest, notably to tourism, on account of those very qualities.

The destination manager in a rural area needs to be sensitive to these characteristics. Apart from the intrinsic value of the resources and landscapes, various forms of tourism can be related to them. Why do people visit the countryside? A range of motivations are involved, with a historic and cultural basis. In prehistoric times nature was feared for its awesome power to destroy man's works. Subsequently it became primarily a source of wealth (agriculture, timber, minerals etc.). In the 'Romantic Era' (from the early to mid-18th century) writers and poets such as William Wordsworth began to appreciate nature as a source of inspiration (*www.dickinson.edu/~nicholsa/Romnat/wordsworth.htm*). This coincided with an awareness by some that nature was increasingly threatened by the power of man.

The 'Frontier Era' in North America, faced with the apparently limitless abundance of the continent and coupled with the rise of industrialism, once again saw nature as a foe to be conquered. In modern times, nature is truly in retreat in much of the world and once again there is a surge of interest in nature-based tourism.

Who are the rural tourists?

In the UK some 80 million visitor nights per annum are spent in rural destinations. In 1993 637 million day visits were made, with an average trip of 27 km and a duration of three hours (Countryside Recreation Network, 1995). The Day Visits Survey (*www.countrysiderecreation.org.uk*) is carried out to improve the quality and comparability of information on day visits in the UK, by a consortium of national agencies; in 1998 these included the Countryside Commission (*www.countryside.gov.uk*), the Countryside Council for Wales (*www.ccw.gov.uk*), the (former) Department of National Heritage (*www.culture.gov.uk*), Scottish Natural Heritage (*www.snh.org.uk*), the Scottish Tourist Board (*www.visitscotland.com*), Wales Tourist Board (*www.visitwales.com*), the Forestry Commission (*www.forestry.gov.uk*), British Waterways (*www.britishwaterways.co.uk*) and the Department for Culture Media and Sport (*www.culture.gov.uk*).

Exercise

Statistics

Use the websites of the agencies just listed to check the availability of up-to-date, online statistics on the usage of specific types of countryside for an area of interest to you.

The demand for rural tourism is influenced by several factors. Car owners are three times more likely to visit the countryside than non-car owners, more than half of all visits to the countryside (52%) were made by only the 4.2% of the population who are in social groups ABC1 (1990 figures, Countryside Commission, 1995). Overall, the typical rural tourist is more likely to be younger and more affluent than the average, in professional or managerial employment, a car owner who lives in or near the countryside. Women and ethnic minorities are groups which are under-represented in the countryside visitor profile and this example of social exclusion requires consideration.

Exercise

Countryside visitors

Consider the range of factors that may discourage 'under-represented' groups from visiting the countryside as tourists or day visitors.

As well as women and ethnic minorities what other groups may make less than average use of the countryside for recreation?

Make recommendations for projects that would tackle these issues.

'Push' and 'pull' factors determine this profile. Push factors influence the individual into deciding on a particular choice of tourism according to his/her personal, psychological needs. This may be through a 'need to escape' from the pressure of work, family commitments or poor housing, but *response* to the 'push' can only be made if the opportunities are available. Not having a car may be one factor. Being a mother – as opposed to a father – may make 'escape' more difficult since equality in responsibility for childcare is not yet the norm in many countries. Pull factors are the attributes of a particular destination or site – the nature of the countryside and the activities that can be pursued there – and the 'pull' exerted will vary according to the particular 'type' of rural tourist.

The supply of rural tourism

Response to the demand for rural tourism and its supply are crucial issues in destination management. Imbalance between the two will result in dissatisfied tourists and/or degraded countryside and the possible disillusionment of farmers and other rural dwellers 'encouraged' to diversify their core activities into tourism. Rural tourism 'suppliers' are represented in the private, voluntary/not-for-profit and public sectors. The diversity conveys the breadth of the term 'rural tourism'.

The private sector

In the private sector in the UK 'mainstream' companies such as Thomson Holidays (*www.thomson-holidays.com*) offer country cottage rentals and small organisations such as 'Scottish Farmhouse Holidays' (*www.scotfarmhols.co.uk*) offer 'centred holidays' (staying at one farmhouse or croft) or 'touring holidays' (where the stay is at several farmhouses or crofts). In each case the guest is staying in a family home. In contrast 'inland resorts' are offered by companies such as CenterParcs (*www.centerparcs.com*) – 'a family-oriented cottage park with sport facilities and a sub-tropical swimming pool', operating in the Netherlands, Belgium, Britain, France and Germany; also by Oasis Villages (*www.oasishols.co.uk*) which provides modern accommodation and, in some resort–villages, ' "climate-controlled" internal environments set in pleasant countryside for swimming and lazing-by-the-pool, alongside opportunities for walking and cycling in the local countryside'.

Exercise

Rural tourism?

Are the purpose-built 'villages' of, for example CenterParcs and Oasis Villages, examples of rural tourism or are they 'mainstream' tourism developments *incidentally* located in the countryside?

In France and Belgium the gîte is well established (*www.itis-fr.com*). This is privately let, furnished, tourist accommodation characterised by its rural character and the personal welcome given to the tourist, but also by the standards provided which are ensured by government regulation. Rural camping sites were until recent years 'unsophisticated', compared to the highly developed coastal sites, although there is increasing diversity perhaps at the expense of the *camping municipal* – simple, clean and cheap sites run by the local communes.

In the middle of the accommodation range the voluntary hotel chains such as Logis de France (*www.logis-de-france.fr/uk/index.htm*) and Auberges de France are small, rural, one- and two-star hotels with restaurants, the conditions of membership of the chain including the offer of a personal service to guests and services reflecting aspects of the rural destination, e.g. regional and local dishes. In Ireland the Village Inns Hotels are comparable and are selected 'for the essential role which they play in the village in which they are placed'.

At the upper end of the market Relais et Châteaux in France (*www.relaischa-teaux.fr*), Paradores in Spain and Manor House Hotels in Ireland are themselves significant examples of the rural heritage – castles, palaces and stately homes – and also play an important role in attracting visitors to the countryside (Davidson, 1992: 146). A range of accommodation types is available in established rural destination areas, from budget to luxury, and many of these are examples of 'traditional' architecture which, without the income from tourism, might fall into decay.

Youth hostels have increasingly widened their membership to include those who can no longer consider themselves youths and continue to provide in many countries good, cheap accommodation, including, as well as the 'traditional' communal rooms, 'family rooms' (*www.syha.org.uk*; *www.yha.org.uk*; *www.auberges-de-jeunesse.com/anglais/default.htm*).

A wide range of companies offer 'special interest' short breaks and longer holidays, based on themes such as heritage, history, wildlife, photography, walking, cycling etc. Generally, their themes necessitate visits to popular tourist areas, but also remoter parts of the countryside where there is potential for service provision by local people. Access issues arise in some areas. In the UK, for example, there is no general 'right of access' to the countryside. The majority is privately owned – some 87% is the figure estimated by Shoard (1980). There are public rights of way and on the wider areas the norm has been a 'tolerance' from the landowners towards informal use. Increasing numbers of commercial companies taking or encouraging their clients to walk or cycle in popular areas has, however, contributed to government assessment of the situation since the 'access issue' has risen to prominence. Even in Sweden, where there is an age-old right of access to uncultivated land – *Allemansrätt* (everyone's right) – landowners are increasingly arguing that 'commercialised access' by growing numbers causes measurable environmental impacts and consequently incurs costs for repair which must be covered 'somehow'.

The history of attempts to gain access to the British countryside for recreation and of the 'access debate' in the UK conveys a long struggle to achieve what many consider a 'right' of all (*www.ramblers.org.uk/factshts*). Two of the earliest known campaigning groups were the Association for the Protection of Ancient Footpaths in the Vicinity of York, formed in 1824, and the Manchester Association for the Preservation of Ancient Footpaths, formed in 1816. The Scottish Rights of Way and Access Society was formed about 1822 by an Edinburgh university professor, Adam Black, and continues today as a voluntary body which records and liaises with local authorities to protect and enhance rights of way in Scotland. James Bryce MP introduced the Access to Mountains (Scotland) Bill in Parliament in 1884 which, although unsuccessful, began the first moves towards a concerted access movement. It was 1945, however, before the Ministry of Town and Country

Planning published a report by John Dower that suggested where and what these parks should be, the National Parks and Access to the Countryside Act becoming law in December 1949. Legislation concerned with access to the countryside continues to be a significant issue (*www.snh.org.uk*).

The voluntary/not-for-profit sector

This sector comprises bodies ranging from a local wildlife trust that owns a small woodland that it maintains and keeps open to the public to bodies such as the Royal Society for the Protection of Birds (*www.rspb.org.uk*) which owns many sites in Britain. Similarly, the National Trust (*www.nationaltrust.org.uk*) and the National Trust for Scotland (*www.nts.org.uk*) are major landowners, the latter owning well-known areas such as Glencoe.

While access to many of these properties is free, visitors see them as destination areas and may spend several days or longer in the wider area spending money on accommodation, food and drink and other tourist-related services. The National Trusts also own numerous buildings of architectural and historic significance and these are further sigificant visitor attractions.

The public sector

The public sector's role in the supply of rural destinations is primarily one of setting the broad framework of, for example, rural landuse policy, legislation for development/conservation/access and subsidy/support for appropriate development. This is overwhelmingly the situation in the UK where, for example, even 'national' parks are not owned 'by the nation'. The challenges this poses for destination management and development are considerable, necessitating skills in using a combination of 'carrot and stick' policies – financial incentives and limited rural planning powers and other regulations (see Chapter 5) – as well as maintaining the degree of mutual tolerance between landowners and users. Such tolerance is generally present, although it is subject to grave uncertainties where land changes hands in the marketplace.

Important historic buildings are conserved by the state in many countries and increasingly some tourism facilities may be developed, generally as 'heritage' and interpretive centres. In the UK these facilities have sometimes been criticised as being less interesting/exciting than in privately run attractions, perhaps related to uncertainties as to whether they were 'educational' or 'recreational' in nature. That old dichotomy is steadily giving way to high-quality interpretations of their subjects. The additional expense, sometimes heightened by a reluctance to introduce admission charges, is necessitating 'creative' approaches to management. A 'destination' approach is encouraged – attractions which on their own are 'uneconomic' can associate with related attractions within the destination area so cooperative marketing can be undertaken. Heritage trails can connect them, leading the tourist along a coherent route of interest in itself.

Issues in supply

Conservation areas

Various 'designated areas' in many countries are covered by protective legislation introduced by central government and/or local authorities. In the UK these include

121

national parks, regional parks and country parks where tourism and recreational use are promoted to varying degrees alongside the conservation of their natural resources and associated cultural activities. There are also national scenic areas, areas of outstanding natural beauty and other designated areas where the outstanding beauty of the areas is uppermost; and various sites where natural resource conservation is priority and visitors will be permitted but not strongly encouraged – such as national nature reserves and sites of special scientific interest. These are UK designations; there are also European Union and international designations (see the discussion on conservation in Chapter 5).

As with the National Trust properties, these public sector properties are often seen as destinations themselves or as the main 'pull factors' of wider destination areas and, consequently, are of great significance to destination management. Provision of visitor facilities within designated areas is generally confined to interpretive centres and trails and perhaps campsites. Carparks will be provided, increasingly on the periphery of the area to discourage motor vehicles within the area. Private concessionaires are generally licensed to supply food and beverages and the supply of accommodation will also be a private sector role, though certain environmental and other 'quality' standards may be required from operators who wish to be officially recommended by the park or area (see the Cairngorms case study in Chapter 10).

CASE STUDY

National park designation – Scotland

Context: 'British National Parks' (England and Wales only) – 'Protected Landscapes'

Characteristics:

- No single body has overall management and planning powers.

- A complex ownership pattern of private/voluntary/public owners.

History of park proposals for Scotland:

- *1876* – World's first national park established – Yellowstone, USA

- *1890* – Yosemite, USA established, as a result of Scottish-born John Muir's campaigning

- *1898* – Bryce's 'Access to the Mountains' Bill – parliament rejected it

- *1947* – Scotland excluded from England and Wales national park proposals

- *1970s* – Park system for Scotland introduced: urban, country and regional parks established; no 'special parks'

- *1990* – Countryside Commission for Scotland report, 'Management and Conservation in Scotland's Popular Mountain Areas', proposed four initial areas for national park status:

> - Cairngorms
> - Loch Lomond/Trossachs
> - Ben Nevis/Glencoe/Black Mount
> - Wester Ross
>
> *Popular support*
>
> - 80% in Scotland pro national parks (survey)
> - International opinions – strong support
> - Working parties (with government appointees) set up to reexamine situation, *again*
> - Merger of Countryside Commission for Scotland and Nature Conservancy Council to form Scottish Natural Heritage (1991) (all government bodies)
> - Natural heritage areas proposed, based on 'voluntary approach' to protection, access etc.
> - Cairngorms and Loch Lomond working parties set up to prepare more reports. Main report supports government reluctance to designate national parks. 'Minority report' recommends Cairngorms National Park. Report recommends Loch Lomond National Park (in all but name)
> - 1998 New (Labour) government committed to establishing Scottish National Parks
> - 2002 Loch Lomond and the Trossachs National Park to be established
> - 2003 Cairngorms National Park established
>
> (See Chapter 10 – Cairngorms case study.)

Rural tourism – how big a market?

The national tourist boards of many countries make annual assessments of the likes and dislikes of overseas and domestic tourists about their trip to the country. For visitors to Scotland, the most mentioned attribute is consistently 'the scenery' – 86% of overseas visitors and 69% of UK visitors (Scottish Tourist Board, 1999). Clearly the image of Scotland is of a predominantly rural destination. This focus is repeated throughout the European Union.

The response of the tourism industry in Scotland is: 'To enhance Scotland's established reputation as a high-quality tourism destination, by building on its history, culture, environment and the hospitality of its people' (Scottish Tourism Strategic Plan, 1999). The key objectives are:

1. Create new facilities and improve existing ones.

2. Promote tourism in a more effective and coordinated way.

3. Enhance skills, including management skills.

Specific targets are to:

- 'Improve visitor perceptions of Scotland.'

- 'Increase expenditure outwith Edinburgh and Glasgow from 71% in 1993 to 75%.'

Increasing attention on rural areas is evident in the 'vision statements' of other national tourist boards.

Specific types of rural tourism

Burton (1995) identified broad categories of nature-based tourism, according to tourist motivations. Each has distinct implications for destination management.

Viewing natural wonders

Examples include: Yosemite Falls in California, USA; Banff Springs in Alberta, Canada; Cirque de Gavarnie in the French Pyrenees; and St Kilda, a Scottish island. The highest standards of conservation management are practised and many are parts of national parks or world heritage sites. Enforcement of strict quotas on visitor numbers and control of activities may be practised.

Taking part in outdoor activities

Rural resources are essential for specific activities such as canoeing, hang gliding and skiing, while a rural setting, such as high-quality landscape, is required for activities such as walking and cycling.

Touring by car or by coach

Touring holidays reflect the sentiment that 'it is better to travel hopefully than to arrive' and require a succession of high-quality landscapes – natural and/or cultural. Management may require liaison with several local authorities along the route for maintenance of lay-bys, picnic spots and interpretive displays.

Experiencing a way of life, the 'rural idyll'

The opportunity to take part in a real (or partially real) rural lifestyle, e.g. holidays on working farms, 'agritourism' etc.

CASE STUDY

Roots in the soil

'Scratch a Frenchman, find a peasant' is a reflection of the proud boast that only a generation or two lies between the urbane French executive and his/her peasant ancestors. Certainly France was a far more 'rural' country than Britain (as measured by population settlement criteria) until the post-war period when migration to the cities that had characterised Britain and other European countries accelerated in France. Many French families would adopt a habit of taking the annual summer holiday back on the family farm.

Exercise

Agritourism

'Agri-tourism is tourism linked to agriculture; farm-based tourism is [...] one element of agri-tourism, but agri-tourism is a broader concept which also covers festivals, museums, craft-shows and other cultural events and attractions' (Sharpley, 1997: 9).

As a destination manager for a predominantly agricultural area, outline a programme of training aimed at enabling farmers and agricultural workers to diversify their activities – i.e. continuing their core activities as 'farmers' but supplementing their (declining) incomes by using the farm and its surroundings as a basis for tourism/recreational activities.

For your choice of farm type, indicate the tourist/recreational activities that might be developed, also considering the wider context of the farm within the destination.

Tourism and the rural crisis

'The rural crisis' is increasingly in the news as it grows in severity. Tourism was seen as the 'salvation' when the problems were those of structural changes and the withdrawal of subsidies. The 'new' problems and challenges of the late 1990s and the early 21st century – genetically modified crops and livestock and in Britain BSE and the foot-and-mouth epidemic – intensify the debate.

Tourism is certainly part of the solution to the problems of the countryside but it has had its own problems. Rural tourism has been viewed as small scale and 'unprofessional'. More recently, commercial interests have moved into the field, as have professional organisations and local authorities and change is taking place. A contemporary challenge is how to retain the 'unique selling proposition' of rural tourism – the beauty and diverse interests of the countryside as well as its sense of a welcome 'difference' from the hustle and bustle and general anonymity of urban life.

The planning, development and management of rural tourism has been generally 'reactive' rather than 'proactive'. This is an inadequate approach in the context of the dramatic changes taking place in rural areas since the 1980s:

- great structural changes
- population decline
- falling employment and income
- diminishing rural services
- loss of identity and culture.

In response to the rise in popularity of rural tourism and recreation, the emphasis has been on 'containing the problems' – through visitor management and conservation – rather than actively promoting the industry. As a result there is a continuing policy implementation gap between:

- recognition of the benefits of tourism and their integration into rural development plans
- perception of tourism as a threat to production activities.

The industry is also fragmented yet interdependent, suggesting the need for more partnerships – e.g. public-private approaches to development.

CASE STUDY

What people think about the countryside: an 'ordinary' rural tourist's/countryside visitor's response to current issues

On the countryside access debate:

'This wild land is my heritage – there should be no restrictions on access to it.'

On field/blood sports debate/animal welfare:

'Fox hunting is morally unacceptable – calling it a traditional rural activity does not justify it.'

'It is cruel to hunt deer – calling it culling is no excuse. Maybe wolves should be reintroduced to do the job as nature intended, but wouldn't they attack sheep and even people?'

On the (Scottish) national parks debate:

'Why should Scotland be denied an approach to conservation and recreation that the rest of the world adopted long ago? After all, it was a Scot – John Muir – who started the international national parks movement.'

The 'ordinary' countryside resident is likely to hold the conviction that those who live in the countryside and earn their living from it know best how to manage it. Also, that they should be left alone to get on with their jobs, providing food for the nation, preferably with continuing subsidies.

The perspectives of those visiting and those living in the countryside are markedly different from each other. It is the politicians' role to attempt to achieve some acceptable compromise, informed by professionals including destination managers. In many countries initiatives have been set up to ease the financial and other burdens that accompany the process of change. One example in the UK is the Scottish Rural Challenge Fund, which 'encourages people based in local rural communities to initiate projects which find new ways to tackle particular rural problems or which create a wider range of opportunities in rural areas. [...] the Fund's objectives complement the Scottish Executive's priorities, notably promoting social inclusion and partnership'. The fund's objectives for 2000–2001, in no particular order, are:

- Helping disadvantaged communities in rural areas, through tackling social exclusion and poverty.

- Better health/quality of life for local people through access to adequate and affordable services, facilities, housing and innovative forms of transport provision.

- Improving community confidence, for example by reducing crime and fear of crime and decreasing the isolation of minority, ethnic and other disadvantaged groups.

- Bringing communities into decision making.

(Scottish Executive Rural Affairs Department, 2000)

Tourism can clearly contribute indirectly to these objectives, but is not specifically targeted. Destination management in a rural area could, however, encourage a community to apply for such funding, devising a scheme focused on tourism but respecting these core priorities. Moreover, political objectives are controversial: an opposition party might have a very different view of tourism's role to that held by the party in power.

CASE STUDY

Political controversy: an opposition party perspective

Tourism is not the 'be-all and end-all' for Scotland. We must not depend on tourism. We will welcome thousands of people to our country and to this constituency, a land of amazing sunsets, where people would walk for miles and pay money to see that, but we have to relish the real excitement and pride in this land and work for regeneration. Tourism can only ever be the icing on the cake, that extra bit, but what people want to do on holiday is to watch other people at work. [...] we have to be much more creative and get this land of ours back to work.

(Adoption meeting of Scottish National Party candidate for Member of the Scottish Parliament for Caithness, Sutherland and Easter Ross, February, 1999)

The Scottish Secretary (Labour) subsequently accused the SNP's candidate of undervaluing the tourism industry. His Industry Minister called the remarks 'an insult to those employed in this vital sector'. He went on to say:

I am deeply concerned that the SNP seem not to take this vast industry – one of Scotland's largest – seriously. [...] This government [...] certainly does not believe that tourism is 'the icing on the cake'.

The SNP candidate responded:

Tourism, developed sensitively, supported generously and promoted passionately undoubtedly has its place. However, without the traditional and new industries that contribute to the mixed economy that is the Highland economy, there will be little tourism. [...] Tourism grows from strong communities. Strong communities do not grow from tourism.

The Labour MSP candidate for the area retorted:

But tourism is not a threat to the development of other industries. On the contrary, the more people who visit us in their leisure time, the more people will realise what a marvellous, unspoiled and hospitable part of the country this is, and what great potential it has. And that can only make it more likely that we will attract new ideas and inward investment.

He claimed that the potential value of Highland tourism will not be realised until it casts off the 'Cinderella' image which many people have of it. The chip on the shoulder attitude which treats the holiday trade as somehow a second-class industry must end. It is the second biggest industry in the Highlands, with 14% of the workforce employed in accommodating and serving the annual throughput of two million visitors:

There is quite rightly some resentment going back to Victorian times of the Highlands being a playground for the rich. The proper place for that resentment, however, is in the history books.

Clearly tourism policy is a matter of some controversy in the north of Scotland. Similarly conflicting perspectives are found in other parts of the UK and other countries. Policy making is an area in which destination management and tourism generally must play an active role (see Chapter 5).

Exercise

Attitudes towards rural tourism development

For a rural area with which you are familiar discuss the type of rural tourism you would encourage to develop the area as a destination. Consider the views of the student group outlined below.

In response to the political exchange outlined in the preceding case study a group of people involved with a rural tourism study group sponsored by the Workers' Educational Association and based in the area in Kinlochbervie in the Scottish Highlands made a suggestion based on their own experience:

It is unrealistic to expect that tourism alone will reverse the depopulation, lack of employment opportunities and cultural decline experienced by many of our local areas. Certainly tourism can bolster community pride and sustain livelihoods but only as part of a wider integrated approach to development. The real challenge is to put our rural areas back into good heart.

A recent illustration of this is the achievement of the people of Alness who built on their success in the 'Britain in Bloom' competition (*www.britain-in-bloom.-co.uk*) by winning some of the categories in the 'Nations in Bloom' competition. Certainly visitors to the area will enjoy the flowers, but it is thanks to young and old in Alness working together that is strengthening pride in the area and recreating a more vibrant attractive community.

The alternative is to create some kind of artificial veneer which some people called tourists are directed towards. This bears no relation to the reality of living in the Highlands and Islands.

It seems to us that [. . . the SNP candidate's] comments point towards a more authentic form of tourism that plays a central role in the regeneration of our communities and reawakens a shared sense in the regeneration of our communities and reawakens a shared sense of wonder in our rich natural and cultural heritage.

There is an opportunity for those of us who care about the future of our rural areas to get involved in creating a local tourism we can be proud of – surely that is worth working for.

For your area:

1. What local resources are available?

2. 'Who' are the stakeholders i.e. the various interested parties?

3. Are these groups equally strong?

4. Is there a prevailing community attitude towards tourism?

5. How would you try to influence that attitude?

6. *Should* you try to influence it? As a destination manager for the area, to what extent should you be 'biased towards tourism'?

Resolving conflict in the countryside

The contrasting views of selected stakeholders in the countryside debate suggest the scale of the challenge faced by destination managers and other professionals in developing rural tourism destinations. While this author can, as might be expected, identify with the 'rational, comprehensive, considered' perspective of the 'academic/professional', each perspective is equally 'real' from the point of view of the different stakeholders. 'Building bridges' between these groups – consensus building and mediation – is no less important in rural areas than it is in urban situations. The romantic notion that the countryside – unlike the town – is a place where everyone lives in harmony, since everyone has a place and 'knows his place' is long gone.

The destination manager has a number of 'tools' available for helping to build concensus with a rural community. The interpretive planning process (*Interpretation*) creates opportunities for local communities to identify their key resources and the heritage they wish to share with tourists. It is part of the destination manager's role (perhaps delegated to a specialist in his/her organisation or a consultant) to foster and encourage local enthusiasm while tempering it with the economic realities of a competitive industry still viewed with scepticism by some of the local stakeholders.

Consensus building and mediation is a significant challenge in rural destination management. Various techniques have been developed in recent years, generally focusing on the abilities of the manager or other professional to respond to, but also to guide, the stakeholders in a development proposal.

In this context interpretation is a further technique, here having a complementary role to its more familiar one as a visitor information service – that of visitor management.

A guiding principle for interpreters is: 'Through interpretation, understanding; through understanding, conservation'. In other words if visitors *understand* why they should not do a certain action, they are more likely to follow the request than if they are simply *told* not to do it (see Figure 3.7). Various techniques are used – from simple signposts to elaborate, state-of-the-art, interactive video presentations

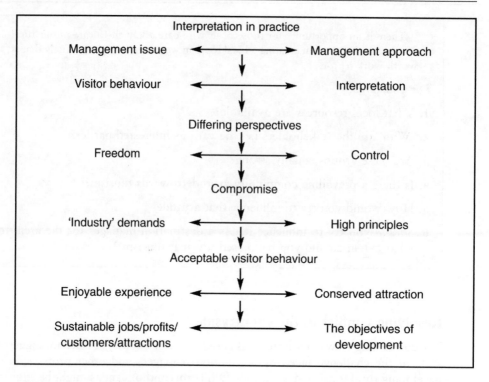

Figure 3.7 *Resolving conflict*

– the choice being guided by another tablet of stone in the interpreter's collection: 'I read and I forget; I see and I remember; I do and I understand'. In today's less deferential world a further line is perhaps required at the end: 'But I pay and therefore I expect...'.

Figure 3.7 conveys the links between the two professional objectives of sustainable resource management and customer service, while recognising that generally, 'He who pays the piper, calls the tune ...', namely the customer.

As an indication of the gulf between the 'rational' perspective and that of the 'countryside establishment' (at least as represented by one of main magazines targeting this group in the UK), Courtauld (1994) refers to this as 'sociological claptrap ... rubbish ... advertising agency jargon ... gobbledygook!'

Critics have referred to this establishment perspective as a long outdated view of the countryside, one of 'traditional values' where 'everyone knew his place and was contented with it'.

The 'ordinary countryside visitor or tourist' probably finds it difficult to understand how such simple activities as having a walk or a picnic in the countryside can possibly cause any damage or how even specialist activities like hill walking or wildlife watching could have adverse impacts. Conversely, he/she probably cannot see how these activities could ever replace traditional countryside activities such as farming.

Planning, development and management of tourism within a rural destination

Planning for rural tourism has been generally reactive, rather than proactive, notably in response to the great structural changes since the 1980s:

- population decline

- falling employment and income

- diminishing rural services

- loss of identity and culture.

The emphasis has been on 'containing' the alleged negative impacts of countryside recreation and tourism as a threat to production activities, rather than a proactive approach of effective visitor management integrated with conservation. There have been exceptions such as the work of L'Association Tourisme en Espace Rural (France) (*www.cnrter.asso.fr/*) and the European Rural Tourism Association, sponsored by the Council of Europe and many local organisations in various countries (*www.rural-europe.aeidl.be/*). Generally, however, there has been a 'policy implementation gap' – recognition of the real benefits of tourism in *policies* has not always resulted in actual rural development *plans*.

The rural tourism industry is also fragmented, unhelpful in an industry that required interdependence. There is a strong need for partnerships in development, where tourism, as in many urban areas, can be a catalyst for regeneration.

Criteria for tourism developments in a rural destination

Rural tourism can be defined simply in terms of where it takes place, but this is of limited help to the destination manager who may be called on to advise on whether or not to support a proposal for a particular tourism development or indeed to take part in the planning process for an area.

In many countries, notably where agriculture is or has been a significant element in the national economy, there has been recognition of the significance of rural tourism and positive moves to encourage growth of the industry. Financial incentives have been significant in the development of tourism, one early UK example being through the development powers of Section 4 of the 1969 Development of Tourism Act grants whereby up to 49% of the total capital costs of an approved development were supported by grant. This 'Section 4 assistance' was of considerable benefit to the early 'modern' tourism industry in the period from its introduction to when it was abandoned. The conditions attached to award of the grant enabled specific forms of tourism development to be encouraged and directed to particular areas and for certain social and environmental policy objectives relevant to the destination area to be supported.

The European Union has a number of measures relevant to tourism development and these also enable specific types of development to be encouraged. Ironically, it is EU agricultural policy that has led to the decline of certain types of farming (through subsidy reduction and withdrawal) and consequently the need to develop tourism as a supplement to farmers' (declining) core activities. This diversification cannot have a standard approach since Europe's farming is itself varied on account of the diversity of landforms and climates of the continent. This is a positive factor for tourism destination development, enabling the regional landscapes and cultural heritage to be enhanced as attractive tourism products while simultaneously restoring and conserving the landscapes which have been degraded by intensive rural landuses and maintaining the incomes of local populations.

Exercise

Rural tourism support from the European Union

Use the internet to explore examples of support for rural tourism and rural development.

Choose a search engine, for example *www.yahoo.com*, to find 'official' bodies in this field and explore their sites. Relevant topics for a 'search' include: Common Agricultural Policy; regional policy; LEADER; rural enterprise; rural tourism.

A few sites to get you started are:

europa.eu.int/pol/agr/index_en.htm
europa.eu.int/comm/enterprise/whatsnew/
www.rural-europe.aeidl.be/
europa.eu.int/comm/commissioners/index_en.htm
members.tripod.com/~WynGrant/WynGrantCAPpage.html

The various forms of financial support for rural tourism development are accompanied by guidelines and conditions designed to direct tourism. An outline of the broad direction EU rural tourism should take was provided by the 1987 report, 'Rural Tourism in the 12 Member states of the EC'. It made seven 'propositions':

- To arrive at a more precise definition of rural tourism.

- To clarify the notion of agritourism.

- To codify rural tourism products.

- To popularise the principal elements of rural tourism.

- To harmonise tourist road signposting.

- To promote centres of rural tourist attraction.

- To encourage Europe-wide cooperation of organisations involved in rural tourism.

The outcome was to be the creation of new and the improvement of existing rural products, in conjunction with the operators. An implicit message was that rural tourism products are inadequately defined – comparison of apparently similar products between and even within countries was not possible. The proposed 'codification' should not, however, lead to any loss of regional distinctiveness; rather, this should be strengthened. Marketing of the rural tourism products would also be enhanced through clearer product identities. Further, it would enable the operations with genuine potential for tourism development to be the focus – rather than the larger, industrialised, agri-businesses which are often based on mono-cultures of one single crop and offer no sense of the 'rurality' sought by tourists. This broad set of guiding principles continues to be relevant.

At the level of the individual or group tourism impacts are generally low. It is with mass tourism that there has existed a problem and this is evident in many developments which it could be argued represent an urbanisation of the country-side. Pigram (1993) notes that this is a trend that occurs where the urban dweller perceives that the rural surroundings are a part of their 'personal recreational space' and seeks to impose urban values in the rural environment. At the opposite extreme, the preservation of perceived rural qualities may well result in the 'fos-silisation' of the countryside (Lane, 1994). This occurs where a stereotype image is perpetuated in tourism literature and may act as a severe constraint on development appropriate to local needs. In this regard, in central and eastern European countries there is a body of opinion that wishes each country to modernise and become a member of the European Union. At the same time each country is at the mercy of the incoming tourism trade due to tourism's powerful influence over the relative weakness of their economies.

This may result in social progress; alternatively, the outcome may be the recreation of an idealised version of the past for the benefit of the tourists. Examples of the latter have taken place in, for example, Bulgaria (Collins, 1996), Wales (Gruffudd, 1994) and Ireland (Stocks, 1996). While visiting a rural community there may be certain images the tourist 'expects' to see: handicraft industries (Collins, 1996; Unwin, 1996; Zarza, 1998) or the traditional Irish cottage (Stocks, 1996).

These notions of 'countryside' and 'nature' are 'social constructs' (Clark et al., 1994: 11; also Macnaghten and Urry, 1997). Such development may be a consequence of, and a reaction to, intensive agriculture which many feel has swept away precious qualities of life and had a despoiling level of impact on ancient landscapes (Harvey, 1998: 154):

> In a county of vast, regimented landscapes of winter wheat and sugar beet, the unimproved pastures of Old Spilsby were an echo of a more intimate countryside, an agriculture of the human scale. [...] In the culture of agribusiness such places are an anathema. [...] Soon after came the land drainage machines, preparing this quiet countryside for intensive arable production.

The affective feeling for the countryside being destroyed in this way was great, but the local communities were comparatively powerless against the economic might of the agri-businesses. The more powerful stakeholders of the village and the area were able to overrule the 'ordinary' people of Old Spilsby. There was no real scientific value to the site so the developers had no legal obligation to maintain it as it was. In Murphy's (1985) conceptualisations of the 'community approach' the overwhelming will of the local community should triumph, but in this case it didn't.

To Hughes (1995) it could be said that the failure to apply Murphy's concept to an example like this is reflective of the lack of a political dimension to the model (see Chapter 5). Further, it can be seen that scientific and rational evaluations prevailed over the affective desires of the local community – because a rational evaluation had taken place and it was found that there was nothing important enough to preserve. Yet the images described by Harvey clearly meant a great deal to the villagers who lived with this environment. Hughes states that the discourse of sustainability is dominated by this scientific and rational viewpoint. While this is essential, it should also be tempered by the affective and the ethical perspectives.

Hughes' solution (p. 58) to the over-rationalisation of sustainability is to recognise the 'communities of affect' as the embodiment of the 'felt experience'. By approaching the issue of sustainability from this perspective the *process* can be seen as just as important as the desired *result*. Zarza (1998: 109) concurs with Hughes on this point when he states that:

> Fostering local dynamics is both a means and an end. The population which is mobilised and supported in the project will generate both considerable motivation, and a positive image which the rural population will internalise.

Also placing emphasis on the rationalisation and categorisation viewpoints are the various classifications of 'rurality' and 'wilderness'. For example, Lane's (1994: 12) '[c]ontinuum [c]oncept' – ranging from sparsely populated remote wilderness, to the 'ultimate expression of urbanisation at the other end of the scale' with an intermediate level somewhere in between. Similarly, Higham (1998: 43) seeks to identify physical indicators of 'artefactualism', 'naturalness', 'remoteness' and 'solitude' to determine the level of 'wilderness purism'. However, such physical indicators may be misleading. A more realistic indicator may be *perceptions of solitude* (ibid.). Concurring with this view is Mather (1997: 197) who in his study of East Grampian hill walkers found that there were conflicting opinions expressed in 'the hills are for all' sentiment yet there were still 'too many people' present. Such concepts of 'rurality' or 'wilderness' may in the end come down to the level of social and power relations present in the community (Murdoch and Pratt, 1993 after Pahl, 1970). For instance, Pahl found that in rural communities there was a close relationship between working and middle classes (ibid.). Similarly in wilderness the main sort of relationship sought after could be said to be one in which the walker/hiker/backpacker communes *alone* with nature.

This raises the other strand of Hughes' (1995: 58) dual approach to the implementation of sustainability, namely the 'restorative' nature of tourism as an antidote to the pressures of modern living and the 'risks' which the individual increasingly has to manage alone, due, for example, to the decline of the nuclear family, etc.

Rural tourism and nature-based recreation can thus provide an escape from the pressures of modern life. There are, however, many different perceptions of 'nature' (Ralton, 2000). For instance, Mackay (1995) examined the perceptions of wild moorland of a sample of Perth city dwellers. Showing them images of wild moorland evoked comments ranging from 'peaceful' to 'bleak' to 'desolation' (p. 106). This echoes the evaluation of certain public attitudes to moorland by the Chief Executive of Scottish Natural Heritage: 'MAMBA' (Miles and Miles of Bugger All – so why bother to preserve it?), reminding us that without some understanding of the ecology of such landscapes it is difficult to appreciate their value (Crofts, 1995, after Wilkinson and Waterton, 1991).

Yet the need to preserve wild moorland has to be argued on ethical as well as scientific and rational grounds. It must be preserved because of the diverse nature of species and their habitats that it contains; also, landscapes of this character are attractive wildernesses to walkers. They are also used commercially for grouse and deer shooting. A symbiotic relationship between a properly managed shooting estate and good habitat creation can exist (Magnusson, 1995), but there is some doubt as to whether recreation/nature-based tourism and shooting can (Ratcliffe, 1992, in Cox, 1993: 274):

> [The] wonderful freedom of the spirit and uplift of the senses that goes with untrammelled access to wild places can easily be diminished, if not completely destroyed, by the sense that others object to my presence there and seek to prevent it.

There are various levels of ability and desire for access to wild country. These range from: 'passive', 'casual', 'vigorous', 'rugged' and 'arduous' as defined by Millward (1991: 242; 1993: 40). The last three forms of access can be seen to be catered for by the type of 'wilderness' landscapes previously discussed. But what about the walkers preferring a more gentle form of exercise or indeed encouraging those people into the countryside who are unaware of the potential benefits and do not participate in any way at all?

Millward uses the cartography of an area to establish the varying levels of access existent (ibid.). From this information he argues that a more equitable provision of access can be made through a rational analysis and evaluation. However, provision of access is one thing, but the desired customer actually using it is another. A marketing approach is necessary, therefore, seeking first to understand the 'latent demand' (Kay and Moxham, 1996: 178) for access, then to provide it and then to continue the dialogue to ensure that an optimum use through understanding is maintained. The Ramblers Association (*www.ramblers.org.uk/*) has been critical of the unfulfilled communication to the general public from the authorities in regard to public access agreements involving private landlords, as mentioned earlier (Bishop and Philips, 1993).

Another example of a set of principles for tourism in the countryside is that prepared by the English Tourist Board/Countryside Commission, 1989.

Principles for tourism in the countryside

Enjoyment

The promotion of tourism enjoyment in the countryside should be primarily aimed at those activities which draw on the character of the countryside itself, its beauty, culture, history and wildlife.

Development

Tourism development in the countryside should assist the purposes of conservation and recreation. It can, for example, bring new uses to historic houses, supplement usage and incomes to farms, aid the reclamation of derelict land and open up new opportunities for access to the countryside.

Design

The planning, siting and management of new tourism developments should be in keeping with the landscape and wherever possible should seek to enhance it.

Rural economy

Investment in tourism should support the rural economy, but should seek a wider geographical spread and more off-peak visiting both to avoid congestion and damage to the resources through erosion and overuse and to spread the economic and other benefits.

Conservation

Those who benefit from tourism in the countryside should contribute to the conservation and enhancement of its most valuable asset, the countryside, through political and practical support for conservation and recreational policies and programmes.

Marketing

Publicity, information and marketing initiatives of the tourism industry should deepen people's understanding of and concern for the countryside leading to fuller appreciation and enjoyment of it.

Few examples of rural tourism will successfully integrate all these principles. Rural tourism in the Austrian Tyrol comes close to doing so and is a frequently quoted example (Davidson, 1992). Austrian traditional farming gave way to modernisation very abruptly and from 1960 to 1980 employment halved. Rural tourism development was seen as a way of maintaining rural populations. This was considered important socially, but so too is the role played by farming in landscape management. This was critical in maintaining the powerful image of Austria as a land of Alpine meadows, forest and mountains but also in avalanche control. Thus social and environmental policy – as well as tourism policy – provides the framework. Farmhouse accommodation is at the core. Farming families continue to own their property but manage it according to government guidelines. These protect existing tourism businesses in the area while encouraging farmers within the 'farmhouse circles' to offer 'traditional', regional products and to market their products collectively, taking advantage of centralised booking services. The scheme integrates well with rural activity holidays, although Davidson (1992) concluded that: 'Rural tourism is a response to a shrinking summer market generally. A further "rediscovery" of the countryside is necessary'.

Exercise

Development in a rural area

You are part of the team concerned with destination management for a rural area. The local newspaper has taken a fairly 'hostile' attitude to tourism development in the area – some (influential) readers argue that there is no 'vision' for tourism in the area.

You must prepare a response – a short article that will convey the 'vision' that your (public sector) organisation is guided by. Include reference to certain current enquiries about availability of development assistance in your area, indicating which you would support, with reasons. Illustrate with reference to several examples of tourism development, e.g. small farm-based tourism initiatives; a 'CenterParcs' type resort; wildlife-based tours; guided walking tours; new golf courses, motor-sport centres, etc.

Exercise

Rural tourism and destination management

Give a critical discussion of existing and potential conflicts in rural tourism. Illustrate with reference to a destination of your choice, making appropriate comparisons with other UK and European Union experience.

Broadly, you are required to show understanding of the management of physical and biological resources in the context of sustainable tourism development in a rural destination.

Specific aspects to address include:

- the importance of integration of visitor management with natural resources management for rural tourism and countryside recreation

- the contemporary context of rapid economic, political, demographic and environmental change as it affects rural areas

- the roles of the public, private and voluntary sectors in development, management and training for rural tourism and countryside recreation

- appropriate tourism/recreation industry responses to demand and conflicts within the industry and with other industries

- the adequacy of existing policies.

Bibliography

Ashworth, G.J. (1989) Urban tourism: an imbalance in attention in C. Cooper (1990) *Progress in Tourism, Recreation and Hospitality Management*, Volume 1. John Wiley & Sons. Chichester.

Buhalis, D. (1994) Information and telecommunications technologies as a strategic tool for small and medium tourism enterprises in the contemporary business environment in A.V. Seaton *et al.* (1994) *Tourism State of the Art*. John Wiley & Sons. Chichester.

Butler, R. (1996) Problems and possibilities of sustainable tourism: the case of the Shetland Islands in Briguglio *et al.* (1996) *Sustainable Tourism in Islands and Small Island States: Case Studies*. Pinter. London.

Buttle, F. (ed.) (1996) *Relationship Marketing, Theory and Practice*. Paul Chapman Publishing Ltd. London.

Cameron, N. (2000) Architecture – Edinburgh Park. *The Scotsman*, 19 May 2000, 15.

Cherry, G. E. (1993) Changing social attitudes towards leisure and the countryside in Britain, 1890–1990 in S. Glyptis (ed.) (1993) *Leisure and the Environment: Essays in Honour of Professor J.A. Patmore*. Belhaven Press. London.

Clark, G., Darrall, J., Grove-White, R., McNaughten, P. and Urry, J. (1994) *Leisure Landscapes: Leisure, Culture and the English Countryside: Challenges and Conflicts*. Centre for the Study of Environmental Change, Lancaster University. Lancaster.

Collins, V.R. (1996) Putting the heart back into the village. *Planning Week*, 48:8.

Countryside Commission (1995a) *Countryside Recreation and Tourism*. CC. Cheltenham.

Countryside Commission (1995b) *Sustaining Rural Tourism: Opportunities for Action*. CC. Cheltenham.

Countryside Commission for Scotland (1984) *Survey of Leisure Use of the Countryside*. CCS. Battleby.

Countryside Recreation Network (1995) *UK Day Visits Survey 1993*. CRN. Cardiff.

Countryside Recreation Network (1996) Consensus in the countryside. CRN. Cardiff.

Courtauld, S. (1994) Baffled by Eco-speak. *The Field*, September.

Cox, G. (1993) Shooting a line?: field sports and access struggles in Britain. *Rural Studies*, 9 (3), 267–76.

Crofts, R. (1995) *The Environment – Who Cares?, Scottish Natural Heritage Occasional Paper No 2*. Scottish Natural Heritage. Battleby.

Deal, S. (2000) All aboard the rough guide to Leith. *Edinburgh Evening News*, 2 May.

Department of the Environment, Transport and the Regions (1998) Sustainability counts: consultation paper on a set of 'headline indicators' of sustainable development. Department of the Environment, Transport and the Regions. London.

Durrell, L. (1969) *The Spirit of Place*. Faber. London.

Edinburgh Business School (at Heriot Watt University) (1995) [online]. Available protocol: *http://www.ebs.hw.ac.uk/EDC/facts-and-figures95/transport.html*. [2000, 28 May].

Edington, J.M. and Eddington, M.A. (1986) *Ecology, Recreation and Tourism*. Cambridge University Press. Cambridge.

English Tourist Board/Countryside Commission (1989) *Principles for Tourism in the Countryside*. ETB. Cheltenham.

Federation of Nature and National Parks of Europe (1993) Loving them to death: sustainable tourism in Europe's nature and national parks. FNNPE. Grafenau, Germany.

Gartner, William C. (1997) Image and sustainable tourism systems in S. Wahab and J.B. Pigram (eds) *Tourism. Development and Growth*.

Getz, D. (1994) Event tourism: evaluating the impacts in J.R.B. Ritchie and C.R. Goeldner (eds) (1994) *Travel, Tourism and Hospitality Research* (2nd edition). John Wiley and Sons Inc. New York.

Gilbert, D. (1989) Rural tourism and marketing: synthesis and new ways of working. *Tourism Management*, March, 39–50.

Gilpin, S. (1996) *Relationship Marketing: Theory and Practice*. Paul Chapman. London.

Glasson, J. (1994) Oxford: a city under pressure. *Tourism Management*, 15 (2).

Glyptis, S. (ed.) (1993) *Leisure and the Environment: Essays in Honour of Professor J.A. Patmore*. Belhaven Press. London.

Gruffudd, P. (1994) Selling the countryside: representations of rural Britain in J.R. Gold and S.V. Ward (eds) *Place Promotion: The Use of Publicity and Marketing to Sell Towns and Regions*. John Wiley & Sons. Chichester.

Hall, C.M. and Jenkins, J.M. (1995) *Tourism and Public Policy*. Routledge. London.

Hart, E.J. (1983) *The Selling of Canada*. Altitude Publishing Ltd. Banff, Canada.

Harvey, G. (1997) *The Killing of the Countryside*. Vintage. London.

Henry, I. and G.A.M. Jackson (1996) Sustainability of management processes and tourism products and contexts. *Journal of Sustainable Tourism*, 4 (1), 17–28.

Higham, J. (1998) Sustaining the physical and social dimensions of wilderness tourism: perceptual approaches to wilderness management in New Zealand. *Journal of Sustainable Tourism*, 6 (1), 26–51.

Howie, F. (1996) Skills, understanding and knowledge for sustainable tourism in *Tourism in Central and Eastern Europe: Educating for quality*. Atlas. Tilburg, Netherlands.

Howie, F. (2000) Establishing the common ground: tourism, ordinary places, grey-areas and environmental quality in Edinburgh, Scotland in G. Richards and D. Hall (eds) *Tourism and Sustainable Community Development*. Routledge. London.

Hughes, G. (1995) The cultural construction of sustainable tourism. *Tourism Management* 16 (1), 49–59.

Hughes, G. (1996) Tourism and the environment: a sustainable partnership. *Scottish Geographical Magazine*, 112 (2), 107–13.

Hughes, G. (1999) Urban revitalisation: the use of festive time strategies. *Leisure Studies*, 18, 119–35.

Innes, N. (1998) Tourism transport in Scotland. In MacLellan and Smith *Tourism in Scotland*. International Thomson Business Press. London.

Judd, D.R. (1995) Promoting tourism in US cities. *Tourism Management*, 16 (3).

Kay, G. and Moxham, N. (1996) Paths for whom? Countryside access for recreational walking. *Leisure Studies*, 15, 171–83.

Lane, B. (1994) What is rural tourism? *Journal of Sustainable Tourism*, 2 (1) and (2), 7–21.

Louis, N. (1997) *Voices of the Old Sea*. Penguin. London.

Lynch, K. (1984) *The Image of the City*. MIT Press. Cambridge, MA.

Mackay, J. (1995) People, perceptions and moorland in D.B.A. Thomson, A.J. Hester and M.B. Usher (eds) *Heaths and Moorland: Cultural Landscapes*. HMSO. Edinburgh.

Macnaughten, P. and Urry, J. (1997) Towards a sociology of nature in P. McDonagh and A. Protheroe (eds) *Green Management: A Reader*. The Dryden Press. London.

Magnusson, M. (1995) in D.B.A. Thomson, A.J. Hester and M.B. Usher (eds) *Heaths and Moorland: Cultural Landscapes*. HMSO. Edinburgh.

Mather, A.S. (1997) Mountain recreation in the East Grampians. *Scottish Geographical Magazine*, 113 (3), 195–8.

Mathieson, A. and Wall, G. (1982) *Tourism Economic, Physical and Social Impacts*. Longman Scientific and Technical. Harlow, Essex.

McCannell, D. (1990) Nature incorporated in D. McCannell (ed.) *Empty Meeting Grounds: The Tourist Papers*. Routledge. London.

McCrone, D., Morris, A. and Kiely, R. (1994) *Scotland the Brand: The Making of Scottish Heritage*. Edinburgh University Press. Edinburgh.

Middleton, V. (1994) *Marketing in Travel and Tourism* (2nd edn). Butterworth-Heineman. Oxford.

Millward, H. (1991) Public recreational access in the countryside: concepts and measures of physical rigour. *Journal of Rural Studies*, 7 (3), 241–51.

Millward, H. (1993) Public access in the West European countryside: a comparative survey. *Journal of Rural Studies*, 9 (1) 39–51.

Murdoch, J. and Pratt, A.C. (1993) Comment: rural studies: modernism, postmodernism and the 'post-rural'. *Journal of Rural Studies*, 9 (4), 411–27.

Murphy, P.E. (1985) *Tourism: A Community Approach*. Methuen. New York.

Murphy, P.E. and Keller, C.P. (1990) Destination travel patterns: an examination and modelling of tourist patterns on Vancouver Island, British Columbia. *Leisure Sciences*, 1 (1), 49–65.

Organisation for Economic Cooperation and Development (1994) *Tourism Policy and International Tourism in OECD Countries 1991–1992*. Special Feature: Tourism Strategies and Rural Development. OECD. Paris.

O'Riordan, T. (1976) *Environmentalism*. Pion. London.

Page, S.J. (1994) Perspectives on tourism and peripherality: a review of tourism in the Republic of Ireland in C. Cooper and A. Lockwood (eds) *Progress in Tourism, Recreation and Hospitality Management*, Volume 5. John Wiley & Sons. Chichester.

Parlett, G., Fletcher, J. and Cooper, C. (1995) The impact of tourism on the Old Town of Edinburgh. *Tourism Management*, 16 (5), 355–60.

Pigram, J. (1993) Planning for tourism in rural areas: bridging the policy implementation gap in D.G. Pearce and R. Butler (eds) *Tourism Research, Critiques and Challenges*. Routledge. London.

Poon, A. (1993) *Tourism, Technology and Competitive Strategies*. CAB International. Oxford.

Raban, J. (1974) *Soft City*. Fontana. Glasgow.

Ralton, A. (2000) Unpublished honours dissertation. Queen Margaret University College, Edinburgh.

RASP (1997) The Northern Cairngorms: an alternative strategy.

Reid, R.D. and Sandler, M. (1992) The use of technology to improve service quality. *The Cornell HRA Quarterly*, June, 68–73.

Richards, G. and Bonink, C. (1994) Marketing cultural tourism in Europe. *Journal of Vacation Marketing*, 1 (2), 173–80.

Riley, R.W. and Van Doren, C.S. (1998) Movies as tourism promotion, a 'pull' factor in a 'push' location. *Annals of Tourism Research*, 25 (4), 919–35.

Scottish Executive Rural Affairs Department (2000) *Rural Challenge Fund Bidding Guidance, 2000–2001*. Scottish Executives. Edinburgh.

Scottish Farmhouse Holidays (2000) *Annual publication*. Scottish Farmhouse Holidays. Ladybank, Fife.

Scottish Natural Heritage (1996) *Working Together: The Natural Heritage in Rural Development*. SNH. Edinburgh.

Scottish Natural Heritage (1997) *Jobs and the Natural Heritage: The Natural Heritage in Rural Development*. SNH. Edinburgh.

Seabrooke, W. and Miles, C.W.N. (1993) *Recreational Land Management* (2nd edn). E & FN Spon. London.

Sharpley, R.J. (1997) *Rural Tourism: an Introduction*. International Thomson Press. London.

Shoard, M. (1987) *This Land is Our Land*. Paladin. London.

Shoard, M. (1999) *A Right to Roam*. Oxford University Press. Oxford.

Steinbeck, J. (1962) *Travels with Charlie*. Heinemann Ltd. London.

Stocks, J. (1996) Heritage and tourism in the Irish Republic – towards a giant theme park in M. Robinson, N. Evans and P. Callaghan (eds) *Tourism and Culture – Towards the 21st Century, Conference Proceedings: Image, Identity and Marketing*. Centre for Travel and Tourism in association with Business Education Publishers Ltd. Sunderland.

Thatcher, M. (1982) On the Falklands campaign, speech to Scottish Conservative Party Conference, 14 May 1982 (Young, 1990) cited in A. Partington (ed.) (1992) *The Oxford Dictionary of Quotations* (4th edn). BCA. London.

Thibal, S. (1988) *Rural Tourism in Europe*. Council of Europe. Strasbourg.

UK Government, Cabinet Office (2000) *Sharing the Nation's Prosperity*. HMSO. London.

Unwin, T. (1996) Tourist development in Estonia: images, sustainability, and integrated rural development. *Tourism Management*, 17 (4), 265–76.

Urry, J. (1990) *The Tourist Gaze*. Sage. London.

Urry, J. (1994) Cultural change and contemporary tourism. *Leisure Studies*, 13, 233–8.

Wahab, S. and Pigrim, J.B. (1995) *Tourism and Public Policy*. Routledge. London.

Warren, P. (1999) Five-star service via your TV screen. *Scotland on Sunday*, 17 January, 8.

Wilkinson, P.F. (1994) Tourism and small island states: problems of resource analysis, management and development in A. Seaton *et al.* (eds) *Tourism State of the Art*. John Wiley & Sons Ltd. Chichester.

Wood, K. and House, S. (1991) *The Good Tourist*. Mandarin. London.

Zarza, A.E. (1998) The LEADER programme in the LA Rioja Mountains: an example of integral tourist development in B. Bramwell, I. Henry, G. Jackson, A.G. Prat, G. Richards, and J. Van Der Straaten (eds) *Sustainable Tourism Management: Principles and Practice*. Tilburg University Press. Tilbury, Netherlands.

CHAPTER 4

Marketing places

INTRODUCTION

No matter how good the planning, development and management of a place is, unless tourists know what it has to offer and believe – or can be persuaded to believe – that it is worth visiting, it will remain a place with merely the *potential* to become a tourist destination. It must also be considered that: 'Choice of holiday destination is a significant lifestyle indicator for today's aspirational consumers and the places they choose to spend their increasingly squeezed vacation time and hard earned income have to be emotionally appealing with high conversation and celebrity value' (Morgan *et al.*, 2002: 4). The World Tourism Organization (*www.world-tourism.org*) concurs with this: 'The next century will mark the emergence of tourism destinations as a fashion accessory. The choice of holiday destination will help identify the identity of the traveller and, in an increasingly homogeneous world, set him [sic] apart from the hordes of other tourists' (Lurham, 1998: 13).

Given the 'fickleness' of the contemporary tourist and the resultant risk that this year's 'place to be seen' can be tomorrow's unfashionable destination, whether a place *should* become a destination is a significant question to be addressed by its citizens, business people and civic leaders. It is not a question to be taken lightly for it *will* change the nature of that place, but at least it can be addressed in a rational manner. Then with the benefits of hindsight that the history of tourism development offers, the options can be reviewed and it may be decided that the place *has* the potential to be a sustainable tourism destination that will benefit both the residents and the tourists.

MARKETING AND THE TOURIST DESTINATION

Marketing is an essential element in achieving that goal and maintaining the place as a successful tourist destination. Marketing as understood today has been recognised as a formal activity since the early 1900s, although the process of satisfying customers while making a profit has been around since civilisation began. Marketing differs from 'selling' in that while selling focuses on exchanging what one has to sell for money, marketing is concerned with examining what potential customers want and adjusting supply to meet that desire. The modern concept has been defined as 'the management process responsible for identifying, anticipating and satisfying customer requirements profitably' (The Chartered Institute of Marketing, 1984: *www.cim.co.uk*). Middleton (1988) referred to the combination of resources and services provided by a destination as the 'total tourism product', later defining tourism marketing as the 'total market reflecting the demand of customers for a wide range of travel related products' (Middleton, 1994). Marketing is therefore an exchange process between the customers buying or using products and producers supplying and selling the products and services. Can this be applied to the demand for the experience of places just as it is to the demand for cars, computers, toiletries and food and drink? A significant point is that while the sale of toiletries, for example, has no limits other than what the customer wants and is prepared to buy, the number of 'consumers of places' or 'tourists' in a given destination at a given time may have a very real impact on actual numbers in the future since the quality of the experience of that place is diminished when popularity pushes the number of visits beyond its environmental or social carrying capacity. This does apply to other products such as car sales to an extent – oversupply may lead to intolerable levels of road congestion and can reduce the 'exclusiveness' or 'snob appeal' of a particular brand.

Burgess referred to 'selling places' as early as 1975 but the concept was implicit in the 'selling' of the Canadian Rockies in the mid-1800s (see Chapter 10). Ashworth and Voogd (1988: 65) referred to 'geographical marketing', considering this 'new paradigm' as 'a planned action (which) implies an explicit and simultaneous consideration of both the supply-side and the demand-side for the way cities are marketed'. Although this appears to be a modern concept, they suggest the approach has in fact been around for quite some time. They refer to one of the earliest examples of place marketing when the legendary Viking, Leif Ericson, recruited settlers for a certain northern and ice-bound land by naming it 'Green land'. History does not record what those he convinced thought of their new home but today they would have grounds for claiming 'misleading advertising'. Ashworth and Goodall (1990) used the term 'place marketing' and asserted that: 'Tourist destinations can indeed be treated as products. They are logically the point of consumption of the complex of activities that comprises the tourist experience and are ultimately what is sold by place promotion agencies on the tourist market'. Kearns and Philo (1993) described 'selling places'. Kotler (1997) described marketing as a 'superior value delivery system'. Applying this to a market-led destination, the management organisation will purposefully use its knowledge of its tourists' needs and wants to achieve its policy objectives; and will develop strategies to maintain tourist satisfaction at this new level. It will also have the means to adjust strategy – even towards 'demarketing' the destination should there be evidence that visitor pressure is causing physical damage to, for example, the physical fabric of heritage buildings or social/cultural damage or annoyance to local residents. A modified strategy may aim at maintaining the annual total of visitor numbers but respond to increasing customer/tourist dissatisfaction by 'extending the season' i.e. demarketing the peak summer season and encouraging a 'second peak' (or more) at the 'low' or 'shoulder' seasons – *if* there are sufficient quality resources available at these times. Edinburgh, for example, introduced its Spring Fling, Autumn and Christmas/Hogmanay events (see Chapter 6). In marketing terms, a destination management organisation would work with 'the mix of controllable marketing variables that the firm uses to pursue the sought level of sales in the target market sector'.

Nielson *et al.* (2001) applied the marketing 'paradigm' to a study of Galway City in Ireland, which aims to 'develop its tourism product while maintaining its environment'. They emphasised the distinctiveness of place and the necessity of identifying:

> the design of the right mix of features and services, the development of an image that is attractive to the target market, the delivery of the destination's products and services in an accessible way and the promotion of the destination's values and image so that potential users are fully aware of the place's distinct attractions.

The authors opined that destinations must determine not only the numbers of tourists they want, but also the 'kinds' of tourist. In this they were referring to a further element of the established marketing approach, namely 'market segmentation', where *current* users of the product are identified but it is the *target stage* of the campaign that determines the market segments or the 'types of visitor' that destination management wishes to attract. The marketing strategy adopted will then be one of: (a) undifferentiated *marketing* – targeting the whole market and ignoring segments; (b) differentiated *marketing* – targeting several market segments and designing separate packages/offers for each one; or (c) concentrated marketing 'where large shares of one or more small segments are pursued'. They emphasise that there is no 'off-the-peg package' for destination marketing which will guarantee success but have no doubt that places can indeed be marketed as products. There are several requirements for successful destination marketing:

- the right mix of features and services
- an image that is attractive to the target market
- the products and services must be delivered in an efficient and accessible way
- the destination's values and image must be promoted effectively to ensure that potential users are aware of the place's distinct advantages.

A marketing strategy should also consider that as a 'product' a destination goes through the 'destination life cycle' (see Chapter 2) and therefore the type of customer is likely to be different at different stages. The marketing messages must therefore evolve in response to change in the destination (and monitoring of change should be part of the general destination management ethos) and in the context of the destination plan.

Returning to the question posed at the outset, can techniques and ideas developed for selling goods and services be successfully applied to places? When the intention is purely to increase visitor numbers there is little doubt. Today's tourist is, however, an experienced and demanding customer and more ready to complain about 'faulty goods' or misleading claims. In an evolving 'blame culture' in the UK, the organisation responsible could be faced with litigation. Destination marketing must therefore stay within appropriate boundaries, resisting certain opportunities that modern marketing techniques offer. When the promoting agency is a public body it is likely to have 'broader civic responsibilities' (Ashworth and Goodall, 1990) and the power of marketing will be tempered by the wider considerations that that entails. Indeed, the techniques of marketing may be used to meet such contemporary 'problems' as *over* success in attracting visitors to a destination. For example, in the late 1990s Edinburgh began cautiously to 'demarket' its highly popular 'Edinburgh's Hogmanay' on grounds of public safety and of socio-cultural impact (*www.edinburghshogmanay.org*). The number of visitors attracted to the city represented success, notably in one important respect – extending the tourism 'season', a desirable objective. However, the huge numbers that came to celebrate found themselves in a potentially hazardous situation where the crowd control procedures that had been carefully determined could not cope with the actual numbers within the limited confines of the city centre. The sheer 'pressure of people' represented a safety risk. The quality of the tourist experience was similarly diminished for those who found they could not see the performances and, more seriously, those who experienced the fear of being crushed against safety barriers. This early experience led to improvements in both respects. The socio-cultural impact of the event is indicated by the complaints received by the local authority and given extensive coverage in the local press. Many were irritated that a lack of transparency surrounded the availability of tickets – there were allegations that most were distributed to hotels and other commercial tourism operators for distribution to their customers; others were concerned that a more insidious process was present – the 'commercialisation' or 'commodification' of a traditional, community event – even if this was by default rather than through deliberate action.

Other cities have raised similar concerns. Venice is a notable example: for over a decade it has restricted the former overeasy access to its highly constricted site and, in consequence, to its cultural treasures. National parks and other designated areas may also wish to balance success – as measured by the number of visitors – against the quality of the tourist experience as well as the physical impact of visitors on the resources the parks were established to conserve. Here too achieving a range of both tourism and conservation objectives can benefit from the creative use of marketing techniques.

Exercise

The problems of success

Using a search engine of your choice (e.g. *www.yahoo.com*) select the 'Advanced search' option, then 'Matches on all words' and enter 'Venice tourism overcrowding'. Select several of the websites offered and using these as a source of information write a short summary of the 'problems of success' of tourism marketing. Suggest how marketing could avoid creating these problems.

PLACE MARKETING TODAY – MULTIFUNCTIONAL RESPONSIBILITIES

It is well established that a tourist attraction such as a theme park or a heritage attraction can be regarded as a 'product'; so too a hotel or a guesthouse and in the transport sector a cruise ship or a train, although the latter may be only partially a 'tourism' product since it is also used by 'non-tourists'. The amalgam of all the 'sectors' of the industry represented by these examples, plus the many non-tourism functions normally found in a city, region or country, is the *destination*. It is now well established that such a large, complex and 'special' entity as a destination can be marketed as a product. 'Spain' is a long-established example, marketed and sold to many millions of consumers since the beginnings of mass tourism in the 1950s for its 'sun, sand and sea'. As tourists became more experienced they became more demanding, however, and the destination acquired a reputation for poor service and facilities. In response, 'in the early 1980s the Spanish government began what was to become one of the most consistent and successful brand-building exercises in destination marketing supported by a significant financial commitment – which is ongoing today' (Morgan *et al.*, 2002). The 'suprabrand' of Spain – España – remains – the associations of 'sun, sand and sea' retain their popularity and are symbolised in the marketing imagery. To cater for increasingly discriminating tourists and the growth of special interest tourism the national associations of culture and heritage are also continued; however, 'second level brands' (Morgan *et al.*, 2002) were given new prominence – the dynamic and youthful city of Barcelona (*www.barcelonaturisme.com/turisme/home2.htm*) and the capital, Madrid; also, the regions of Andalucia and, in the north and offering a very different 'green' Spain, Galicia (*www.tourspain.es/turespai/marcoi.htm*).

'Everything under the Sun' – the Spanish Tourist Authority campaign slogan from 1984 gave way to 'Passion for Life' in 1992, replaced by 'Bravo Spain' in 1997. This last slogan was successful in the UK, although there had been concerns that associations with bullfighting might have been made by the increasingly 'green' tourists of the key markets, Britain, Germany and France. The contemporary product is thus a highly diversified one. This approach reflects evolving tourism and other policies, themselves responses to changing consumer tastes and social priorities with marketing as a powerful 'tool' in the armoury of commercial and government agencies.

Tourism is, of course, only one of many actual or potential uses of a specific place. Some 30 miles (20 km) south of San Francisco, in California, an area was promoted as the ideal location for companies developing 'new technology'. Through the success of the marketing campaigns it became known as 'Silicon Valley' (*www.siliconvalley.com*). Given the reality that there are generally many different objectives for a given place at a given time, place management and increasingly destination management have the task of reconciling tourism with the other competing or collaborating industries and services, working with more established professional areas such as planning and the legal system which enable the physical regulation necessary to minimise or resolve conflict – the essence of the planning philosophy. 'Tourism is, in this case, one function within the multi-functional place to be managed on the basis of professionally determined norms and political decisions about the role it should play in the wider spatial setting for the attainment of municipal goals' (Ashworth and Goodall, 1988). They discussed the several 'philosophies' for place management. Rarely does one industry or landuse have absolute priority; more commonly there will be a prioritising of uses that varies between places. The *preservationist* philosophy emphasises the natural and cultural resources and their intrinsic values in determining the nature of the place; their preservation is a measure of success. *Redistribution* is another philosophy, asserting the unacceptability of 'social exclusion' i.e. the existence of a sizeable percentage of the place's population who are excluded from social and other basic 'rights' on account of limited educational and other opportunities which determine their earning power (*www.onecity.org.uk*). The *marketing phi-*

losophy is superficially similar to that of planning (see Table 4.1), but Ashworth and Voogd (1993) expressed reservations:

> [It is not] merely a matter of substituting a new terminology and renaming the various procedures of the planning process. Tourism supply becomes the tourism product to be 'positioned' in relation to competing products, demand becomes the customers, which need 'segmentation' according to product purchasing behaviour, and management becomes market planning undertaken in a 'development' or 'promotion' department.
>
> [...] marketing simply takes a new set of planning procedures that claim to be customer or client-orientated [...] existing and potential demand conditions are compared with 'product analysis', i.e. inventories of the facilities and attractions of places, in the light of such demands and in comparison with competing places. Deficiencies are thus highlighted and dealt with by a mixture of new investments on the supply side and market promotion on the other.

Table 4.1 *Planning versus marketing*

Planning	Marketing
Tourism supply	Tourism product
Tourism demand	Tourism customers (segmented)
Management	Market planning

Adoption of a marketing-led approach can meet resistance within a place. From the perspective of a place as a whole, and where the public authority is the lead body in determining the direction of destination development, there is commonly a resistance to substituting 'market responsiveness' for the 'professional normative response'. The planning approach has traditionally managed tourism through legislation founded on 'good practice' – familiar concepts include 'carrying capacity', 'conforming landuses', 'acceptable functional mixes' and, more recently, 'sustainable development'. In the entrepreneurial climate of the early 21st century the objective is increasingly a balance between 'traditional' public sector philosophies and the largely economics-driven market perspective of the local chambers of commerce, major investors and other influential bodies representing the private sector businesses. (This is discussed further in Chapter 5: Destination planning and policy.)

SPECIFIC MARKETING CONCEPTS AND THE DESTINATION

The place as product

If someone says, 'I didn't enjoy that meal', the product is clear and the hotel or restaurant that served it may not see that customer again. It is in the interests of the establishment to find out the reasons for the dissatisfaction and do something about it. If a tourist (or more importantly a significant number of them) says, 'I didn't enjoy Cambridge (or New York, or Provence or Poland ...)', the challenge to the destination manager is much more complex. What aspects of the destination does he/she mean – the 'so-called friendly people', the unhelpful landlady, the lack of things to do, the weather, the littered streets, the traffic ...? The destination is a complex of both tangible and intangible elements, any or several of which may be at fault from that particular 'consumer's' point of view. The destination is where the facilities and attractions are, but is also the 'product' itself; and each tourist defines his/her own distinct product according to their individual tastes and interests. The 'friendliness' of local residents is a destination attribute that many tourists seek and is often referred to in promotional brochures of marketing departments. In many destinations it ranks considerably above 'tangible' features such as the range and quality of accommodation or the food and drink as clearly shown in the annual surveys of the national tourist boards in the UK (*www.star-uk.org.uk*). However, it is largely beyond the direct influence of destination management due to the 'heterogeneity' of tourism products: 'Service products are often referred to as being *inseparable*, which means the product is often consumed and produced simultaneously. Because there is less opportunity to pre-check a tourism or hospitality product, it can vary in the standard of its service delivery' (Cooper *et al.*: 1998, 355–6).

A frequently mentioned and important feature of many destinations, 'the scenery', is obviously a physical feature made up of land and its topography, vegetation and the outcomes of human activity. While there is increasing acknowledgement of the need for more active management of the countryside for a wider range of objectives – including tourism – 'scenery' is an 'intangible' quantity existing as much in the 'mind's eye' of the tourist as in the real world (as discussed in Chapter 10). As such, marketing 'Super Natural British Columbia' (*www.gov.bc.ca*) or 'Herriot Country' (*www.hambleton.gov.uk/hambleton/herriot.nsf/pages/herriot. html*) brings some risk of raising unattainable expectations, given that 'super natural' may be misinterpreted and that 'James Heriot' is a fictional character, while both 'marketing concepts' refer to real places, the former a Canadian province, the latter a part of Yorkshire. Moreover, terms such as 'the countryside' and 'scenery' are 'loaded' terms carrying with them a range of meanings, not all of which will be experienced on an average tourist visit (see Table 4.2).

Destination management organisations are also increasingly proactive in tackling urban environmental quality issues such as littering, air pollution and urban planning and design issues including the provision of 'public squares' and other traffic-free areas as 'people places'. Generally, they work with local authorities and public–private partnership bodies (*www.nyrp.org*, *www.pps.org*). These issues are attaining new significance for tourism and all are influenced by intangible qualities such as 'perception' and 'atmosphere'.

'Service' is a major element of the 'intangibles' of the destination 'that has specific characteristics that set the product apart from the more general goods sold in the market-place [...] emphasis is increasingly placed on the service provider to develop a deeper understanding of the linkages that correspond to consumer benefits sought and the nature of the service delivery system itself' (Cooper *et al.*, 1998: 354). Many service products are 'intangible' and generally they cannot be tried out before they are bought, as is common practice; yet the 'annual holiday' is one of the most expensive purchases most people make. The would-be tourist has to rely on trust that the holiday that has been paid for perhaps six months or more in advance will be 'as discussed' with the travel agent or described in the travel

Table 4.2 *Overseas and British tourists' reactions to Scotland, 1998*

Attractive features	All overseas visitors	All British visitors
Scenery	86%	69%
Friendly people	74%	53%
Castles, churches, museums and sites of historic interest	73%	32%
Peace and quiet	48%	60%
Natural wildlife	34%	36%
Range/quality of accommodation	34%	50%
Good food and drink	28%	45%
Unattractive features	All overseas visitors	All British visitors
Poor weather	33%	23%
Difficulty in travelling around	10%	6%
Lack of wet weather facilities	8%	4%
Poor quality food	6%	2%
Poor quality accommodation	6%	1%

Source: Adapted from Scottish Tourist Board, 1998

brochures or on the website. Referring to the future development of 'marketing tourism in cyberspace' (WTOBC, 1999: iii), the World Tourism Organization (*www.world-tourism.org*) noted, 'The Internet is having a greater impact on the marketing of travel and tourism than any technology since the invention of the television. It has already established itself as a crucial distribution channel via which tourism organisations can promote their destinations and products offered by their service providers'. The organisation noted the significant point that generally there is no confirmation that the information contained on a website is accurate and up to date and proposed the idea of a 'Website approval mark' that would provide a benchmark for quality assurance. WTO could operate an approval scheme, allowing inspected websites that meet its standards to carry a WTO approval mark. A simple link would allow those approval standards to be scrutinised, so that it could be well regarded. (World Tourism Organization, 1999: 145).

Such standards are as near to 'tangible' as the product can be at the point the money is handed over. It raises the issue of 'trust' that is central to the transaction and the issue of 'authenticity' or misrepresentation. This is discussed further in Chapter 11, where, for example, the increasing availability of digitally enhanced or altered photographs can convey a 'digital destination' which may correspond to a popular 'organic image' of a destination (Chapter 3) but may lead to disappointment on experiencing the actual place (*www.digitaldestinations.co.uk*).

The *'perishability'* of tourism products is a further distinguishing characteristic. A museum, gallery or theatre ticket or a hotel bedroom or a place on a special interest tour package which is not sold represents lost profit to the operator. While the product can continue to be sold at other times, the potential sale on that particular day cannot be recovered. A 'non-perishable' product such as a camera or a souvenir which is unsold on one particular day can be sold the next day without representing loss to the seller. Conversely if a heritage centre, for example, on a particular day or month experiences crowds that exceed its capacity – as determined on grounds of safety or the quality of the individual visitor experience – it can draw in its maximum income for that occasion – but cannot expect the disappointed who are turned away to return another day. They may have come to the end of their holiday and returned home or are generally disappointed with the crowding in the destination at 'peak season' and refuse to return another day and queue up. 'Seasonality' is a major challenge to most destinations and a common response is to try to 'extend the season' so levelling out visitor numbers throughout the year. (see the discussion on Edinburgh's Hogmanay in Chapter 6). New attractions or festivals may be developed and lower, 'off-season' prices offered to help overcome the reluctance of many tourists to change their 'natural' holiday period or their inability to take holidays out of the main 'summer season'. Established school holiday dates and employer resistance to change of holiday periods – even when general social trends indicate the desirability of it – may, however, continue to be a significant barrier. The crowding of many destinations in the peak season and the resultant queuing as well as the 'premium' prices charged by many attractions at this time may eventually result in general consumer pressure that will change deeply ingrained social 'norms'.

The *marketing mix* that is offered to prospective visitors to a destination, the 'target market', will determine the emphasis placed on its specific attributes. Of course, the key elements of a destination – the 'physical' attractions – are not themselves 'perishable' except over very long periods of time: even the Eiffel Tower or Buckingham Palace will one day crumble to dust or will reach a state of decay where, on public safety grounds, they must be demolished.

The marketing plan

The marketing plan will evolve with the changing strategy of the destination. In response to change, the plan will address what is to be done and when; the estimated costs; which agencies will be involved in implementation; and how to measure change and the effectiveness of the response. Kotler referred to the marketing variables which a firm (or in this context a destination management and development organisation) can control as the *'marketing mix'* of the '4 Ps': *Product*, *Price*, *Promotion* and *Place*. Here the *product* is the destination – the totality of the place, including its tangible features and its intangible characteristics (see Chapter 3). Certain other attributes which are marketing concepts – the place's branding and its positioning – can also be influenced.

Aaker (1991: 7) defines a brand as 'a distinguishing name and/or a symbol (such as a logo, trademark, or package design) intended to identify the goods or services of one seller, or group of sellers, and to differentiate those goods or services from competitors who attempt to provide products that appear to be identical'. In this context it would refer to whether the destination (or product) has a distinctive and recognised name which makes it 'stand out' from rival destinations. Positioning is concerned with whether it is considered to be the best, or among the best, in its category of destinations or merely 'just another place'. It is what a brand stands for in the minds of customers and its prospects, relative to its competition, in terms of benefits and promises (Ritchie and Ritchie, 1999). To have validity, this standing has to be determined according to criteria recognised by the tourism industry, as in Edinburgh's 2001 travel award.

Box 4.1 *Edinburgh is prestigious publication's favourite UK city*

Readers of Condé Nast Traveller magazine have ranked Edinburgh as the best city in the UK in the esteemed publication's 2001 travel awards. Edinburgh, which was second in the same awards last year, beat London into second place. This is the first time that a Scottish destination has topped the rankings. The holiday magazine, which is aimed at independent travellers all over the world, is regarded as the 'Bible' of the travel industry and is highly respected by leading travel writers and journalists. The awards are, based on strict criteria including value for money, quality and range of attractions, culture, cleanliness and safety.

Source: Edinburgh and Lothians Tourist Board website (*www.edinburgh.org.uk*)

Price is less clear when referring to destinations, although common reference is made to prices being higher in the 'capital' (e.g. London, Amsterdam, Rome etc.) than in the 'provinces' or smaller towns and higher in the centre of the city than in the outskirts. 'Value for money' is perhaps the more useful idea, although it is subjective and dependent on the visitor's level of affluence.

Promotion is vital to the destination since it generally cannot be sampled in advance and a wide range of promotional materials is available. Authenticity in advertising promotional materials is an important element since these contribute to formation of the 'induced image' of the destination (see Chapter 3) which in turn determines the subsequent reaction of tourists on finally experiencing the destination after a lengthy period of anticipation.

The fourth P is *Place*, referring not to the destination itself, but to where the decision to select and purchase the product/book the holiday is made. It is affected by each of the other Ps and there is a wide range of 'distribution channels' for the purchase of a product. A familiar example is booking a 'package holiday' through a travel agent, while direct booking (and paying) through the internet is growing rapidly in popularity (see Chapter 11).

In addition to the familiar '4Ps' Booms and Bitner (1981) added a further three 'Ps' for service products such as tourism. These are *People*, all the staff the tourist will deal with at different stages of the holiday, notably their characteristics; the *Physical evidence*, the environment in which the service is delivered; and the *Process*, corporate policies and procedures of the organisations the tourist has to deal with. This could have increasing relevance as concepts such as 'ethical purchasing' become more mainstream, as environmental accreditation schemes such as the Scottish Tourist Board's 'green award' schemes (*www.visitscotland.com*) become established and are entered by more and more businesses, and 'green' tourism advisory organisations are available to advise on good practice (see Figure 4.1).

A marketing plan would also include a statement of the financial, human and physical resources necessary for its implementation.

The Adventure Travel Society (ATS)
ats@adventuretravel.com
www.adventuretravel.com/

American Society of Travel Agents (ASTA) Environment Committee
johnb@astahq.com
www.astanet.com/www/astanet/news/environm.html

Conservation International (CI)
ciwash@igc.apc.org
www.ecotour.org

The Ecotourism Society (TES)
ecomail@ecotourism.org
www.ecotourism.org

Ecumenical Coalition on Third World Tourism (ECTWT)
contours@caribnet.net

End Child Prostitution in Asian Tourism (ECPAT)
ecpatbkk@ksc15.th.com
www.ecpat.net

Environmental Conservation Tourism Association, Inc. (ECTA)
ECTAinfo@aol.com
www.desocom.com/ECTA

International Institute for Peace through Tourism (IIPT)
conference@iipt.org
www.iipt.org

International Society for Eco-Tourism Management (ECOMANAGE)
www.ecomanage.com

Pacific Asia Travel Association (PATA) Foundation
76215.1735@compuserve.com
www.pata.org

Partners In Responsible Travel (PIRT)
www.pirt.org

Tourism Concern
www.tourismconcern.org.uk

World Tourism Organization (WTO) Environment Committee
www.world-tourism.org/committe/envcomm.htm

World Travel and Tourism Council (WTTC) ECoNETT & GREEN GLOBE
www.wttc.org

Figure 4.1 *Environmental and ethical tourism destination advisory organisations*

BRANDING

Branding is concerned with what a product offers to potential 'customers' – both tangible and intangible elements – and with creating an image from these, i.e. giving a product an identity or a 'personality' which clearly distinguishes it from any other product. Branding has its origins in the practice of physically 'branding' cattle and other livestock with a red-hot branding iron or dye to demonstrate ownership. Coincidentally (?) the image of the cowboy branding cattle in the 19th-century American West is retained in the marketing of a major cigarette brand, the powerful and evocative imagery of a lifestyle of freedom and individuality continuing to persuade millions of urbane smokers who may never have seen 'cowboy country' to stay with the brand and to persuade others in former Soviet countries to switch to it, implicitly as a demonstration of their liberation from the former Communist subjugation.

The sheer power and influence of some of today's global brands has resulted in increased political and environmental backlash against them, while in tourism it is fair to say that the use of branding is still at an early stage. In the contemporary commercial context there are three parts of such a created identity: the *brand name* – using the written or spoken word; the *brand mark* – a symbol or design; and the *trademark* – its legal designation. From the consumers' perspective the benefits of branding are that it readily identifies a product, implies a certain level of quality or performance and suggests a desirable psychological reward for purchasers who become associated with it or the real or imaginary lifestyle it represents. From an organisational perspective, branding adds value to the product being offered, helps develop loyalty towards it and 'positions' the product in the marketplace.

Creating an *identity* for a product involves establishing a means of identification. This is usually attempted through the use of a name, symbol, design or colour (or several of these) and establishing legal protection for the specific combination of them. It is also concerned with establishing what the brand should stand for. For a chosen target market clear meanings must emerge from the associations expressed in the brand's advertising and today a diversity of media are available to integrate colour, music, events and personalities into powerful print/television/film/internet images. These will be reenforced throughout the organisation or, in this case, the destination, in signposting, transport livery, stationery, literature etc.

Destination branding

Branding a tourist destination presents challenges beyond those experienced in a simple product. Schmitt and Simonson (1997) offer a useful perspective – 'marketing aesthetics' or the 'marketing of sensory experiences in corporate brand output that contributes to the organization's brand identity' – which offers alternative approaches to the branding of products and services. Their focus is 'on the experiential benefits provided by a company or a brand as a whole and the aesthetic planning that is essential to developing and implementing a corporate brand or identity'. Ritchie and Ritchie (1998) interpret the marketing of aesthetics as about *experiencing* a brand/company. They quote the examples of 'Starbucks' coffee, 'Absolut' vodka and 'Nike', where the 'experience' embraces look, feel, taste, smell, touch, colour, typeface, sound etc. and they assert that Schmitt and

Simonson's 'paradigm' is relevant to tourism. A significant element of their conceptualisation of branding is the strong warning against commoditisation – i.e. an avoidance of the current situation where 'we are awash in high quality look-alike/me-too products and services' (Schmitt and Simonson, 1997: xii). Ritchie and Ritchie (1998) regard this as an 'aggressive, in-depth response to a major policy concern regarding the "homogenization of destinations" identified by some 100 international experts in tourism at a policy forum held nearly a decade ago'.

They consider this to reflect a growing recognition among strategic thinkers in tourism that rather than emphasising only the high quality of service, a greater emphasis needs to be placed on providing 'high-quality experiences' (Otto and Ritchie, 1995). The 'travel experience' is thus a series of individual service transactions. They quote Keeley (1992) who expressed a similar view: 'There is an overall trend away from product attributes towards lifestyle or value systems'; and Schmitt and Simonson (1997) who write: 'The consumer of today makes choices based on whether or not a product fits into her or his lifestyle; whether it represents an exciting new concept – a desirable experience'.

The implications for today's tourism destination management are clear. Value is provided by satisfying customers' experiential or 'aesthetic' needs. Rather than a focus on the attributes and benefits of the destination's products and services, there is increasing attention to the diversity of *sensory* experiences that the destination provides and which can be further enhanced.

In the destination context, destination residents are themselves part of the 'visitation experience' and thus the destination brand (Ritchie and Ritchie, 1999). This contributes both positively and negatively to the challenge of successful destination management. A traditional product or service can usually be moved from one location to another without significantly altering the nature of the product/service. By contrast, the 'friendliness' of a host population – or, conversely, their level of irritation with tourism (see Doxey's Irritation Index in Chapter 2) – can be a significant influence on the quality of the visitors' experiences, although clearly the residents cannot be moved around for the convenience of tourists. Neither can destination managers 'control' the activities or influence the priorities of the local residents and businesses to any great extent. For example, local residents may resist proposals for a new conference centre on the grounds of unacceptable construction noise and subsequent increased volumes of traffic in 'their' neighbourhood. Destination managers would see a planning decision that supported the residents and turned down the application for the conference centre as a lost opportunity to add to the international prestige of the destination and to augment its brand image, as well as a loss of potential income and new jobs for the city ... possibly for some of the residents opposing the development. 'Perhaps it is too much to expect that a brand can capture and allow for these types of political and social shifts. Nevertheless, the reality is that they affect the perception of a destination brand' (Ritchie and Ritchie, 1999).

Developing a successful brand identity takes considerable time and effort on the part of the destination management and marketing team, but there is evidence that such investment is sound, since successful destination brands seem to have a long life (Ritchie and Ritchie, 1999). They quote Coca-Cola as a supreme example of a long-life product, the more so since pressure to change in response to social trends and new technological possibilities for innovation leads to rapid product turnover. The very nature of tourism destinations – places determined by their geography and the built environment – limits the possibilities for rapid change. Clearly, however, destinations *are* subject to the destination life cycle (see Chapter 2) as infrastructure ages or, more dramatically, as tourist preferences change, fuelled by the emergence of 'new' destinations that emerge through political or economic changes or by becoming more readily accessible through technological advances in transport.

The most successful destinations are those with brand identities based on enduring values and Ritchie and Ritchie (1999) identify the '*I ♡ NY*' campaign (*iloveny.state.ny.us*) and the '*Super Natural British Columbia*' (*www.travel.bc.ca*) market positioning as examples, while world-class heritage features that have become icons such as the Eiffel Tower, the Pyramids of Egypt and the Great Wall of China 'are the kinds of unique and enduring symbols that DMOs [destination management organisations] are prepared to die for'. Contemporary buildings rarely have that symbolic appeal, perhaps because iconic qualities require the passage of time to allow associations and the 'patina of age' to develop. The Twin Towers of the World Trade Center in Manhattan, destroyed by terrorists with great loss of life in 2001, were acquiring that quality and ironically, and tragically, were attacked because of it.

CASE STUDY

'*Scotland the Brand*'

' "Plaid too staid" say critics of Scotland's latest trademark. Logo to highlight quality produce is dismissed as anodyne', *The Scotsman*, 11 September 1997.

This referred to a logo commissioned by 'Scotland the Brand' (*www.scotlandthebrand.com*), an organisation backed by the government agency Scottish Enterprise (*www.scotent.co.uk*). The logo uses tartan and the name of the country to sell Scottish products abroad. It was intended to be a new official stamp of quality but was immediately criticised by certain designers and academics for trying to sell a 'saccharin' image of Scottish business. Representatives of business, tourism, manufacturing and the arts did, however, give support to this 'country of origin device', the logo's aim being to create a brand identity that Scottish companies and organisations of all sizes would be encouraged to use. 'Scotland the Brand' would provide a 'consistent and distinctive way of authenticating the source of Scottish products and services, worldwide'. It was estimated that the new image would provide a further £30 million of new sales over the next three years for companies adopting its use while Scotland the Brand had a £3 million budget over three years to promote and develop the idea. The Scottish Secretary of State considered the new image was 'very Scottish, strong and colourful and one of great quality' while others asserted that consistent use of the device would provide a powerful additional means by which companies and organisations can differentiate themselves in increasingly competitive global markets.

Companies using the logo would have to demonstrate that their operations employ 'rigorous quality standards' with a European standard used by 'Quality Scotland' as the benchmark. The chief executive of the Scottish

Tourist Board, said: 'The values associated with Scottishness that emerged from research are quality, reliability, integrity and authenticity. These are hugely strong brand values for any product of service. The immediate benefits will be substantial for Scottish consumer goods and will lead to a greater brand equity for Scotland plc. We should be aiming to position Scotland as a byword for quality'.

Not everyone was convinced the logo would be a success. Other design and advertising experts argued that the imagery was not dynamic enough and, even for traditional products like whisky, insufficiently distinctive. The general academic reaction was that while the logo would be more effective abroad, it could be 'counterproductive' for less traditional products such as new technology wishing to break with stereotypes, while many Scots see tartan and notably 'tartanry' as tacky and question its very authenticity (*www.thetatgallery.com/*). Certain marketing academics differed and argued the traditional case that the design capitalised on Scotland's strong international reputation for (they alleged) honesty, quality and hard work, while the use of blue is strong and identifies with team colours and the Scottish flag; adding that tartan is something that is immediately recognisable in the world market as Scottish, despite many Scots having become blasé towards it.

The 'Scotland the Brand' debate arose at the time of further questioning of national stereotypes in the context of political devolution for Scotland and Wales. The UK Prime Minister Tony Blair broke with tradition for the Commonwealth Heads of Government Meeting in Edinburgh in 1999 by abandoning the traditional state trappings of Scottish identity – drums, pipes, kilts, tartan. Critics asked whether these most recognisable traditional cultural symbols are now 'a liability or a priceless asset thrown away at our peril'.

The Scotsman attempted a moderate stance:

> Aside from the special case of tourism, it can be justly claimed that the perception of marching pipes and twirling drumsticks offers us few economic benefits. Granny's Hielan' Hame may help to sell Baxter's soups or Walker's shortbread, but it does nothing to help consolidate or promote further success in those sectors of industry and commerce which are now fundamental to our survival as a nation: electronics, oil and financial services.

It added that 'these icons are by no means universally popular in Scotland'. The newspaper continued (rather critically) that the Prime Minister was not attempting to rebrand Scotland, but rather was attempting to repackage the whole of the United Kingdom (*The Economist*, 1997: 43–4).

DESTINATION IDENTITY AND STEREOTYPES

Marketing is, however, *customer* focused. If the tourist associates certain icons with a destination, should he/she not be given the opportunity to see them? Is it wise to rebrand a destination and attempt to deny them 'bagpipes, tartan and haggis' – no matter how unrepresentative of the 'real' Scotland – if that is what they expect? What aspects of a destination's heritage should be projected? One critic of the post-devolution debate in Scotland warned that it is vital to avoid ending up with 'Scotland the bland' rather than 'Scotland the brand' even though pageantry no longer defines Scotland's (and Britain's) identity in the modern world. However, despite the customer orientation that marketing must take, destination branding should be done with the active involvement of – or at least consultation with – the destination's residents. They too are part of the reality as well as the marketing mix of the destination and marketing professionals cannot afford to be out of touch with the 'message on the street'.

The majority of Scots probably *are* fed up with Scottish logos which constantly use the 'traditional' tartan-bagpipes-thistles iconography, just as they despair of the companies that feel the need to put 'Scot' in front of their names to identify themselves: 'Scotmid, Scotfresh or whatever. You don't get companies south of the Border calling themselves Engwatch or Engspend' (Reid, 1999).

A 'non-tartanised' Scotland should be given the opportunity to breathe and grow, meanwhile asking what else a country has to offer. Reid (1999) asserts that 'there is a place for haggis and heather if the customer wants to buy into that, but if we want to say we're a small, dynamic and modern country, then that sort of image simply isn't appropriate'. Eighty per cent of Scotland's population now lives in and around cities and whether the romantic 'Braveheart' type of image is a valuable way for a modern nation to present itself is highly debatable. New imagery for Scotland, the distinctive things that mark out the country today could include, for example, other aspects of its heritage such as in science and discovery, inventions, intellectual skills, the quality of its education and contributions to philosophy – increasingly important skills in a global economy that is becoming ever more knowledge based. 'These sort of images are far more important than using the branding of a guy running amok with a cleaver' (Reid, 1999).

But would they attract tourists?

In fact, the latest brand research commissioned by VisitScotland (2002) and put into practice in the Autumn Gold 2002 campaign (*www.scotexchange.net*) develops the 'senses' theme of the spring campaign with new seasonal variations incorporated into the brand positioning: 'Live it. Visit Scotland.'. All marketing campaigns will build on the senses campaign, developed around the five senses: 'See it, touch it, hear it, taste it smell it' (see Chapter 3).

The research 'showed that Scotland could be summarised in 3 words: enduring, dramatic and human. Together they form the essence of Scotland's brand. [...] 'Scotland is enduring. Our buildings, tradition, and culture convey a sense of timelessness. And in a world that seems to change every time we turn around, people seek out the things that inspire a sense of permanence. They find them in Scotland'. As for 'drama', Scotland has 'dramatic scenery, beautiful light and the drama of the changing weather'; while 'human' reflects the finding that 'the Scots are seen as down to earth, innovative, solid and dependable but full of integrity and pride. The survey showed that people felt they got the genuine article when they came to Scotland and that there was nothing synthetic about Scotland.'

The marketing of Scotland would appear to have turned full circle.

Bibliography

Aaker, D.A. (1991) *Managing Brand Equity: Capitalizing on the Value of a Brand Name.* Free Press. New York.

Ashworth, G. and Voogd, H. (1988a) Marketing the city: concepts, processes and Dutch applications. *Town Planning Review,* 59, 65–80.

Ashworth, G. and Voogd, H. (1988b) Can places be sold for tourism? in G. Ashworth and B. Goodal (eds) *Marketing Tourism Places.* Routledge. New York.

Booms and Bitner (1981) *Marketing's 3 Ps.*

Cooper, C., Fletcher, J., Gilbert, D. and Wanhill, S. (1998) *Tourism Principles and Practice* (2nd edn). Longman London.

The Economist, (1997) A new brand for Britain, 43–44.

Keeley, (1992) in J.R.B. Ritchie and R.J.B. Ritchie (1999).

Kotler, P. (1984) *Marketing Management: Analysis, Planning and Control* (5th edn). Prentice Hall. New Jersey.

Kotler, P. (1997) *Marketing Management: Analysis, Planning and Control* (9th edn). Prentice Hall. New Jersey.

Lurham, D. (1998) World tourism: crystal ball gazing. *Tourism, the Journal of the Tourism Society,* 96, 13.

Middleton, V. (1994) *Marketing in Travel and Tourism* (2nd edn). Butterworth-Heinemann Ltd.,

Morgan, N., Pritchard, A. and Pride, R. (2002) *Destination Branding: Creating the Unique Destination Proposition.* Oxford. Butterworth-Heinemann.

Neilsen, M., Murnion, P. and Mather, L. (2001) Destination marketing and cultural tourism: the Galway city case study in J. Butcher (2001) *Innovations in Cultural Tourism, Association for Tourism and Leisure Education.* Tilburg University. Tilburg.

Reid, D. (1999) Creative partner for the 1576 Agency, Edinburgh in *The Scotsman,* Edinburgh.

Ritchie, J.R.B., Hawkins, D.E. *et al.* (1993) *World Travel and Tourism Review: Indicators, Trends and Issues.* Oxford. Oxford University Press.

Ritchie, J.R.B. and Ritchie, R.J.B. (1998) Branding of tourism destinations: past achievements and future challenges. A basic report prepared for presentation to the 1998 *Annual Congress of the International Association of Scientific Experts in Tourism,* Marrakech, Morocco, September 1998.

Schmitt and Simonson (1997).

VisitScotland (2002) *Live it. Visit Scotland.* STB. Edinburgh.

World Tourism Organization Business Council (WTOBC) (1999) *Marketing Tourism Destinations Online – Strategies for the Information Age.*

CHAPTER 5

Destination planning and policy

INTRODUCTION

'Planning' is a very human activity, one of our defining characteristics being the ability to 'think ahead' rather than making purely instinctive and spontaneous responses to prevailing environmental conditions. The remains of ancient cities that are today treasured cultural heritage attractions show clear evidence of 'rational planning' to meet the increasing needs of growing populations in terms of housing, workshops, shops and markets, water supply and defence as well as more intangible qualities such as ambience and beauty:

> Town planning in Britain has evolved from historical bases over a period of approximately 2000 years of urban development, from the Roman period to the early mediaeval towns, progressing through the Elizabethan age of regulations and the rebuilding of London, to seventeenth and eighteenth century geometric planning. [...] The methodical and visual placing of people and buildings on land is the art and science of (town) planning, and encompasses far more than mere town building.
>
> (Morris, 1997)

A number of cities have been awarded the accolade 'world heritage site' (*www.worldheritage.org*) on account of their well preserved extensive 'planned' districts such as Edinburgh's (17th-century) New Town (see Chapter 6) but also indicating the timelessness of quality environment.

Despite the clear importance of planning, it is sometimes regarded as almost synonymous with 'interfering bureaucracy'. This is unfortunate and unwarranted. 'Planners' in a local authority or in a consultancy firm are professionals, generally graduates and those with a degree in planning or other closely related subject areas are likely to be members of a professional body, in the UK the Royal Town Planning Institute, allowing them to use the title 'chartered town planner' (*www.planning.haynet.com*).

A BRIEF HISTORY OF MODERN TOURISM PLANNING

In the 'world's biggest industry', tourism, tourism planning is a comparative newcomer. Early tourism development was founded on a basic assumption – tourism is an 'intrinsic good'; that is, 'it can do no wrong'. This was founded on tourism's apparent use of existing 'free resources' (beaches, countryside, fresh air, cities etc.) and on the 'non-extractive' nature of the industry, i.e. it did not 'use up' these resources. The expected economic benefits to investors were great, while it was assumed there would be 'spin-off' benefits to local communities and the environment. Early tourism development responded in an ad hoc manner to changing markets and with the advantages of hindsight it is clear that this resulted in lost opportunities – it was generally what is now regarded as non-sustainable tourism.

An example of this approach is the development of Disneyland, California (1952). For its time the approach was fairly progressive, involving both economic and physical plans with market assessment the foundation of the physical plans:

> [the goals were] to locate the best area, taking account of freeways and population growth patterns. We wound up with little more than 300 acres of orange groves in Anaheim, California. [...] a neon jungle of motels, gas stations, restaurants, and other tourist support facilities. It was an aesthetic nightmare.
>
> (Disney Corporation quoted in Gunn, 1988)

In other words, there was a lack of adequate foresight about changing tourist trends and the resultant demands and little or no awareness of the side-effects on the local area – what today we would call the environmental and social impacts of tourism development – the consequences of a 'non-integrated' approach to tourism development.

By the mid-1960s integrated planning for development was more common. There was recognition of the need to accommodate the 'external effects' of tourism development on the regional and environmental context. The late 1980s and early 1990s saw an increasingly experienced and demanding tourist and public and increasing awareness of the adverse effects of tourism development, while the tourism industry from the 1990s to the present has the objective of 'optimum development' (see Figure 5.1). There is increasing acceptance that this requires planning for achievement of wide-ranging objectives within a context of sustainability. In this context 'tourism planning' shares a great deal with 'planning' or 'urban and regional planning, as practised in the UK and many other countries, which aims to encourage the 'right' development in the 'right' place to achieve the widest range of benefits for the many stakeholders.

COMPONENTS OF THE CONTEMPORARY PLANNING SYSTEM

The UK planning system is a well-established and statutory approach for the reconciliation of objectives in environmental planning and landuse and the approach is broadly similar elsewhere in western Europe and other social democratic countries.

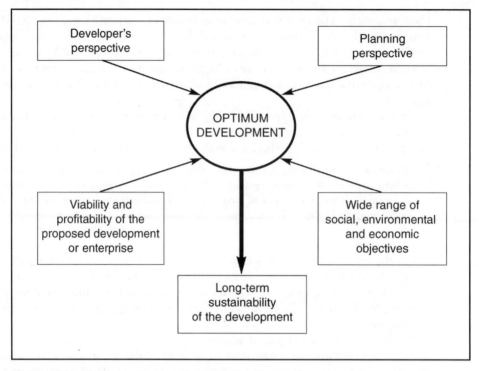

Figure 5.1 *The development and planning context*

The UK *planning system*

Two components of the system affect the outcome of a proposal for development: (a) development control, which is site specific dealing with discrete proposals for a comparatively small area such as plot of land for a house, a hotel or a visitor attraction; and (b) plan making, which is area based, e.g. plans for a small town or for parts of a city ('local plans') in which tourism is one of many activities to be harmoniously and profitably integrated.

From 'proposal' to reality
The initial stage is where the would-be developer/entrepreneur 'has an idea' (see Figure 5.2). It may arise intuitively or it may be the result of a great deal of critical thought based on long experience. Subsequent stages develop from this.

Is this developer's perspective too narrow? Or does the developer 'know best'?

The planning perspective on a given development can be described as 'interventionist' – the planner 'intervenes' on behalf of the 'wider community of interests' or the other 'stakeholders' (see the Largs case study in Chapter 8). Several characteristics can be recognised in any development proposal.

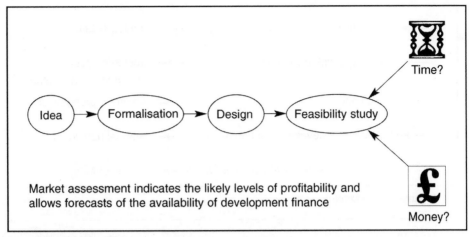

Market assessment indicates the likely levels of profitability and allows forecasts of the availability of development finance

Figure 5.2 *The developer's perspective*

There are many 'interested parties' or 'stakeholders' and planning must attempt to satisfy all of them. A 'social remit' is present as well as the more 'familiar' economic imperative. The NIMBY syndrome ('Not In My Back Yard') may have to be confronted – people are reluctant to accept change in their locality unless they can see benefits to themselves. 'Planning gain' or 'spin-off' to the wider community from the development is desirable in the forms of new jobs; improved infrastructure; amenities, etc. As far as the 'community' is concerned, tourism is only one possible 'use' or form of development for 'their' given locality.

The would-be developer must submit the formalised 'idea' to 'the planners', i.e. the statutory framework for development control, generally located in the local authority for the area within which the development is proposed. Only if planning permission is granted may the development legally go ahead. The process inevitably requires a period of time, depending on the 'complexity' of the development proposal and/or the proposed site, generally (in the UK) around two months. While this can lead to a rather 'negative' image of planners, the process is highly democratic and open to scrutiny.

There are two main elements of the planning system at 'local' level.

Development control
This can be seen as a series of steps:

1. Informal discussion between developer and planning officers. This is optional, but recommended as likely to save time in the later stages.

2. Formal submission of the development proposal by the would-be developer to the planning authority.

3. Planning officials examine the proposal – in the context of existing development, proposals for the area and local public opinion. A public meeting may be held to gauge the views of the local community in the area where the development is proposed. (Public meetings are discussed later in this chapter.)

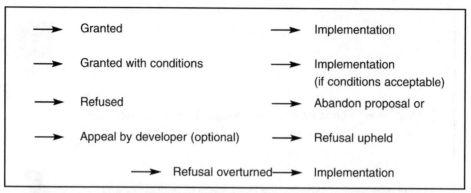

Figure 5.3 *Planning permission*

4. Planning officials' recommendations are made – for submission to the planning committee.

5. The planning committee's approval (or otherwise) of recommendations is given (see Figure 5.3).

The gaining of planning permission is a significant step for a developer. An awareness of the procedures – and a realisation that development control is actually development *enablement* – is likely to contribute to gaining planning approval for a proposed development. The planning authority is not against development; the objective is to encourage appropriate development in a specific location.

Another local authority department which would-be developers may also have dealings with is 'building control'. It is largely concerned with the 'internal'/structural details of building construction or renovation and is empowered to issue 'building warrants' for proposed new buildings or alterations to existing buildings so allowing these to go ahead where they meet appropriate safety and other legal standards.

The planning system – 'plan making'
'Development control', i.e. planning decisions on individual development proposals, must be in conformity with the 'development plans' for the wider area in which the development is proposed. Preparing plans for an extended area, with a diversity of landuses, land values, activities and ownerships is complex. A number of historical stages in its evolution can be identified, reflecting the growing complexity of the process, in turn determined by the increasingly complex demands of society.

HISTORICAL STAGES IN MODERN PLANNING (UK)

Era of the 'master plan' (1960s on)

The master plan approach owes its origins to the early days of modern planning that drew on the work of late 19th-century figures such as Patrick Geddes

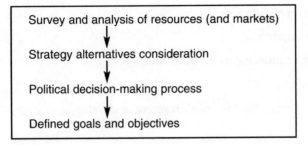

Figure 5.4 *Guidelines for development*

(*www.cce.ed.ac.uk/geddes*) who argued the case for an approach based on: 'Survey → Analysis → Plan'. For all parts of the UK there was a comprehensive detailing of guidelines for development (see Figure 5.4).

Although a considerable advance, its weakness was the fact that it was a 'once-over' method: 5-yr plan → obsolescence → 5-yr plan → obsolescence → ... (cycle repeats).

The plan is increasingly 'out of touch' with changing circumstances.

Planning in the UK (1970s on)

Planning took a more flexible approach – a 'systems' or 'strategic' approach which permitted:

- added awareness of socio-economic factors (in addition to physical landuse) via cost-benefit analyses

- increased public consultation.

The present phase in UK planning (mid-1990s on)

The present approach is characterised by:

- acknowledgement of 'constant change'

- continuous monitoring (feedback) and response

- continuous revision.

This is the basis of 'systems approach' planning. There is also an increasing recognition of tourism/leisure as a major industry.

Contemporary planning increasingly incorporates management into planning for tourism, now embracing a wider range of 'tools' and activities such as:

- marketing and publicity

- information and interpretation

- traffic management.

There is an increased integration of people and place management and of the interdependence of the tourist and the host community. For example, 'people control' may be essential to preserve the quality of the tourist experience or the attraction itself at popular 'heritage' sites but this can be achieved through 'soft' approaches such as:

- information and interpretation services
- the availability of alternatives
- the (subtle) directing of movements and activities
- the fostering of 'goodwill'.

This approach can, in turn, lead to more responsive development control and plan making.

TOURISM PLANNING AND PRACTICE IN THE UK

Tourism planning has been largely confined to:

- designated areas such as national parks and heritage coasts
- 'subject plans' (plans which focus specifically on tourism/leisure)
- tourism/leisure as one topic in development plans for an area.

While a specific focus on tourism development may seem attractive after a history of benign neglect of the industry, such 'sectoral' approaches can suffer from a lack of coordination with other sectors. For example, a new network of footpaths/cycle tracks in a rural area may benefit local bed-and-breakfast or hotel operators, but with inadequate coordination with agricultural interests in the same area may lead to problems for both industries. Walkers may unintentionally disturb cattle or sheep, perhaps at sensitive times such as the lambing season, hardening farmers' attitudes towards tourism and leading to closure of access to privately owned land, even where access is a legal right.

In the 1980s it was regretted that: 'Tourism is so ripe for some corporate treatment, [yet] there are few signs of holistic approaches being adopted' (Healey, 1981). The 1990s saw the beginnings of integration of tourism development into general area development. As but one example, it may be ironic that the outbreak of foot-and-mouth disease in cattle and sheep in the UK in 2000/2001 drew attention to the true economic significance of tourism – six or seven times the economic value of agriculture – perhaps encouraging these industries into a new, more collaborative partnership.

Who are the tourism planners?

Modern tourism development owes much to the skills and risk taking of private sector entrepreneurs. The public sector – notably in the UK – took little interest in the young industry until comparatively recently when it moved from a largely 'regulatory' role to one of more active, frequently proactive, tourism development increasingly in active 'partnership' with the private sector. Despite this, it must be considered that (in the UK and in other EU countries):

A further feature of the last fifteen years [prior to 1997] has been the declining role of the public sector as a source of development demand and its replacement largely by the private sector. Instead the public sector role in many fields of service provision has been redefined as an enabling and co-ordinating one of which this local plan will be a component. A more direct control over redevelopment is possible for the council in relation to the several key city centre sites which are in its ownership. In recent years also the council has helped to initiate and come to rely on co-operation and partnership arrangements to achieve its wider objectives [with local enterprise companies and the private sector].

(City of Edinburgh Council, Central Area 1997)

This trend is likely to continue as we see major institutional change including European integration and moves to devolution and regionalism and increasing central government focus on policy integration issues such as 'joined-up thinking' and working across departmental boundaries. Local authorities are now subject to many practices common in the private sector such as competitive tendering for the provision of services, delivery plans, output measurement and evaluation and the concept of 'best value' (Roberts, 2001). Sustainable development, social inclusion and community plans are further examples of this process of change. They affect tourism planning and development as profoundly as they affect any other sectoral interest and will entail ever closer collaboration between the public and private sectors. Planning 'is not an unchanging subject. Planning policies reflect changing viewpoints and fashions as to what is "right" at a particular time in a particular place – often with amazing swings in opinion as evidenced by the present condemnation of modern architecture and the return to traditional styles and the emphasis on conservation. But once a policy is agreed upon and implemented anyone who contravenes it by building the "wrong" building in the "wrong" place will soon find themselves subject to the full force of the law' (Greed, 1996: 11).

The planning authority

In the UK planning is largely a local government responsibility. For example in Edinburgh, the City of Edinburgh Council is responsible for plan preparation and development control. Regional councils (such as the former Lothian Regional Council), which existed until the late 1980s when there was local government reorganisation, were responsible for preparation of higher level strategic or regional plans as well as transportation plans. These 'regional' functions are now undertaken by groupings of neighbouring councils.

Development plans

Development plans are of two types and contain a wealth of information for developers – including tourism developers – as well as interested citizens. Their formats are prescribed by central government, and must conform to a series of national planning guidelines (NPGs) which provide statements on policy on nationally important landuse and other planning matters. These are important input to plans and provide considerations for development control. Central government also publishes planning advice notes (PANs) which provide advice on good planning practice (*www.planning gov.uk*). European Union 'directives' are also a part of the framework.

Structure plans

These are strategic policy overviews for a region and generally consist of a 'written statement' and a 'key diagram' (rather than a detailed 'map'). They take a 'broad brushstroke' style and cover a large area.

Local plans

These consist of a 'written statement' and a 'proposal map' and are site specific and highly localised, covering an area such as 'the central area' of a city. The plan brings into one document all the local council's policies and proposals for the use of land and development in the area it covers. It builds on past policies and seeks to develop these into a comprehensive and coherent framework to guide future development and conservation activity and the operations of development control. Its success will depend largely on how effectively it has anticipated and addressed future development issues and pressures and exploited new development opportunity to enhance environmental quality (City of Edinburgh Council, 1997).

Subject plans

These are topic specific, addressing a particular sector, for example:

- tourism/leisure
- transport
- housing
- financial plans
- enterprise zones.

CASE STUDY

The place of tourism in a city centre

Any local plan must consider all policies for the use of land and development in the area it covers. In a given area, tourism may or may not have an important role – in many cities its role is significant. In the context of a local plan for the centre of a UK city that is also a world heritage site, tourism must develop alongside other key urban issues. In the Central Edinburgh Local Plan, for example, 'leisure and tourism' is one among several important elements of the Council's policies for 'multiple use' of the area:

- conservation and design
- green environment
- economic development
- shopping
- housing
- leisure and tourism
- education, health and other community services
- transport.

A local plan must integrate these various elements and so there are further chapters on 'Context and strategy' and 'Implementation'. Appendices provide an 'Area profile', 'Schedule of sites with development potential', 'Shopping frontages' and 'Conservation areas', the last two reinforcing 'tourism' in defining the city centre as an area of high status and aesthetic quality:

> The strategy for the local plan is founded on the Council's concerns to encourage developments which will create jobs and wealth and further the role of the city centre as a major urban centre. This requires a positive response to the demands and pressures which are at their sharpest in and around the city centre. These must be managed to improve the environment and assist in area renewal and revitalization. New developments must not undermine the qualities of vitality and diversity which are the hallmark of a city centre. On large sites in particular this is a consideration which argues for mixtures of uses capable of fulfilling different planning objectives.
>
> (City of Edinburgh Council, 1997)

The Edinburgh case study (Chapter 6) discusses tourism in Edinburgh in detail. Here we are concerned more with the general principles of tourism development in the context of a local plan where a wide range of topics and issues must be given consideration and the significance of tourism in the specific local plan area must be established.

'Leisure activity and tourism has increased dramatically in the course of several decades. It is now a major part of the City's economy with significant potential for further growth and job creation.' (City of Edinburgh Council, 1997.) The plan identifies various categories of leisure and tourism since in the planning context each has distinct landuse and other requirements and differing impacts on the other legitimate uses of the city centre. The categories of tourism and leisure provision are:

- museums, galleries and historic buildings open to the public

- theatres, cinemas, concert halls and similar entertainment facilities associated with frequent, intense, evening use and which carry major traffic and parking implications

- sports venues catering for spectator sports ('their use may be occasional but overwhelming')

- active leisure facilities, including swimming pools and fitness clubs which are used on a casual basis

- commercial leisure provision – a great diversity including restaurants, public houses, bingo halls, cinemas, dance halls, night clubs, saunas and, latterly, sex-oriented establishments. (see the discussion on grey area tourism in Chapter 6)

Certain new, key developments make a significant contribution to the city's leisure role and interest. A statement from the Edinburgh plan could apply to many cities: 'The outdoor environment, its streets, parks and urban spaces may be the location for much casual leisure and sometimes formal entertainment, from pavement cafes to street theatre'. Many of these uses of the area are shared by both tourists and local residents. This emphasises the need for an understanding of the general interactions between uses, of the environmental, social and economic impacts of tourism on these other activities and of these activities on tourism.

Accommodation provision is a further major element of a city's role in tourism. In many cities the majority of the hotel and guesthouse accommodation is in the central area. In the peak summer season these may be barely adequate but may be supplemented by seasonal accommodation in private houses (B & Bs) and student residences. The planning authority will have a significant role in determining the location of new hotels in conjunction with private sector developers. Developers will generally desire the most attractive and accessible sites, while the planning authority may already have zoned these sites for other legitimate uses. Such landuse conflicts are generally resolved with reference to the local plan. Developers can save themselves much time and therefore money by making use of these plans to determine whether their chosen site is considered appropriate for their type of proposed development. Challenging these land allocations would be a lengthy and expensive process – they have been made on the basis of technical assessment and consideration of social, environmental and economic considerations. Securing planning permission for their proposed developments on 'inappropriate' sites would almost certainly require a lengthy process of consultation with a wide range of stakeholders. This process is illustrated in the case study of a canal-side development discussed later in this chapter.

Types of planning

As well as local plans, structure or strategic plans and subject plans, certain other categories of planning are commonly referred to.

Economic development planning has grown in importance in recent decades as many older industrial areas lose their economic viability. Docklands, coal-mining areas, 'steel towns' and others were among the earliest to fall foul of the structural changes taking place in most industrialised countries as the Industrial Era gives way to the 'technological era'. 'Urban regeneration' is a term commonly used to describe the responses to the subsequent social, environmental and economic problems that arise in cities. The Edinburgh case study (Chapter 6) describes the process in the 'Edinburgh Waterfront' which embraces the areas of Leith and Granton, where tourism is now a major element, at least partially replacing former dockland and other industrial activities. A further example is the recent development of a new financial district in the centre of the city which also generates more business tourism.

Physical landuse planning is the process of allocation of appropriate uses to generally undeveloped land. In heavily developed countries and regions such 'virgin' land is extremely rare while in 'less developed countries' physical landuse planning is a desirable alternative to the unregulated, exploitative land development that sometimes takes place. Examples include instances of tropical rainforest clearance for grazing land where the fragile soils are likely to be washed away by the heavy tropical rainfall; also, certain early examples of mass tourism development where inadequate survey and analysis led to an unsustainable industry – either in economic, environmental or social terms. Certain national parks areas have also suffered from inadequate or poor landuse planning – for example in the Cairngorms case study (Chapter 10) it can be argued that skiing developments should not have been permitted in the central mountain core – 'wilderness preservation' rather than 'recreational use' is the appropriate 'landuse'. Conservation and park planning can be regarded as specific examples of physical land planning, for example the planning for Scotland's first two national parks, the first being designated in 2002 (see Chapter 10).

Infrastructure planning is concerned with transportation, power, water and/or waste disposal, etc. The Edinburgh case study (Chapter 10) discusses traffic management for one of the city's main tourism areas, Princes Street. The encouragement of appropriate, sustainable transport to meet the needs of both tourists and residents is the objective.

Social facility planning addresses the provision of educational, medical and recreational facilities and services etc. A leisure plan is prepared for many cities and the facilities that are developed may serve a dual function as part of the 'tourism' infrastructure of the destination. Increasingly, cultural facilities are regarded as both a social/leisure provision (i.e. for the residents) and also elements of the tourism industry e.g. theatres, conference centres, museums, sports grounds, visitor orientation centres as well as major festivals which, although not necessarily permanently located in a particular building or buildings, are of increasing significance.

URBAN AND REGIONAL PLANNING

This is comprehensive planning which integrates all the subject-specific types of planning just discussed. It is established throughout the UK and in its contemporary form displays certain key characteristics:

- continuous, incremental and flexible, incorporating 'feedback'/checking mechanisms and periodic revision

- comprehensive and integrated

- recognises that all development sectors and supporting facilities and services are interrelated *and* related to the natural environment and society of the area (as a system)

- acknowledges that all components of the 'system' must be understood in order to optimise development.

The systems approach

The above list characterises the 'systems approach' adopted by modern urban and regional planning and founded on the necessity of sufficient information about the system to properly understand and analyse it and so plan for development. In the planning context the 'system' can be a city, a city and its region or a part of a city and, in the tourism planning context, whatever area is defined as the destination is the system.

Computer technology and information systems are essential to handle the great amounts of data and these permit:

- demand analyses

- evaluation of alternative strategies

- analysis of economic, environmental and social impacts of proposed development

- preparation of economic and financial analyses of projects

- preparation of architectural and landscape design perspectives etc.

The systems approach is discussed further, in the context of policy making, later in this chapter.

Community involvement

The basic premise of community involvement in comprehensive planning is that active participation is good for the residents of the area, allowing them, as principal stakeholders, to influence the future development of their locality. In the contemporary context of sustainable development it has become recognised that the 'good' of the community is intrinsically linked with wider economic and environmental forces and therefore local opinion has to be informed opinion. The process is time consuming. Various degrees of participation in decision making are possible and it essential to be aware of which level is present in a given situation so that the real significance of the decisions agreed at such a meeting can be determined. For example, a local community meeting to discuss an important development proposal may be poorly attended. Can it be concluded, therefore, that local people 'just don't care'? 'Apathy' is certainly a possibility: an hour or two of popular TV 'soaps' may be a more attractive way to spend an evening. Contrariwise, local people may feel 'alienated' from the decision-making process and the 'experts' and lack the confidence to make their opinion heard or even to attend. Another possibility is that while a meeting may be well attended, there may be awareness that there is little probability of the outcomes of the meeting being acted upon – holding a public meeting is mere 'tokenism'. The several possible levels of effective participation have been described as a 'ladder' or set of steps, ranging from non-participation to full participation (see Figure 2.3).

CASE STUDY

Public participation in planning

Background
One 'definition' of planning is that it is about ensuring 'the right use of an area of land, at the right time, for the right people'. But how to respond to the different opinions that will be expressed on any particular development? That is part of the planner's task. More significantly, how can the 'perfect compromise' be arrived at? In fact, can everyone ever be pleased?

This dilemma has become known as the 'NIMBY syndrome'. The letters in the acronym stand for 'Not In My Back Yard'. The implication is that everybody wants the benefits of a development, but none of the disadvantages – they can go in somebody else's backyard. This can lead to the decision makers concluding that everyone is only out for their own ends.

Is it true? Could you present a case for or against a given development proposal that sounds as if you had considered the local situation, the wider context and the developer's point of view and come up with a proposal that is beyond criticism?

If the planner's role is to find this 'perfect' compromise he needs to know: the facts *and* the feelings or attitudes towards the proposed development.

The facts – or at least the 'facts' as they appear to the developer – are usually clearly stated. The feelings towards the development may not be so clear. The people who will be affected by the development may not know they have a right to be heard may not know how to go about being heard or may not put their point of view over in a way that the planners can react constructively to or understand.

For a destination manager, who certainly will be involved in development, or for an individual or a group of stakeholders, learning to communicate with the planners and developers is vitally important. Certain skills are needed do it well. The case against (or in support of) a proposed development must be well prepared, based on understanding the likely effects or impacts on the community, on the wider public or specific business interests and based on understanding of how developers, planners and any other 'interested parties' are going to present their cases – in other words, how they see the situation. Armed with facts and that understanding, stakeholders can certainly increase their chances of influencing the decision on a proposed decision (see Figure 5.5).

'You' have a right to participation – opportunities for involvement, knowing your rights
You can join in the debate – as a developer, as an individual, as a group etc.
So can anyone else! – there are differing points of view and no single 'right' view
The local/community response is important, so must not be regarded as unimportant
The local/regional/national perspectives – the 'wider' perspective is easily overlooked – you and your organisation/ community are part of the wider scene
Cost-benefit analysis is needed to weigh up the pros and cons of a proposal
Resolution of conflicting views may require compromise by some or all parties. A proposed development may have to be modified

There are only three ways in which the planners can respond to the application to carry out a development:

- grant permission to develop as described
- grant permission to develop, but with certain required modifications to the proposal – 'conditions'
- refuse permission to develop.

Figure 5.5 *Some points for a stakeholder to consider in planning permission discussions concerning new developments (in the UK)*

Once a stakeholder group has thoroughly examined a proposal it is necessary to be clear on the direction in which they want to influence the decision. Remember too that 'the planners' are not as powerful as some think – the professionally qualified 'planners' in the development control section of the planning department make only recommendations on a particular development proposal (although the reasons will be clearly justified); the real decision is made by the councillors, locally elected politicians serving on the planning committee.

Remember also that the developer can 'appeal' against the decision given by the planning authority. Carefully researched notes should not be thrown away in despair or rage! They may be needed again.

Exercise

Scenario – a local development proposal

Introduction
The local planning authority, the City of Edenville Council, has received a planning application concerning development of a distinctive site, which has been semi-derelict for some years. However, 'a 'semi-derelict site' means different things to different people. The planning system must by law give the opportunity for all these different people to have their say on how, or whether, this site should be developed. Only then can the planners respond to the application for consent to go ahead and develop that site.

The proposed development
A planning application has been lodged in respect of property near the Unity Canal at The Old Landing, Lammington Road. The application is for planning permission to construct a licensed premises – a bar/restaurant – adjacent to a largely disused canal. The premises would be distinctive in that a restored barge would be moored alongside on the canal, allowing customers to have a meal/drink while enjoying a cruise.

The site
The site of the proposed development is within an area which is mainly residential with 'compatible' uses. Most dwellings are in substantial blocks of flats, three storeys in height with commercial premises on the ground floor. There are also a number of detached houses with large walled gardens. The area is well served with local shops, while there are several local public houses and cafes nearby. A substantial number of commercial premises are vacant (see Figure 5.7).

A number of small workshop premises are located on the canal banks near to the site. These are generally in a poor state of repair. A brewery occupies much of the opposite bank of the canal.

The land has been disused for many years, while the adjacent canal is a 'remainder waterway' no longer carrying commercial traffic. The owner is a public sector body, British Waterways Board. The area is used for informal recreation, although is locally considered a dangerous area at night due to the poor condition of footpaths and inadequate lighting. The canal itself is regularly used for fly tipping (illegal disposal of rubbish). The canal banks and the canal itself are partially overgrown with vegetation.

Photograph 5.1 *Unity Canal – the site*

The site is generally in a poor condition. A narrow access road links the site to two nearby arterial roads into the city centre, which is less than half-a-mile distant.

An opportunity to participate
The Planning Authority has notified local residents and others likely to be affected by the proposed development. Copies of the planning application are available for inspection at the offices of the Planning Department.

A group of residents have decided to call a public meeting to discuss this proposed development, which they consider likely to have considerable effects on their neighbourhood. They have publicised the event locally, through notices in the windows of local shops and a small advertisement in the local newspaper. They have sent written invitations to the meeting to the developers, the planning department, local councillors, the owners of the land and the last known secretaries of a local neighbourhood association (Gilton Neighbourhood Association) and a local traders association, both of which were once active but have not been heard of in recent times. Other special interest groups are hoped to be in attendance at the public meeting (see Figure 5.6).

Note that a consensus of local opinion may emerge at the meeting ... or it may not. A wide range of interested parties will be present who have not previously been aware of any common interest and who have not previously tried to respond to a planning application for a development which would affect all. A group from the Tourism Studies Department at Edenville University College have agreed to assist interested local people in understanding the workings of the planning system and in making a strong representation to the local planning authority. They will be present at the public meeting.

A PUBLIC MEETING

To discuss the proposed development of a bar/restaurant and floating barge at Lammington Road

Will be held in The Community Hall Lammington Road

Time: 7.00 pm
day, month, year

A representative of the city planning department will attend

ALL WELCOME

Interested parties expected to attend the meeting:

Developer
Land/property owner
Local residents
Conservation group
Recreation and leisure interests
Tourist board
Local traders' association
Edenville Council, Department of Planning
Lammington Ward, Edenville Councillor
The local newspaper
Tourism planning students

Figure 5.6 *Public notice of a meeting*

Group exercise: stage 1
There should be a chairperson and a minutes secretary.
   At least one person should represent each of the organisations/stakeholders listed.
   From each stakeholder point of view, give what is considered to be a realistic 'presentation' to the meeting.
   At question time, the chairperson asks for questions from the audience.
   The chairperson keeps order (with assistance as necessary).
   Conclusions from the meeting are summarised for submission to the Planning Committee for consideration.
   Note that 'realistic assumptions' about the development and the wider tourism etc. context may be made where insufficient detail/information is available to answer questions from the audience.

Group exercise: stage 2
Assume the role of the Planning Committee (local councillors/members of the Planning Committee).
   Discuss the planning application and the representations from the local meeting.
   Recommend a decision:

• award planning permission to develop as proposed

- grant planning permission to develop, with conditions

- refuse planning permission.

Notes for game play
Various facts/figures/speculations can be introduced to vary the exercise. The exercise can be related to 'real' places within the experience of the players or can be entirely imagined locations whose details are carefully listed and agreed by players.

CONSERVATION – A GENERAL OVERVIEW

Conservation is broadly understood to refer to the careful management of resources and environment. The word and its general implications have been in common use for some time, for example in the writings of John Muir (Chapter 10) and others in the late 19th century, to the many contemporary writers since it has acquired a new prominence in the context of sustainability and a general acceptance of the need to 'look after the environment'. Nature conservation, built environment conservation, resource conservation, heritage conservation and other forms are common topics in planning matters and in conservation policy. A tourism destination which can boast such areas generally has enhanced tourism because of its intrinsic qualities and character and also the 'benchmark' of quality such designations bring. The awarding of such a designation to an area is likely to enhance existing tourism levels. In the context of Scotland's very late entry into the international 'club' of countries with national parks (2002) – i.e. almost every country in the world – despite a resistance by some tourist boards and many entrepreneurs to the assumed 'restrictions' that national parks would bring, there is now a clamour to be included within the proposed boundaries of the new parks in anticipation of the economic opportunities that result.

In rural areas conservation of the natural environment is achieved or at least supported by conservation policy and legislation that derives from it. National parks and other 'designations' are examples (as discussed in Chapter 10). In urban areas, conservation of the built environment is fostered through a number of designations.

Conservation areas are areas of quality, special character and interest. When they are designated by a local authority it is effectively a statement of intent to maintain and enhance their special character. New developments and change to existing buildings or the general environment must be 'in character' with the area, either complementing or enhancing it. Guidance and enhancement schemes will be prepared by the local authority and generally cover aspects that contribute to the area's character and the local sense of place. Examples are listed buildings and others of townscape interest, boundary walls and railings, historic gardens, trees and landscape features, traditional and natural paving materials and street furniture and the historic pattern of streets and spaces.

Listed buildings

These are buildings 'listed' by central government bodies in the UK which gives them statutory protection under the relevant Town and Country Planning Acts. To be 'listed' a building must be of outstanding historical or architectural interest. All buildings dating from before 1700 are listed, the majority of those built between 1700 and 1840, a considerable number from 1840 to 1914 and a small number from 1914 to 1939. Individual buildings are also 'graded' according to their merits. In some countries equivalent schemes also 'list' brand new buildings if they are of sufficient merit.

'Scheduled monuments' and buildings looked after by the national trusts (non-governmental, 'membership' bodies) in the UK are also given special conservation consideration.

The spirit of place of destinations

Quality in the built environment and the distinctive spirit of place of destinations are increasingly sought by tourists – conservation of the elements that contribute to this is achieving new significance. In many locations the remaining older buildings reflect the climate and the topography of their region which in pre-industrial times determined building sites and materials. 'Communication was always a problem – water was the main form, using rivers and coastal waters. Wild rural hinterland forced towns onto fertile coastal strips or river valleys. A distinct [...] tradition of coastal towns and seaside architecture evolved. [Political] instability prevented [...] the development of styles in Europe being integrated into the development of a unique national style in the [...] "lesser" houses [which] still clung to the native or "vernacular" style' (Edwards, 1986).

In upland areas in the UK there is a prevalence of stone construction – walls of irregular stones from the vicinity used 'random rubble' construction. 'Harling' of pebbles and mortar was applied in a thin layer to walls to protect them from the weather and this was painted – white, commonly, although also other 'earth' colours. This gives rise to the 'colour palette' of a region (see the Culross case study in Chapter 7 and the Dunbar case study in Chapter 8), in which both places share a similar 'East Coast' vernacular style – reflecting the similar climate and underlying geology of the sites. Other characteristics of the style are small windows and steep roofs of 'pantiles' – red, curved tiles recalling the influence of the old sea trade with Holland – and with 'crowstep' gables, since with mediaeval technology it was difficult to cut sandstone on a diagonal. An alternative explanation is that planks of wood could be placed across the 'steps' enabling access for tile repairs etc., the historical uncertainty merely contributing further to the fascination of the tourist who takes time to 'stop and stare'.

Town form can also be 'read' and interpreted. It too reflects climate and the functional and cultural influences through trade and commerce. For example, the principal components of mediaeval towns remain in many tourist destinations – the market square, the tollbooth, the meandering 'organic' form of the streets (see the Edinburgh case study in Chapter 6). Later towns, from the 18th century on, reveal increasing affluence through a concern for amenity as in formally planned squares and woodland planting around the town. There may also be evidence of increasingly formal town planning, e.g. a new settlement adjacent to the original old town.

Photograph 5.2 *Modern architecture integrated with earlier styles*

Evidence of the 19th century may be visible in the products of Victorian technology, for example iron bridges, some protected by conservation legislation. From the early 20th century on there are signs in many towns and cities of the decline of traditional industries and evidence of the 'Modern Movement' (1930s) 'which brought to an end the age-old relationship between built form, the urban tradition and climate. Concrete, brick and plate-glass replaced traditional materials and town form changed from closely-knit and protective to open plan and windswept' (Edwards, 1986).

While 'modern architecture' is often criticised, it can be part of the spirit of place:

> Bring people together and they create a collective surplus of enjoyment; bring buildings together and they can give visual pleasure which none can give separately. [...] there is an art of *relationship* just as there is an art of architecture. Its purpose is to take all the elements that go to create the environment: buildings, trees, nature, water, traffic, advertisements and so on, and to weave them together in such a way that drama is released.
>
> (Cullen, 1971: 9–10)

By developing sensitivity to these relationships the destination manager can influence development proposals to the advantage of a neighbourhood important to both residents and tourists.

The influence of tourism itself is now part of the evolving pattern of many destinations. Tourism brought positive influences such as new jobs and income which permitted community continuity rather than the continuing decline of certain traditional industries and livelihoods which can continue in response to the contemporary desire for the conservation of old buildings and features. It is these characteristics that can be profitably and discretely interpreted for tourists giving them the deeper insights into the places that increasingly they seek. Tourism can also bring negative influences in the form of a demand for 'historic' images which perhaps never existed. Such kitsch can undermine the integrity of a place, although

177

with the powers that planning authorities have – as well as limited grant aid – 'authentic' restoration can often be achieved. (These ideas can be explored further at 'The Tat Gallery': *www.thetatgallery.com.*)

The role of 'heritage' conservation in tourism destinations

'Heritage' is a term which covers the best and, arguably, the worst aspects of conservation. While the word itself is old and well established it has acquired new connotations in recent years. It is used descriptively (or patriotically?) as in the titles of UK government departments and agencies such as English Heritage and Scottish Natural Heritage. It is also used ironically, in the context of 'the heritage industry', a term coined by the writer–historian, Hewison (1987), who argues that commercialisation by the tourism industry of something as important as a nation's heritage is a serious concern: 'Heritage means everything and it means nothing, and yet it has developed into a whole industry'. The related term 'culture' is also criticised on account of the connotations of elitism. Dictionary definitions of heritage are along the lines of 'what is or may be inherited'. In Britain this implies values, traditions and ideas over and above actual artefacts such as art works, historic buildings, machinery etc. The National Heritage Memorial Fund (GB) (1980) described heritage as:

> a representation of the development of aesthetic expression and a testimony to the role played by the nation in world history . . . also includes the great scenic areas, the fauna and the flora.

The United Nations has attempted to give internationally acceptable definitions of both cultural heritage and natural heritage (UN Convention concerning the Protection of the World Cultural and Natural Heritage, 1972 and 1975) (Burton, 1995: 108).

Heritage centres such as the Jorvik Centre in York – the first of its type in the UK – opened in 1984 (*www.jorvik-viking-centre.co.uk*) – and Vikingar! (*www.vikingar.co.uk*) in Largs (see Chapter 8) have gained in popularity. By comparison, museums have become regarded by some people as dull, old fashioned and lacking in excitement. Traditional crafts may also have suffered as cheap 'heritage souvenirs' are purchased by tourists instead of 'genuine articles', a cultural impact of tourism (*www.thetatgallery.com*).

'Heritage' seems to embrace all these currently favoured associations while 'heritage tourism' is tourism centred on what a place, a country, a continent or even the world has inherited, e.g. 'European heritage' or 'world heritage'. It includes historic buildings (from stately homes to 'ordinary' domestic architecture), works of art and craftsmanship, beautiful and or representative scenery and industrial artefacts. At the same time nostalgia for a bygone, former time has become popular, delivered by the tourism industry in the form of 'theme parks' and heritage trails.

Exercise

'Heritage' of the future

Is it conceivable that Disneyland Paris (*www.disneylandparis.com*) or a 1990s high-rise office block will be considered 'heritage' in 20 years' time?

Consider what aspects of the contemporary scene in your city/town/region will be regarded and cherished as 'heritage' in 20 years' time. How would you – as a destination manager – go about ensuring their protection meantime? What threats might you expect to meet?

Heritage attractions in the destination

Various categories of cultural heritage are now the basis for the tourism industry in widely diverse destinations – industrial heritage (The Union Canal, Edinburgh, *www.millenniumlink.org.uk*; Ironbridge, Shropshire, England, *www.iron-bridge.org.uk*); military heritage (Culloden in the Scottish Highlands, *www.nts.org.uk/culloden.html*); religious heritage (Lourdes, southern France, *www.lourdes-france.com*) etc. Despite the sometimes contentious nature of the term, much of the criticism targeted at it applies to tourism in general.

CASE STUDY

A new heritage and visitor centre as a 'gateway' to a destination

Dumfries and Galloway is an attractive, 'underdiscovered' region in south-west Scotland (*www.galloway.co.uk*; *www.dumgal.gov.uk*). While it lies close to the busy M4 motorway, the main tourist flows (from the south generally and the north of England in particular) are targeted on Edinburgh and Glasgow and the Highlands. It would take something very special to detract them into another destination. Beautiful rolling hills, peace and quiet, coastal scenery, market towns, history are not enough.

An opportunity
A village in the region may have the potential to supply the necessary 'detraction'. In the village is a redundant mill, now largely in ruins – a 'romantic ruin' – with strong industrial/historical associations. Moreover, the village is a 'conservation area', a formal status granted on account of its urban design and architecture and its historical associations. There is also an active and informed local community.

The context and the 'motivations' for development are complex. The local community desires 'appropriate' tourism development. At regional level the local authority wishes to encourage new employment opportunities and increased tourism could contribute both directly and indirectly to that objective. At the national level the tourist board and the countryside commission have complementary interests – encouraging tourist dispersal into less visited areas in accordance with national policy; and restoring a historic building while creating a new interpretive centre for the region as a whole.

The village has a small tourism industry. It is well established and based on return visits, but the main market is elderly and is not replacing itself. Local businesses would like to see more tourists, but in general they share with local residents the concern that developments should not be brash and intrusive on the life of the village. Young people would like more job opportunities and more 'life' in the village and have fewer 'reservations' about tourism development and the changes or impacts it might cause.

A feasibility study was conducted – a rapid overview of the main parameters, with limited detail and a focus on the factors determining viability. At this stage there was no direct community involvement – to avoid raising local hopes – as the study was required to be objective and might reveal there was no potential for cost-effective restoration and hence tourism development.

Key questions include:

1. Does the old mill and associated village present a range of heritage resources which lend themselves to interpretation and tourist interest?

2. What forms might this take?

3. What numbers and types of visitor might be attracted by these options – to the attraction itself, to the village and to the region?

4. How financially viable is each option and what are the possible sources of funding?

Objectives by which alternative development options might be evaluated are as follows:

1. Generate sufficient revenue to cover running costs (as a minimum).

2. Provide direct and indirect employment.

3. Provide benefits, minimise costs to local community.

4. Contribute to tourism development in region.

5. Provide an enjoyable experience attractive to the majority of visitors to region.

A market-led approach is prioritised. Primarily, it must determine the needs and wants of visitors in relation to how they can be met by the proposed centre. Second, (although this aspect is intimately related) conservation of the buildings, their surroundings and the sense of place must be achieved.

Interpretive themes
The criteria for interpretation drew on established guidelines (the Carnegie Interpret Britain Award and others (*www.heritage-interpretation.org.uk*)) and were: authenticity – drawn from the natural and cultural heritage resources of the region, validation by local community, community involvement (residential and business) integration into local goals; and adaptability to changing economic circumstances. Integration of local community interests and resources, tourism development and business were likely to be achieved by development. Moreover, local character and spirit of place could be enhanced:

> a small attractive town, with a distinctive history, set in beautiful countryside, with evidence of long interaction between nature and man [...] a cultural landscape.
>
> (Howie 1987)

This should be the foundation for tourism in the area.

Would increasing numbers of tourists visit this destination? What motivations are present and therefore what type of tourisms should be developed? Available statistics showed that 'small numbers, frequent return visits, above average spend' characterised the present situation. Local people suggested the development objective should be 'more of the same'. However, the local authority and a national countryside agency – which would be providing funding – questioned whether this were viable. Supported by consultancy research they asserted that the market was changing and that 'novel' developments might be required to attract the highly desirable, higher spending 'new tourist' (Poon, 1993) who seeks 'REAL tourism'. The focus should be on the 'new tourist', but the attraction must also have broad appeal to a wide audience. In other words, as well as authentic themes there must also be other facilities ... for profitability.

Resource appraisal

The resource appraisal determined that the Old Mill was indeed a 'romantic ruin' but not particularly special. It was in a good location – near to the town yet sufficiently far away from it to be 'another world' with, moreover, adequate space for the creation of car parking.

This blend of the authentic and the pragmatic was the basis for development recommendations. The mill area was not very visible – directional signposting would be required. Buildings would be restored and conserved. The ruins would be interpreted through an appropriate interpretive centre constructed in harmony with them while conserving the 'romance' of the site, its distinctiveness and its drama, notably the water features which brought industry to this location in the first place. 'A sense of stepping into an enclosed and different world' would be maintained.

The nearby town was itself of great significance to the regional destination as a whole. With the new attraction it should become a 'gateway' to the region (very important since a key policy objective is boosting tourism within the wider regional destination). The town is 'neat and orderly' since it originated as an early planned settlement and is therefore historically significant. The associated parkland/estate has historical associations with personalities 'both great and lowly'. The remains of the mill lade and the river connect the site to the wider regional landscape.

These are pieces in a jigsaw relating to the early industrial origins of the town. Heritage interpretation would create potential new visitor experiences – transforming 'a casual, disinterested stroll down the main street' into 'an intriguing and rewarding trail of discovery/a treasure hunt'. The wider landscape is an area of hill, woodland and rocky shore protected by several conservation designations including national scenic area and site of special scientific interest, having both protective and potentially promotional value. There were opportunities for recreational activities and developments based on the historic and literary associations.

From a policy perspective, a key question was: what can development of this site contribute to the principal objective – economic development of the region through encouraging visitors to stay longer; how can the existing pattern of day visits be converted to one of staying tourists? The newly developed attraction should complement existing attractions in the area and the wider region – the Tourist Information Centre in the town and other information centres in the region, nature trails and hiking trails managed by the Forestry Commission and cafes, pubs, shops in the adjacent village. Competing attractions should be avoided.

It was concluded that the early proposal of the local community 'draws its specification too narrowly from the industrial heritage of the mill. Therefore, we recommend [...] that neither a "museum" nor a "heritage centre" as defined is the appropriate role model, though elements of each are relevant. The ability to adapt to changing needs is essential. Themes, expanded themes and further developments are essential to contribute to continuous change while respecting "unchanging" core values'. This would meet the objectives of both the town and the wider regional destination as recognised by the client public sector agencies.

This case study has illustrates the boundary between the plan for a specific development and the wider 'policy context' within which planning operates. The remainder of this chapter explores the latter that important area.

POLICY MAKING AND THE DESTINATION

Policy making takes place in both tourist destinations and in private businesses, i.e. policy making is both a public and a private sector activity. At the level of the tourism operation – a heritage centre or a hotel – it is concerned with the business and its internal affairs, primarily its economic viability. This often fails to recognise that the business's plans and subsequent operations have effects on the wider community; and that the effects on the wider community in turn affect the success of the business:

> Public sector policy objectives which may be sought from tourism include the creation of income and wealth; job creation; maintaining and improving the image of the area, its environment and the quality of life; maintaining and improving links within and between nations; and contributing to the nation's balance of payments position.
>
> (Hartley and Cooper, 1993)

How can these wider objectives be integrated with the essentially 'self-centred' objectives of a private business? To answer this question requires an understanding of the nature of policies and policy making.

Policy and policy making

It is useful to begin with a caution. While arguing the case *for* tourism policy making, Hall and Jenkins (1995) wrote: 'Policy making is a value laden and political activity [...] too often we are passive in our acceptance of government activity in tourism [...] The role that power, values and interests play in tourism policy and research requires far greater attention than has hitherto been the case.' In this context, they question even everyday words like 'facts'. 'Facts are open to question according to one's values, position and power and can be interpreted and used accordingly.' Policy is no more and no less than 'a set of statements, based on relevant considerations'.

Goldsmith (1980: 22) asserted that public policies 'include all actions of governments, not just stated intentions [...] as well as an understanding of why governments sometimes chose to do nothing about a particular question'. Hall and Jenkins (1995: 5) give an insight into that important 'why':

> Policy is [...] a consequence of the political environment, values and ideologies, the distribution of power, institutional frameworks, and of decision-making processes [...] public policies stem from governments or public authorities. A policy is deemed a public policy not by virtue of its impact on the public, but by virtue of its source.
>
> (Hall and Jenkins, 1995: 5)

Policy making is therefore an important activity but it should not be regarded as impartial and objective (as 'planning' purports to be); rather, it reflects values. Public policies are experienced by citizens and tourism entrepreneurs alike as regulations, rules and guidelines prepared by politicians – who have been elected to positions of authority by the public in order to make such decisions – for society to adhere to and operate by. Hill (1997: 377) however, expresses concern about the reasons behind policymaking: 'It is widely established that politicians do not work in a systematic way from ideology to policy but are rather engaged in calculations relating ideology to electoral considerations to anticipated problems with current policies to demands from pressure groups'.

It is important for the destination manager – or the concerned citizen – to be able to distinguish 'values' from 'facts'. For example, in challenging (or supporting) proposed developments within a destination, it may be useful to identify the 'type' of policy-making process that is operating in the destination, since some types give more weight to 'values' than to 'facts'.

Henry (1993: 3) describes four categories of policy: *distributive* policies, which benefit all or most citizens indiscriminately; *redistributive* policies which generally favour a segment of the population at the cost of other segments; *constituent* policies, which define procedures in a democratic society such as election laws; and *regulative* policies, designed to control the behaviour of members of the community. Tourism policies can take the form of three of these categories. It can be distributive, e.g. implementing a policy that benefits the whole country or region; it can be redistributive, e.g. favouring one region over another to reduce economic disparity between them or to create economic regeneration where one region's traditional industry base has declined, or it can be regulative, e.g. restricting activities that are not environmentally favourable.

The above categorisation of policy types is useful – it reveals the differing fundamental objectives to be met by prevailing policies. Understanding of that is helpful to the destination manager in seeing how his/her objectives match or conflict with them.

As noted previously, policy making takes place in both the public and the private sectors. The courses of action and general directions to achieve specific objectives can be at odds, both setting their own preferred parameters within which actions can take place. The private sector (small businesses to large corporations) has the fundamental objective of maximising returns on investments and is thus generally characterised as opportunistic, individualistic, speculative and willing to take risks. The public sector (central and local government and various agencies) has the more complex (or as critics would say, 'woolly') objective, 'the public interest', focusing on welfare benefit maximisation while minimising adverse effects or disturbances, using such means as regulating behaviour, raising or lowering taxes and influencing the distribution of benefits. The policies of the public sector are characteristically cautious (although they can also be creative), development-oriented and generally strategic or coordinating. They are subject to ideological influence, most obviously when there is a change of government, and are authoritative, meaning they are backed by an act or a regulation (*www.hmso.gov.uk/acts.htm*). They are generally program related, for example transportation, education or revenue generation and are 'universal', meaning that they apply to the whole country or region. They can be oriented towards conflict resolution and may be motivated (if covertly) by compassion, as in social policies.

Despite the high ideals of public policy, in a democratic society they are generally put into practice on a basis of gradual, small-scale change. At the end of the day they are based on value judgements emanating from a specific political party that must win continuing support from the electorate. The authority may weaken in its total commitment to the original stance when it detects that the electorate is tiring of its clearly ideology-based policies or when it is has difficulties with policy conflicts, e.g. between tourism and transportation since the 'theoretical to real-world' translation may prove difficult. There may be short-term difficulties that interfere with long-term objectives or costs of critical services may have risen. Sooner or later a majority of the electorate will change its values or will simply 'want a change' and at the next election will vote for another party. The public sector cannot maintain continuity; it is at the mercy of the voters and the electoral cycle. This may be seen as a problem of the democratic system or its great strength.

Policy models

Various 'models' have been developed to guide and to explain the approaches taken to policy making. Thomas Dye, an American political scientist, wrote a 'classic' textbook on public policy in which he discussed the pros and cons of various types of policy model: 'Most public policies are a combination of rational planning, incrementalism, competition among groups, elite preferences, systematic forces, political processes and institutional influences' (Dye, 1987: xii).

The simplest 'model' a government might adopt is encapsulated in the saying: 'You can't please all the people all the time, so we'll do things our way, to the best of our abilities and hope for the best'.

But public policy formulation is, by its nature, complex and that simple ideal is inadequate. Models are abstractions/simplifications of the 'real world'. A number of policy models exist and it is useful for people in general and destination managers in particular to be aware of their respective strengths and weaknesses. Models have several purposes: to simplify the (complex) subject matter; to identify the main aspects of a problem; to aid understanding; to chart linkages between elements and outcomes. There are three main categories of policy model: 'apolitical', 'political' and 'hybrid'.

Apolitical model

'Apolitical' models aim to address the problems to be solved, unhindered by the 'complications' introduced by politics. They can then more readily reveal the problems to be addressed and systematically and comprehensively gather information to try to understand the needs and wants of society. Solutions can then be generated and possible courses of action evaluated. While they can achieve comprehensive information inputs of society's needs and wants and so profess to offer the 'best' solutions for achievement of these ends, their weakness is their intrinsic detachment from 'political realities' and their consequent idealistic assumptions. Because of this performance standards are almost impossible to achieve. They are also highly resource demanding and unlikely to be fully achieving in the 'real world'. There are three types of apolitical model: the *rational*, the *incremental* and the *systems* model.

The *rational* model aims for comprehensive inputs of information on society's needs and wants and the 'best' solutions. Its weaknesses are its idealistic assumptions which are unlikely to be fully achieved in the real world and the fact that it is highly resource demanding. The *incremental* model tries to achieve its goals through a step-by-step approach with attendant fine-tuning of the methodology and frequent reviews of findings, although its weakness is that it cannot cope with major policy change. It is criticised as 'blundering through', regardless of changing circumstances. The *systems* model has attracted a lot of attention since the availability of the modern and cheap PC/personal computer with its highly efficient data-handling abilities which greatly assist the systematic, scientific and methodical approach. The model considers:

- 'inputs' (demand, political support, etc.)

- the 'conversion process' (i.e. the political system)

- 'outputs' (i.e. recommendations).

It is limited largely by the people operating it and the political environment.

Political models

There are three types of 'political' model: the *elite*, the *group* and the *institutional*. They are all heavily influenced by 'narrow' sectoral interests (the tourism lobby is one!) and ideological values, sometimes at the expense of the 'public good'. Political models do, however, reflect the nature of society – essentially an unequal division of power and influence.

The *elite* model is favoured by those who consider that policy making should be in the hands of a knowledgeable and powerful elite body that would determine policy direction (generally, but covertly, by manipulation). Its supporters would assert that 'the masses' are apathetic and are quite happy to delegate to 'the elite', their 'betters', responsibility for major policy decisions. It views society as hierarchical, with an 'elite' at the top of the 'pyramid' and 'the masses' at the bottom (see Figure 5.7).

The main weakness of the elite model is that the elite may be unrepresentative of society as a whole and may not be accountable – the policies they make may not be in accord with the values of the 'public interest' or society. The elite or the 'power brokers' may be, for example, 'financiers', 'the media', 'entrepreneurs', 'trade

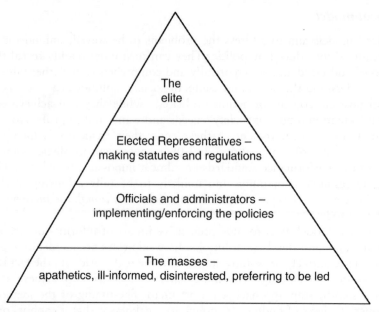

Figure 5.7 *Elite model of policy making*

union bosses' or 'landowners'. In other words, there can be an elite of 'the Left' or of 'the Right' in politics.

The second political model is the *group* model. Its strengths are based on the belief that 'the community' acts best if it forms into groups, creating coalitions as required, each acting to achieve outcomes favourable to its own interests. The group is viewed as a link between government and 'the masses' and policies are formed at the point of balance between groups. The model's weaknesses are alleged to lie in the common knowledge that well-informed and resourced groups (or organisations) tend to have greater influence than their numbers justify – the 'public interest' may be espoused but in reality it is the interests of the persuasive minority that are being 'pushed' and the 'group' may not be representative of the wider 'society'. Also, group dynamics change over time as activists come and go, leading to unstable political agendas.

Exercise

The role of groups: 'environmentalists'

With reference to the exercise on p. 172, concerning the public meeting to discuss a planning application for a waterside restaurant and floating barge, consider the role of the environmentalist/conservation groups who attended the meeting and how representative of 'wider society' their position was.

Which of the following do you agree with? Give your reasons.

1. The statements they made are not representative of wider society, the group had an idealistic and impractical attitude towards a worthwhile development which should be encouraged.

2. Their views were far sighted and recognise the wider realities. Green spaces

are essential for a healthy urban environment and should not be sacrificed for the short-term economic gain of a private company, despite the minor 'improvements to local amenity' (?) that were on offer.

The *institutional* model is the 'classic' policy model. It embraces a process where public policy is arrived at through a series of logical steps: Policy is proposed → adopted → legitimised (e.g. by statute) → universal (or targeted) → implemented → enforced.

Policies therefore need the support and the structure of the institutions of government. The weakness of the institutional model is that it is not apolitical, being operated by a government of a particular ideology which is inevitably susceptible to personalities and to persuasion by groups and elites. However, the safeguard is the public service, although critics argue that civil servants and officials can be 'politicised' so removing the safeguard.

Hybrid models

There are several types of 'hybrid' models. They range widely, from those having a basis in rationalism to those based in incrementalism, all with the shared weakness of tending to be more political than apolitical. Examples are the *extra-rational*, the *satisficing*, the *mixed scanning* and the *management by objectives* models. In the 'real world' most models are to a degree hybrid in that they contain elements of various other models, purpose designed for a particular policy context.

In the *extra-rational* model, 'experience' is added to the attributes of the rational model. Experience modifies idealism, so the model is less dependent on 'perfection'. But is this any more than policy making by intuition? Does the well-meaning, experienced policy maker always serve the public interest? The *satisficing* model aims at meeting basic objectives at the minimum threshold. It uses rational methods and does not pretend to be comprehensive or seeking the 'best solution' – only what are satisfactory means for achieving policy goals. The *mixed-scanning* model also seeks 'acceptable' means i.e. policies which adequately address the problems in the way of achieving the goals. It uses a repeating process of:

- rationally breaking down ('disaggregating') complex problems or goals into simpler components
- looking for ('scanning') partial solutions to the components of the problems
- combining the partial solutions (reformulation)
- reaching progressive partial solutions.

The *management by objectives* model is based on modern management practices. Results are achieved through matching the action necessary with the resources needed to achieve desired outcomes.

A criticism of the satisficing, mixed-scanning and management by objectives models is that they are open to manipulation to achieve a narrow rather than a comprehensive outcome.

No single policy model is 'perfect' – however, the systems model is more attuned to the 'real world' than most for a number of reasons. It is based on a rational

1. Inputs – sources of demand and the structure of political support

2. The political system – the conversion process, where manipulation of inputs takes place, producing policy positions

3. Outputs – a finely-tuned end product, or a specific policy with linkages to other policy areas plus a monitoring and review

Figure 5.8 *The systems model*
Source: Dye, 1987

process involving logical progression, feedback loops, monitoring and inter-relationships of components and is responsive to sets of factors outside the expected policy framework.

The systems model usually involves three interrelated and sequential phases (see Figure 5.8).

Positive characteristics of the systems model include:

- an open structure – all components are open to influence by all others

- recognition of the influence of various forces: elites, pressure groups, incremental change, institutions, etc.

- every component is interconnected in an evolving decisions-forming network but one which does not aim at producing 'blueprints'

- government has clear responsibility for implementation of public policy.

Whatever the policy model in vogue at a particular time and under a specific administration, in a democratic society the voting system allows citizens to exercise their right to make changes and it is on the basis of the expressed policies of rival political parties that votes are cast and parties rise or fall. Public policy towards an activity or industry (and tourism is no exception) changes with time and with public opinion and since it is 'the public' that elects governments to power – at least indemocratic societies – politicians must pay close attention to changing public attitudes.

Henry (1993: 24) gives a striking historical example of historical change in attitudes towards leisure (and tourism) in the UK. In the early 19th century the emphasis in the state's role in leisure was the suppression of 'disruptive' leisure forms, while the commercial sector – small-scale entrepreneurs notably publicans – were replacing the traditional squires as patrons of popular recreations. By the late 19th century a less laissez-faire approach to social and economic policy was having its influence and there was increasing emphasis on 'improving' forms of leisure activity through state support for sports stadia, music halls, railways. The early to mid-20th century saw the beginnings of the 'welfare state' in the form of 'increasing recognition of leisure as a legitimate concern of government in its ownright' (Henry, 1993: 24). This trend was to mature as leisure was added to the portfolio of welfare services – it became 'one of the community's everyday needs' – and to continue until the late 1970s, when a radical government of the right was elected in Britain committed to 'new economic realism' and the restructuring of the welfare state. By the late 1980s and into the 1990s the 'marketisation of service provision' (Henry, 1993: 24) and the use of leisure and tourism as a tool for economic rather than social regeneration had transformed attitudes towards the role of government in leisure and tourism. In the late 1990s and into the early 21st century, centre-left government in Britain has not significantly changed this trend (see Figure 5.9).

1780–1840	Suppression of popular leisures
1840–1900	Erosion of laissez-faire approach to social/economic policy
1900–1939	Social reforms – laying foundations of the welfare state
1944–1976	Growth and maturing of welfare state
1976–1984	'New economic realism' – restructuring of the welfare state; 'Thatcherism'
1985–1990s	State flexibilisation and disinvestments
1990s on	More leisure time ... or less? Impact of new technology

Figure 5.9 *Brief history of development of leisure sectors*
(*Source*: Adapted from Henry, 1993)

Exercise

Leisure trends and policy changes

Consider the effects on and implications for tourism of the leisure trends and policy changes of the 1990s onwards. Examine the most recent policy changes for your city/region/country and consider their effects on tourism.

What is tourism policy?

Hall and Jenkins (1995: 8) define tourism policy simply as 'whatever governments choose to do or not to do with respect to tourism'. Meethan (1998) writes 'in terms of policy, there are a variety of levels to be considered – European, national, regional, county and district. What they all share in common is a realization that tourism needs to be incorporated into broader strategies of planning and economic development'. Amoah and Baum (1997) offer a more explicit explanation of tourism policy. Tourism policy can be seen as a set of guidelines that will help identify specific actions and objectives to be taken to meet the needs of a given area. They are referring to tourism policies in smaller areas, rather than national policies. They add that policy is not only a product, but also a process.

Tourism policy is, therefore, policies aimed at the tourism industry, with the objective of guiding, directing or even coaxing the industry to make choices and develop in a direction that will be beneficial to the area, region or nation for which the policy is intended. The benefits of a good tourism policy can be numerous:

urban regeneration, reduced unemployment, economic regeneration, sustainable development, conservation of culture and nature and encouraging people to stay in rural areas rather than creating urban 'megaplexes', which leaves the countryside desolate (Baum, 1994).

Who makes policies?

It may appear from the preceding arguments that government or politicians are the sole 'authors' of policies. In a sense they are, because it is usually politicians who, in the end, decide what should be written in the policies. But preceding the final policy is a long and often complex process. There are many 'stakeholders' who influence and advise politicians when making a policy and sometimes they cooperate with politicians in making the policies. When creating a new national environmental policy for example, an approach might be to establish a committee to ensure that the interests of a broad range of people are represented. The members of the committee could represent government, parliament, administrative sectors, organisations of business and industry, trades unions, various interest groups, non-governmental organisations (NGOs), citizens' organisations and the news media. The range of representation would make it difficult to agree on a strategy that would please everybody, but at least it ensures that no single group would make decisions that would influence a whole nation.

CASE STUDY

Cambridge Tourism Strategy, 2001–2006

This *policy strategy* may be compared and contrasted with a *local plan* – for convenience, that for Edinburgh discussed earlier in this chapter. Both cities are major international destinations and historical university cities where tourism is an important element in the economy and an important contributor to the cosmopolitan feel of the cities. While the local plan is concerned with actual, site-specific proposals and developments, a strategy (in this case a tourism strategy) is a *policy* document and aims to provide *broad guidance* on:

decisions, policies and work programmes of the Tourist Information Centre and all other sections of the Council involved with tourism. The tourism service is financially supported by the City Council but is not the only player influencing tourism. This is a *strategy* to be delivered through *partnerships*. It will act as a *catalyst* for initiatives and projects working in partnership with the County Council, South Cambridgeshire, the East of England Tourist Board and the tourism industry.

The strategy coves a *5-year period* and is based on a *vision for tourism* in the city – *discussed with all* involved in tourism in the city – and giving due regard to issues of *sustainability*. It relates tourism in the city of Cambridge to the *national* UK context, as described in 'Tomorrow's Tourism', the national tourism strategy, published by the Department of Culture, Media and Sport in

1999 (*www.culture.org.uk*). It also relates Cambridge tourism to the regional context, the East of England, assessed in 'The Strategy for Developing Tourism in the East of England 2000–2010', published in 2000 by the East of England Tourist Board. This sets out a strategic framework for action in the region, based on five key principles:

- partnership

- quality

- sustainability

- competitiveness

- accessibility.

Typically, a strategy document addresses broad themes (again, in contrast to a *plan* which is more concerned with specifics). In Cambridge these are:

- providing the right framework within which tourism can flourish

- developing and spreading quality

- encouraging the 'wise growth' of tourism.

The strategy includes a *key message*: 'tourism is important to the economy and needs to remain attractive and competitive'; and a *key pledge*: 'to increase access to tourism for all, including those with disabilities and the elderly'.

In summary, the Cambridge document is a model of its type, identifying broad, strategic issues and objectives at city level, relating this 'up' to regional and national tourism strategies and 'down' to local planning issues 'on the ground' in the city. While concerned with tourism strategy, it acknowledges that it must feed into other strategies, for example the 'County Cultural Strategy' and the 'Community Strategy' which will set the long-term goals for the future of Cambridge.

POLITICS AND IDEOLOGY – THE ROLE OF GOVERNMENT

In the 1980s – the period of 'Thatcherism' in the UK (after the Prime Minister of the time, Margaret Thatcher) – the Conservative government's policy approach was to reduce the power of government to 'interfere' with the workings of a free, market economy, withdrawing as much as possible and leaving accountability to the industry and market forces. Expressions of this were deregulation, privatisation and elimination of tax incentives.

In 1997 a Labour government was elected to power – a 'centre-left' government inclined to more attention to social equity in their values and ideologies – and they incorporated into their objectives a shift towards providing funding for regeneration and development with a stronger role for community consultation and involvement. Their strategies of regeneration came through monitoring local services including employment, housing, crime prevention and education (Foley and Martin, 2000).

Tourism, policy and politics

There has been a paucity of policy making for tourism, notably in the UK. Britain has a 'mixed economy' where 'the public interest' or 'society' is fostered and protected by the government from the 'excesses' of the private sector or 'business interests' (notably 'big business' and latterly 'international capitalism') while the government is also dedicated to supporting 'business' and 'enterprise'. Arguably, this has led to a less than wholehearted commitment to regulation or 'interference' in development than has been the case in some other countries. In France, for example, democratically elected governments have tended to take a much less inhibited approach to 'centrally controlled' development. As described in Chapter 9, the Languedoc-Roussillon region was the subject of large-scale tourism planning and development where the national government prepared the grand plan and retained firm regulatory power over private development within the scheme. Within different democratic countries there can be strong differences in approach to the 'public–private' power balance and different interpretations of the role of each 'sector'. The 'balance' between private and public control takes its most extreme form in countries with totalitarian regimes, for example the former USSR, where a Communist government had total control and the private sector was essentially non-existent. Extreme 'left-wing' regimes are matched by extreme right-wing governments in their exercise of power. Perhaps surprisingly in such 'intolerant' regimes, tourism was a major element of concern to governments, although there were distinctive characteristics. In the Soviet countries citizens were rewarded with holidays. Policy dictated, however, that citizens would travel only within their own or other Soviet countries. This policy avoided the adverse economic impact of the 'leakage' of wealth from the Soviet bloc through international tourism and the adverse social impact of attitudes arising from glimpses of life in 'free countries'. Outsiders (inbound tourists) were not permitted into the country for the same reason. An example of tourism's impact in right-wing countries is provided by the beginnings of mass tourism in Franco's Spain in the 1950s. While the dictator enthusiastically supported tourism development for its potential to bring in foreign capital, he overlooked the fact that the comparative affluence and liberal morals of these tourists would stir discontent among his own people, eventually contributing to the downfall of his regime and the return of Spain to democratic Europe.

One of the most dramatic examples of changing political attitudes towards tourism is that of modern China. China is a developing country with a Socialist economy and a government that has been actively addressing tourism development through a variety of policy initiatives (Zhang, Chong and Ap, 1999: 471–5). The country's policies towards tourism changed with the ideological premise that tourism should be developed in the socialist market economy model, resulting in initiatives to open tourism further to foreign investors and allow overseas travel for Chinese nationals. These measures will affect the cultural and social environment within China increasingly as it is forecast by the World Tourism Organization (WTO) that the country will be the world's number one tourism destination by the year 2020, surpassing even the United States (Luhrman, 1998: 13). Public policy initiatives do, however, remain firmly in the control of the government.

By contrast, the United States is firmly committed to the capitalist ethos, distinctly more so than the UK, and it is the market that dictates policy on many issues. The United States Travel and Tourism Administration (USTTA), the main government agency with responsibilities for tourism policy, was a victim of disagreement between politicians and industry leaders and was closed in 1996. Tourism is very important to the domestic economy, 'yet the industry's size does not translate into a strong tourism policy' (Brewton and Withiam, 1998: 51). This is partly because US policy makers have always considered the domestic market the most important so there has been less pressure to develop the international tourist market, as most countries do. The closure of the USTTA is also notable – in most countries governments make great efforts to encourage collaboration with other sectors: 'US tourism has been characterised by weak and limited authority, little regulatory ability and unreliable government support. [...] Some thirty three other nations, including Cyprus and Indonesia, put more money toward international tourism than does the United States' (Brewton and Withiam, 1998: 54).

Within the European Union governments are generally strongly supportive of tourism, although there are distinctly different national tourism policy objectives reflecting both economic and cultural factors. In Austria the focus of tourism policy is on earning 'hard currency'; France has eight priorities and has adopted a policy of restricting the use of credit cards overseas by non-business travellers (Brewton and Withiam, 1998: 56), perhaps a small incentive to its citizens to holiday within France.

Tourism has been regarded for most of its history as a non-damaging and entirely beneficial industry. As discussed in Chapter 2, it is only within the last 20 years or so that awareness of the full implications of the economic, social and environmental consequences of tourism have become clear resulting in the industry now being subject to a degree of public policy influence. Today, in most countries with a highly developed tourism industry, there is some control through a range of approaches. Compliance with policies can be enforced or 'encouraged'. There is 'control' by regulations and legislation, penalties for non-compliance with these and incentives for compliance. Government has subtle influence over the industry through use of the media. Most powerful of all, government can create new policies that will reflect its own political 'shade'.

Despite this apparent power, governments in mixed economies are limited in their exercise of power through policy making. Public opinion is a powerful force, itself influenced by corporations through advertising and by the media which in turn influence government. It might be asked: 'Are the public and the private sectors in competition, or are they complementary to each other?' Another question is: 'Is the public sector "less efficient" than the private sector?' It may seem so at times. For example, would-be developers frequently complain about the length of time they must wait for planning permission for a development that they consider to be uncontroversial and capable only of bringing great benefit to an entire neighbourhood of a city or a whole region. Although overly simplistic, it is largely true to say that in the interests of the public, government must pursue a wide range of policy objectives – social and environmental as well as economic – while the private sector 'merely' seeks profitability. In a mixed economy the overall goal must be complementarity between public and private interests.

ROLE OF THE PUBLIC SECTOR IN TOURISM

Policy issues in Britain in the 1990s, in a context of radical right of centre politics, centred around the 'privatisation' of whatever functions of central and local government could be taken out of the public sector. There was much debate concerning how far this process could go in defining 'the minimum, essential, core responsibility of government'. Remaining public services that could not be 'privatised' would no longer be subsidised: rather they would be brought into the realm of 'market forces'. They would be subject to 'compulsory competitive tendering', meaning they would have to bid to maintain 'ownership' of a service against any other interested parties, so ensuring that the 'customer' received the most cost-effective deal. 'Intervention' in this 'free market' would not be permitted except in very special circumstances.

There are instances where the alleged 'inefficiency' of the public sector is a fair criticism. The 'protectionism' of inefficiency – whether in the collection of refuse or the delivery of the highest standards of customer care in a city's tourist information office – is unacceptable. However, many services to the public are justifiably 'protected' from the marketplace where the 'lowest bidder' wins the contract. Deeper questions must be asked. For example, consider the following.

How does an 'independent' bus operator survive while charging very low fares? Maybe because it operates on only the most 'profitable' routes. The public sector may be operating a full service on a wide range of routes, including 'unprofitable' rural routes and running a 'night service' for only small numbers of users. This is possible because the 'expensive' fares subsidise these 'unprofitable' but arguably 'essential' public services. An extrapolation of this scenario might see the public bus service withdrawn and the private sector remaining as the sole provider. In the absence of competition, the private operator might then end the low price regime and raise all fares to 'economic' levels, perhaps higher than those charged by the public service.

How is a museum/interpretive centre able to operate with no admission charge? The local authority that 'owns' it is able to transfer funds to it from its other income-generating services, on the 'ideological' assertion that museums 'should be' free of charge – a 'public service'.

The objective of sustainable tourism raises further the question of the nature of public services and the role of government. 'Limits to development' as indicated by measures of the carrying capacity of certain locations may require enforcement of 'unpopular' policies e.g. the restriction of hours of operation of certain businesses, 'cushioned' perhaps by financial compensation given to the private operators 'hit' by this. By the same taken, from the private operator's perspective, it may seem grossly unfair that he/she should have to suffer any interference with the operation of the business.

Exercise

Interference?

List other examples of government/local authority 'interference' in the activities of private tourism businesses. From both perspectives list arguments for and against these restrictions.

At the scale of an industry as a whole, only the public sector in the form of government can create and enforce policies. A striking example is the commitment to tourism. The tourism 'balance of payments' is the difference between the income to the country generated by inbound tourism (from other countries) and the money 'lost' through citizens of that country taking their holidays and business trips overseas. In many countries this simple measure reveals a 'tourism deficit', for example in the UK this worsened in recent years, while at the same time tourism in the UK was considered a 'growth industry' (NEDC, 1992). The arguments for government support for tourism – expressed in policy form and in various packages of financial encouragement for the industry – are complex and extend beyond tourism itself. For example, governments and local authorities continue to stimulate tourism in areas where 'traditional' or former industries have declined when it may be many years before that investment will be 'justified' in money terms. Social benefits – in the form of new jobs – are generally one of the reasons for such action. Environmental improvement of the run-down industrial area is a further common reason – it is a catalyst for action, a clearly visible sign that 'something positive' is happening in the area and is a recognised 'green flag' to private sector investors to get involved. The broad, undisputed view is that controlled development is beneficial to a quality tourism industry.

WHO SHOULD BE IN CHARGE OF TOURISM?

That government *should* be involved in tourism is acknowledged in most countries. 'Where' that involvement should be located – i.e. in which government department – is subject to changing attitudes towards the industry and consequently the tourism policies that are formulated for it. In the UK for example, responsibility for tourism policy was part of the portfolio of a parliamentary under-secretary in the Department of Employment. In 1992 it was transferred to the new Department of National Heritage, a broad cultural/media department, where a minister of cabinet rank was given responsibility for tourism and where the interlinking and often interdependent interests of tourism, the arts and sport were clear. Currently, the national strategy for tourism is part of the remit of the Department for Culture, Media and Sport (*www.culture.gov.uk*) that is responsible for museums, galleries, libraries, heritage, the arts, sport, education, broadcasting, media and tourism, as well as the Millennium Dome and the National Lottery. The president of the (UK) Tourism Society (*www.tourismsociety.org*) has voiced the (personal) opinion that the Department of Trade and Industry (*www.dti.gov.uk*) would be a more useful location (Thurso, 2002) (see Figure 5.10).

Exercise

The benefits of tourism development

What other benefits can arise from tourism development? Add your suggestions to Figure 5.10.

Economic
Job creation
Taxation of businesses
Economic regeneration
General contribution to wealth

Social
Many tourist facilities can also be used by the local community
Local pride can be boosted
Diversity can be increased

Environmental
Quality environment attracts investment
A successful tourism industry depends on quality in the built and natural environments
General sense of well-being

Interrelationships
Tourism can contribute to both business and environmental objectives.
Creation of favourable conditions attracts private sector investment
Visible success contributes to government popularity (political gain)
Sustainable development is encouraged

Figure 5.10 *Tourism development – benefits created and government motives*

Role of government incentives

'The underlying motive of government support for tourism is political gain' (Ward, 1989). If this is so then tourism will be favourably supported by government by policy and other instruments which positively discriminate in favour of developments which are 'in tune' with the governments ideological stance. The means employed will be both direct and indirect, e.g. the removal of barriers in the way of a private developer and reducing the appeal to the private sector of alternative (but less favoured) projects.

TOURISM ORGANISATION

Central government

As discussed earlier, 'central government' is the highest or national level of government and has a key responsibility for policy making. Central government departments or agencies are concerned with ensuring these policies are reflected in actual development 'on the ground', whether that development is carried out by the agencies themselves, by private developers or, increasingly, by 'public-private partnerships' (PPPs), where the agency retains overall control through a share of the funding, while the implementation and in some cases the subsequent operation of a development is by a private company.

Also at national level are various semi-independent bodies known as quangos (quasi autonomous non-governmental organisations). Examples are the national tourist boards within the UK: the Scottish Tourist Board/'VisitScotland' (*www.visitscotland.com*); the English Tourist Board (*www.travelengland.org.uk*); the Wales Tourist Board (*www.wtbonline.gov.uk/start/en*); and the Northern Ireland Tourist Board (*www.interknowledge.com/northern-ireland/default.htm*) and other organisations with relevance to tourism such as the Forestry Commission (*www.forestry.gov.uk*); Scottish Natural Heritage (*www.snh.org.uk*), English Nature (*www.english-nature.org.uk*) and others. These quangos are funded by central government, but are independent while accountable in how they pursue their objectives. Their objectives are derived from central government policy.

Local government

Local government is organised at several levels. There may be a 'regional' council, a 'district' council and a 'community' council, each concerned with a distinct 'level' of activity and having specific responsibilities or 'functions'. In Britain, for example, 'housing' has been generally a 'district'-level function, while transport was a 'regional' matter. The community level generally had no 'powers', although it had a right to be informed and listened to. In the regional and district councils are 'councillors' (elected members) and 'officials' (professional and other employees), the latter carrying out the official business of the council, which had been agreed by the elected councillors as representatives of the people of the area. In this way, through its planning department, a local authority has direct responsibility for the control of landuse and the directing of landuses to the most appropriate locations – the councillors making the final decisions while acting on the recommendations and advice of the professional staff.

International level

Above national level there is a hierarchy of levels of organisation, many of which have tourism responsibility. The degree of authority held does not, however, increase with level and many of these bodies, though prestigious, are largely advisory.

At the 'continental' level, the European Union is probably the most familiar. Its 'Directorate General' or DG XXIII (*http://europa.eu.int/comm/enterprise/index_-en.htm*) has a significant tourism remit. European Union 'directives' have major influences on the tourism industry of all 15 countries (in 2002) including, for example, issues such as the minimum wage of employees, environmental legislation and support for agriculture. Harmonising these policies through the Union, while maintaining national and regional distinctiveness or 'spirit of place' is a major challenge (see Figure 5.11).

Exercise

The functions of tourism organisations

Find the URLs/web addresses of the national and local organisations indicated in Figure 5.11 in general terms for your area. Then visit the websites and note the functions of each organisation.

World Tourism Organisation (*www.world-tourism.org*)
United Nations (*www.un.org*)
Organisation for Economic Co-operation and Development (*www.oecd.org*)
National Tourist Board
Local or area tourist board
Local authority (tourism or other named department)
Local enterprise company
Local traders/business organisation

Figure 5.11 *Organisations concerned with tourism at global to local level*

TOURISM DESTINATIONS AND TRAVELLER HEALTH

Many diverse issues concern the tourism industry at a global level – both directly and indirectly. Tourist health is an example of the former. Is it possible to establish an internationally agreed level of 'freedom from unacceptable levels of health risk' for the tourist, wherever he/she travels throughout the world? This seems scarcely credible when standards of health for the citizens of countries throughout the world remain extremely wide. Tourist safety presents similar, perhaps even greater, challenges when it is considered that the tourist may be the deliberate target of violence in a robbery or, through the killing, kidnapping or injury of a tourist by a 'terrorist' group since this is likely to have a severely detrimental effect on the next few years' inbound tourism and, consequently, a major blow may be struck against a government.

Foreign aid and the elimination of foreign economic exploitation are other 'global' issues that indirectly affect the tourism industry and that require an international approach. International organisations have, at this time, a largely advisory role and little real power to enforce that advice, far less turn it into binding policies. Perhaps the best known global organisation, the United Nations (*www.un.org*), has drawn up the 'Charter of Human Rights' and numerous 'declarations', although even these cannot be enforced. The World Tourism Organization (WTO) (*www.world-tourism.org*) has given the industry the Tourism Bill of Rights and Tourist Code, the Acapulco Document and the ManilaDeclaration on World Tourism, although again with a 'moral authority' rather than real powers of enforcement. The Organisation for Economic Co-operation and Development (OECD) (*www.oecd.org*) is an international organisation helping governments tackle the economic, social and governance challenges of a globalised economy.

Some of these issues are discussed further in Chapter 11, in the context of the longer term prospects for tourism. Governments tend to have as their planning/policy 'horizon' the date of the next election, i.e. five years or so. There is growing need for a longer term and truly international perspective in the context of the global economy and a truly global industry, tourism.

Exercise

The effects of tourism development

Consider the effects of a proposed (or potential) tourism development in your village/town/city/region bearing in mind the likely range of 'interested parties'.
Categorise these effects as:

* economic
* social/cultural
* environmental.

Explain which are beneficial/harmful from the destination perspective.

Exercise

Tourism development at the strategic level

Planning and policy frameworks for tourism – at local, regional or national level – are rare in Britain, more common in other countries. Policies and strategic plans have existed for some time for most important economic and social activities. Now that tourism is a major economic and social force it requires similar frameworks for defining objectives and guiding actions:

The tourism industry will be faced with some difficult challenges over the next few years. Managers and executives, faced with making present and future policy decisions on tourism issues, will need a managerial framework for analysing the various alternatives so that a course of action can be selected.

(Edgell, 1988)

Eight years on...
In 1994 the first Scottish Strategic Plan for tourism was published. '[The Plan] analyses the current performance of Scotland's tourist industry and identifies the action which needs to be taken by those who provide the support to the industry, by the industry itself, and by the organisations working in partnership if the industry is to meet successfully the challenges which face it in the years ahead' (Scottish Tourism Strategic Plan, 1994).

What are the challenges of devising a national or regional strategy for tourism; or specific aspects of tourism at the regional or national level? Many countries have a strategic plan for tourism, however, it would be difficult for *you* to prepare a report on such a major, wide-ranging topic. A more practical alternative is suggested.

Consider the regional context of development of a heritage centre (or other tourist attraction) on a given site of *your* choice. You should reread the 'heritage' case study given on page 179. Alternatively, what would be the wider implications of general development of tourism within a specific town or village you know? You could also 'invent' an 'imaginary' one, describe it in sufficient detail and similarly consider the wider implications on tourism development.

What social/cultural, environmental and economic factors would you have to consider? What are the 'real' reasons for this tourism development?

Hint

Is the rationale for development to 'replace' former heavy industry now in decline (as discussed in the Culross case study in Chapter 7)? Or is it to regenerate an existing, but declining destination (as discussed in the Dunbar case study in Chapter 8, and the Aviemore case study in Chapter 10)?

Exercise

Sites for development of tourism related projects

Imagine that you are a destination manager working with a specialist planning consultant to advise you on sites appropriate for tourism development. The subsequent developments will be public sector led, although considerable investment and development will be carried out by the private sector through a 'PPP' (or public–private partnership). As a destination manager you wish proactively to identify sites for potential developers, rather than passively waiting for prospective developers to choose sites which may be – from a destination-wide perspective – inappropriate.

Consider sites for a range of potential clients interested in small to medium size developments in a city of your choice. (Refer to the Edinburgh case study in Chapter 6 for guidance.) Go on the basis that your client has not specified a particular sector of tourism – they simply wish to invest in this expanding industry. Inspect the site and evaluate its potential for tourism development. You are primarily concerned with a general overview of the site and its location:

- the site's suitability for development for a *specific* tourism use (you choose this)

- the issues likely to be considered in the application for planning permission; advise your client on possible responses to these issues.

Points to consider:

- current use(s)

- location (city centre, suburban, urban fringe/rural)

- access (main, trunk, lesser roads; bus and rail services; parking; pedestrian/cycle routes etc.)

- area (square yards/square metres/acres/hectares) and shape of site (irregular/'long and narrow' etc.)

- existing condition of site, briefly covering:

    - natural environment – ground cover (mature trees, grass, builders' rubble etc.); topography (slopes, depressions etc.); drainage (e.g. boggy areas)

- aspect, i.e. views into site from surroundings and out from site (to be retained or concealed); also, views your proposal might obscure

- built environment – onsite and adjacent buildings, e.g. architectural styles; heights and scale (two/three storeys, high-rise etc.); uses (e.g. residential, commercial, office, educational, institutional etc.).

• overall character of site (spirit of place/'*genius loci*').

Note: Do not go onto private land without permission or place yourself in any dangerous situations! If you are questioned by anyone, clarify that what you are doing is a student project.

Bibliography

Baum, T. (1994) The development and implementation of national tourism policies. *Tourism Management*, 15 (3), 185–92.

Brewton, C. and Withiam, G. (1998) United States tourism policy alive, but not well. *Cornell Hotel and Restaurant Administration Quarterly* 39 (1), 50–59.

Centre for Environmental Intepretation. *Journal of Environmental Interpretation*. Manchester Metropolitan University. Manchester.

City of Edinburgh Council (1997) *Central Area Local Plan*. CEC. Edinburgh.

Community participation in tourism planning (1994) *Tourism Management* 15 (2), 98–108.

Cooper, C. (1990) Resorts in decline: the management response. *Tourism Management*, March.

Cullen, G. (1971) *The Concise Townscape*. Architectural Press. London.

Dawood, R. (1989) Tourists' health – could the travel industry do more? *Tourism Management*, December.

Department of Culture, Media and Sport (1999) *Tomorrow's Tourism*. DCMS. London.

Department of the Environment, Welsh Office (1992) *Planning Policy Guidance: Tourism*. DoE. London.

Dye, T. (1987).

Edgell, D. (1994) International tourism policy and management. In R. Ritchie and C. Goeldner (eds) *Travel, Tourism and Hospitality Research* (2nd edn). John Wiley & Sons. New York.

Edwards, B. (1986) *Scottish Seaside Towns*. BBC. London.

European Commission (1994) *Tourism Policy in the EU. Background Report I*. SEC/B24/ 12/94.

European Community (1991) Community action plan to assist tourism. *Official Journal of the European Community*, L231, 26–31.

Foley, P. and Martin, S.J. (2000) Perceptions of community led regeneration: an analysis of community and government viewpoints. *Regional Studies* 34, 783–7.

Frank Howie Associates (1987) *A Heritage Centre Feasibility Study*. Dumfries and Galloway Regional Council.

Goldsmith (1980).

Greed, C. (1996) *Introducing Town Planning* (2nd edn). Longman. London.

Gunn, C.A. (1988) Vactionscape: Designing Tourist Areas. Van Nostrand Reinhold. New York.

Gunn, C.A. (1994) *Tourism Planning: Basics, Concepts, Cases*. Crane Russak.

Gunn, C.A. (1997) *Vacationscape: Developing Tourist Areas* (3rd edn). Taylor & Francis. London.

Hall, D.R. (ed.) *Tourism and Economic Development in Eastern Europe and the Soviet Union*. Belhaven. London.

Hall, M.C. (199?) *Tourism and Politics: Policy, Power and Place*. John Wiley & Sons. Chichester.

Hall, M.C. and Jenkins, J. (1995) *Tourism Policy*. International Thomson Business Press. London.

Hartley, K. and Cooper, N. (1993) Tourism policy: market failure and public choice and perspectives on tourism policy. In P. Johnson and B. Thomas (eds) Mansell.

Healey, (1981).

Henry, J.P., (1993) *The Politics of Leisure Policy*. Macmillan.

Hewison, R. (1987) *The Heritage Industry, Britain in a Climate of Decline*. Methuen. London.

Hill, (1997).

HM Government (1992) *Planning Policy Guidance: Tourism*. *www.planning.odpm.gov.uk/ppg*.

Inskeep, E. (1991). *Tourism Planning: An Integrated and Sustainable Development Approach*. Van Nostrand Reinhold. New York.

Krippendorf, J. (1982) Towards new tourism policies. *Tourism Management*, September.

Krippendorf, J. (1989) *The Holiday Makers*. Heinemann. London.

Lee, G. and Barrett, G.W. (1994) EC support for tourism in ACP states and regions. *Tourism Management*, 15 (3), 200–202.

Lickorish, J.L. (1991) Trends in tourism in J.L. Lickorish, *Developing Tourism Destinations*. Longman. Harlow.

Light, D. and Prentice, R. (1994) Market-based product development in heritage tourism. *Tourism Management*, 15 (1), 27–36.

Luhrman, (1998).

McCarthy, P. (2000) Tourism Policy and the Community. Unpublished dissertation. Queen Margaret University College. Edinburgh.

McIntosh, R.W. and Goeldner, C.R. (1990) Tourism's future in *Tourism*. John Wiley & Sons. Chichester.

Meethan (1998).

Morris, E.S. (1997) *British Town Planning and Urban Design*. Longman. London.

National Economic Development Council (1992) *UK Tourism: Competing for Growth*. NEDC. London.

National Heritage Memorial Fund. *www.caledonia.org.uk/land/bwilson.htm*

Organisation for Economic Cooperation and Development (1997) *Tourism Policy and International Tourism in OECD Member Countries* (on diskette). OECD.

Pearce, D. (1989) *Tourist Development* (2nd edn). Longman Scientific and Technical. Harlow.

Petty, R. (1989) Health limits to tourism development. *Tourism Management*, September.

Prentice, R.C. (1993) *Tourism and Heritage Attractions*. Routledge. London.

Ritchie, R.J.B. and Goeldner, C. (eds) (1994) *Travel, Tourism and Hospitality Research* (2nd edn). John Wiley & Sons Inc. New York.

Roberts, G. (2001) Change for the 21st century. *Journal of the Royal Town Planning Institute*, 20 April, 23.

Scottish Office Industry Department (1992) *Structure of Local Government in Scotland: Tourism*. HMSO. Edinburgh.

Scottish Tourist Board (1994) *Scottish Tourism Strategic Plan*. STB. Edinburgh.

Theobold, W.F. (1994) *Global Tourism: The Next Decade*. Butterworth-Heinemann. Oxford.

Thurso, V. (2002) *Annual Reports and Accounts of the Tourism Society*. The Tourism Society. London.

Tourism Society (1989) Structure of the UK tourism industry: the case for government policy and support for the tourism industry. *Tourism*, October.

Uzzell, D. (1989) *Heritage Interpretation* (Volumes 1 and 2). Belhaven.

Van Doorn, J.W.M. (1994) *Tourism 2000: A Strategy for Wales*. Wales Tourist Board.

Ward, T. (1989) Role of government incentives. *Tourism Management*, September.

Williams, A.M. and Shaw, G. (1988) *Tourism and Development: Western European Experiences*. Belhaven.

Williams, A.M. and Shaw, G. (1991) Tourism policies in a changing environment in A.M. Williams and G. Shaw (1991) *Tourism and Economic Development* (2nd edn). Belhaven.

Witt, S.F. (1991) Tourism in Cyprus. *Tourism Management*. March.

Yale, P. (1991) *From Tourist Attractions to Heritage Tourism*. Elm.

Zhang, H.Q., Chong, K. and Ap, J. (1999) An analysis of tourism development in modern China. *Tourism Management*, 20, 471–5.

Websites

Association for Heritage Interpretation	*www.heritageinterpretation.org.uk* *europa.eu.int/comm/enterprise/index_ en.htm*
Department for Culture, Media & Sport	*www.culture.gov.uk*
Department of Trade & Industry	*www.dti.gov.uk*
Directorate General/DG XIII	*europa.eu.int/comm/enterprise*
English Nature	*www.english-nature.org.uk*
English Tourist Board	*www.travelengland.org.uk*
Her Majesty's Stationery Office	*www.official-documents.co.uk*
Forestry Commission	*www.forestry.gov.uk*
Jorvik Centre, York	*www.jorvik-viking-centre.co.uk*
Northern Ireland Tourist Board	*www.interknowledge.com* *northern-ireland/default.htm*
Organisation for Economic Cooperation and Development	*www.oecd.org*
Patrick Geddes Centre	*www.cce.ed.ac.uk/geddes*
Royal Town Planning Institute Journal	*www.planning.haynet.com*
Scottish Natural Heritage	*www.snh.org.uk*
Scottish Tourist Board	*www.visitscotland.com*
The Tat Gallery	*www.thetatgallery.com*
Tourism Society	*www.tourismsociety.org*
Vikingar!	*www.vikingar.co.uk*
UK Central Government – culture	*www.culture.org.uk*
UK Central Government – planning	*www.planning.gov.uk*
Wales Tourist Board	*www.wtbonline.gov.uk/start/en*
World Tourism Organisation	*www.world-tourism.org*

CHAPTER 6

The historic–cultural tourist city

[*Note:* In your reading of the case studies in Chapters 6–10 consider which of the detailed aspects of each specific destination are transferable – with modifications – to other 'same type' destinations which you may wish to study.]

INTRODUCTION

Cities are key elements in the development of every country or nation state and 'urbanisation' is a global trend. The 'sustainable city' is the desired objective but always there are barriers to be overcome – cultural, environmental and economic. Less developed countries face great problems arising out of the decline in traditional rural employment and migration to urban areas and in certain cases political upheaval and violence; elsewhere, inadequate planning and/or weak policy making can result in ecological, social and economic challenges. Half of the world population now lives in cities and with a growth rate of around a quarter of a million a day by 2025 the figure will have risen by around two thirds – 'the equivalent of a new London every month' (Rogers, 1996: 4).

A capital city has particular remits in that it represents the nation as a whole and so consequently has certain responsibilities to it. Recent years have seen some cities regain a former status through a degree of devolution of political power from central government – for example in 1999 London regained a Lord Mayor after a gap of many years and after several centuries Edinburgh is again the home of the Scottish Parliament.

Tourism generally has a role to play in cities, notably in the forms of special interest tourism focusing on the arts and culture, and business tourism (including conference tourism and incentive tourism). Conservation is likely to be a significant issue where the built environment and the wider historic heritage contributes to the status of the city and of the nation as a whole. Conservation of such priceless assets may be in conflict with certain plans for development which some would argue are equally if not more 'essential' to the status of the city. Thus commercial interests frequently argue that new roads and other transport developments are vital to the development of the city – criticising opponents of these developments as preferring the city to be 'pickled in aspic', i.e. preserved just as it is.

EDINBURGH

In Edinburgh one of the oldest 'unofficial' or 'voluntary membership' civic associations is the Cockburn Society (*www.cockburnassociation.org.uk*) which attempts to tread the challenging line between conservation and development,

Figure 6.1 *Edinburgh's location*

while an example of a 'younger' organisation with a more specific focus is 'Spokes' (*www.spokes.org.uk*) which campaigns for better conditions for cyclists and for sustainable transport generally under the slogan, 'Expanding roads to fight congestion is like loosening your belt to fight obesity' (see Figure 6.1).

In the urban context it is therefore common to find tourism development and management discussed alongside other significant issues and concepts including: public–private partnership working; economic regeneration; the national economy; tourism as an economic catalyst; heritage, arts and cultural tourism.

205

All these issues and challenges are present in Edinburgh, the capital of Scotland and a city that entered a period of rapid change in the 1990s heightened by the devolution of political power in Britain in the late 1990s.

The establishment of the Scottish Parliament in 1999 (*www.scottish.parliament.uk*) is initiating major structural and economic changes with highly positive economic impacts on the city. This also heightens the 'economic divide' between the capital and the rest of the country, notably the City of Glasgow (www.glasgow.gov.uk). The two cities are historically characterised more by their rivalry than a spirit of cooperation. This is increasingly unacceptable – for their mutual interests as well as the national interest. Edinburgh City Council leaders now refer to the two cities as a: 'world-class combination ... [where] the success of the two cities is crucial to the success of our rural areas, and key to the overall economic success of Scotland [...] the cities are the gateway to wealth and work'. For example, the 'Twin Cities Promotion' seeks to 'link the attractions of Scotland's two main city destinations in easily bookable packages combining transport, accommodation and added value offers. [..] The primary objective is to achieve sustainable medium-term growth in off-season business from overseas markets in order to support quality year-round employment in tourism' (Edinburgh Action Plan, 2000).

The complexity of city planning and development, plus the increasing significance of tourism has encouraged many city authorities and business organisations to create new senior posts such as 'destination manager' and 'city centre manager'. Edinburgh Council in conjunction with business interests established a city centre management company in 2000 and the City's first Director of the City Centre Management Company was in post later that year. The remit of this senior position – as an example of the growth of opportunities in the wider field of destination management – is indicated in the advertisement for the post (see Figure 6.2).

Images of Edinburgh

The image of Edinburgh is a topic of regular debate (see Chapter 1).

There has been a prevailing view of Edinburgh, along the lines of 'Edinburgh is beautiful, but a little boring. One day I'll visit it – when I'm retired/grey-haired/older'. A distinct change is taking place and this is noted in several travel guides: Edinburgh is trendy, and the publicity from the book/movie *Trainspotting* has made the city even more cool and popular (*Dagbladet*, Norwegian newspaper, 28 June 1996, referring to the work of Welsh, 1994).

Edinburgh is widely recognised as a beautiful city, benefiting from a unique architectural heritage and magnificent natural setting. It is also a forward thinking and progressive European Capital City. The city centre is the shop window for the whole city and it is crucial to the city's future that the centre remains strong economically.

It is designated as a World Heritage Site, provides a centre for employment, shopping and leisure for East Central Scotland, is the centre of Government, a renowned tourist destination and the hub for administration, education, finance, health, law and transport for Central Scotland. An innovative company structure has been developed to achieve this objective and an essential element is the development of a City Centre Management Company for delivery of a range of services in the city centre.

An outstanding director is sought to lead this company in promoting the city centre and delivering/procuring direct services. Candidates should have a proven track record in delivery of multifunctional services, marketing, commercial and strategic management and strong communication skills.

The director will be employed by the City Centre Management Company and report to the Board. Remuneration will be in line with the high profile of the post.

Interested parties should send CVs to _____

Figure 6.2 *Director of the City Centre Management Company advertisement*
Source: Advertisement in *The Scotsman*, 2000

The *Rough Guide to Scotland* (1996) takes a similar tone: 'a great drinking city [...] there is a youthful presence for most of the year – a welcome corrective to the stuffiness which is often regarded as Edinburgh's Achilles Heel'.

Lonely Planet (1999: 9) writes:

Studded with volcanic hills, Edinburgh has an incomparable location on the southern edge of the Firth of Forth. The city's superb architecture ranges from the Greek-style monuments on Calton Hill (for which it was called the 'Athens of the North'), to the extraordinary 16th-century tenement, to monumental Georgian and Victorian masterpieces.

But it adds: 'The flipside to all this, however, is the grim reality of life in the bleak council housing estates surrounding the city, the serious drugs scene and the distressing AIDS problem'. The *Edinburgh Evening News* (16 July 2002) notes that Lonely Planet's Edinburgh 2002 edition refers to the city as one of 'all-night parties and overindulgence' and that a 'tide of testosterone and alcohol means that several streets are best avoided by female visitors on weekend nights [...] [though Edinburgh is] safer than most cities of a similar size'. The newspaper went on to quote some local, angered pub and club owners, one of whom responded with: 'If ladies don't want to be lonely on this planet, they should not stay away from Edinburgh, but come out and enjoy the varied and exciting nightlife'.

The *Good Tourist in the UK* (Howie, in Wood and House 1992: 148) noted one of the contradictions of the city:

It is a medical centre of world standing – its famous doctors and scientists are household names – yet in some of its peripheral housing estates, products of well-meaning but sadly misguided planning in the 1960s, the levels of AIDS and HIV infection are the highest in Britain.

Bill Bryson (1995: 302–10), the popular contemporary travel writer describes his pleasure at arriving by train at Waverley station right in the heart of 'such a glorious city' on a fine winter's evening:

> To a surprising extent, [...] Edinburgh felt like another country. The buildings were thin and tall in an un-English fashion, the money was different, even the air and light felt different in some ineffable northern way.

His favourable first impressions were dampened by the winter rain and a cooler perspective. Princes Street had diminished in grandure as a world-class street as a result of the demolition in the 1950s and 1960s of many of the great Victorian and Edwardian buildings and their replacement by nondescript concrete blocks.

Edinburgh, like the characters of one its famous literary figures, can appear to have a 'Jekyll and Hyde' personality. 'You'll have had your tea then' is an approach to hospitality that still lingers on in a few places, as implied by Reid (1998: 55):

> When the icy wind slaps against your cheeks or the spooky sea-mist called the 'haar' rolls off the North Sea, Edinburgh's hospitality takes on a rather aloof, you'll-like-it-or-leave-it persona.

Edinburgh has more than one persona, however – like any real place it is multi-faceted. In a student's guide to Edinburgh, Cousins (2000) enthuses about these – 'the Asian shops of Leith Walk, the Jewishness of Newington, the gay scene of Broughton, and the student quarter of the Southside'. Perhaps because of its beauty, character, history and contradictions, Edinburgh ranks third behind London and Rome among European cities in terms of hotel occupancy (City of Edinburgh Council, 1999). Page (1995) includes Edinburgh in 'the popular overseas visitor "milk run" of organised coach tours, which commences in London and incorporates Oxford, Stratford-upon-Avon, Bath, Chester, Edinburgh, York, Cambridge and London'.

Current situation and wider context

What is the 'product' of Edinburgh and how does it compare with other city destinations – notably other 'rival' European city destinations?

Edinburgh achieved World Heritage Site status in 1997 (*www.ewht.org.uk*). The designated area embraces the mediaeval Old Town and the Georgian New Town.

Conservation

> Edinburgh was not desecrated in the 1960s as were some others: our Old and New Towns are as built – marvelous architectural jewels to have. We've very much a sense that the city is on loan to us, and it's to be passed on, preferably in better condition but certainly at least in as fine a condition as when we were entrusted with it. [...] There are (though) tangible economic reasons for making the most of World Heritage Site status over and above its potential for bringing even better quality of life to our townsfolk.
>
> (Hazel/City of Edinburgh Development, 1997)

The 'official' view of Edinburgh is clearly positive, while recognising the 'obligations' its high status brings. The well-informed tourists drawn to the city – at least partially because of this accolade – will expect the very highest quality it implies and will make comparisons with other such sites. For example, Krakow (Cracow) in Poland was one of the first 12 designated world heritage sites in 1978 (*www.krakow-info.com/unesco.htm*). Major work is going on in this historic old city 'in order to protect and preserve this heritage at a time of transition to a market economy [...] the question is whether the visitor management and the planning controls will do justice to the city's past' (Airey, 1998 in Shackley, 1998).

The mediaeval city of Rhodes in Greece achieved World Heritage Status in 1988 (*whc.unesco.org/nwhc/pages/sites/main.htm*). The city can offer Edinburgh inspiration from the pedestrianisation that has been widely implemented in its city centre, making for a generally pedestrian-friendly environment. However, this has also resulted in an overflow of goods from shops onto the pavements of some already narrow streets making for a rather cluttered appearance in places and repetition of somewhat tacky souvenirs.

Socio-economic profile of Edinburgh

The city has a population of approximately 450,000. It is likely to increase in absolute terms more than most other Scottish local authorities, apart from Aberdeenshire and West Lothian (City of Edinburgh Council, 1999) (*www.ebs.hw.a-c.uk/EdWeb.html*). There are, generally, high skill levels making it a centre for 'new technology' or 'sunrise industries' – including telecommunications, information technology, bio-technology, artificial intelligence. Other major industries within the destination include education, brewing, publishing and finance. Recent years have seen rapid and ongoing construction and development of the new financial district to the west of Lothian Road on the outskirts of the city centre. Jobs in government are increasing, greatly enhanced by the presence of the Scottish Parliament (*www.scottish.parliament.uk*). Employment in the 'ACE' industries, i.e. arts-cultural-entertainment, are growing rapidly. Some 85% of all jobs are in the service industries, 20,000 of them in tourism.

Despite this affluence there are some severely disadvantaged communities. The affluent status excludes the city from certain UK government/European sources of finance for development but the city has a firm commitment to tackling 'social exclusion'.

The City Council supports the major festivals and tourism generally but is not permitted to retrieve a share of the income generated to reinvest in the city. The strong historical character of the city is moderated by its three universities, one university college and several further education colleges. These contribute to the growing 'youth culture' exemplified by the rise in clubs and other entertainment facilities and, arguably, a 'liberal' atmosphere. Analogies are increasingly made with other European capitals as Edinburgh tentatively moves towards '24-hour city' status (see Figure 6.3). This trend is not without its critics and references are occasionally made by conservative elements to the 'negative associations' of 'rivals' such as Amsterdam (*www.amsterdam.nl*) – prostitution and drugs – arguing that 'traditional' images of historic capital cities have proven worth and should not be discarded for transient fashions. A compromise is suggested in Berlin (*www.berlin-tourism.de*) where the 'Long Night of the Museum' is a tourist favourite. Rather than restricting the '24-hour city' concept to pubs and clubs, for some years a number of the city's museums, art galleries and other cultural venues have stayed open until dawn, with strong support. It has to be added, however, that in the wake of that success the city's bordellos held a 'Long Night of the Brothel' in 2002, with a view to 'changing the "seedy" image of prostitution' (*The Scotsman*, 2002).

- Home of the Scottish Parliament since 1999
- Saturation levels of tourism (arguably)
- Traffic congestion
- Opening up of less visited places
- More provision for families with young children
- Nurturing of the urban villages
- 'A place of vision and lively debate'

Figure 6.3 *Edinburgh – major opportunities and challenges*
Source: City of Edinburgh Development (1997)

Social exclusion

There is a significant divide between rich and poor in the city. Many studies have been conducted into the links between poverty, ill health and premature death. According to the Lord Provost's Commission on Sustainable Development (City of Edinburgh Council, 1998: 75, para. 5.179):

> [T]he death rate in Granton was 50% higher than the city average and three times that of the area with the best record [Balerno]. Such discrepancies cannot exist in a sustainable city.

In a truly sustainable city – which Edinburgh is committed to becoming – this is unacceptable. In the poorer areas tourism has a role to play. The resident community should be empowered and involved in the planning and enhancement of the amenity and heritage sites in their area with a view to developing 'grey area' tourism (Howie, 2000: 102), as part of a wider urban regeneration programme. In this way planning for the community is integrated with added value for visitors. Environmental improvement plus provision of proper infrastructure are keystones for investment, job creation and training.

Social exclusion, culture, heritage and tourism

In defining 'social exclusion' and the 'socially excluded', Prime Minister Tony Blair (Newman and McLean, 1998: 143–53) implicitly recognises the key role of culture and heritage in tackling them. Both are significant factors in tourism: '[P]eople who do not have the means, material or otherwise to participate in social, economic, political and cultural life'.

The City of Edinburgh Council (199x:11) acknowledge this problem:

> Tourism and a growing international reputation have generated immense economic benefits for the City, with all the evidence pointing to continuing growth. However, there are tensions over the differential spread of the costs and benefits. [...] How can the economic spin-offs from tourism be circulated more widely to the local population?

In several areas of the city such initiatives are already underway in the form of priority partnership areas – PPAs. *Craigmillar and Niddrie* is one such area, a 'peripheral council housing estate', to the southeast of the City. The area was once Edinburgh's agricultural backdrop and included the historically significant mediaeval Craigmillar Castle, although in ruinous condition. The post-war surge in population put increasing pressure on areas such as these for housing construction. By unfortunate coincidence the local industries of brewing, cream production and coal mining declined from the 1950s onward and with it came unemployment and lack of opportunity. The Craigmillar Festival Society was set up by a small number of local people in 1962, determined to tackle the problems (Crummy, 1992), a pioneering example of using 'the arts' as a focus for community involvement and civic pride.

The growth of tourism in Edinburgh is part of the rationale for establishing a country park in the area, centring on the now restored castle. While the park will benefit local people, their priorities are good-quality housin,g and decent jobs. 'Heritage' comes some way behind, although there is some potential for small-scale tourism-related employment as a spin-off of these assets. It is inconceivable that tourism can provide the answer to all their problems, but it may contribute to the 'feel good factor' and act as a marker of rich history, which would do much to change a negative image of the area (Ralton, 1999).

Wester Hailes at the opposite, western side of the City inherited part of Edinburgh's industrial past in the form of the Union Canal. From its construction in the 18th century this waterway was used to transport coal and clay through the central belt to where it met up with the Forth and Clyde Canal at Falkirk which continued the east–west water link through to Glasgow and the west coast. As Wester Hailes developed to become a major housing area the (then disused) canal was built over in the 1960s. Thirty years on, with recognition of the tourism and leisure potential of the canal and a successful bid to the Heritage Lottery Fund, the entire canal is being reopened. At Wester Hailes redevelopment of the historic waterway involved the restoration to the surface of the underground piped section and associated landscaping works.

The overall scheme – 'The Millennium Link' (*www.millenniumlink.org.uk*) – was completed in 2002. The associated developments will also contribute to the strengthening of the 'collaboration' between Edinburgh and Glasgow discussed earlier in this chapter. The restored, heritage waterway is likely to become a significant recreational/tourism attraction (Howie, 1989). At the Edinburgh 'terminal basin' commercial and residential development are underway linking a former industrial and semi-derelict area with the financial centre of the City. Tourism/recreational developments are under consideration.

A third area, *North Edinburgh*, has a rich industrial and fishing past. As part of a multi-million pound improvement the waterfront area is proposed for development incorporating the redundant gasworks at Granton, where the three holding towers of the gasworks are to be preserved as industrial heritage, having been granted 'listed building' status (as discussed in Chapter 5).

While controversial, the sky-blue towers are a distinguishing feature of the landscape. Alongside there is to be new housing, a college campus, an improved yachting marina and cycle and walkways.

211

Exercise

Industrial buildings as 'heritage'?

Why is there some resistance to considering industrial buildings/constructions as 'heritage' (see Chapter 5)? In a destination known to you identify similar industrial 'remains'. Find out whether they are protected in any official way and comment on why you feel they are worthy of such a status (or not).

(Note that 'The Millennium Link' is classified as industrial heritage yet there was little controversy over whether it should be conserved and considerable public and private money spent on its restoration. Why is there such a difference in attitude?)

Further west along the coast at the more affluent community of Cramond, there are substantial remains of Roman settlements and future development will present these to both local people and tourists. To the east, the unique sense of community which developed alongside the former fishing villages is documented in the New-haven Fisheries Museum.

Much of the coastline of North Edinburgh will become known as 'Edinburgh's Waterfront', the largest waterfront development in Europe (*www.edinburgh-waterfront.com*). A major element of this is the retired Royal Yacht *Britannia* berthed in the area in 1997 (*www.royalyachtbritannia.co.uk*). Against intense competition from cities around the UK Edinburgh was successful in its bid to become *Britannia*'s new home. It is now owned by The Royal Yacht Britannia Trust, a charitable organisation whose sole remit is the maintenance of *Britannia* in keeping with her former role. The ship is now permanently moored in Edinburgh's historic port of Leith and already a highly successful visitor attraction. Commercial, retail, residential and leisure facilities are also under development creating a new tourist focus which contributes greatly to the economic and social revival of Leith. A major element is Ocean Terminal, opened in 2001. This is a 444,000 sq ft/ 41,248 sq m shopping centre development including major national department and specialist stores, restaurants, multiscreen cinema and, accessible from the main building, the Royal Yacht *Britannia*.

As an outcome of the Ocean Terminal development alone 1,500 jobs have been created in Leith, while overall unemployment in the area has been reduced from 5,000 to 1,900 (at 2002). The Scottish Executive is located in an adjacent building accommodating 1,500 employees. The old port of Leith has progressively, since the 1980s, changed its reputation from a slightly seedy, former industrial and docklands area to a fashionable area of quality restaurants and local character.

Urban waterfront regeneration is common in many coastal cities with an industrial base, notably where former industries are in decline. Tourism and leisure-related developments are generally a significant component (*www.atlantic-planners.org/whatnew/confsj98/sources.htm*). Notable examples include London (*www.london-docklands.co.uk*), San Francisco (*www.sfport.com*) and Vancouver (*www.portvancouver.com*). Vancouver's regenerated waterfront incorporates 'Canada Place', the Canadian government's landmark investment in British Columbia. The facilities include public areas, entertainment venues, restaurants, offices, retail outlets and parking space, plus – of increasing significance – excellent

Photograph 6.1 *Vancouver waterfront development*

public transport links. It has become the focal point for BC's thriving tourist and international trade sectors and 'a meeting place for all Canadians'.

Edinburgh and sustainable development

These developments reflect the strong commitment of the city to sustainable development in its true sense. The City of Edinburgh Council established the Lord Provost's Commission on Sustainable Development in 1998, the first of its kind in the UK and followed the model of an independent royal commission, steered by a committee of private, public and voluntary representatives from the fields of health, business, academia, etc. Social exclusion was emphasised as a key concern in the sustainable development of Edinburgh, as important as the environmental factor and intrinsically linked to it.

Sustainability

The major task faced by the commission was initially to audit the current status of various sectors of Edinburgh life; provide a more sustainable blueprint for the future; and be an advocate of sustainability in the community at large. There were differing views on just what sustainability meant. According to some witnesses who were asked to submit evidence it was obvious that economic sustainability held more sway than the social or environmental factors (Mittler, 1999).

The intentions and achievements of the commission have been positive; however the proposed successive convening of the commission failed to materialise. This was perhaps linked to the controversy where several developments given the go-ahead by the City Council seem to pay little regard to sustainable principles: for

213

instance the development, and extension, of out-of-town shopping centres to the south, west and east of the city at Straiton (IKEA), the Gyle and Kinnaird Park respectively. While there have been subsequent plans to link the last two areas with bus and rail links, there is no such plan for the IKEA development which caused no small controversy as it rode roughshod over the council transport policy (Mittler, 1999). The developments have led to considerably increased flows of private cars when the wider policy context is one of developing means of reducing dependence on the private car. Newman and McLean (1998: 151) describe the related problems such development can cause: 'The trend to create out-of-town retail parks and city centre shopping malls creates city centres which are empty and dangerous places to live after rush hour'.

This too is at odds with the City's desire to revitalise the city centre and re-establish Princes Street as a world-class shopping and sightseeing boulevard.

The future sustainability of Edinburgh as a World Heritage Site and as a city of inclusion and of economic and environmental balance will depend to a large extent on the uptake of the commission's recommendations. The Edinburgh Tourism Action Group, established in March 2000, is a partnership between the public and private sectors that aims to coordinate tourism in Edinburgh. It integrates this commitment as one of the key objectives of its Edinburgh Tourism Action Plan (December 2000): 'Create greater synergy between the different elements of the tourism industry, and encourage inclusion, innovation and entrepreneurship'.

Exercise

Edinburgh: destination appraisal – a 'virtual field trip'

Guidance notes
This virtual field trip and guidance notes put you in the role of a destination manager charged with evaluating a number of sites within Edinburgh which illustrate aspects of the city as a tourist destination and also – a key aspect of this approach to destination management – as a living, working *place*. There are three main elements:

1. the image of the city

2. the 'anatomy' or basic 'components' of the city

3. tourism provision – i.e. specific provision for tourism and the impacts of tourism on the city and its residents.

For each of these elements, a number of specific locations are identified for you to 'visit'. Guidance notes are provided referring to relevant policies and issues which must be considered in drawing up destination management recommendations for these sites.

The image of Edinburgh

There is no single image that 'sums up' or epitomises Edinburgh; like any real place there are many images that a local resident becomes familiar with over time or a perceptive tourist can glimpse even in a short visit. The amalgam of the tangible and intangible qualities create the spirit of place of any destination and generate in the tourists – if successful – 'endearment' towards the place and enhance the probability of making return visits.

The stereotype/cliché/imagined/romanticised images of Edinburgh are found on tins of shortbread biscuits, sweets and bottles of whisky and on postcards and calendars. They include certain buildings – the Castle, Holyrood Palace, Scott Monument and St Giles Cathedral; statues such as Greyfriar's Bobby and the floral clock in Princes Street Gardens. These have created for many (potential) tourists an 'organic' image of the city that is a narrow version of the whole. A more contemporary image of the city is unobtrusively being 'induced' by a more mature tourism industry (see the discussion on image theory in Chapter 3).

CASE STUDY

Image and change: the Edinburgh Military Tattoo

There is a proposal to move the internationally famous Edinburgh Military Tattoo. This takes place annually during the Edinburgh International Festival but it is separate from it. Preparations include erecting a large scaffolding-supported seating area, which creates considerable disturbance to local residents. The Tattoo could be moved to a permanent site in Princes Street Gardens where the existing – and aging – 'Ross Bandstand' could be replaced by a 'national stadium' of a design befitting this exceptional site and also able to cater for a range of musical and other performances.

The image of the Tattoo against the dramatic background of the Castle is highly cherished and there is considerable opposition to the proposed move.

Exercise

'Out-dated' but 'much-loved'

Should the proposed move to a new location for the Edinburgh Military Tattoo be supported? What are the arguments for and against such a move?

Consider an event or building in a destination you know which has 'out-lived its usefulness' according to 'the authorities' but is 'much loved' by local people. From a destination management perspective what (if any) compromise could you suggest?

The 'Real Edinburgh' is all around the visitor but it is more subtle to perceive than the famous or 'iconic' features of the city. Dahles (1998) argues that in today's context 'culture', 'tourism' and 'everyday life' have become much more integrated.

Cultural tourism can include intangible pleasures such as simply absorbing the 'atmosphere' of a destination, as well as sampling local food or exploring 'non-touristy' neighbourhoods and visiting the homes of local people ... if informal contacts can be made. Dahles attributes the success of a number of smaller cities, such as Edinburgh and Dublin, to their decision to enhance their distinctiveness – 'rediscovery of local vernacular styles [...] city culture is redefined here as the amalgam of structures and practices, characteristic of the aestheticised consumption spaces of many contemporary metropoles, where the arts, sports, leisure, and tourism come together symbolically segmented space'.

Examining the contrast between these two sets of images – the organic and the induced – can assist in clarifying the strengths and weaknesses of Edinburgh as a destination. The tangible aspects include architectural styles, levels of traffic, degrees of pollution, purpose-built tourist attractions etc. The intangible aspects are atmosphere, ambience, a sense of congestion or of spaciousness, a sense of a 'safe city', walkability, cycle-friendly streets and other factors. Together these determine the spirit of place or *genius loci* of the city and strongly influence the experiential quality of the visit. Edinburgh is generally placed high in national 'liveability' surveys and – officially – aspires to being regarded as a 'green' destination.

'Green destination' has been a rather vague term, but increasingly specific criteria are now available addressing both environmental and social aspects. In such a destination high standards of environmental quality are encouraged and maintained, embracing 'hard' elements such as air quality (which match or, better, exceed European Commission standards); also 'soft' elements such as the proportion of the city devoted to 'green spaces' – parks and walkways/cycleways, low levels of litter and graffiti and the presence of 'people places' such as public squares and pedestrianised areas. The recent proliferation of outdoor eating, drinking and 'people watching' places in the city – for example, the Grassmarket – proves that even in an 'unpredictable' maritime climate 'people spaces' are popular.

CASE STUDY

Litter in Edinburgh

Edinburgh Evening News, 22 December 2000:

> The modern lines of a new litter bin will soon become a familiar site across the city as more than 2,000 are installed in the next two years. Specially designed for the Capital, the bins boast graffiti-resistant corrugated sides, ashtrays and lockable lids to make them secure when VIPs visit. [...] Heritage campaigners, tourism leaders and senior councilors have already welcomed the design. [...] The 2,145 bins are part of a multi-million pound deal struck by the council with advertising giant Xxx who will pay for the bins and also provide 76 bus shelters, nine automatic public toilets and ten bike racks. In return, the council has allowed the firm access to key advertising sites across the city.
>
> Edinburgh is the first city in Scotland to have become involved in an initiative of this kind which will provide £3.7 million pounds of street furniture. The move

follows the revelation that the council received 7,000 phone complaints last year about Edinburgh's litter [...] At the same time we are hoping to develop a campaign which will lead to a situation where littering will become as unacceptable as drink driving. [...] It is a win–win situation for everybody. The council gets to keep its money to spend on top priorities, the public get new street furniture and our shareholders are happy.

Exercise

Advertising and litter

How acceptable is a 'proliferation' of advertising within a world heritage site? Is this a good 'trade-off'? How do other comparable destinations respond to the costs of maintaining high standards of litter control?

Good role models from other cities have helped to overcome doubts about certain destination management issues and warn against others. Barcelona (*www.bcn.es/english/ihome.htm*) has successfully reestablished its traditional 'street life' that had been repressed under the 'Franco regime'. Closing streets to vehicles is increasingly accepted through different 'degrees' of closure and many squares have now returned to social use. La Rambla is 'Spain's most famous street ... the place to head for a first taste of Barcelona's atmosphere [...] dotted with cafes, restaurants [...] enlivened by buskers [...] rarely allows a dull moment' (Lonely Planet, 1999).

Barcelona has also 'solved' that proverbial tourist challenge – especially for those with young families in tow – of 'finding a toilet'. Cafes, bars and other establishments in certain popular areas have an informal agreement that their toilets may be used without charge by non-customers/passers-by on the basis that this is one further step towards creating 'people-friendly' areas that tourists will want to visit.

CASE STUDY

Noise pollution

'No sax please we're trying to sleep'
Edinburgh Evening News, 22 December 2000:

Outdoor concerts by well-known jazz saxophonists [...] have been cancelled after noise complaints against the Princes Street venue they were due to play. The move was made after [the musicians] said they were unwilling to play within a 90-decibel noise limit imposed by council environmental health chiefs. [...] The council's decision to impose a noise limit came in the wake of complaints from guests at a nearby three-star hotel over noise from the 250–seat tent venue. Club promoters [...] have also pulled out, describing the scaled-down sound system as 'pathetic'. 'You can't ask DJs of "X's" standing to play at a venue where you can hear yourself talk on the dance floor', they added.

Residents living in the area had also been affected. 'This temporary venue should never have been licensed to open 25 yards away from a major hotel', said the general manager. 'It's not on for residents to have to listen to this music until 3am on a Sunday.' [...] A council spokesman confirmed that environmental health officers had set the 90-dB limit after the band's first week-end. 'We tried to agree noise levels in advance of the venue opening, but it proved difficult with the promoter. Ninety decibels is a standard restriction for a venue of this size in this area and no further complaints have been received'.

Editorial comment:

The City Council deserves praise for its decision to host Edinburgh's first Capital Christmas festival this year. The success of the Hogmanay celebrations in recent years has proved that both local residents and visitors can be tempted into the city centre – even in the depths of a miserable winter – if there are first-class attractions on offer. It made sense to spread the party atmosphere across the whole festive season. But as recent events have shown, a festival is only as successful as its forward planning and there have been some major mistakes made in the run up to this first capital Christmas.

Officials did not secure the appropriate consents for the giant Christmas Ferris wheel which currently dominates the Princes Street skyline. [...]

A 90-decibel sound limit on gigs would have made a mockery of the [artists'] music. [...] The question remains as to why no one anticipated these problems arising. [...] It is all very well coming up with great ideas like a giant Ferris wheel in Princes Street or a music tent in the gardens, but attractions must be practical as well as exciting if the Christmas festival is to emulate the success of 'Edinburgh's Hogmanay'.

There has been added sparkle to the city's celebrations this year. Let's hope the lessons have been learnt and next year's events go ahead smoothly, without all the controversy.

Exercise

Noise pollution

What is the optimum solution here? 'Clubbers' are accustomed to very loud music – within a club. At an outdoor venue should that level have to be 'tolerated' by 'non-clubbers'? What are the implications in the (possible) context of Edinburgh (or a city/large town you know) as a '24 hour city'?

Another 'noise-pollution' issue: the highly popular Edinburgh visitor attraction 'Our Dynamic Earth' (*www.dynamicearth.co.uk*) includes a large semi-permanent 'tented' annexe that has been rented out for functions generating a significant income for the main visitor attraction. The area the attraction is in was predominantly industrial and is now an 'up-and-coming' development area, now including recently built 'up-market' flats, the owners of which are objecting to the noise of music etc. from the functions. Consequently, certain types of functions cannot now be held if they generate noise into the night, resulting in a very considerable drop in income for the attraction.

Is this reasonable? What are the priorities in such a 'multifunctional' area of a tourist destination? What compromises would you suggest?

Should an exception to noise level limits be granted to 'traditional' musicians, for example (in Edinburgh) bagpipers? There are increasing complaints to the local council – by residents and workers/businesses in the area – about the number of pipers playing in the area on most summer days. However, most tourists love them. ... Or do they?

CASE STUDY

Air quality

In Edinburgh, air quality still falls below European standards in several parts of the central area during peak traffic flow times. Transport choices in the city have until recently prioritised the private car, although the city authorities are now committed to reducing dependence on the car through working towards a viable range of alternatives. 'Greenways' (bus priority lanes), reopened suburban railway links, cycle ways, widened pavements, improved bus timetable information and bus punctuality, street closures and one-way traffic flows are improving the situation, although years will be required to change public attitudes significantly. 'People places' are particularly dependent on appropriate transport developments and the resultant improvement in air quality.

Local residents in Edinburgh's various communities and neighbourhoods are taken into account in planning and developing the city, whether with tourism or other sectors in mind. A number of initiatives show that success can follow such local focus (or 'locus') approaches. Edinburgh can therefore be regarded as a 'green destination', the term being almost synonymous with 'sustainable destination' since it implies that environmental and social factors are given appropriate consideration alongside the 'traditional' economic measures of 'success'.

The 'anatomy' or 'components' of Edinburgh as a destination

'Corridors'

Main through traffic corridors, such as Princes Street, have benefited from the removal of traffic that was 'incidentally' in the city, through construction of the city bypass in the 1980s. More recent and ongoing street modifications are the introduction of 'speed bumps', lower speed limits and widened pavements. These are gaining in acceptability as motorists themselves choose to or have to walk and consequently begin to appreciate the resulting people-friendly streets.

Princes Street demonstrates that 'corridors' are more than mere traffic conduits! Other cities have long known this: consider the boulevards of Paris and La Rambla in Barcelona.

Field notes

Princes Street lies along the southern boundary of the 'New Town'. The overall street plan of 'gridiron' parallel streets intersected by perpendicular streets and the resultant vistas and focal points play an important role in creating the sense of spaciousness in the area. The design dates back to 1766 when the architect James Craig won a design competition for the layout of the 'New Town'. The Georgian buildings are an essential element of this design having the key characteristics of formality and regularity, scale and attention to decorative detail. This is exemplified in Charlotte Square. The formal layout of the New Town complements the informal, organic layout of the Old Town – a key element of Edinburgh's World Heritage Site status.

Exercise

Architecture and planning

Consider the architecture and planning of Princes Street as an example of an internationally famous street. Is there 'room for improvement'? What might this be and what general principles should constrain such development?

Note

The 'migration' of businesses from the New Town to premises in the new Financial District is initiating major change – a reversion to the original residential use of the area – and necessitating further building work.

Read the following case study and consider whether it suggests general principles that might be applicable to a city destination of your choice.

CASE STUDY

Key locations, notable buildings and contemporary issues in Princes Street

Caledonian Hotel (West End)

One of Edinburgh's top hotels. A 'fin-de-siècle' building built in the 19th century for the Caledonian Railway Company and formerly named the North British Hotel. It is: 'An unlikely blend of Dutch Baroque and French Second Empire plus some Renaissance detail for good measure reflecting the 19th-century railway barons' views on architecture – "any style as long as it's impressive"' (Ward, 1985: 65).

Exercise

Architecture and urban design

Does the distinctiveness of this building contribute significantly to the quality of the tourist experience of Princes Street (and Edinburgh)? Does it (and other 'distinctive landmarks) offer guiding principles for the future development of Princes Street? For a destination you know, identify the 'iconic' or highly distinctive buildings that deserve to be preserved despite the 'inconvenience' they may bring to 21st-century traffic movement and other activities. What 'inconveniences' are caused by 'your' buildings? What solutions or compromises do you suggest?

Exercise

Transport management

In 2000 restrictions were imposed so that cars may only drive westwards of Princes Street; buses, taxis and bicycles may drive in both directions. Pedestrians have subsequently benefited from pavement widening. The next phase of the plan will prohibit cars completely.

Should this 'world-class' street be closed to cars and further pedestrianised? Where then would these 'displaced' cars go? What are the implications for these other areas? Is driving along this scenic boulevard one of the pleasures the city should be promoting? Given that 'everyone' may not want to (or be able to) walk this 'mile' can you suggest other 'novel' forms of transport appropriate to a historic city?

Exercise

Princes Street Gardens

Consider the 'vacationscape' (Gunn, 1997) of the Castle/Old Town skyline from Princes Street. This 'world-class' vista is protected by planning legislation, but there is increasing pressure to allow certain developments to go ahead. Waverley Station development proposals would improve the functionality of this 'transport node' and permit an extended shopping area to be constructed. This would require raising the present height of Waverley Station's roof which would then 'intrude' to a small degree – on this vista.

From a destination management perspective should this proposal be supported? Does a small height increase really interfere with the view? If so, what conditions should be imposed?

For a destination you know, identify 'views' that deserve preservation. What 'threats' do they face today or in the near future?

Transport nodes

The main railway station (Waverley) and the main bus station (St Andrews Square) entered a phase of major redevelopment in 2000. Both termini had been criticised as old-fashioned and the bus station as run-down and unbefitting a capital city. Unfavourable comparisons had been made with Glasgow bus station, which is user friendly and even incorporates popular sculptures. In each transport mode, shopping will be a significant element: the retail function encourages investment in the projects and on completion is expected to contribute to the maintenance and ambience of the areas.

Exercise

Transport nodes/termini

Transport 'nodes' are significant in creating first – and last – impressions of a destination. What qualities should be built into redevelopment plans generally and specifically for the transport nodes of a destination with which you are familiar?

Shopping

Princes Street is losing out to out-of-town shopping malls and to the city of Glasgow. There is a proposal to build an underground shopping mall beneath Princes Street. Existing stores now require more space and could expand into this area, while others retailers would move in. Unlike in many malls the shoppers' experience would not be one of being 'underground' – large windows would look out to Princes Street Gardens and the vista of the Old Town beyond.

Exercise

The place of malls in a cool climate

From a destination management perspective should this proposal be supported? What conditions should be set? If the proposals are rejected, what alternatives are there?

In general, are underground malls the 'way to go'? Do people really enjoy shopping underground? Give arguments for and against them.

Critics have argued that recent and current shopping proposals for Princes Street remove the last vestiges of the 'unique selling point' from this famous street. They argue that rather than encouraging further conformity (e.g. of brands and 'big names') the street should feature distinct or unique shops and reintroduce the 'character' that Princes Street once had. They refer to the department store 'Jenners' as a role model, one of the few traditional stores remaining in Princes Street (due to progressive 'modernisation') whose 1895 'baroque' façade attempts to out-decorate the neighbouring Scott Monument, a gothic fantasy and icon of the city. 'Boots the Chemist' occupied a comparable highly decorative building which was demolished and replaced with a 1960s' 'modern' building.

CASE STUDY

Shopping

The proposal for shopping and redevelopment of Princes Street itself should be viewed in the wider context. In 1997 a ten-year plan to revitalise the original New Town of Edinburgh was unveiled. This area was designed in the 1760s by James Craig and is bounded by Princes Street, Queen Street, St Andrew's Square and Charlotte Square. It was until recently the heartland of Edinburgh's business life. The plan included proposals to pedestrianise George Street 'in an attempt to turn it into one of the world's finest shopping thoroughfares – a 'Bond Street of the North', a comparison with London's famous street. The plan envisages public and private sector investment and collaboration and was welcomed by the city's Chamber of Commerce, which said it could help to beat off increasing competition from Glasgow, Livingston and other shopping areas where in total one and a half million square feet of new shopping space is opening.

The City of Edinburgh Council and the local enterprise company, Scottish Enterprise – Edinburgh and Lothian (*www.scottishenterprise.com/about/lecs/edin*) predicted a steady transformation of the first New Town while preserving the historic buildings and townscape which helped to win Edinburgh its World Heritage Site status. The public sector – the City Council and SEEL – would have major involvement in environmental and streetscape works and National Lottery funding assistance (*www.lotterygoodcauses.org.uk*) would be sought for heritage conservation works within the plan. If the proposals were carried out, it is predicted there would be a 28% increase in the population of the area, a 5% reduction in traffic volume, a 25% increase in housing and treble the present number of pedestrians in George Street.

Among the specific proposals are a business quarter for the small-office commercial sector such as legal and financial services, a high-quality approach to shops, housing principally for young people above shops making possible a 28% increase in the population and increased cultural and tourism activities centring on the Assembly Rooms in George Street and the National Portrait Gallery in Queen Street. There would be wider pavements on Princes Street and restoration of the gardens in Charlotte Square and St Andrew's Square. The area would be promoted as a quality location for businesses, shops and residents. New shops would be allowed to have frontages on the street, but only high-quality shops and stores of international repute (e.g. Versace, Armani, Harvey Nichols and Conran). The street would also have a large number of restaurants and cafes and the growth of a 'cafe culture' would be encouraged.

The study was commissioned jointly by the City of Edinburgh Council, Historic Scotland (*www.historic-scotland.gov.uk*), LEEL (now SEEL) (*www.scottish-enterprise.com/about/lecs/edin*), Scottish Homes and the Edinburgh New Town Conservation Committee (*www.ebs.hw.ac.uk/EDC/guide/newtown.html*) in response to fears that offices in the area were lying empty. While there was some truth in this, the first New Town (the original part) is not in economic decline. In the wake of the construction of the new financial district office vacancy rates are dropping, retail spending is rising and the number of people living in the New Town is increasing.

The broad plan was welcomed by Edinburgh's politicians and business leaders and it reinforces the council's planning and economic development policies for the city centre. It creates a balance between conservation in the World Heritage Site and appropriate forms of development and provides an opportunity for the New Town to continue to play a vital role in the economic vitality of Edinburgh city centre and 'to enable Edinburgh to retain its competitiveness'. In late 2000 it was confirmed that the prestigious store Harvey Nichols would open a branch in St Andrew's Square in 2002, forming a major focus within this new up-market area. It will also be the significant development that will make possible the complete renovation of the currently run-down bus station.

Entry points/gateways to the destination

The city has been slow to recognise the truism that 'first impressions count' – the visual impressions of the 'arrival' – and 'departure' – points are in need of strengthening, with arrivals at Edinburgh by road, rail, air and water.

Exercise

Gateways/first impressions

What are these 'first impression' points and where are they? Where is the Edinburgh that is pictured in the 'mind's eye' first noticed? Are these critical 'first impressions' well managed and enhanced or unnoticed and neglected? How can they be enhanced/improved?

Apply this practical exercise to a destination of *your* choice.

Zones (central/urban, suburban, rural 'hinterland' and remote)

Edinburgh's central zone is experiencing major activity, prompted by the devolution of political powers to the new Scottish Parliament based in the Holyrood area. This in turn is leading to expansion of the city population, to increasing housing demand and housing prices. New land for housing is sought on green field sites on the city's boundaries.

The suburban zones attract housing and retail developments, the latter having arguably contributed to the decline of Princes Street as a major shopping area for both tourists and residents. Certain new retail proposals for Princes Street are aimed at reducing this trend.

The surrounding areas of the Lothians are inevitably less popular than the city itself. Ironically, the success of the city in tourism is resulting in localised overcrowding and traffic congestion and this can benefit the towns, villages and countryside of the surrounding areas as certain tourists turn to these quieter areas. For tourists travelling further afield there is a clearly defined 'milk run', although many tourists may be reluctant to leave the many attractions of the city itself. Localised congestion, high prices and parking problems may affect this picture. A policy objective of the Edinburgh Tourism Action Plan (2000) is a commitment to

Photograph 6.2 *A 'first impression' of Edinburgh by road*

'encourage greater visitor dispersal and retention throughout Edinburgh, the Lothians and the rest of Scotland'. This harmonises well with Scottish tourism policy for a greater degree of dispersal throughout the country, notably to areas with problems of economic decline.

Tourism provision: specific provision for tourism

Figure 6.4 gives information about plans already discussed for bringing more tourists into Edinburgh.

Figure 6.4 *Edinburgh Tourism Action Plan: Wanted! As many tourists as possible. Discussion* in Edinburgh Evening News, *8 December 2000. Ian Swanson*

Anyone who's tried to negotiate the crowded pavements at Christmas and Hogmanay will find it hard to believe there's a need to attract more visitors to Edinburgh. But the city's tourism industry has just launched an action plan to increase its share of the market. The new drive to make Edinburgh one of Europe's 'must see' destinations includes city breaks targeted at different age groups, offering events and festivals outside the normal tourist season and measuring the capital against places like Barcelona, Vienna and Copenhagen.

The private sector is to take the lead role in promoting the city – and there will be a much bigger emphasis on the internet. Jack Munro, chief executive of the Edinburgh and Lothians Tourist Board, claims information technology will make tourist brochures redundant within three years. 'We can't any longer sell Edinburgh on the back of a nice brochure,' he says.

'By 2003, tourism will be the biggest single category of product sold over the internet. Some 230 million North Americans and 202 million Europeans will have internet access.

Our customers want to buy the Edinburgh tourism product in a completely different way from before. By using the internet, they want far more information and far more detail.'

The action plan has been praised by industry groups, but some experts and interested parties enter a note of caution. Bill Anderson of the Forum of Private Business in Scotland says the internet is important, but 90% of bookings still come by conventional means. 'We do need to use the internet, but it is not the answer to everything. You can't ask the internet about specialist diets because you're allergic to ice cream or if you can leave your dog in a car outside the hotel. Personal contact is very important. We still need guidebooks, telephone numbers and people at the end of the line to answer questions.'

Tourism lecturer Frank Howie, from Edinburgh's Queen Margaret University College, acknowledges the internet is not yet part of most people's daily lives – but says that will come. 'We are already seeing relatively cheap internet-access TVs and that will make a difference. The internet will become like another TV channel. At the moment, it is special-interest tourists wanting to customise their own holiday who are more likely to use the internet. Once they can log on on their TV ordinary tourists will probably follow. It will be more convenient.'

Tourism is worth £1.2 billion to the Edinburgh economy and until recently the city has managed to buck the downward trend in tourist numbers seen for Scotland as a whole. In 1999 Edinburgh and Lothians saw a 16% increase – the highest ever – in UK visitors and the capital retained its 13th place in the world league of conference destinations, staying ahead of London and overtaking Paris. But there was a drop in overseas visitors. Final figures are still being calculated, but it could be as much as 10%. The industry blames the strong pound.

Ivan Broussine of the Scottish Tourism Forum says despite its obvious attractions, Edinburgh cannot afford to rest on its laurels. It must compete, for example, with cities like Venice, Amsterdam and Paris as a weekend break destination. 'People don't have to come to Edinburgh and they will only do so if word of mouth says the service here is good,' he says. 'Business will not automatically come here. It has to be worked at. Even if Edinburgh has performed better than the rest of Scotland, it must retain its competitive edge. If you don't change with the market, you're in danger of losing the market.'

Jack Munro says the action plan will try to bring tourists to Edinburgh throughout the year. 'We will be promoting the Christmas market, Hogmanay and city breaks, continuing to develop events and festivals outside the peak season.' But he says there is strong competition. 'People want to know why they should come to Edinburgh rather than Barcelona or Vienna. Instead of general inquiries, we are almost having to bid for individual travel.'

Frank Howie, who specialises in destination planning and management, is sceptical about giving the lead role in tourism to the private sector. 'The private sector does certain things very well. They can put their money on a winner – but they can also pull out. The public sector is in there for the longer term, but that doesn't mean it has to be a "dead hand".' And he believes today's tourists are more mature than in the past. 'They've been to the tourist sights. When they come back, they want something different – romantic Edinburgh, literary Edinburgh, poetic Edinburgh, youth Edinburgh. All these "other Edinburghs" are out there waiting. Tourists are becoming more experienced, more demanding and more prepared to complain. The attitude is "Been there, done that, bought the t-shirt, what's next?" Maybe parts of Edinburgh are overheating and we need to look at developing other parts of the city for tourism. The Hogmanay celebrations show we can be almost too successful. We definitely don't want to stop tourists coming to Edinburgh, but we may need to disperse them a bit. Leith has *Britannia*, but tourists are effectively jumping from the centre down to Leith and back again. Why do we not create more tourist attractions in Leith itself?' And Mr Howie says that, with a bit of effort, even the local neighbourhoods of Gorgie and Dalry could find a place on the tourist trail. 'I was in Barcelona recently for a couple of weeks' holiday. The first three or four days was doing the sights, then I said to my Catalan friends, "That was great, now show me the real Barcelona." That's what we need to do in Edinburgh. There are many more young, adventurous tourists these days, who read the *Rough Guides* and *Lonely Planet* – the cool travel books – and they are looking for "ordinary" places, relatively untouched by tourism. With a bit of tender loving care ordinary places like Gorgie-Dalry could become interesting.'

Exercise

'Ordinary places' and their potential

For a city/large town of your choice – whether it is currently a tourist desti-nation or not – identify 'ordinary' areas that you believe could be of interest to the 'New Tourist' of today who is looking for 'REAL' tourism.
See the discussion on new tourism and REAL tourism in Chapter 1.

Impacts of tourism on the city and its residents

Residential and business communities

Generally, both these 'communities' recognise the contribution tourism makes to the city's economy, although there are regular criticisms expressed to the media such as overcrowding of central area streets and, more insidiously, the loss of local shops that become tourist-oriented, rather than catering to neighbourhood needs. While there is, allegedly, less general 'warmth' towards tourism in Edinburgh (or the UK as a whole?) than in some destinations – perhaps related to a less developed 'service mentality' – tourists generally regard the city as a friendly place. As a step towards enhancing this the City Council introduced 'City Centre Representatives' in 1998 to be the 'public face' of the city and able to provide information and assistance to all city centre users – businesses, visitors and residents. Glasgow also took a similar step (*www.glasgowworks.co.uk/cityreps/city_centre_reps.htm*). They are also trained in basic first aid and have a working knowledge of at least one foreign language. As a further example of measures that benefit both tourists and residents, a 'Safe City Strategy' was launched in 1996 on the rationale that 'feeling safe at home and in the street is essential to everyone's quality of life'. A significant element of this is the use of closed circuit television (CCTV) to improve safety in public places and commercial centres. The initial 'Capital Eyes' project covered Princes Street, Lothian Road and the Grassmarket and is expanding in coverage (*www.scotland.gov.uk/library/pan/pan59–17.htm*).

Exercise

Privacy

Is there a danger of infringement of privacy in the widespread use of CCTV? Should further expansion be supported? Give your answers for and against, from a destination management perspective.

Response to climate/weather

Responses can be reflected in the buildings, facilities and services offered in all the tourism sectors. The realisation that an unpredictable maritime climate can be moderated by good design in outdoor eating, drinking and general 'people watching' areas – as well as in bus shelter design – is being demonstrated in new developments. Arguably, the 'new tourist' who visits Edinburgh is less dependent on 'good' weather.

Tourism provision

Edinburgh: destination summary

All sectors of the tourism industry are represented in the city: accommodation, transportation, attractions (natural; cultural; man made), retail and information services. Accommodation has diversified in recent years, as seen in the growth of independent hostels and budget to mid-range hotels catering for more youthful travellers and families. Transport in this affluent city is dominated by private car use although alternatives are gaining wider support.

The attractions sector has been boosted by a major new attraction – 'Our Dynamic Earth' (*www.dynamicearth.co.uk*) at Holyrood – while the traditional historical and cultural attractions generally hold their ground. The retail sector has lost out to other cities and to the out-of-town shopping complexes, but a resurgence of 'up-market' speciality shopping may reverse or slow this trend.

Impacts of tourism and responses to this suggest Edinburgh may be considered to be at the 'mature' stage of development as a tourist destination (see Chapter 2).

CASE STUDY

'Mega events' – Edinburgh Hogmanay

Edinburgh's 'Hogmanay' new year festival is arguably one example of the recognition that there are 'optimum' levels of development beyond which the 'carrying capacity' of a place is exceeded and the quality of the tourist experience is diminished. In fact, in this example it was public safety considerations that prompted serious consideration of crowd size which is now in operation. Applying this concept to the destination as a whole is important – given the implications of decline – but it is also controversial. Clearly, few local businesses would welcome the prospect of reduced numbers of tourists if it meant reduced business. More recognition that where the tourist experience is enhanced the tourist will stay longer and generally spend more money is beginning to win over the business community. A related example is reduced opposition to traffic restrictions. The historic Royal Mile in August was until recent years a busy traffic corridor. Progressive 'traffic calming' through the reintroduction of 'setts', the traditional – and relatively bumpy – road surface, and road narrowing have produced a quieter, less polluted and pedestrian-friendly street. Temporary closure of part of the street during the height of the summer festival period showed the great popularity of 'continental-style' pavement cafes and bars. In late 2000 plans were announced to close that part of the Royal Mile – between Cockburn Street and the City Chambers – from 8 am to 6 pm all year round. Blanket opposition to such measures has largely disappeared in the city – concern now focuses on where 'displaced vehicles' will go and how long it will be before improved public transport provides a genuine alternative to the appeal of the private car.

As tourists (and residents) in destinations increasingly rediscover the use of their legs as a means of transport the levels of detail within the environment must change – a slower pace allows more enjoyment of smaller details, but also lowers tolerance of graffiti and litter including the urban blight of chewing gum dropped indiscriminately onto pavements (*www.zer-ogum.org.uk*), not to mention the problem of dog droppings, another international problem (*www.district.north-van.bc.ca/article.asp?a=538&c=424*).

While 'signing' for vehicles is part of the 'cityscape', there is more need for pedestrian-scale directional and interpretive signing. The City Council has begun a comprehensive programme of high-quality, legible yet unobtrusive directional signing as befits a world heritage site. There is a parallel need for interpretive signing. A number of 'heritage trails' exist in the city, for example the 'Patrick Geddes Heritage Trail (Howie, 1986). Ironically, the conditions demanded by the local civic trust for the placing of interpretive plaques resulted in their being 'missed' by the great majority of tourists.

There is a double irony here in that the trail is based on the approach of Geddes, a 19th-century Edinburgh pioneer in the planning of cities and regions (*www.cc.ed.ac.uk/geddes*). In the spirit of his approach to education and to 'civics', the trail uses his technique of 'provocative interpretation'. It asks the user to stop and look closely at the townscape visible from each of the stations on the trail and consider the question: 'Could things be better organised at this point?'

A number of other self-guided 'trails' exist in the city, focusing largely on architecture/design and history. In recent years a number of private companies have offered walking tours and these have become popular. They focus largely on 'murder and mystery' or the supernatural but also cover the literary, historical, cultural and film/media associations of the city.

Current controversial issues in the city – 'grey area' tourism

Howie (2000) has referred to 'grey area tourism'. These are issues in tourism, or initiated by it, on which the 'official' tourism bodies do not have a clear or agreed approach.

Red light zone

Exercise

The sex industry

Should there be official recognition (and regulation) of the sex industry in the City, as exists in Amsterdam and other larger, but comparable European city destinations?

A century ago, one of Edinburgh's most famous literary sons, Robert Louis Stevenson, 'began to discover a side to Edinburgh which was far removed from the middle-class drawing rooms of his sheltered childhood [...] the underworld howffs of Leith' (Desebrock, 1983:14 in Stevenson, 1983). Irvine Welsh, author of the novel *Trainspotting* (1994), may or may not have been aware of Robert Louis Stevenson's earlier accounts of this 'other Edinburgh' when he proposed that Edinburgh, as an aspiring European capital city, adopt the Amsterdam approach to the sex industry:

> A good way to promote tourism would be to turn Leith into a social policy experimental area like Amsterdam, with drugs and sex liberalisation to the fore.
> (*Edinburgh Evening News*, 28 January 1997)

A 'controlled but cooperative' policing approach to prostitution is established in the city. Contemporary examples include 'saunas' where prostitution is known to be practised – in areas of Leith and other less affluent neighbourhoods in the city. Reducing the incidence of prostitution on the streets is regarded as desirable for the safety of sex workers and for the welfare of local residents. Not prostitution but regarded as part of the sex industry, naked, erotic dancing has become available in certain bars in more salubrious neighbourhoods of the city centre, both on stage and as 'lap dancing', with comparatively little evidence of complaint.

Ryan and Kinder (1996) argue that sex tourism should not be perceived as 'a form of deviance', its general treatment in the tourism literature, and that it is hypocritical to discuss urban tourism with no reference to prostitution, since it is a widespread urban phenomenon. They also note that in Auckland, New Zealand, 30% of the value of the sex industry comes from 'out-of-town clients and others who could be described as tourists'.

There are arguments for localisation of sex tourism in areas where issues of health and policing can be assured – but where? Planning and other records for (sex-selling) saunas, generally suggest an initial hostility from local residents, often taken up by the press, then if permission is granted a 'settling-in' period, when the matter largely disappears from public debate. Amsterdam is frequently mentioned as a good example of a contemporary tourist city. As well as its undoubted attractions in the arts and culture, its architecture and urban design and its friendly residents, it has a reputation for tolerance and liberalism. This extends to its red light district. Dahles (1998) has cast doubts on this – suggesting that Amsterdam needs a new identity – at a time when Edinburgh may consider it a potential role model. She refers to growing 'dirt and disorder' allegations and a loss of its

Photograph 6.3 *Sex in the city – erotic dance in city centre bars, Edinburgh*

attractiveness in an expanding tourist market; also, the fact that in 1991, Amsterdam dropped from fourth to eighth place in the most popular cities in Europe league table, 'outpaced by Dublin, Vienna, Budapest and Edinburgh and threatened by Madrid, Brussels, and Berlin' (Dahles, 1998). She adds that image research shows that 78% of visitors are drawn by the cultural–historic aspects – museums and exhibitions – while over 50% by the liberal atmosphere of the city. 'Hot issues' like a red light district, 'dirt and disorder' and drugs are certainly issues in Edinburgh but they do not appear to have a significant adverse impact on the actual tourist numbers; indeed, in the absence of research evidence, they may contribute positively to its image as a modern, cosmopolitan city.

Exercise

'Sex in the city'

The 'sex industry' exists in many, if not most, cities in formal recognised guises but also as an informal, covert activity. What are your views on it? Should it be banned? Should it be ignored? Should it be 'brought out of the dark' and recognised (and regulated and taxed) like any other industry/commercial activity? Is it present in a destination you know? What forms does it take? Is it one of the many assets of that destination or a disincentive to mainstream tourists?

Development sites

From the mid-1980s to the late 1990s Edinburgh had been infamous for its 'holes in the ground' – i.e. cleared/derelict sites where redevelopment has been 'indefinitely postponed' for various reasons – primarily an unsatisfactory financial climate.

The Edinburgh financial district

Until only a few years ago the following was true:

> For all its financial wealth, there is no downtown business district of glass tower blocks and there are no motorways. Business is conducted in the elegant sobriety of converted Georgian townhouses and in ornate Victorian banking halls and board-rooms. Edinburgh, with its over-powering and civilising sense of history seems to have resisted the urban excesses of the 20th century, much as Florence or Vienna have done.
>
> (Ward, 1985)

In 1994 the Edinburgh International Conference Centre (*www.eicc.co.uk*) was completed and the new financial district of which it is a part is nearing completion, transforming the west side of the city, strengthening Edinburgh's transition towards becoming a European city of distinctive neighbourhoods – such as the Paris 'quartiers' – and precipitating major change in the New Town. Business had been conducted in the Georgian town houses of the New Town. However, the New Town was originally built as a residential area for the 'well to do', keen to escape the squalor of the 18th-century Old Town. Much later, in response to socio-economic change, substantial parts of it became the business district. Now the New Town is about to see demographic change once again as its vacated offices are coveted as desirable residences.

The vanguard (or 'early warning'?) of what was to come was the completion of the Sheraton Hotel in 1984. It is variously described: 'a plain stone-faced monolith with faint neo-classical tinge' (McKean, 1998) and more appreciatively as a 'modern hotel [whose] stone-clad, gabled façade and glistening interior re-interprets the Edwardian luxury evident in the Caledonian Hotel' (Ward, 1985).

Exercise

New neighbourhoods

(Use the Edinburgh examples as exemplifying general principles and a basis for comparison with a destination of your choice.)

The financial district/Conference Centre (EICC)/Sheraton Hotel:

1. Does this major development mark the beginnings of an 'arrondisement'/
'quartier' approach to city development (with reference to the distinctive districts of Paris)? What are the pros and cons of such an approach to urban planning and design?

Are these new buildings complementary to – or in unacceptable contrast to – the historic architecture of the city? Are they fine examples of con-temporary architecture or are they unworthy of such a prominent location in a capital city? Consider the adage 'form–function–feasibility' (i.e. the form should be related to the function of a building, and this should be feasible to achieve).

2. What impact(s) will the EICC and related developments have on the surrounding neighbourhood? Consider the small traders, pubs, cafes and local residents. What changes in the neighbourhood might be anticipated?

3. Festival Square lies in front of the Sheraton Hotel, adjacent to Lothian Road. Is it a *public* space or is it the property of the hotel? Such uncertainties prevent it taking its rightful place as a public square – a feature in short supply in the city. Latterly, this perceptual problem has been recognised by the City Council – public art is invited, up-market 'international' markets have been held and more public use is made of it, adding to the informal use long made of it by young skateboarders.

A number of other major developments are now underway or recently completed, such as the previously noted 'Our Dynamic Earth' (*www.dynamic-earth.co.uk*), a major visitor attraction opened in July 1999 in the vicinity of Holyrood Palace. It was financially assisted by the Millennium Commission but unlike several other similarly supported attractions which have failed to meet their visitor targets, this exceeded expectations by 48%, drawing in just over half a million visitors, as opposed to the 350,000 budgeted for, by the end of 2000. It also became a successful venue for corporate hospitality, hosting more than 200 events by that date.

Other developments are taking place in this area – hotel, retail, major newspaper and media headquarters and, notably, the new Scottish Parliament expected to be completed by 2004.

Sites such as these illustrate a number of aspects of Edinburgh as a destination. Not unexpectedly, a city is essentially 'multifunctional' – it serves many purposes, of which tourism is only one. Edinburgh, a 'tourist–historic' city (Ashworth and Tunbridge, 1990: 79) presents particularly sensitive considerations. A central aim of destination management in Edinburgh is to integrate the demands made on the city in such as way as to attain an optimum pattern and level of development and to sustain this for the benefit of tourists, residents and the business community.

The Old Town of Edinburgh

The appeal of Edinburgh as a World Heritage Site has been attributed to the contrasts between the New Town and Old Town. Whereas the built environment of the New Town is characterised by its 'formality', the pattern of development of the Old Town is one of 'organic growth', that is, unplanned, gradual change over the centuries in response to changing demands and changing fortunes. The mediaeval, Victorian, modern and postmodern eras are represented, all playing a functional rather than solely a decorative role within the area. This is at the heart of the destination management challenge – integrating tourism with the everyday functions of a living working place.

Destination management issues

The Royal Mile is the 'must see' heart of the Old Town, running downhill from the Castle to Holyrood Palace. Traffic–pedestrian conflicts are significant and the pros and cons of pedestrianisation – in part or in whole – have been long debated. Local residents express concern over the declining proportion of local shops as they give way to tourist shops and the question of 'tourist tat' vs authentic Scottish souvenirs is raised (*www.thetatgallery.com*). New developments have engendered heated debates as to their integration with the existing urban fabric.

CASE STUDY

Architectural styles and new developments

St Mary's Street, just off the Royal Mile, exemplifies the popular 'Scots-Baronial' style – crowstep gables, mock defensive turrets, stone construction and decorative detail. It is 'iconic' – instantly identified as 'Scottish', although some critics have rather haughtily referred to it as a 'bastard' style, lacking a true pedigree.

The style is found in 'ordinary' flats and local shops as well as in more prestigious buildings in the Royal Mile and loosely interpreted in buildings elsewhere in the city – and the country. Over the years, modern buildings have steadily encroached on the Old Town.

Contemporary architecture such as the former Lothian Regional Council Offices (built 1968) at the George IV Bridge/High Street intersection contrast strongly with the adjacent buildings, 'its horizontality and the large scale conceding little to the verticality and fine grain of the Lawnmarket' or the weakly classical former Midlothian County Council Buildings completed in 1905 (McKean, 1992).

Exercise

Old and new architecture

Should new buildings be required to copy or incorporate elements of the existing buildings into their design or should they be free to introduce new elements into a heritage townscape?

Should the aim be harmony or (stimulating?) contrasts within an area?

Is a sense of 'human scale' the key element?

The Crowne Plaza Hotel (formerly the Scandic Crowne) built in 1989 in the High Street draws on the Scots-Baronial style, while being system built of prefabricated concrete panels. It is an attempt to combine modern function with (at least superficially) traditional style.

Comment on the integration of this 'contemporary' building with the surroundings. It attempts to emulate the traditional, architectural form of neighbouring buildings though the fine detail of the hand-crafted product is missing from this product of modern industrial construction methods. Is it successful or is it an unacceptable 'pastiche'?

Should a building always be 'of its time'? In today's postmodern era should designers and developers be free to treat 'heritage' less reverentially? Perhaps in an area such as the Old Town – part of a world heritage site – strict rules of conservation should apply? Or should the philosophy be one of concern to maintain a human scale and a respect for the past with a willingness to integrate the best of present-day architecture and urban design?

These ideas and others on the role of city and regional planning and human impact on the environment generally were discussed and presented to citizens and visitors by Patrick Geddes (1854–1932) at the Outlook Tower, now regarded as the 'world's first interpretive centre' a short distance from the Castle down the Royal Mile. He used the audio-visual equipment of his day – the *camera obscura* – which projected live images of the city onto a screen (*www.cce.ed.ac.uk/geddes*) (Howie, 1986).

IN CONCLUSION – EDINBURGH AS A DESTINATION

A major review of Edinburgh, carried out in 1989, focused on the city as a destination in the context of its competitors. It concluded that the city has certain great advantages:

1. the setting – a great location, comparable to that of Prague (*pis.eunet.cz*)

2. the historic Old Town – comparable to that of Heidelberg (*www. e-heidelberg.com*) with its dramatic 'ribbed spine from fortress to palace'

3. the New Town – its elegant, planned townscape which is also functional

4. the people of the city.

It also identified issues where action was required to enable the city to compete successfully in a European and global market:

1. attractions, events and accommodation

2. a new vision for Old Town

3. infrastructure

4. training and employment

5. marketing.

The study took a historical perspective, noting the tradition of enterprise and achievement in Edinburgh – for example in medicine and science – notably from the period of the Enlightenment in the 18th century, stating that 'now' (i.e. 1989), just as then, there is a need for new visions for the city. It proposed a focus on tourism development, with the residents in mind, and what it must therefore supply – satisfying jobs in a famous and prosperous city.

Given the great importance of tourism it warned against complacency. The 'do nothing' option was unacceptable. The city would slip down the destination league table. Once relegated the result would be fewer tourists, less revenue and less inward investment.

This vicious circle could even become a downward spiral. The 'new tourist' was recognisable – more experienced and more demanding – a product of a shrinking world offering more destination choice. Exotic new destinations were becoming available at very low prices, often subsidised by governments anxious to develop tourism, while Edinburgh was in direct competition with Paris, Amsterdam and York for short breaks. Other UK destinations were more active than Edinburgh – they were spending far more money to attract visitors: while EU visitors to UK had increased by 30%, in Edinburgh they had increased by only 5%. Direct air routes to Edinburgh were very limited – a longer term issue that had to be addressed. Half of all overseas visitors were from North America, a risky overreliance susceptible to political and economic variations. The tourist season was only 13 weeks long – 'shoulder weeks' had to be developed. That was the perspective in 1989.

Edinburgh's attractions

Edinburgh was second only to London, with 60 major attractions, in 1989. The problem was that the visitors visited too few of the range of attractions – on average only '2.4' attractions each. While the Castle had one million visitors per annum, many of these visitors raised the question, 'what is there to do next?' and left the destination after seeing little else. The study recommended that 'events' tourism should be encouraged. Religion and history were established in this field, but many other themes are more recent. For example, in the comparable destination of Saltzburg, the Arts Festival generated £15 million per year, demand for tickets generally outstripped supply and 3,000 jobs were directly related to it, while the city has only a quarter the population of Edinburgh (1989). Both destinations are 'burghs/burgs/burchts', as their names imply (Ashworth and Tunbridge, 1990: 79) – i.e. they are both defensible towns situated on high ground. They both have old and new towns and both capitalise on their historic, cultural and literary heritage. Each city has much to teach the other in terms of managing tourism and their cities.

More than a decade after this detailed study, the benefits of taking up these recommendations are clear. Development in all the recommended action areas has created the situation where, at a time when Scottish and UK tourism has declined over several years, Edinburgh's continues to grow, now requiring the city to once again devise a vision for itself and its future. Edinburgh's spirit of initiative has always turned a problem into an opportunity and the city has been involved in many of history's great movements – 'Today's trade wind is tourism' (Edinburgh Tourism Action Group, 1989). The key issue today is how best to respond to the challenges that success brings, embracing both the 'traditional' associations of Edinburgh and its recently acquired 'cool' image.

Bibliography

Airey, D. (2000) in M. Shackley *Visitor Management*. Butterworth-Heinemann. London.

Archaeological Institute of America/Kenneth Dasdan (1997) 'Roman Lioness' [Online]. http://www.archaeology.org/9707/newsbriefs/lioness.html [19 October 2000].

Ashworth, G.J. and Tunbridge, J.E. (1990) *The Tourist-Historic City*, Belhaven. London.

British Waterways Board (2000) Millennium Link [Online]. *www.millenniumlink.org.uk*.

Bryson, B. (1995) *Notes from a Small Island*. Blackswan. London.

City of Edinburgh Council (Annual) *Edinburgh: The Capital City. Official Guide*. CEC. Edinburgh.

City of Edinburgh Council (1998) *The Lord Provost's Commission for Sustainable Development*. CEC. Edinburgh.

City of Edinburgh Council City Development (1999) *Towards Sustainable Growth*. CEC. Edinburgh.

City of Edinburgh and Patrick Geddes Group (1988) *Patrick Geddes Heritage Trail*. CEC. Edinburgh.

Cousins, M. (2000) *The List Student Guide 2000*. Student Publications. Edinburgh.

Crummy, H. (1992) *Let the People Sing! A Story of Craigmillar*. Freepress. Newcraighall.

Dagbladet (1996) Edinburgh is cool. 28 June.

Dahles, H. (1998) Redefining Amsterdam as a tourist destination. *Annals of Tourism Research* 25 (1), 55–69.

Edinburgh Tourism Action Group (1989) *A Multi-agency Tourism Study of the Status of Edinburgh's Tourism*. ETAG. Edinburgh.

Gunn, C. (1997) *Vacationscope: developing tourist areas*, 3rd edition. Taylor & Francis. Washington.

Hazel, G./City of Edinburgh Development (1997) *Edinburgh: A City whose Past is also its Future*. Supplement. Royal Town Planning Institute. London.

Howie, F. (1986) The Patrick Geddes Heritage Trail, Royal Mile, Edinburgh. *Environmental Interpretation*. Centre for Environmental Education. Manchester.

Howie, F. (1992) Edinburgh, the Lothians and Fife in K. Wood and S. House, *The Good Tourist in the UK*. Mandarin. London.

Howie, F. (2000) Establishing the common ground, in Richards, G. and Hall, D. (eds) *Tourism and Sustainable Community Developments*. Routledge. London, pp. 101–18.

Insight Guides (1988) *Scotland: The Insight Guide*. APA. London.

Lonely Planet (1999) *Barcelona*. Lonely Planet. Melbourne.

Lonely Planet (2002) *Edinburgh*. Lonely Planet. Victoria and London

McKean, C. (1998) *Edinburgh: An Illustrated Architectural Guide* (2nd edn). Royal Incorporation of Architects Scotland. Edinburgh.

Mittler, D. (1999) Sustaining Edinburgh: The Lord Provost's Commission on Sustainable Development for the City of Edinburgh. *Scottish Affairs*, 29, 104–20.

Newman, A. and McLean, F. (1998) Heritage builds communities: the application of heritage resources to the problems of social exclusion. *International Journal of Heritage Studies*, (4) 3 and 4, 143–53.

Page, S. (1995) *Urban Tourism*. Routledge. London and New York.

Ralton, A. (1999) Unpublished honours dissertation. Queen Margaret University College. Edinburgh.

Reid, D. (1998) Touching the heart of Scotland. *Wanderlust*, August/September, 29, 55–8.

Rogers, R. (1996) *Cities for a Small Planet*. Faber & Faber. London.

Rough Guide (1996) *Scotland: The Rough Guide* (2nd edn). Rough Guides Ltd. Edinburgh and London.

Ryan, C. and Kinder, R. (1996) Sex, tourism and sex tourism: fulfilling similar needs. *Tourism Management*, 17 (7), 507–18.

Schaber, W. (1985) [English translation by Gail Schamberger] *Salzburg Town Guide*. Residenz Verlag. Salzburg.

The Scotsman, (2002), 1 June.

Smallman, T. (1999) *Edinburgh*. Lonely Planet. Melbourne.

Stevenson, R.L. (Reprint 1983) *Picturesque Old Edinburgh*. Albyn Press. Edinburgh.

Ward, R. (1985) *The Spirit of Edinburgh*. Richard Drew Publishing. Glasgow.

Welsh, I. (1994) *Trainspotting*. Minerva. London.

Wills, E. (1998) *What is the City but the People?* The EDI Group Ltd. Edinburgh.

CHAPTER 7

Village and small town

In this chapter the 'transferable material', i.e. facts, ideas, experience etc. which may be applicable to other destinations of this 'village/small town' type of your choice, includes destination image and rurality, industrial and agricultural heritage and its interpretation, local architectural styles, approaches to small-scale regeneration and development and 'priorities' in allocating scarce funding.

CULROSS

The well-preserved village of Culross is a surprising find in what was until recently a predominantly industrial area:

> The historic burgh of Culross lies on the northern shores of the Forth, some 20 miles from Edinburgh – a peaceful little town which seems to tumble down to the sea. The small white-harled houses, with rust coloured pantiled roofs, look very like they did in the 17th century when they were occupied by the merchants who brought wealth to Culross. Those days, when Culross harbour was full of sailors and merchants from Dutch and Baltic ships, are long gone. Now the foreign voices heard in the causies of Culross belong to tourists.
>
> (National Trust for Scotland, 1995)

Location

Culross is a village with a population of less than 500, located on the shore of the Firth of Forth, some 6 miles/10 km west of Dunfermline, West Fife, Scotland, UK (*www.dunfermlineonline.net*; *www.culross.org.uk*). The local tourist board is Fife Tourist Board (*www.standrews.com/fife*), the local authority is Fife Council (*www.fife.gov.uk/links.htm*) (see Figure 7.1).

Image

Guidebooks give a clue to how the village is perceived. Key words identify the induced image favoured by the writers. Positives include 'architectural gem', 'unchanged', 'romantic', 'picturesque' and 'quaint', negatives include 'out of the way' and 'little to do'. Other recurring words refer to its distinctive 'vernacular'

Photograph 7.1 *Overview of the village of Culross and its locality*

architecture – 'white-harled houses', 'pantiled roofs', 'causies' (causeways) and ...
tourists.

Strengths

Strengths of the village as a tourist destination include its distinctive architecture
and historical associations, its proximity to Dunfermline, a historic town of some
tourism note, 5 miles/8 km away (*www.dunfermlineonline.net*), and to Edinburgh,
20 miles/14 km away; also the fact that the village remains a living community and
not a 'museum'.

Weaknesses

Weaknesses include the rather narrow focus and level of tourist services and
infrastructure. Accommodation and places in which to eat/drink are limited,
although in a village only limited increase in provision may be possible without
unacceptable levels of change in the character of the place. This also applies to the
provision of parking places. Interpretation of the historical and architectural
interest is fairly specialised and is arguably too discrete – even inspite of the
importance of maintaining the sense of authenticity of the village as both a historical and a living place. Culross is also perceived as remote in terms of public
transport and signposting from the main roads – although it is only a short detour
off the main north–south tourist routes as they cross the Forth Bridge. There is 'not
enough to do' according to many visitors, notably those with children, while circulation within the village and visitor–resident 'congestion' during the summer
require attention.

Figure 7.1 *Location of Culross*

Destination portfolio

The distinctive qualities of the village are due to its urban form, its well-preserved 17th-century vernacular architecture and its historical associations. Culross is the most complete example in Scotland today of a burgh of the 17th and 18th centuries. This includes little houses with red pantiled roofs and crowstep gables lining narrow cobbled streets converging on the Mercat Cross. There is a 12th-century church with well-preserved interiors, the 16th-century home of a notable early industrialist, complete with original interiors and mediaeval gardens, the Abbey which was founded as a Cistercian monastery in 1217 and continues in use as the local parish church, the Town House which was built in 1625 and is now used as the National Trust for Scotland Visitor Centre and The Study, with its distinctive, corbelled 'Outlook Tower'.

The village's social and historical heritage goes back to the 6th century when it was an important religious centre. In the 15th century the village was granted a charter by the Cistercian Abbey, making it a barony and therefore giving it economic privileges such as the right to buy and sell goods within its boundaries, to hold a weekly market and an annual fair. The monks were among the earliest to engage in coal mining and this permitted the companion industry of salt panning to be developed – sea water was run into large iron 'pans' and evaporated by coal fires. Coal, salt and other tradeable goods were exported to Scandinavia and the Low Countries. The returning ships used the red pantiles produced in the Low Countries simply as ballast, but these progressively replaced the turf roofs of the little houses of Culross and indeed other coastal villages in the region which came to resemble in design those across the North Sea. Coal mining grew in significance under Sir George Bruce who gained the lease of the Abbey's collieries in 1575. King James VI of Scotland (James I of England) was so impressed and keen to increase the royal revenues that he granted Culross the status of Royal Burgh which permitted it to take part in the lucrative import and export trade (NTS, 1995).

For such a small place, there is a wealth of buildings of architectural significance and strong historical associations which give the village much of its tourist appeal. More recent historical connections focus on Valleyfield Woodland Park some 2 km east of the village which forms part of a landscape created in 1802 – the only commission of its kind in Scotland to be carried out by Humphrey Repton (1752–1818), the notable English landscape gardener.

Tourism status

The architectural qualities and religious significance of Culross are clear and rightly form the basis of its contemporary tourism industry. Can the equally fascinating social history be developed for tourism?

Industrial heritage is the focus of tourism in many destinations. The industry of salt panning and the related buildings are the main attractions in several locations including Northwich in Cheshire (*www.saltmuseum.org.uk*) and the Isle de Nourmatier (*www.enjoyfrance.com/magazine/zoom/00/page1_us.htm*) in the Vendée region of France. At Northwich, the Salt Museum works to conserve and promote the history of the Cheshire salt industry and the communities of the Cheshire salt towns since salt mining is 'an activity which has had an incalculable effect on the region's history and development. [...] Through original artefacts, models, re-constructions, old photographs, paintings and interactive exhibits the Salt Museum tells the story of a unique industrial heritage'. The Isle de Nourmatier's wealth still comes from its local production and the salt merchants harvest the marshes each summer. There the museum and tourist trails are based on significant material remains of the industry and its continuing importance. At Culross all significant traces of these industries have long disappeared, other than Preston Island in the River Forth where much of the industry took place. The island is now, however, within a lagoon, although this may make access more feasible, potentially for tourism.

241

Photograph 7.2 *Street-scape of Culross*

Photograph 7.3 *Distinctive regional architectural details – The Study*

The historically significant coal mining industry existed in the area until relatively recently – the 1970s – although preservation of machinery, buildings and other features was not considered for tourism development despite its historical significance. This contrasts with mining heritage centres such as the Scottish Mining Museum (*www.scottishminingmuseum.com*) at Newtongrange, near Edinburgh, established in 1984. It is a nationally registered independent museum which was founded to preserve and present Scotland's mining heritage. It includes a visitor centre, a recreated underground roadway and coalface, the pithead, and the massive winding engine as well as a restaurant and shop. This has 'put the area on the map' once again and while this level of tourism certainly cannot replace the jobs and wealth created by the now defunct mining industry it does play a significant role in the area.

The economic and social history of Culross is the basis for its current popularity as a tourist destination. There is also some tourist appeal in the nearby woodland while the shoreline of the estuary is the habitat of regionally significant seabird populations. Within its immediate environs there is potential for the development of other attractions. However, this raises a fundamental question: *Should* tourism in Culross be further developed? In answering this, several other questions must be raised.

Alternative futures – a question of priorities

The community of Culross did not drift apart when the area lost its core activities. Small-scale tourism founded on its successfully conserved architecture contributed to this. A key factor was the foresight of the National Trust for Scotland – back in the 1930s – in also 'conserving' the local community by encouraging them to continue living in their (restored) homes as tenants, albeit with certain restrictions on alterations to the houses (*www.nts.org.uk/culross.html*). Thus in the 1970s, when coal mining ended, the village was already both an established tourism destination *and* a working village. Arguably, with the clearance of the 'unsightly' coal mining industry, it actually increased in attractiveness as a place in which to live, at least for those not dependent on that industry for a livelihood. Tourism and other compatible 'uses' helped arrest disintegration and preserve community life. The village has become, to an extent, a 'commuter village' like several others in this part of the Fife. Workers in the capital, Edinburgh, who cannot afford the high housing prices there, find an alternative in living within 'easy commuting distance' in a pleasant village.

How has this impacted on the 'spirit of place' of the village? Could more tourism be developed within the village?

In emerging tourism destinations in central and eastern Europe – such as Poland and Bulgaria – villages and the countryside are increasingly attractive to western European tourists, largely because they seem to capture the essence of 'rurality' that parts of rural Britain have lost (see Chapter 9). This counters the rather 'dark' and heavy industrial image that then Soviet areas acquired during the Cold War and which dominated tourist perceptions until recent years. In western Poland, near the border with Germany, diversifying the use of the outdoor activities centre of a university to cater for tourist use has benefited the university which continues to use the (now improved) facilities at other times used by tourists, while the nearby village is able to sell fresh produce locally and some of the villagers are employed directly in tourism.

Collins (1996) studied several Balkan villages, which, with government funding for rebuilding, have become 'museum villages' successfully acquiring a new prosperity while preserving the 'essence' of village life. They capitalise on the premise that increasing numbers of tourists want to experience what life was like in a traditional village, seeing, for example, revived local crafts. One such village is Koprivshtitsa which formerly traded throughout the Balkans. 'Several houses have been restored to the condition they were in at that time ... although there are a few concessions to modern comfort, such as indoor bathrooms and electricity. [...] The houses are then "adopted" by families to clean and look after, in return for a percentage of income. Most guests eat in the restored village pub, which has a restaurant and provides a place to meet the "neighbours".'

A company supervises the villages in the scheme. Careful 'target marketing' of the product is an important part of the management notably to 'special interest' tourists, such as 'academics' and 'ethnic' tourists seeking out their family 'roots'. Visitors can see, for example in Koprivshtitsa, lace makers in their own homes, once again using the traditional practice of weaving horse hairs into the lace for added strength and can commission work directly. Another village, Arbanassis, features its restored fortress–villages that date back to the Ottoman occupation. Here it costs 'ten times the price of a modern house to restore one of the old dwellings, but so popular is the restoration programme that people are happy to undertake the commitment'. Incomers can buy a house if they are prepared to restore it and this brings in a steady source of employment for village craftsmen.

The restored Bulgarian museum villages take several forms reflecting the wishes of their residents. In Bozhentsi they opted to be a 'day village'. On payment of a fee visitors can wander around the restored homes during the day and the locals are left in peace in the evenings.

Richards (1999) highlighted the role of marketing in revitalising craft production, in the context of developing cultural tourism in Europe. Culture, crafts and tourism were identified as the 'vital partnership' and the definition of 'culture' was taken to include 'living culture' and 'popular culture'. Traditional crafts and cottage industries, such as textiles production, were important elements and tourists' purchase of locally produced goods and souvenirs was regarded as an important contributor to the local economy.

The Alto Minho in northwest Portugal (*www.rtam.pt*) was one of the regions discussed. This is a predominantly rural area dominated by the fertile valleys of the Lima and Minho Rivers which run from the mountains of the Peneda Geres National Park (*www.eurobirding.co.uk/peneda_geres_national_park.HTM*) to the Atlantic coast. The region is only recently being discovered by tour operators and independent tourists from the UK and other northern European countries and this market is still small when compared to international tourism elsewhere in Portugal, such as the Algarve. In the Alto Minho the traditional production of textiles for local use was increasingly being replaced by a more commoditised approach as more were sold outside the region, but a lack of entrepreneurship and marketing skills was holding back the potential. Richards considered there was a poor linkage between textile production and tourism whereas the potential for the basically high-quality products (and the need) for tourism in the interior of the region was great.

Opportunities for tourists to see the production taking place should be developed and local outlets such as in the villages would make it easier for craft producers to sell their products. 'Cultural tourists do not want to simply purchase a textile craft. They want to buy the whole experience behind it. They want to know that the linen was cultivated and spun locally as tradition dictates' (Fernandes *et al.* in Richards, 1999).

This raises questions on the nature of 'tourist tat' (*www.thetatgallery.com*) – what is the rational for cheap, generally imported, poor-quality 'souvenirs' dominating tourist outlets when high-quality, locally made crafts could be more effectively developed?

A further example may be drawn from British Columbia, Canada. An area that was wholly dependent on the local forestry industry now has its villages that cater for the needs of ecotourists. It raises a key question as to whether dependency on one industry should simply be replaced by dependence on another:

> After more than 100 years of large-scale timber exploitation in this province, and despite considerable negative attention focused on our forest industry, we remain one of the most sought after wilderness tourism destinations in the world. In fact, the tremendous opportunity for growth in eco-tourism has been, in part, created by an infrastructure made possible by resource extraction: roads, railways, airports, utilities and communities are all in place to foster expansion and diversification [...] obviously, diversification, rather than attrition, is essential to a stable and healthy economy.
>
> (Lawson, 2001)

These examples of village tourism raise several points. An increasing percentage of contemporary tourists are inclined to be 'independent travellers'. The majority, however – while forsaking the 'excesses' of certain hotel-based packages – still want comforts such as bathrooms and decent food as well as meaningful contact with local people (Howie, 1999). The physical restoration of 'traditional' villages can preserve the ambience of the built environment, but can it restore or recreate the social and cultural values associated with village/rural life? Some would question whether 'all' aspects of former village or rural life *should* be recreated – some, such as 'subservience to the local squire or master', should presumably be confined to the history books! In some villages there may also be 'difficulties converting a traditional working class community to the fresh disciplines of tourism, but they are not insurmountable' (Collins, 1996). Tourism has a significant opportunity here in contributing to the rebuilding of communities.

In the wider context, the impact of information and communication technology is likely to have significant impacts on villages and rural life generally. The opportunities it opens up for 'tele-cottaging' – living and working in a village yet being fully in contact with one's work in 'the city' – are running in parallel with certain social trends such as disillusionment with city life and lifestyle choices such as 'voluntary simplicity' – an up-dated versions of the 1960s' 'back to the land' vision. Whether these trends are in opposition to or are running parallel to current interest in the preservation of traditions and the physical environment, the diversification of employment opportunities, the restoration of communities, as well as other village, small town and rural questions, is the basis for evaluation of alternative futures for former traditional villages as tourist destinations. These 'futures' may be tourism led, but they should not be tourism dominated.

CULROSS – EVALUATION OF POTENTIAL

Just how much further potential does the village and its environs have? Perhaps more controversially, would the development costs be justified by the revenue generated by increased tourism? Are other areas more in need of the investment that would be required? Are there other reasons – apart from the economic – for development of this particular tourist destination? Might there be a stronger case for reducing the adverse impacts of tourism within the small village while encouraging tourism within the wider area?

The area tourist board has a remit for the whole of Fife – its primary objective is to increase tourism-generated income within the region. Several local authorities exist within the region. They have a role in tourism development and each argues its own case for development within its own boundaries. Development is expensive and risky. With limited funding a strong case has to be made as to why tourism development should take place in a particular locality, in this case Culross, where there is already a successful – if small – tourism industry. Other local authorities in Fife may present a stronger economic argument for successful development – for example a new golf-related facility in the east of the region building on the existing strength of St Andrews – the 'Home of Golf'; or an area where traditional industry is currently in decline may present a strong social argument for a tourism development on account of the job creation potential. Resolution of this debate may centre around an impact assessment of potential developments – addressing socio-cultural, environmental and economic factors. In such a context 'destination management' must truly be a 'multidisciplinary' activity with a wide-ranging ethos.

An example of such an impact assessment is discussed in Chapter 5. That chapter also considers the significance of conservation – as a 'stimulus' of tourist attraction, but also as a constraint on certain forms of development.

Bibliography

Collins, R.C. (1996) Putting the heart back into the village. *Planning Week*, 48:5.

Dunfermline Local Plan (2000) Fife Council.

Edwards, B. (1986) *Scottish Seaside Towns*. BBC Publications. London.

Howie, F. (1999) Ordinary places in G. Richards (ed.) *Tourism and Sustainable Community Development*. Routledge. London.

Lawson, P. (2001) Village tourism. *Branch Lines*, 12 (1) Faculty of Forestry, University of British Columbia, Vancouver, BC, Canada.

Moody, D. (1992) *Scottish Towns: Sources for Local Historians*. Batsford. London.

National Trust for Scotland (1995) *Culross*. NTS. Edinburgh.

Richards, G. (ed.) (1999) *Developing and Marketing Crafts Tourism*. Atlas. Tilburg, Netherlands.

CHAPTER 8

The resort

INTRODUCTION

In this chapter the 'transferable material,' i.e. facts, ideas, experience etc., which may be applicable to other destinations of this resort/seaside resort/cold water resort type, includes destination image and changing fortunes, approaches to regeneration and development and 'priorities' in allocating scarce funding.

TYPES OF RESORT

Resorts are towns or villages that have developed significant specialist tourism functions. They can be classed as coastal, inland, mountain or scenic resorts according to their location. Alternatively, they may be classified in terms of the character of their development (Robinson, 1976:168):

1. Centres which have developed exclusively as tourist resorts either by adding artificial attractions and infrastructure to pre-existing natural attractions, e.g. Niagara Falls, Canada (*www.niagarafallstourism.com*) and Blackpool in northwest England (*www.blackpooltourism.com/portal.asp*) or by developing tourist infrastructure in the absence of striking natural resources.

2. Towns which have developed a tourist industry as an incidental part of their normal functions, e.g. Stratford-upon-Avon (*www.stratford.gov.uk/stratford/tourism.nsf/pages/tourism.html*) Aviemore (discussed in Chapter 10) and most capital cities (see Edinburgh case study, Chapter 6).

3. Planned and developed destinations such as those of coastal Languedoc-Roussillon (discussed in Chapter 9) may be regarded as exemplifying a third resort type, being recently planned and developed 'new' destinations where facilities and services have been purpose built.

In this chapter the focus is on coastal resorts, although many of the points made are applicable to other types of resorts, the common factor being that tourism developments are a significant element within the locality.

Over a decade ago Cooper (1990:63–7) examined the threats facing 'cold water resorts', primarily the coastal resorts of northern Europe, as opposed to the 'sun, sand and sea' destinations of the Mediterranean coasts. He collated the views of a number of researchers in the field and produced a checklist of the threats they faced (Figure 8.1).

- Diminishing share and volume of domestic holiday market
- Growth in low social status, low spend tourists and day visitors
- Competition from holidays abroad and new domestic tourism facilities in northern resort locations
- Dependence on the long holiday market and difficulty of breaking into short holiday market
- Limited appeal to overseas visitors
- Highly seasonal destinations
- Outdated, poorly maintained accommodation and amenities
- Lack of wet weather facilities and out of season activities
- Poor information and interpretation
- Poor access and traffic problems
- Local opposition to tourism as the residential role increases
- Political interference on decisions
- Financial restrictions and low budget
- Lack of professional, experienced staff
- Local government reorganisation leading to more distant and larger authorities and short-term planning horizons due to planning and budgeting deadlines
- Low priority given to strategic thinking
- Lack of confidence in tourism by the business community
- Demands for increased operational efficiency and entrepreneurial activity by local government
- Shortage of research data

Figure 8.1 *Threats facing cold water resorts*

As well as these threats identified by Cooper, further 'threats' these resorts face lie in the changing nature of tourists. The characteristics of the contemporary tourist include:

- increased spending power per capita

- more leisure time

- greater experience of travel (and so, more discernment)

- a more active, ageing population

- more single adults

- later marriage

- two-income families.

It should also be noted that today fewer people work in 'sedentary' occupations and so are less in search of 'passive' holidays, where the minimising of effort was the goal.

ENVIRONMENTAL ISSUES

Increasing general awareness of environmental issues further contributed to the changed status of resorts, the media regularly reporting incidences of visual pollution and contaminated water at well-known resorts (see Figure 8.2).

- Solid debris – plastics, 'sanitary goods', condoms, timber etc.
- Oil – industry effluent and leakage from ships
- Other chemicals – industrial waste; farm fertilisers
- Sewage – raw or treated from cities
- Hot water – from power stations (changing the local ecosystem and encouraging, for example, algal growth)

Figure 8.2 *Beach pollutants*

Whereas all pollutants, notably the first two categories, can affect the visual attractiveness of a beach or coastline for tourism, some are also health hazards. For example, along the coastline near Musselburgh, a small town some 10 miles/16 km east of Edinburgh, once famous for its shellfish (notably mussels, hence the name) signposts still warn against eating these 'fruits of the sea'. Coastal and beach clean-up is expensive and the chemicals used for the treatment of oil spills can be more harmful biologically than the oil itself. The upgrading of sewage treatment has commonly been regarded as 'uneconomic', since the high levels of pollution were seen as a 'summer-only' problem. Sometimes water pollution is a direct result of the influx of tourists causing the capacity of treatment plants to be exceeded. However, the reaction of the contemporary tourist to this problem is no longer temporary – they are deterred from visting the destination, sometimes permanently. It is generally accepted today that 'prevention is better than cure' and is, in the longer term, also cheaper. European Union standards and enforcing regulations are leading to higher standards. 'Blue Flag' beaches are preferentially chosen by increasingly 'aware' tourists (*www.seasideawards.org.uk/blue1.htm*).

In Britain in 1988, 22 of 392 monitored beaches (including Blackpool's) failed to meet the standards necessary for the 'Blue Flag' award. Many areas have introduced their own standards to complement the EC standards. Lothian region's 'Clean Forth' campaign, begun in 1993, is leading to higher standards benefiting Edinburgh's waterfront (including Portobello, discussed later in this chapter) and eventually allowing traditional mussel fisheries to reestablish. In 2001 the sparling, a fish that disappeared from the Forth in the late 1960s due to overfishing, changes in habitat and pollution, reappeared as a spawning population. Since this fish is a key 'indicator species' of unpolluted water its reappearance is a clear sign of improving water quality.

STRATEGIES FOR RECOVERY

Diamond (1988) identified four possible strategies for tackling the problems faced by coastal resorts in decline.

Turnaround strategy

This would require public and private sector bodies to take action to reverse falling visitor numbers by investment in development and substantial planning and promotional efforts. The Isle of Man's approach – discussed later in this chapter – is one example.

Sustainable growth strategy

Where the resort's external conditions (such as access to the resort) are unfavourable, the objective is to maintain existing markets while attempting to achieve a low level of growth to supplement the loyal repeat visitors. This could be exemplified by the Largs approach, discussed later in this chapter.

Incremental growth strategy

New markets are sought – cautiously. New products are test marketed and according to the results development projects are undertaken in a phased, step-by-step manner. Dunbar illustrates the tentative search for new markets.

Selective tourism strategy

The resort's continuing strengths are identified. Only these are developed and target marketed appropriately. Examples of selective markets include family holidays and the education sector. 'Gambling' is a further example.

CASE STUDY

'Blackpool places its bets on casinos for resort future'

A survey conducted in 2000 revealed that 71% of residents who responded support the move to turn Blackpool (*www.blackpool.gov.uk*) into the 'Atlantic City of Europe'. The proposals are led by the public–private consortium Blackpool Challenge Partnership (*www.bcp-ltd.co.uk*) and include building up to six resort casinos, shopping malls, large theatres and conference facilities as well as increased gambling floor space. 'Blackpool has a huge number of parallels with Atlantic City on the eastern seaboard [of the USA]. It suffered comparable economic problems and is now thriving as a result of similar projects,' said the BCP manager. 'More than 25,000 jobs could be created by the proposals, which have been backed by developer

Leisure Parcs.' The managing director added that he wanted gambling taxes to be 'ploughed back into local regeneration projects' (Royal Town Planning Institute, 2001: 1).

The scheme hinged on a proposed change in the UK gambling laws. This would allow Blackpool and other coastal towns to host resort casinos. The review body reported to the government in 2001 and the chances of Blackpool becoming the 'casino capital of the north', or even 'of Britain', increased when the government announced proposals to relax laws which could pave the way for plans for resort casino hotels in Blackpool. In the wake of this the Blackpool Challenge Partnership reaffirmed its aim to work towards improving life for the whole of the seaside community – for tourists, industry and local residents. The 'resort casino hotels' concept meets with its criteria. Under the private developer, Leisure Parcs', proposals, Blackpool's famous 'Golden Mile' would make way for a 'Golden Triangle' of hotels, entertainment venues and a state-of-the-art conference centre. This is expected to create up to 25,000 new jobs in Blackpool and by the year 2020, the resort could be attracting 30 million visitors a year, spending £2bn. Close examination would be made of two existing, successful resorts where gambling is a major element – Las Vegas which upgraded its image of a rather seedy place into a respectable family resort and 'convention capital' of the USA; also Atlantic City which used the introduction of hotel gaming as 'a tool of urban development'. All aspects of tourism development would be considered, including job opportunities, hotel accommodation, conference facilities, community safety, nightlife and transport.

Exercise

The Blackpool proposals

Select a resort or resorts you are familiar with and decide which aspects of the Blackpool proposals might apply to them. Give your reasons. What specific new developments not noted above would you suggest? Has sufficient consideration been given to the climatic differences between the American 'role models' selected and British resorts, with their notorious 'changeable' maritime climate? What 'weather-related' responses would you build into your proposals?

As far back as 1985 the English Tourist Board launched a competition to raise awareness of the need for such strategic thinking. Resorts were asked to submit strategies that would be judged according to:

- level of local society commitment
- level of political support
- extent of 'corporate thinking' and involvement

- evidence of partnership with other public agencies, voluntary bodies and commercial interests

- attitude and commitment of the local tourism industry

- potential and ability to capitalise on strengths and opportunities

- the need for tourist board involvement.

Torbay and Bridlington were the winners and they received Tourism Development Action Programme status. TDAP status areas receive UK government aid for tourism while also involving the private sector. They are areas with major opportunities for tourism development or which demonstrate a need for tourism development on economic grounds. The creation of the 'English Riviera' was a further step to 'rebrand' or create a new identity for the area (see Chapter 4) (*www.torbay.gov.uk/index.asp?page=370*).

The perspectives discussed above give a framework for analysis of the responses to the challenges faced by the resort of Dunbar and the other resorts discussed in this chapter.

DUNBAR, EAST LOTHIAN

Photograph 8.1 *Dunbar*

Dunbar is a small town of 6,518 inhabitants (1991) situated some 20 miles (36 km) east of Edinburgh, in the district of East Lothian (*www.geo.ed.ac.uk/scotgaz/maps/1246.imagemap?380,138*).

It has been a popular seaside resort since Victorian times, although it has experienced decline since the late 1950s. During the 1980s significant efforts were made to reverse the trend, although there is concern that the longer term decline has only been concealed.

Key destination problems

Key problems and opportunities were identified by the 'Dunbar Initiative' – a partnership of public and private bodies – led by the local authority and the Scottish Development Agency in the late 1980s. The approach was aimed at tackling the regeneration of the destination comprehensively, rather than continuing the previous 'piecemeal' approach that had failed to reverse the trend of declining visitor numbers. The decline of Dunbar was caused by the same social and technological changes that afflicted many UK and other northern European resorts. Dunbar, however, had been slow to react due to distinctive local circumstances. A new power station was to be constructed only some 6 miles (10 km) southeast of the town. The fact that this was to be a nuclear power station gave rise to considerable protest by anti-nuclear campaigners. The development did, however, go ahead.

It would be difficult, but not impossible, to determine the impact of such a development on the image of Dunbar. No matter how well screened it might be, to many the mere presence of a nuclear power station would be considered a factor against Dunbar as a tourist destination. It should be considered, however, that the highly popular destination of Edinburgh is only a further 20 miles (30 km) or so from the now operating Torness nuclear power station and this is rarely raised as a factor against visiting Edinburgh. What was more significant locally, in the short term, was the fact that the large workforce necessary for the power station construction required accommodation and a significant percentage of the incoming workers found that in Dunbar – in this way supporting the town's underused hotels and guest houses.

Completion of the power station resulted in the departure of the construction workforce, ending the 'reprieve' from its declining tourism income. Meanwhile the decline in popularity of 'cold water, northern European resorts' had continued, leaving Dunbar – 'cushioned' for so many years – less prepared than other similar resorts for the harsh economic realities.

The problems of the town were:

- insufficient and outmoded attractions

- a low level of attractiveness – and continuing deterioration

- a fragmented, if well-intentioned, approach by the local authority

- insufficient visitor information

- insufficient promotion

- lack of specific tourism data

- insufficient local tourism organisation. Local opinion held that local government reorganisation in the 1970s, which substituted the wider district of 'East Lothian' for 'Dunbar' as the local authority, had strongly contributed to a loss of identity and resources.

These problems were common to many formerly popular northern European resorts at that time. 'Whether the progress of the resort life cycle [...] takes 20 years (as in the case of the Spanish Costas) or 200 years (as in the case of Scarborough) before the resort reaches maturity, destinations eventually reach the point where turning point decisions are necessary' (Voase, 1995: 125). The necessary changes were taking place in the USA, and other countries now well into the 'post-industrial' era. Popular conversation had already been enriched by expressions such as 'the rust belt' and 'sunset industries' reflecting major structural change leading to the decline of traditional 'heavy' industries and their dependent cities, accompanied by unemployment for their workforces. Tourism was widely regarded as a 'panacea', which would provide new economic futures for these areas; and tourism tastes were broadening and demanding new types of destinations and attractions.

'Traditional' resorts and the type of holiday experience associated with them had indeed gone out of fashion. The 'traditional British seaside holiday' had acquired a Monty Pythonesque image of men in rolled-up trousers with knotted handkerchiefs on their heads, of deck chairs and fat ladies and skinny men, of 'naughty' picture postcards and ice cream cones.

Perhaps giving a more contemporary view, referring to the Kent coast resorts of Margate, Ramsgate and Broadstairs (*www.tourism.thanet.gov.uk*) in particular, Johnson (1993) wrote in the *Guardian*: 'It's easy to see what they [the English Tourist Board, 1993] mean in Margate, where boarded-up and abandoned guest houses and neon signs proliferate along the beach front. In the almost toy-sized shopping centre, tattooed young men swear loudly at each other'.

The self-esteem of the local communities of aging resorts was simultaneously declining. The image projected through the media had a determining influence on decision taking. As Voase (1995: 125) noted, major change was necessary to create a new image and justify it with actual material change: 'The essential problem of the domestic seaside is one of a spiral of decline in which contracting business inhibits investment, which in turn contributes to continued deterioration of the product and continued contraction in business'. The changes in tourists' tastes and opportunities, which began in the 1950s and accelerated in the 1960s, were due to technological change (the availability of new passenger jet aircraft), social change (increase in holidays with pay and the 'Swinging 60s') and increasing spending power. Tourists who had traditionally spent their two weeks' annual holiday at a comparatively nearby resort could now head for the guaranteed sunshine of the Spanish Costas.

Larger resorts were able to respond more rapidly and more successfully to the changes. There the tourism industry was comparatively strong economically with access to private capital and significant political and economic strength within the local area. Examples include Bournemouth, Scarborough and Blackpool, in contrast to the smaller resorts where the local authority was the main and, probably, the only investor (Voase, 1995: 139) (*www.northyorks.gov.uk/tourism/default.shtm*).

Resorts such as Dunbar faced becoming increasingly unfashionable if not extinct. The problems were heightened by government curbs on spending by local authorities that made it difficult for local authorities to fulfil their responsibility for capital investment (Voase, 1995: 125). In the wider social and economic context, this time of significant change saw 'traditional' industries, such as coal mining throughout Europe and iron and steel towns in the USA, declining along with their dependent towns and communities. Is tourism as an industry any different? Importantly, it is – in the global context tourism was and is expanding rapidly. It shares this growth with information technology and other 'hi-tech' industries, as opposed to the old 'smokestack' industries in the 'rust belts' which are rapidly declining. If the declining resorts are to take advantage of these trends they must reposition themselves in the marketplace. This requires significant change in the destinations without 'throwing out the baby with the bathwater', that is the fundamental resources that give the resort its distinctive spirit of place. It also needs considerable investment and effective marketing.

Destination regeneration strategy – the Dunbar approach

For Dunbar it was necessary to identify:

- the key land and human resources with potential to solve problems
- the level of community (residential and business) commitment and support
- the key issues to be focused on
- the attractions of the resort and their attractiveness (including new image potential).

Development of concepts and recommendations for the regenerated destination was to be based on a programme of research identifying new activities and information needs and recommending promotional approaches. A number of main themes or topics emerged, all taking as keystones 'authenticity' of the products and maintenance of the 'spirit of place' of the destination. These were:

- health and fitness – a possibility
- countryside recreation – a certainty
- architectural heritage – a possibility
- fishing industry heritage – a certainty
- historical associations – a certainty.

It was also considered that there was potential in resurrecting the old epithet, 'Dunbar – the Ancient Gateway to Scotland', although the main A1 road north, passing near Dunbar, which gave credence to this was increasingly criticised as below 'A road' standards and was losing popularity to the M4 motorway on the west side of the country.

An exhibition and an audio-visual presentation were prepared to communicate the regeneration ideas to the local residents and the business community and to stimulate discussion (Howie, 1988b). Following this consultation on the outcomes would form the basis for a market analysis.

The market analysis would identify:

- the commercial viability of the selected themes
- the catchment population (of potential tourists) – considering access/transport corridors etc.
- other relevant factors to be addressed as they were identified.

Implementation

The implementation phase of the regeneration of Dunbar would address selected recommendations:

- for the natural environment – improved access and interpretation
- for the built environment – construction of a new swimming pool; a town centre improvement scheme
- for customer services.

An 'image campaign' and appropriate marketing would underpin the success of the regeneration programme which would include both minor change/fine-tuning of existing facilities as well as innovatory change if the need for this were established. The programme would be monitored and evaluated providing 'feedback' which would trigger adjustments as necessary to achieve the stated objectives.

Status report

The programme for the regeneration of this resort was carefully formulated and drew on the best available examples of contemporary good practice. By the mid-1990s, however, it was clear that while Dunbar had experienced improvement, there was a failure to 'break through'. While there were many possible reasons for this outcome, the following was one possibility.

Hypothesis

The 'incremental' (step-by-step) approach to regeneration failed to catch the attention of potential new tourists. A 'big bang' (such as a major new development) approach might have been necessary to 'put the destination back on the tourist map'.

An alternative response to the only partial success in regeneration would have been to consider 'non-tourism' futures for the town. Dunbar had been a successful tourist destination for over a century – that 'role' suited the times. But tourism was a comparative 'newcomer' – for all the town's previous history other activities were its 'bread and butter'. Was tourism the only future?

A non-tourism scenario

Dunbar could have 'rebranded' itself as a 'retirement town'. The natural and cultural facilities that made it an attractive tourist destination lend themselves well to this new identity – delightful countryside and coast, 'fresh air', local shops and services, golf courses and large hotels. Although the hotels were mostly rather run down through lack of investment capital, some could readily have been converted into residential homes for elderly people. The town was already an established 'commuter settlement', with good road and rail links for residents working in Edinburgh and this role could have been part of a symbiotic relationship with the 'retirement model'.

The survival of existing hotels, however, may have meant *not* having a residential home next door! The 'retirement/commuter town' identity might have contributed to a negative and 'dull' image of the town, unattractive to contemporary tourists – the resort's internal conflict. The relaunched 'tourism option' was favoured since it was held to lead the way to regeneration – although the residential and commuter roles of the town would continue unobtrusively. The 'step-by-step', fragmented approach had failed to turnaround the fortunes of this traditional, seaside resort. In a more demanding marketplace, a 'big bang' was required.

Development of a major new visitor attraction

Development of a major new visitor attraction is a costly and risky undertaking. Sound evaluation must underpin decisions – evaluation of the resources available and of potential themes for the attraction, paying close attention to the viability of these in the contemporary context. A decision was reached to create a major visitor centre around one of the major historical figures associated with the town and to capitalise on the inherent qualities of the local natural environment. The theme would also be in line with increasing contemporary interest in the sustainability of the global environment.

Project proposal: the John Muir Environmental World

John Muir is a founding father of what has become the international conservation movement and he was the inspiration for the creation of national parks. He was born in Dunbar in 1838, emigrating with his family to the USA. In the USA and other countries his achievements are widely commemorated, while in Scotland, his birthplace, he remains little known (Howie, 1988). A John Muir heritage centre in Dunbar would certainly meet a key requirement of authenticity and, arguably, attract an international following of tourists to the town:

John Muir Centre (proposed), Dunbar (*www.cs.strath.ac.uk/contrib/JMC/*)

John Muir exhibition, USA (*www.sierraclub.org/john_muir_exhibit/*)

John Muir Trust, Scotland (*www.jmt.org*)

Current status of the heritage centre proposal (2002)

While the theme of the visitor and heritage centre remains strongly supported there have been several major problems:

- locational controversies – whether the centre should be located in the town or in nearby countryside

- fund-raising problems – failure to win National Heritage Lottery funding, due largely to the inability of local community groups to resolve their locational uncertainties

- competitive threats from comparable visitor centres, notably the recently completed 'Our Dynamic Earth', at Holyrood in Edinburgh, which has an 'environmental' theme.

An impact assessment of the proposed centre had highlighted a major controversy. The initial proposal envisaged it being constructed within the existing John Muir Country Park, on the coast near Dunbar. Some argued that this natural area – part of which is the 'wild, rocky shore' of which Muir had written fondly – should remain wild. These opponents nevertheless wanted a commemorative centre to be set up, but it should be located in an appropriate building within Dunbar.

Since no such building was available, the result was deadlock. The ongoing controversy resulted in failure to gain the sought-after and crucial lottery funding.

Meanwhile, in the nearby town of North Berwick, the 'Scottish Seabird Centre, a 'state-of-the-art' interpretive and visitor centre opened in 2001 (*www.seabirdcentre.org*). This is contributing significantly to the attractiveness of this old established resort town to both 'traditional' and new visitors.

Exercise

Authenticity or compromise?

Just how important is 'authenticity'? Are compromises sometimes acceptable?

In order to achieve the desired John Muir Heritage Centre should compromises regarding its location have been made? If it were the case that the only site available was within a 'wild' area, development of which John Muir (some would say) 'would have' disapproved, should development have gone ahead there? Factors to consider include the fact that the visitor attraction would contribute to regeneration of this destination; also that John Muir's important conservation message would reach a wider audience.

A further controversial issue arose in 2002. John Muir's birthplace – a building within Dunbar – is a small 'traditional' visitor centre (*www.cs.strath.ac.uk/contrib/JMC*). There are current proposals to remove 'all' the internal structures of the building to permit the development of a 'state-of-the-art' interpretive centre. Opponents argue that this would remove the authentic, tangible connection with John Muir. Proponents argue that only the rooms are authentic, all the contents and fittings are simply 'of the time' of John Muir – the reconstruction of the interior of the building (while preserving the outside) would permit the development of an interpretive centre that would befit this pioneer environmentalist ... and attract significant numbers of tourists (see the discussion of heritage interpretation in Chapter 6).

LARGS, NORTH AYRSHIRE

The traditional resort town of Largs offers a comparison for Dunbar, with the added value that it has recent experience of the development of a heritage-based visitor attraction.

Largs is a small coastal town of 10,645 inhabitants, situated on Largs Bay, 18 miles (29 km) southwest of Greenock (*www.geo.ed.ac.uk/scotgaz/towns/townfirst456.html*).

Largs also has experienced a decline in popularity as a holiday destination and struggles with decreasing population and high unemployment. The local North Ayrshire Council works closely with the councils from East and South Ayrshire in policy creation to tackle this and other issues. Many of the inhabitants of the districts are commuters, to employment in Glasgow (*www.ayrshirejsu.gov.uk/structureplan/development.html*).

As in Dunbar, the decision was made that a major, new tourism development was required to turn around the town's fortunes. Vikingar! was developed and opened in 1994/95, part of the £4.2-million Barrfields Redevelopment Project (North Ayrshire Council, 1984). This connected the existing swimming pool and the Barrfields Pavilion Theatre and added the Vikingar! Experience, Winter Garden Cafe, theatre bar, gift and craft shop and the Viking Soft Play area.

The Centre interprets and presents the heritage and influence of the Vikings, specifically the history of invasion and settlement in this part of Scotland and takes the Battle of Largs in 1263 as a central focus. As in Dunbar's proposed visitor centre, the theme is nationally significant and relevant to this region. The expectation of success of the attraction and its potential as a catalyst for further development was based on sound analysis since economic regeneration was a major concern for Cunningham District. European funding was also forthcoming. The local community basically wanted development and although many expressed a preference for an indoor, dry sports area, the decision was made to build a visitor attraction. The local authorities decided to press for what they believed the community needed, rather than what a majority (of those who expressed an opinion) in the community appeared to want (see the discussion of policy models in Chapter 5).

The decision was also in accord with the current Scottish Tourism Strategic Plan (1994 and updates), one of the objectives of this national plan being 'to increase expenditure out with Edinburgh/Glasgow from 71% to 75% [...] and increase the number of jobs in tourism from 171,000 in 1991 to 195,000' within five years. The problem of seasonality is always an issue in UK tourism policies and Vikingar! was planned as an all-weather and potentially all-year attraction. The strategic plan also noted the scope for new attractions and 'things to do', which embraces entertainment, cultural attractions and events and the arts.

Vikingar! began as an all-year attraction, but as the initial excitement of the new product died down and the rest of the town followed the seasons, Vikingar! eventually had to do the same and is no longer open all year round for tourists, only for school visits. Even though Vikingar! had a higher annual throughput of visitors than the Scottish average for comparable attractions and has received several national tourism awards (including the Scottish Thistle Award for marketing), it is not running as successfully as expected. The failure to obtain National Heritage Lottery funding impeded the wider plans for recovery of the destination. The visitor attraction has also changed from being publicly owned (North Ayrshire District Council) to being owned by a charitable trust. The trust has its own policies and one is that projects seeking funding for renewal will have to focus on education. This does not pose a problem for Vikingar! as its lifeline during the off season has been educational visits from schools and the attraction has now been running for more than eight years. Other relevant factors include:

- The centre offers a cultural heritage product that is unique in Scotland, although the original Viking centre in York, Jorvik, could be a strong competitor on the UK and international markets and since 1999 the town of Peal in the Isle of Man has had a major 'Viking' heritage centre (as discussed later in this chapter).

- It has 'other legs to stand on' (it incorporates a swimming pool).

It may be speculated that this experience has contributed to a reduced focus on tourism in the regeneration of Largs. The three districts that constitute Ayrshire have a current joint strategy with comparatively little reference to the industry. The tourism content is largely about the environment and sustainable development, with little reference to culture or heritage, although the general encouragement of economic growth or regeneration implicitly includes tourism (*www.ayrshire-jsu.gov.uk/structureplan/development.html*).

Vikingar! has contributed to economic regeneration in Largs, although the local businesses apparently fail to recognise this. Appropriate renewal of this distinctive product may successfully relaunch it and allow further contribution to the regeneration of the resort. An ongoing challenge is the fact that the destination is 'out of the way' for many tourists – if not arriving by car, the train from Glasgow is the only mode of public transportation (see Chapter 4).

Exercise

Dunbar

Dunbar sought to identify itself as *the* destination. Indeed it blamed its decline at least partially on its earlier absorption into the wider local authority area of East Lothian. Was this a wise strategy? Were there not stronger arguments for identifying and marketing a wider area – with a diversity of attractions and accommodation – as the destination? (Consider the success of the 'English Riviera' discussed earlier in this chapter.)

ST ANDREWS AND THE COASTAL VILLAGES, EAST FIFE

The challenges faced by Dunbar are common to most 'traditional' coastal holiday resorts. The 'destination' need not define a single, precisely defined place. It can be a broader geographical area. The 'East Neuk' of Fife might be regarded as a destination area; alternatively, the 'East Neuk Villages' or the town of St Andrews alone. Whatever approach is adopted, each 'destination' would in fact share a wider 'tourist area', but local economic, social, environmental or political pressures might preferentially place the main marketing effort on a specific locality (see Figure 8.3).

St Andrews is a well-established summer resort with beaches, steep cliffs, a harbour and a modern Sea Life Centre. It is also a historical town, exemplified in its architecture and street layout, and is a former ecclesiastical centre of Scotland with a 12th-century cathedral, now an attractive ruin. The University is Scotland's oldest, established in 1412. It is also internationally known as the 'Home of Golf' and this continues to bring prestige to the town.

The coastal villages of East Fife are St Monans, Pittenweem, Anstruther and Crail. They are former fishing villages, ancient burghs of the 'golden fringe on the beggar's mantle' (a reference to the old county of Fife) which grew in importance in the 15th and 16th centuries as ports trading with the Baltic and the Mediterranean. Many traditional architectural features and the basic urban form have been retained, such as fine old crowstepped, pantiled houses, ancient churches, tollbooths, market squares, boatyards that once made fishing boats and now build leisure craft, a fisheries museum as well as an operational fishery. Offshore is the Isle of May, one of the first Scottish lighthouse sites and now a major nature reserve with a bird-watching station.

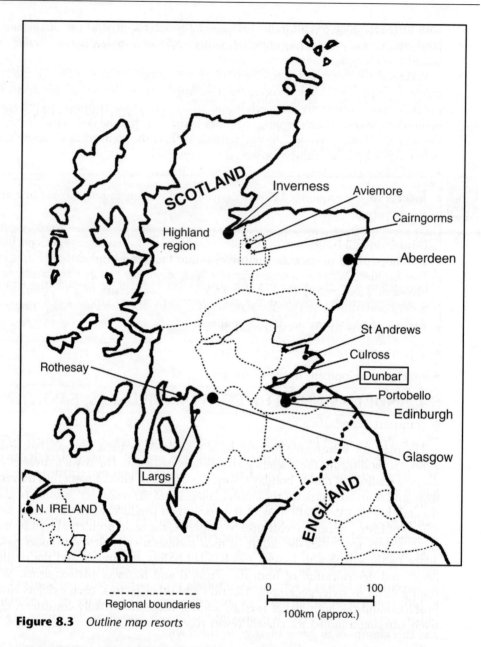

Regional boundaries

0   100

100km (approx.)

Figure 8.3 *Outline map resorts*

As a destination, St Andrews and the coastal villages are popular. St Andrews is, however, overwhelmingly the main draw. In addition to its golfing fame, it is a fine town:

> If anywhere in Scotland captures the national mood in architecture and town-form it issurely St. Andrews. It is the kind of place whose character depends largely upon the elusive quality of townscape. Here on a windy plateau above the sea, we have a distinctively Scottish town, a record in stone of the nation's urban tradition.
>
> (Edwards, 1986)

As a consequence, the challenges posed by overpopularity are significant. In 1993, the St Andrews' Tourism Management Plan was drawn up as:

...a 2 year, pilot initiative in response to the recognition that, as a historic town under increasing pressure from its visitors, an integrated management approach to future tourism development in St. Andrews was needed

(St Andrews and North East Tourist Board, 1995)

The objectives of the plan were:

- to enhance the visitor experience of St Andrews
- to increase the economic benefits derived by the town and its surrounding areas from tourism
- to protect and enhance the built and physical environment
- to improve and protect the quality of life of local residents.

In order to start the move towards sustainable tourism development, a strategy was adopted which comprised five main project or action areas:

- improvements to the presentation of St Andrews
- enhancement of services and facilities
- tourism development in the wider area
- townscape proposals
- transport proposals.

The plan for sustainable tourism in St Andrews has been generally successful, although monitoring the changing situation is essential. The town's diverse 'products' – traditional family holiday resort, the 'Home of Golf', prosperous university town and tourism centre for the coastal villages and the region – continues to give it the stability that destinations with only one main product, which is subject to the whims of taste, cannot have. Unlike St Andrews, the main problems faced by many resort towns arise from the failure of their comparatively narrow product base to adapt to the changes in leisure and holiday habits and trends and the resultant decay and deterioration of both the physical and business environments. While resorts differ in style, geographic location and other factors, each exhibits similar problems and the approaches used to address them are broadly consistent, effectively offering a model for coastal resort regeneration.

ROTHESAY AND PORTOBELLO

Rothesay is a Scottish West Coast Islands spa/resort town which acts as a gateway to the Island of Bute. It was the principal destination of the famous 'doon the watter' trip of Glasgow folklore – the mass exodus of predominantly working-class people during the annual 'Fair Fortnight' in summer, at least until the early 1960s when cheap package deals to Spain became available (*www.argyll-bute.gov.uk/index.asp*).

Portobello is an East Coast seafront beach resort but also a suburb of Edinburgh. It has, in many ways, physically turned its back on the seafront, its greatest asset, its role as a suburb tending to obscure its continuing potential as a coastal resort, with the added value of easy access to the capital city.

The decline of the domestic leisure and holiday market on which both depended has led to the physical decline and deterioration of the building stock and poor environmental quality. This affected the business climate resulting in business closure, lack of business confidence generally and of the resources necessary to stimulate regeneration. Major impediments were the lack of visitor facilities and related investment and the limited availability of development sites suitable for new development, largely as a result of fragmented ownership patterns and conservation area status. Portobello has, however, recovered a desirable status as a residential area since its relatively lower house prices attract young professional families outpriced from Edinburgh (see Chapter 5).

In both Rothesay and Portobello, resources for regeneration were available in terms of:

1. valuable capital assets:

   - fine old buildings suitable for refurbishment

   - waterfront attractions with water- and land-based leisure potential

2. the business climate:

   - appreciation of a need to adapt to new market opportunities and the possibilities of business support and assistance

   - low property values and prices encouraging external entrepreneurial interest and investment. (Keddie, 1995)

As tourist resorts both had declined significantly, to the point where piecemeal approaches on a single problem-solving basis were incapable of changing their fortunes; as in Dunbar, only public sector investment could enable the necessary integrated strategies for redevelopment.

In each case it was the combination and scale of problems and opportunities coupled with attractive settings that present the challenge. The bases for regeneration were identified as:

1. environmental improvement and provision of high-quality facilities

2. provision of all-weather facilities, attractions and events to prolong the visitor season and raise the profile of the resort

3. an adequate supply of tourist accommodation in the resort or nearby

4. a willingness on the part of the local business community to adapt to the needs of a more sophisticated visitor

5. exploration of the resort's unique locational characteristics and advantages

6. an adequately thought through marketing strategy which both exploits the resort's advantages/facilities/characteristics and is well targeted at particular market niches

7. an integrated approach to action by public sector agencies adopting an initiating

role in identifying opportunities for improvement and development and acting in partnership with private sector agencies.

With adequate investment regeneration can be achieved by a programme of small-scale yet locationally significant improvements to create a context for large-scale development – if this is appropriate and capable of integration into the resort. Local aspirations and priorities should be considered, although false hope should not be given where there is no possibility of responding adequately to them. Local support should be gained by clear demonstration of the progress being achieved.

CASE STUDY

Newsflash: A 'Yellow Flag' mini-revival in Portobello's fortunes', Edinburgh Evening News, 2 April 2001:

Hopes of a mini-revival in Portobello's fortunes are growing on the back of a £7 million investment in cleaning up the sea. [...] Portobello has just been told it could be in line for a prestigious 'Yellow Flag', awarded by the Keep Scotland Beautiful campaign, for cleanliness. [...]

But winning the award would involve banning dogs from part of the beach – a move that has proved unpopular in the past with people living nearby. The award would go a long way towards burying memories of the days, just three years ago, when swimming was banned due to fears about pollution. The sea at Portobello was declared out-of-bounds to swimmers in 1995 because it was said by experts to be more brown than blue and full of waste matter. Swimmers were only welcomed back to the sands in 1998 and last year a £7 million project to improve the quality of water at Portobello beach began. East of Scotland Water said the work, carried out as part of a £322 million national investment in cleaner water, involved removing a 1940s outfall pipe and installing two new pipes (www.esw.co.uk/).

The quality of the water has now impressed judges from Keep Scotland Beautiful, who have told the council a prestigious Yellow Flag is within its sights. Although Portobello needs to address several areas to be eligible for the award, which is only one step below the Blue Flag given to Britain's best beaches, hopes are high the beach can meet the strict criteria.

Mr X, owner of The X Hotel in Portobello, said winning a Yellow Flag was likely to bring more visitors to the resort at a time when many businesses were struggling: 'Business is very slow right now and the days of 45,000 on the beach are long gone, but if the upgrade goes ahead, it will boost the local economy. It would give the youths in the area some prospects if we can attract anything like as many visitors to the beach as we used to. Money in the area benefits everyone'.

A three-year development programme is being carried out by Edinburgh City Council and the authority is planning to spend £250,000 to brighten up the promenade and help keep the beach tidier. That could culminate in the Fringe Festival visiting Portobello for a day of entertainment at the seaside. A council spokesman said: 'All rails are to be painted, entrances to the beach are being developed and new signage put in place. We will also fit new benches and new and more litter bins'.

The national director of Keep Scotland Beautiful said: 'We are working with the City of Edinburgh Council to make sure all the criteria for an award for Portobello can be met for 2002. The local community must be seen to be in favour of these proposals, including "dogfree" areas, before any award can be achieved. This would greatly boost Portobello's attractiveness as a visitor attraction and benefit local businesses in the area'.

Among the improvements that Keep Scotland Beautiful insist must be put in place before the Yellow Flag can be awarded are a dog ban at a designated bathing area on the beach, as well as a means of enforcing the ban.

Lifeguards and safety equipment must be provided, along with upgraded toilet facilities, good signage, a zoning plan for different uses of the water, such as jet skis, and adequate parking and access arrangements, including good public transport. The City Council hopes to be able to satisfy the judges next year that Portobello is worthy of a Yellow Flag, but a spokesman said it needed the support of the community to put some of the necessary facilities in place. The spokesman added: 'We are working with Portobello Community Council on these initiatives, but people didn't want dog bans the last time we tried this or lifeguards. Ultimately, it's a local resource, and any changes will only be implemented dependent on funding and the wishes of local people'.

THE ISLE OF MAN

The preceding discussions of individual resorts have made some reference to their roles in the development or regeneration of their regions. In the case of the Isle of Man it is the island itself that is the destination. The success or failure of individual resorts is intimately connected with the changing image and popularity of the island as a whole (*www.gov.im/*).

The Isle of Man is situated in the Irish Sea, midway between Liverpool and Belfast, a disadvantage insofar as it results in a high cost of access and the lack of a day trip catchment to support attractions. Its popularity has declined due to changing tastes away from the traditional family seaside holiday and increased opportunities abroad and the inadequate response is the result – at least partially – of an existing legacy of now outdated infrastructure (Cooper, 1990). An early commitment to tourism as a main industry resulted in a large stock of Victorian and Edwardian buildings – purpose-built guest houses and hotels, music halls, cinemas and shops, catering largely for the working class of northern England. These are largely unsuited to modern tastes and in need of expensive renovation. The sheer scale of the challenge requires a strategic response.

Tourism grew from 90,000 in 1870 to stabilisation at around half a million passenger arrivals per year by the interwar years. A lack of further investment resulted in the destination continuing to offer the traditional working-class seaside product and by 1955 numbers were in decline. A casino and indoor entertainment complex was built in the 1960s in an attempt to overcome climatic disadvantages – now 'heightened' by the easy availability of Mediterranean 'sun-sand-sea' destinations – and to extend the range of attractions. By the mid-1980s the tourism industry was in crisis. Many businesses explored 'non-tourism' options, as the

Photograph 8.2 *Hotels on the seafront, Isle of Man*

many small proprietors – individuals or family concerns – had limited ability to invest and upgrade tourist facilities. Hotels were built with large family-size rooms are now deficient in the modern expectations of en suite bathrooms and lifts. Some were converted into private accommodation, residential homes and other business uses, although many are of architectural merit and entailed even higher costs for renovations (see the discussion of conservation in Chapter 5).

The problem was so serious that only a comprehensive approach would succeed and this required the active involvement of the Manx government. A marketing plan aimed at consolidating the Isle of Man's position in traditional markets, but significantly also pioneered new markets to reduce seasonality. A development plan for tourism addressed the need to update the destination's tourist facilities, since it was disadvantaged in terms of price and product. The marketing strategy identified a number of new markets with potential:

- the 'short break' market – less seasonal, higher spending and attracted to heritage and sporting facilities

- less 'seasonal' markets – club excursions and the elderly

- the visiting friends and relatives (VFR) market

- the business market, enhanced by the island's offshore finance industry.

The basic question that arises is what the destination's 'new' tourism should be based on. Archaeological, historic and natural attractions and good sporting facilities are the main strengths of the resource base to develop, complemented by increasingly high-quality bistros and restaurants, high-quality accommodation, new shopping malls and new heritage attractions to exploit the resource base. Examples are the Laxey Wheel complex, the redeveloped museum in Douglas and the new state-of-the-art heritage centre opened in Peal in 1999 which interprets the island's strong 'Viking' associations. (Note Largs' similar use of this theme.)

As Cooper (1990) noted, the depth of the Isle of Man's tourism crisis could only be tackled by a comprehensive and coordinated tourism development plan which would form the framework for devising effective management solutions. Its administrative independence allowed customised solutions to the specific problems of the tourism industry to be devised. The experience offers lessons for other resorts in a similar position:

- the need for commitment on the part of the tourism industry

- the need for professional leadership from the public sector

- the need for a coordinated promotion and development strategy over the medium rather than the short term in order to match the holiday product to the needs of emergent market segments.

The experience of British and other northern European 'cold water resorts' represents a 'just in time' reponse to the competition they suddenly faced from Mediterranean and latterly other sun-sand-sea destinations, beginning in the late 1950s/early 1960s. By the 1990s, again largely through changing tourist tastes, themselves the result of wider trends, the sun-sand-sea destinations were facing serious problems.

TORREMOLINOS, SPAIN

Torremolinos (*www.costadelsol.net/web/torremolinos/index.htm*) is an archetypal Spanish 'sun-sand-sea destination'. It could have been one of the fishing villages which the veteran travel writer Norman Lewis (1984) described – an almost mediaeval community where life revolved around the seasonal sardine catches, the bar and satisfying feuds with neighbouring villages, where people struggled to sustain their perilous existence and some defended against the entice-ments of an inexorable tourist development.

While the northern European resorts declined, Torremolinos and other former fishing towns and villages benefited and became thriving destinations, but by the late 1980s several began to experience a downturn. A decline in arrivals could have been caused by several factors:

- a recession in the tourism-generating countries – external factors

- a deteriorating image – internal factors (Pollard and Rodriguez, 1993).

The fact that other comparable resorts were continuing to grow in popularity suggested that the problems were intrinsic to the resort itself. Perhaps the destination was entering the 'natural' decline stage of the life cycle (see Chapter 2)? If so, then the 'inevitability' of decline should be challenged – what specific factors were causing it and could they be tackled?

Statistical information confirmed the reality of the downturn in visitor numbers. But what was the cause, or causes? Recession in the main tourism generating countries was certainly a factor, but decline in the wider region – Malaga province – had begun before the recession.

The problems facing Spanish tourism generally were summarised by Pollard and Rodriguez (1993):

- *economic* – emphasis on a restricted market (British and German) – especially on the low margin package tour business
- *surplus bed capacity* in the hotel sector as visitors switched in favour of apartments
- *environmental factors* – both the general social milieu as well as the built and natural environment
- *negative, downmarket image*, notably due to overcrowding, noise, drunkenness and commercialisation
- *building noise*, dust and general spoilation of the natural environment.

These together had led to disillusionment with the basic Spanish tourism product. The media took up the discussion and certainly contributed to the increasingly adverse image of 'mass, sun-sand-sea' tourism.

How important to 'mass tourists' are environmental factors – including the natural and built environment and socially related noise and litter pollution and crime? It might be assumed that the type of visitor predominant in the mass tourism/package holiday resorts surveyed is less concerned with these than more demanding tourists, but Pollard and Rodriguez (1993) revealed their real concerns over quality aspects of the destination.

The tourists' view

The town's image is one of a combination of natural environment factors and the general ambience of the town – its lively atmosphere, nightclubs, nightlife and entertainment opportunities. Cultural factors play only a limited role, for example the Spanish heritage is of little interest to the visitors surveyed at that time (1990). A little over one-quarter of the visitors found no disadvantages worthy of mention. A substantial majority identified specific problems with the highly commercialised nature of tourism, the crowding in the streets, bars, restaurants, hotels and beaches – ironically, since they themselves inevitably contributed to it.

Generally, foreign and Spanish visitors alike were concerned about the cleanliness of the sea, the beach and the town; the ease of traffic movement; noise levels; building design and town planning; and parks and gardens. Many mentioned dirty beaches (litter and dog faeces) and marine pollution as their principal natural environment concerns, although also doubtful water quality since there was inadequate development of sewage treatment. Untreated waste due to limited tidal action and visible rubbish discarded by visitors resulted from an inability for waste treatment to keep up with increasing visitor numbers. In the town itself, dirty streets, broken pavements, roaming dogs and vagrants and 'shady' characters caused greatest concern.

Urban design problems

Pollard and Rodriguez (1993) concluded that the built environment of Torremo-linos 'lacked the order and simplicity of both the traditional seaside resort and its modern planned counterpart'. There were no promenades and backing public gardens, no well-defined visitor and residential accommodation zones or recrea-tional and commercial business districts. The general impression was of a hapha-zard collection of urban activities and landuses, with only a very basic street system allowing access between different areas. Communication between hotel or apart-ment and shopping areas or beach was unclear. The apparent disorder reflected its origins and its subsequent spontaneous growth, unchecked by a planning frame-work. Crimes such as petty theft, pick pocketing and mugging were noted while the availability of drugs, pornographic material and different perceptions of amorality caused some objections.

The current circumstances for resorts

Reviewing resort studies such as the example discussed above, with British resorts in mind, Wright (2000) commented: 'Since 1965, the number of holidays abroad taken by the British has risen from 5 million to over 27 million and the UK seaside has suffered'. He quotes a Consumers Association report (July 1999) as saying, 'The overriding impression of the traditional resorts is one of ageing infrastructure, tired ideas and low quality accommodation'. While referring specifically to the southwest of England, his view is that standards and value for money must rise if resorts generally are to survive since contemporary tourists will not tolerate less. He notes that £4.7 billion a year is still being spent on seaside holidays and 190 million day trippers a year bringing a further £2 billion, while stating that 'In many cases the level of decline will soon reach a point from which effective regeneration will be difficult to achieve'. Referring to the report of the British Resorts Asso-ciation (1998), Wright asserts: 'Many seaside towns and coastal resorts now exhibit problems of economic and social deprivation on a scale hitherto only dis-played in inner-city and metropolitan areas. [...] what is happening is a longer-term structural decline of seaside resorts', behind the (necessary) façade of pre-senting a positive image to holidaymakers, visitors and conference delegates. Major action is now necessary requiring EU and UK involvement.

MAJORCA

Wright (2000) describes the experience gained from a 'benchmarking' visit to Majorca by the Torbay Forum, made up of representatives from the public and private sectors (*www.bitel.es/dir~calvia/khome.htm*).

Calvia on Majorca has a similar tourism history to Torremolinos. It reversed its decline by early recognition of its problems and swift action by the Spanish gov-ernment to decrease the impact of mass tourism on the environment by attracting more profitable visitors. Since 95% of Majorca's income is derived from tourism there was a clear need for government to avoid decline of this vital industry. This required:

- tactical marketing in the short term
- strategic planning in the medium term
- a visionary approach to long-term resort regeneration.

In this case, effective political leadership provided the essential motivation and vision and this led to the emergence of new strategies – significantly, while the resorts were still viable – underpinned by a clear structure and a successful partnership. A powerful island-wide hotel federation was a key force in creating a new, dynamic and focused tourism industry involving local residents, businesses and councils, the island and national governments and the European Union. A collective decision was taken to improve resort infrastructure and accommodation standards. A sustainable approach was adopted, based firmly on Local Agenda 21, addressing urban planning, protection of the environment, local culture and quality of life by:

- reorganising the flow of visitors
- reclaiming the coastal area
- reducing the congestion of town centres
- demolishing unsightly hotels.

This approach led to a new image of the island. Planning and development controls were introduced to oversee new hotel building and inspection schemes ensure that existing hotels were upgraded and refurbished. As a result a higher yield is achieved from fewer bed spaces.

The consensus view on Majorca's tourism future was that there are limits to growth and that tourism development should focus on value rather than volume. The beaches were extended, the 50-mile coastline promenade was widened and existing green spaces were protected and new ones created. The quality and distinctiveness of public spaces was improved, the natural environment was preserved and enhanced and improvements in the quality of the bathing water were maintained – to the extent that all beaches were to attain a Blue Flag status. Street furniture was replaced and safe coastal walking and cycle routes were developed. Numerous schemes were introduced to promote the island's culture, arts, activities and crafts, and to create local distinctiveness. Winter events programmes were jointly funded, resulting in entertainment packages for out of season visitors which were offered free to the guests of those hotels that had helped finance and support the initiative.

From a low point in 1990 when Majorca received 3.98 million visitors, the investment and associated improvements enabled the island's visitor numbers to reach 7.3 million in 1998 – a growth of almost 100%. Drawing on that experience, the report made a number of recommendations for British coastal resorts.

Accommodation

British resorts should aim to increase quality standards by reducing outdated and poor-quality accommodation, by introducing obligatory grading for accommodation listed in official guides and encouraging new hotel accommodation, especially the national budget-style developments where consistent quality standards are part of the company philosophy and operation.

Attractions and events

The Forum recommended that 'green' flagship attractions should be encouraged while the success of existing high-profile visitor facilities should be extended, building on strong links with TV personalities or literary figures. Attractions, cultural, heritage and sporting events and activities should be encouraged all year round – with festivals based on film, heritage, food, maritime, artistic and literary interests. Planning controls should be used to safeguard prime holiday areas and for the protection of natural environments and the enhancement of built environments.

Entertainment/eating and drinking

A diverse but high-quality range of entertainment, catering and bars should be available with licensing hours in selected zones modified to increase their attractiveness.

General

Good-quality retail activities, a reliable transport system and a strong economic base are essential for a healthy, all year round tourism industry. If resort centres and their shopping facilities are to be improved and strengthened, a strong link needs to be forged between those involved in tourism and in retailing.

The road and rail links to resorts and within the region need to be improved; similarly, the use and development of major regional airports should also be promoted. While recognising tourism's role in broadening the economic base, resorts should capitalise on new industries and inward investment.

The Forum also commented on a number of strategic aspects. Online information systems are essential. There should be improved job prospects and training within the tourism industry since trained, motivated and well-paid staff will make a great contribution to the local tourism industry's successful development. Despite strong support for tourism development, economic diversification should be encouraged.

Drawing on the experience of the Forum's benchmarking visit to Majorca, Wright (2000) concluded that achievement of these objectives requires partnership working and visionary, non-traditional solutions to resorts' problems as well as policies and actions for regeneration and investment to meet changing visitor expectations. The natural environment, the biggest asset, should be protected and enhanced. Visitors need to be won back and new markets developed. Six key factors must be present to make this happen:

- vision and leadership

- changes in the business culture

- partnerships and structure

- funding

- up-to-date research

- support from the local community.

Vision and leadership

This should refer not only to the business but also the wider community that needs to share in the vision for the future course of development. Key organisations must demonstrate inspiration, commitment and leadership and direct and monitor progress.

Changes in the business culture

Individual businesses should be encouraged to develop their own business plans, targets and action for improving their operations; they should look for ways of maintaining and improving the quality of their customer service; they need to involve all staff in training and development programmes and keep themselves informed of innovative ideas.

Partnerships and structure

Improved working relationships should result from an improvement in communications between the business community, local authorities and tourist boards. Resorts should work in partnership with key regional and national bodies and seek participation in the EU initiatives.

Funding

The resort should aim to achieve EU Objective 2 status (*www.europa.com*), single regeneration funding and maximise funding from the Lottery and private sector investment. They should lobby for support from the local regional development agency and the national government and for the greater recognition of tourism in the standard spending assessment. To help individual businesses initiate capital improvements, a grant programme should be established.

Up-to-date research

Resorts need to be able to draw on reliable and up-to-date research, not necessarily requiring expensive surveys. Above all the information needs to be relevant to the market and to be capable of informing the vision.

Support from the local community

The industry needs to highlight and promote the role that tourism can play in supporting local culture, heritage, sports facilities and the general quality of life for residents as well as for visitors. A stronger tourism industry will lead to a stronger community. The use of local suppliers and services should be promoted, although the tourist industry needs to recognise that the support of the local community will only be forthcoming when it provides – *and is seen to provide* – economic, environmental and social benefits.

Wright (2000) concludes that if a resort is to prosper then it is vital that a major emphasis is given to quality and value for money issues, while the goals can only be achieved through 'joined-up thinking' and a partnership approach between the public and private sectors at national, regional and local level.

CONCLUSIONS

A number of common threads are clearly present in the Dunbar case study and in each of the resort studies in this chapter. They reflect the changing nature of the contemporary tourist and the greater expectations he/she has of resorts – among the earliest tourism destinations and now requiring considerable action to allow them to respond successfully to demands of the 21st century.

Bibliography

British Resorts Association (1998) *Behind the façade*. Report from the Resort Regeneration Conference held in Torbay on 19 December.

Cooper, C. (1990) Resorts in decline – the management response. *Tourism Management*, (11) 1, 63–7.

Edwards, B. (1986) *Scottish Seaside Towns*. BBC Publications. London.

English Tourist Board (1993) *Turning the Tide: A Heritage and Environment Strategy for a Seaside Resort*. English Tourist Board. London.

Howie, F. (1988a) John Muir – Prophet of the Wilderness. *Heritage Interpretation Journal*. Society for the Interpretation of Britain's Heritage, 4, 27–34.

Howie, F. (1988b) The Dunbar Initiative: exhibition and audio-visual production. Scottish Development Department. Edinburgh.

Johnson, A. (1993) Victorian values washed up on the seashore. *The Guardian*, 9 August, 16.

Keddie, D. (1995) Regeneration by the sea. *Scottish Planner*. Royal Town Planning Institute. London.

Lewis, N. (1984) *Voices of the Old Sea*. Penguin Travel Library. London.

North Ayrshire Council (1994) *Vikingar!*. National Hertage Lottery bid.

Pollard, J. and Rodriguez, D. (1993) Recession or reaction to environment?, *Tourism Management*, (14) 4, 247–58.

Royal Town Planning Institute (2001) Blackpool places bets on casinos for resort future. *Journal of the Royal Town Planning Institute*, April, 13.

St Andrews and North East Fife Tourist Board (1994) *St Andrews, the East Neuk and North East Fife*.

St Andrews and North East Fife Tourist Board (1995) *St Andrews Tourism Management Plan: Review and Proposals for the Future*.

Scottish Tourist Board (1994) *Scottish Tourism Strategic Plan*. Edinburgh.

Urry, J. (1998) Cultural change and contemporary holiday making. *Theory, Culture and Society*, 5, 35–55.

Voase, R. (1995) *Tourism, the Human Perspective*. Hodder & Stoughton. London.

Wright, P. (2000) Regenerating seaside resorts: learning from Spanish practices. *Journal of the Tourism Society*, 103, 8–11.

CHAPTER 9

Regional destinations

In this chapter the 'transferable material', i.e. facts, ideas, experience etc. which may be applicable to other destinations in this 'regional' category, includes destination image, national/regional identity, public–private partnership (PPP) approaches to development, 'peripherality' (for marginalised areas), European Union funding for projects and the 'threat' of emerging rival destinations.

THE SCOTTISH HIGHLANDS

> This is an area of superlatives and contrasts where all the clichés about scenery, hospitality and heritage come true.
> (Highlands and Islands of Scotland tourism promotional brochure, 1991)

Highland landscape, history and dress have given Scotland one of the best known 'national' images in the world. It is not entirely 'authentic', much of it being a creation of the 'romantic' imagination principally of the mid-Victorian era, and it is not representative of the rest of Scotland outwith the Highland region. It also has to be said that many Scottish people are less than happy to be identified with the cliché image of 'bagpipes, tartan and haggis', as indicated by this quote from Womack (1989, in McCrone *et al.*, 1995: 201):

> That all Scots wear tartan, are devoted to bagpipe music, are moved by the spirit of clanship, and supported Bonnie Prince Charlie to a man – all these libels of 1762 live on as items in the Scottish tourist package of the twentieth century.

At a time when Scotland has just regained a parliament after an absence of almost 300 years attention is rightly directed to identifying or creating an appropriate image of the country, including the Highlands, whose image features most prominently in representations of Scotland as a whole. This 'new' image would not lose sight of the appeal (and commercial value) of 'traditional' imagery, yet would address the realities of Highland depopulation and landscape mismanagement and assert the diversity of contemporary Scotland as a whole.

These and other factors underpin the considerations of this look at the Highlands:

Tartanry. The various factors that constitute the popular tourist image of the destination. This generally embraces: (a) 'Balmorality' referring to the associations of the area with the monarchy; (b) the *Brigadoon* factor, (*www.imdb.com*) referring to the power of film in contemporary culture and the rather narrow image of the Highlands and Islands (and Scotland) that it has, until recently, created.

'Tourist tat'. The proliferation of poor-quality souvenirs that are sold as representations of the region/country regardless of the potential of the local craft industry. The ubiquitous 'tartan dolly', one of the most purchased souvenirs, is generally not made in Scotland, not made of local materials and does not employ many local people (*www.thetatgallery.com*).

The *Highlands*.

'Europe's last wilderness'

This phrase has frequently been used in describing the Highlands. In reality much of the region is a 'cultural landscape' with a history of depopulation and exploitative landuse and significant mismanagement issues:

> If wildness means the chance of walking for hours without encountering a road or any habitation other than the occasional farm, and that probably now deserted, this is correct. Yet not an inch of the uplands is unmarked by human imprint.
>
> (Smout, 2000: 116)

A related ironic perspective is reflected in the term, the MAMBA phenomenon – Miles and Miles of Bugger All' – although in introducing the expression Crofts (1995) is in fact arguing that it is a failure to recognise its true worth that leads to the 'why bother to preserve it' mentality.

Rural development

The Scottish Highlands and Islands have been classified as disadvantaged economically on account of their remoteness (see Figure 9.1). They are peripheral to Scotland's power core – the central belt embracing Edinburgh and Glasgow. The European Community has the power to distribute funding to areas such as these under Objective 1 that has the aim of 'promoting the development and structural adjustment of regions whose development is lagging behind' (European Communities, 2000: 133).

The Highlands qualified for this funding, but the area has benefited to such an extent that it is no longer eligible.

All Objective 1 areas are eligible for LEADER assistance, another European Community measure to help disadvantaged areas, LEADER being an acronym standing for *Liaisons Entre Actions pour le Développement pour l'Économie Rurale* (Links between Actions for the Development of the Rural Economy) (*www.rural-europe.aeidl.be/rural-en/euro/p11.htm*).

The Highland LEADER programme had a number of objectives supporting development policies in the Scottish Highlands and Islands, one of the remotest and least populated areas of Europe, and it aimed at combating isolation and the departure of the region's 'living strengths' through economic diversification and the creation of enterprises. It sought to take advantage of the exceptional natural and cultural heritage of the areas concerned and the use of advanced communication

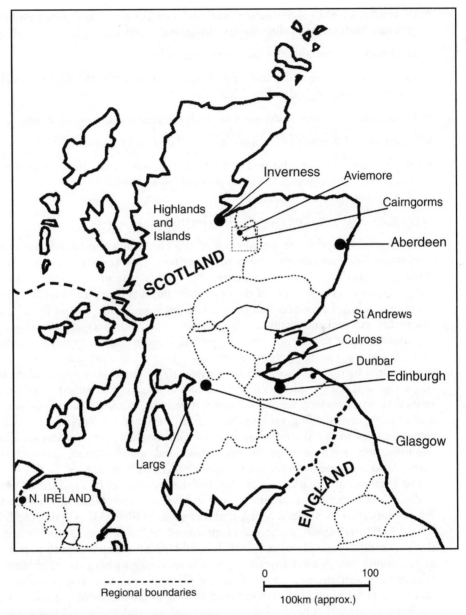

Figure 9.1 *The Highlands and Islands*

technologies. These aims are to be met specifically by the LEADER strategy and its objectives are as follows:

- to promote and/or enhance the local development participatory approach
- to diversify the activities of the areas that are almost exclusively dependent on declining sectors such as agriculture, fishing, energy and military installations

- to reinforce small-scale agricultural activities, to enable local products to generate more added value and to stimulate exports

- to promote sustainable development approaches

- to increase the originality and appeal of tourist products through the exploitation of the natural and cultural heritage

- to encourage the use of information technologies and distance training

- to implement renovation actions in the villages and remote areas

- to promote the use of the Gaelic language for social and economic ends (*www.rural-europe.aeidl.be/rural-en/plr/uk/uk-hi.htm*).

Strengths and weaknesses of the destination

The primary strengths and weaknesses of the Highlands and Islands as a tourist destination lie in its cultural and natural heritage. Its international image is tarnished when the 'tat' factor overshadows the quality anticipated from the induced image. Quality in the delivery of the deservedly popular historical, literary, musical and other cultural products has been raised in recent years but while 'Highland hospitality' is a real and intrinsic value, contemporary tourists generally also expect a professionalism that is not always present. Concerning the 'natural' landscape and wildlife, increasingly informed tourists expect a more authentic product than promotional literature has sometimes promised. As noted previously, while much of the region is remote and 'wild', ecologically it is heavily modified – and reduced in biodiversity – by long human occupation and use. While it is certainly beautiful and capable of providing the experiences of 'wildness' (as opposed to true wilderness except in certain areas) and/or the solitude that many visitors seek, more sophistication is required in its promotion and interpretation, particularly in response to differing national preferences among targeted visitors.

For example, the marketing of Scotland has tended to be targeted at general audiences with images of mountains and valleys, as research has shown that these images appeal to consumers. Morgan and Pritchard (2002: 33) examine the British Travel Authority (1997) 'destination suprabrand' of Britain and its subdivision into the 'subbrands' England, Scotland, Wales and London which are 'both part of, and at the same time, distinct from it'. There is no distinguishing the Highlands and Islands from Scotland as a whole, thus 'the positioning of Scotland as a land of fire and stone is translated into the rational benefit of encountering rugged, unspoilt wilderness, romantic history, heritage and folklore, and warm and feisty people'.

Brydon (1998 in Godde *et al.*, 1998) points out, however, that the German market, which is the second largest consumer, is targeted with images of wild landscapes with only suggestions of limited human influence, such as a small white cottage, while for the French or Italian markets, quite different images are used, emphasising culture and tradition. When visitors arrive, however, all will actually share the same resource.

Status of tourism in the destination

Tourism is one of the Highlands and Islands' most important industries generating some 20,000 full-time jobs and an annual turnover of £500m plus spin-off benefits to other industries. Great improvements within the industry took place during the 1980s and into the 1990s but increasing international competition and rising tourist expectations demand further coordinated action to achieve a quality in service and facilities that matches the undeniable quality of the landscape and heritage.

Destination marketing and promotion

The Scottish Tourist Board, now 'Visit Scotland', has had a base in the Highlands – Inverness – since 1994 in addition to the headquarters in Edinburgh (*www.visit scotland.com*). Highlands of Scotland Tourist Board (HOST) is the lead agency for tourism marketing and promotion in the Highlands (*www.host.co.uk*), covering the mainland only, the Western Isles, Orkney and Shetland having their own tourist boards, while Morayshire is included in Grampian and North-East Scotland Tourist Board. HOST coordinates the promotion of the Highlands as a whole divided into the following geographical areas which have their own literature and promotional material:

Northern Highlands

Inverness, Loch Ness and Nairn

Skye and Lochalsh

Badenoch and Strathspey

Fort William and Lochaber.

There are also numerous 'unofficial' organizations – collaborations and consortiums of tourism businesses which are either not members of the Highlands of Scotland Tourist Board or choose to market themselves using alternative additional channels. Some examples of these are: the Skye and Lochalsh Hospitality Association (*www.skye-hotels.co.uk*), Scottish Highlands Explorer (*www.cali.co.uk/highexp*), Inverness & District Bed and Breakfast Association (*www.invernessbedandbreakfast.co.uk*), The Road to Isles Marketing Group (*www.road-to-the-isles.org.uk*) and HI-ways (*www.hi-ways.org.uk*).

Local authorities within the area include Highland Council (*www.highland.gov.uk*), a main partner in tourism organisation in the Highlands. As with HOST this body covers the mainland of the Highlands only – Moray, the Western Isles, Orkney and Shetland have their own local authorities.

Tourism planning and development is undertaken by local authorities and enterprise companies, within the broad Scottish strategic framework. Highlands and Islands Enterprise (*www.hie.co.uk*) is the lead agency for tourism development in the entire Highlands *and* the Islands.

Local enterprise companies for the area are the following:

Argyll and the Islands (*www.aie.co.uk*)

Caithness and Sutherland (*www.case-lec.co.uk*)

Inverness and Nairn (*www.ine.co.uk*)

Lochaber (*www.lochaberlimited.co.uk*)

Moray Badenoch and Strathspey (*www.mbse.co.uk/innovation*)

Orkney (*www.orkney.com/business/oe/index.htm*)

Ross & Cromarty (*www.race.co.uk*)

Shetland (*www.shetland.hie.co.uk*)

Skye and Lochalsh (*www.sale.hie.co.uk*)

Western Isles (*www.wie.co.uk*)

Highlands and Islands Enterprise (HIE) network's role is an enabling one – 'to unlock the potential of the 400,000 individuals in the region with skills and potential of their own and the more than 8,000 voluntary and community groups and help create a strong, diverse and sustainable economy where quality of life is matched by quality of opportunity. To this end activities include: provision of business support services, delivery of training and learning programmes, assistance for community and cultural projects and measures for environmental renewal'.

Destination portfolio

Attractions and dislikes

The scenery/countryside is generally the main tourist 'like' of the destination area of two-thirds of visitors. This has implications for development such as improved access and better facilities (appropriately 'low key') for outdoor activities and special interest tourism. The recent changes in access legislation and the designation of the first Scottish national parks in 2002 have major significance. The main dislike is 'bad weather' according to a quarter of the visitors, implying the need to give serious consideration to appropriate wet-weather facilities; visitor attractions in the Highlands have limited catchments of residents and must rely on a higher proportion of tourists to visit them (Scott Wilson Resource Consultants, 1997). It can be done – Urquhart Castle (*www.undiscoveredscotland.co.uk/drumnadrochit/urquhart*), operated by the government agency Historic Scotland (*www.historic-scotland.gov.uk*), maintains its position as one of Scotland's top ten tourist attractions with 243,000 visitors in 1996 (ibid.). The main reason for not visiting the area according to one in four visitors is along the lines of 'haven't got round to it/haven't thought about it/not top priority'. A survey by the Scottish Tourism Forum conducted a survey of 675 Scottish tourism businesses and reports that 77% of them say that business had been markedly affected by high fuel prices. In the Highlands this figure rose to 86% (*www.scotiaweb.co.uk/transport/news.html*). The potential of alternative fuels – such as liquid petroleum gas (LPG) – is currently under review, with limited availability a considerable disadvantage to an attractive 'green' alternative to petrol and diesel.

The Highland midge (*Culicoides impunctatus*), a biting insect, is not dangerous, but causes considerable discomfort to many visitors (and locals) yet is rarely mentioned in tourism brochures. 'The place of the midge in human ecology is such that a greatly increased tourist industry to the West Highlands could be encouraged if the midge could be controlled' (Darling and Boyd, 1964: 144). In the development of the Languedoc-Roussillon region of France eradication of the (more dangerous) mosquito was undertaken with the 'simple' objective of removing a 'pest' – the mosquito irritates tourists and spreads disease. The wider implications of the elimination of a species were not given much weight at that time. Such dramatic 'ecosystem engineering' would be much less acceptable today and is unlikely to be applied to the elimination of the Scottish 'midge'. Local biological control schemes using natural predators of the midge are at an early stage of experimentation.

Transport and access

Seventy five per cent of domestic visitors in 1998 came by private car. For overseas visitors, in 1997, the main form of transport to the UK was: air (63%) and then sea/tunnel (37%). Once in the UK, 62.5% used a private vehicle to get to the Highlands. Clearly the private car is the preferred mode, although this may reflect an under-provision of public transport alternatives.

Accommodation

In 1998 31% of UK visitors to the Highlands stayed in a hotel or guest house; 7% stayed in a bed and breakfast; 23% stayed in self-catering; 28% stayed with friends or relatives; 10% camped or caravanned; and 3% stayed in a hostel, university or school. For overseas tourists, in 1995, half stayed in hotels or guesthouses, with other forms of accommodation being used almost in equal proportions, except bed and breakfast which was used by only 1%.

Retail and information services

The tourist information centre (TIC) network plays an important role. In a region of dispersed settlement, a wider role for TICs – for example also providing certain 'non-tourism' services to local communities – is a topic of discussion. For example, they might operate as internet centres, although this has also been proposed as part of a 'survival' strategy for struggling rural post offices with little action so far. The distribution of services, season of operation, the supply and training of guides and facilities to supply the growing demand for special interest tourism are all topics requiring consideration.

Tourism development and impact considerations

An overall, coordinated development strategy is required for this large area of low, dispersed population. An appropriate strategy would:

- recognise and build on current strengths of the tourism sector of the economy
- improve the tourism industry's competitive position
- tackle the contemporary issue of balanced development – i.e. sustainability would be an important principle underpinning development.

Specific strategic priorities would include:

- extending the season and raising occupancy levels
- lengthening stay times and increasing visitor dispersal
- improving the quality of the tourism product
- developing skills, particularly local entrepreneurial and managerial skills
- enhancing the effectiveness of tourism marketing
- integrating tourism development with environmental concerns to strengthen the links between tourism and other sectors.

A possible 'role model' for development in the Highlands and Islands – the 'Road to the Isles'

Origins of the idea

The 45-mile/72.4-km A830 from Fort William to Mallaig is the traditional 'Road to the Isles'. Despite its attractiveness, the area experienced a drop in tourism in the early 1990s. Local businesspeople felt that most visitors coming to the area were only 'passing through' on their way to Skye and that if they could publicise their area properly, more tourists might stay longer, spend more money and generally contribute to the well-being of the area (Ralton, R., 2002).

Funding of £16,000 was secured – 12.5% from the district council, 12.5% from the local tourist board and the remainder from LEADER. This allowed 65,000 copies of a brochure to be printed. The Road to the Isles Marketing Group was able to translate its ideas into action because it pursued its vision purposefully. By organising themselves, agreeing a shared goal, applying for funding and committing themselves to the effort required, members of the working party were able to secure the personnel and financial support they needed to produce their brochure. The brochure was then given to B & Bs, hotels, filling stations and tourist information centres for distribution and display.

The marketing group considers that the brochure has been very effective and that the area has seen an increase in the length of time visitors stay, roughly half of the former one-day visitors now staying for up to three days. Future possibilities include developing a new brochure in conjunction with another group on the Isle of Skye.

Two major strengths of the marketing group were their 'common vision and voice' and their commitment to that agreed objective. Once the money was secured for the project the group's widely supported common goal gave them the ability to focus their limited time and resources effectively. A further advantage was the assistance they received from other agencies, in particular from the local area tourist board, the local enterprise company (LEC) and the funding from LEADER. The involvement of the local tourist board at the early stages was seen as crucial for any tourism marketing project, while a representative of the LEC ensured that the project moved forward by facilitating and joining in group discussions – a genuine 'community exercise' with local ownership that produced positive results.

Although the group had many strengths, the task was not easy. Members acknowledged that the effort required a substantial time commitment which is often difficult for local businesspeople in the Highlands. In areas where people depend heavily on their income from the summer tourist season, it is difficult to keep members and momentum during the summer months. The group dealt with this by getting as much work done as possible during the winter, off-season months.

A further problem the marketing group acknowledged was their lack of a marketing plan, something to address in future efforts. The brochure was sent only to individuals who enquired about the area, but was not sent to *potential* visitors. One member commented that it is 'one thing to create a nice glossy brochure but it is meaningless if it doesn't reach Joe Public in London, America or wherever'. Group members felt that with more planning in the initial stages, in particular more detailed market research and the development of a marketing strategy, they could have better targeted their audience. Local groups could seek advice from the area tourist board on this issue (Herbert, 1997: 12–14).

Continuous monitoring and evaluation was seen as an essential requirement followed up by appropriate reaction, with a comprehensive strategy agreed by many 'players' including the local residential and business communities.

Summary/conclusions

The Highlands and Islands of Scotland is a destination with an internationally recognised and positive image which, nevertheless, requires constructive reassessment in the circumstances prevailing in the early 21st century. Further development of the tourism industry is required, within an overall, coordinated strategy that is essential within a large area of low population density. The traditional strengths founded in the natural and cultural heritage must be complemented by a positive response to perceived deficiencies in quality of services and facilities, so meeting international standards.

LANGUEDOC-ROUSILLON, FRANCE

Image of the region

Languedoc-Roussillon is France's southernmost région, lying on the coast of the Mediterranean and bordering Catalan Spain and the Principality of Andorra (see Figure 9.2). For many tourists it has no distinctive image, although specific towns and areas within it are well known. Certainly it lacks the strong imagery associated with its adjoining région, Provence. Kaplan (1994) offers an image:

> Cumbersome as a name, lacking the instantly memorable, mellow flavor of so many other enticing areas in la belle France, Languedoc-Roussillon all the same has richness and variety that are thrilling to discover. Local passions can be fierce when it comes to the tasty Catalan dishes of Perpignan or the succulent oysters of Bouzigues. You'll find local pride in the region's numerous notable wines, too, from the Costière de Nîmes in the east to the more westerly Corbières, and to Fitou in the southwest.

The region covers a broad sweep of attractive land and seascape. From east to west, the region follows the Mediterranean shore extending from the old Roman city of Nîmes in the east, past the Camargue, renowned for its wild white horses, to the attractive small town and artists colony of Collioure and on to Spain in the west. The dramatic gorges of the Tarn River, the beautiful Cévennes National Park, the Parc Régional du Haut-Languedoc and the snowy peaks of the eastern Pyrenees all deserve to be enjoyed by tourists.

Culturally, the region is diverse still retaining a language that derives from spoken Latin – the *langue d'oc* – once the language of all southern France, sometimes called Occitan or, further east, Provençal. The word 'oc' means yes, differentiating the language and the culture from the French speakers of the rest of the country and their use of 'oui' (see Chapter 3).

Organisation of the tourism industry

The modern région of Languedoc-Roussillon incorporates five départements (Pyrénées-Orientales, Aude, Hérault, Gard and Lozère) and was created politically in 1972. The development of the Languedoc-Roussillon coast is a highly regarded example of collaboration between the public and private sectors and an example of supply stimulating demand. Before 1963 there were only a few existing resorts in the région and they were of limited capacity. Development was planned on a grand scale and involved road construction and the reclaiming of marsh land in the east near the Camargue in an attempt to reduce the nuisance and health risks of the mosquito. Strategically the scheme was also a response to the rapid growth of mass tourism. The French government recognised the irony in the fact that northern European 'mass tourists' were passing over and through France en route to the growing coastal resort destinations of Spain and wanted a share of this booming industry. The government did not, however, wish to have the 'up-market' resorts of the Riviera 'downgraded' by attracting mass tourists to them and so the concept of developing a new tourist destination – for mass tourism but better planned and avoiding the 'excesses' of the Spanish Costas – emerged. There would also be opportunities for some diversification through facilities for certain types of special interest tourism; for example Cap d'Agde became 'the undisputed favourite of international naturism' (*www.naturist.de*).

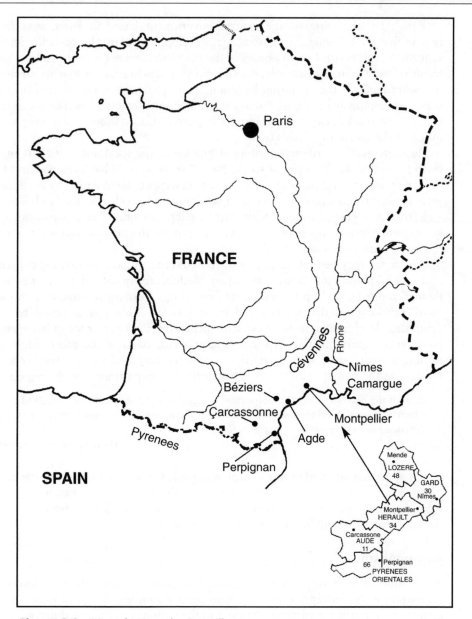

Figure 9.2 *Map of Languedoc Roussillon*

Pearce notes the key role of the public sector, in the form of the central government and the regional authorities, in the development of the region:

A clear and coordinated division of responsibility was required to undertake such a large-scale programme. No one organization had the resources or competence to take everything in hand yet the success of the operation depended heavily on all facets of development being carefully coordinated. The roles of the State, the local and regional authorities and the private sector were therefore defined right from the outset.

(Pearce, 1989: 51, 264)

285

'Paris', i.e. the state or the central government based in Paris, was firstly responsible for drawing up the strategic, development plan, the basis for its subsequent overall control of all phases of the operation. France is, politically, a more 'centrist' state than, for example, the UK and was 'less hesitant' about acquiring the necessary land for the operation by 'compulsory purchase' if negotiation failed. It was also responsible for undertaking the major infrastructural works – construction of the road network, upgrading the ports, afforestation, water supply and much of the mosquito eradication.

The state also contributed additional finance to the local authorities to enable them to undertake the regional work. New resorts were to be developed and four 'mixed economy' companies broadly based on existing local authority boundaries were created to undertake this work of servicing and developing the land acquired – electricity, sewerage, roads, parking areas, telephone lines. The companies would subsequently resell much of the serviced land to the private sector at a price reflecting initial costs and the improvements.

A basic strategy behind the plan was to avoid the 'ribbon development' pattern that was despoiling the coastlines of other Mediterranean coastal areas – i.e. 'front de mer' roads backed up by apartments and shops forming an almost continuous 'wall' blocking off the beaches and coastal vistas. This was achieved by concentrating development in five new settlements, leaving open space in between, so conserving environmentally sensitive and/or scenic parts of the coast, while permitting economies of scale in terms of infrastructure and sharing the economic impacts of the new developments between the five departments of the region:

> Each of the new settlements incorporates a major new resort of 40,000–50,000 beds, which acts as a development pole, and several smaller existing ones which may be expanded or redeveloped.
>
> (Pearce, 1989: 51, 264)

The approach adopted in this scheme is regarded as a good example of the public and private sectors working together with each able to get on and do what it can do best. Responsibility for marketing, however, was not clearly defined and so demand was slower than anticipated in its growth.

Regionalism

The 'vision' of a 'Europe of the regions' has grown in strength. It counters the accusation of 'Eurosceptics' that the European Union will lead towards a bland, standardised European identity, deficient in the national and regional diversity that has been a precious characteristic. According to this vision, development should, therefore, recognise regional 'differences'. Where these differences are considered 'unacceptable' (e.g. because of poverty) they should be phased out; where they are desirable e.g. the local 'spirit of place' or just a sense of 'pride in belonging' – they should be enhanced.

The Languedoc-Roussillon area is classified as an Objective 2 area by the European Commission (see Figure 9.2). Its development is thus an example of 'Economic and social conversion of areas facing structural difficulties e.g. industrial, agricultural, fishing and urban areas' (European Commission, 2000: 133).

The region also receives 'Objective 5b' funding from the Commission on account of it once being a heavily 'industrial area' – wine production or viticulture, although this was of 'everyday' wines and not a great creator of wealth as is the case with the great vineyards of France.

Pearce (1989) comments on the fact that many writers on regional development have concentrated on the transformation of areas from agriculture to industry and have ignored the possibility of growth in the 'tertiary' or 'service' sector of the economy of a region or country. In Languedoc-Roussillon, this process is occurring. Mass coastal tourism has heavily contributed to the expansion of the services sector in the economy (70% of workers), although the holiday resorts created in the 1960s need to find a new lease of life. The two main challenges that the Languedoc-Roussillon LEADER programme aims to take up are the creation of conditions for a lasting recovery bringing together the private and public sector and assertion of their products, tourism and heritage, in order to counterbalance the area's structural weaknesses.

Here, the aim of LEADER is to develop new relations between rural areas and their urban centres, to develop new uses for rural areas according to a tourism/ heritage/local products formula and to develop the impressive cultural, natural and building heritage (Rural Europe, 1998a; *www.rural-europe.aeidl.be/rural-en/plr/fr/ fr-lr.htm*).

However, the resort of Languedoc-Roussillon, while developing and sustaining the regional economy, is focused mainly on the coast. The rich cultural, environmental and architectural heritage of the hinterland is relatively ignored. This can be seen as a *core-periphery* type relationship in which the coastal area is the core and the hinterland is the periphery dependent on the coast for 'overspill' tourists. One of the reasons coastal Languedoc-Roussillon was developed was to intercept tourists on their way to Spain, as noted earlier. Such a strategy might not be appropriate for the hinterland of Languedoc-Roussillon. In the aim to 'capture' visitors there is a danger that the periphery may try to emulate the more successful core and this may lead to homogenisation of both. Boniface (2000: 141) considers that the periphery – in this case the hinterland – is dependent on its core of Mediterranean France and this may lead to such homogenisation.

The comments of a middle-aged inhabitant of a small village in a former silk industry area in the Cévennes foothills, recorded by Bernstein (in Boniface, 2000), reveal the issue to be one of quality and reveal the dilemma of choice of action between whether to provide what the locals deem suitable and adequate or what the outsiders regard as appropriate and necessary and show the influence of conforming to the latter:

> 'We could develop tourism, since we've got the mountains and good weather five months a year. Some people went into gîtes. ... But they were badly done, too primitive. People didn't like them. I was always saying, You've got to give people all the comforts of home, since they're used to them, and if they don't have them they won't come. Now some of the gîtes are better. But people need more than just a pretty view. They need tennis, golf, things like that. The problem is we're too hilly for a real golf course. We don't have the space. Maybe one of those small golf courses that don't take up too much room. I hear they're pretty popular.

The Languedoc-Roussillon coastal resort itself was developed centering on five major areas and these were designed to act as 'honey pots' to prevent environmental damage to the fragile coast in between them (Pearce, 1989). This may indeed act to draw tourists who will bypass or miss the rich hinterland. As Boniface (2000: 138) indicates:

Here the periphery may depend upon its resource-rich companion to provide it with points of entry for access by tourists from a distance and abroad. Nice, Marseilles and Montpellier fulfill the role for the hinterland of the French Mediterranean. But access also needs to be accompanied by information, otherwise the trade and presence of the casual visitor is lost. Of the three airports, probably due to the origin of funding and their ownership, only Marseilles serves some of the interior in anything like an acceptable way, as well as the immediate environment and coastal area. Public transport links into the interior are weak, perhaps not least because of the difficulty of the terrain; an important exception being the railways leading from Nice to, respectively, Digne and Tende in the pre-Alps, the former of these deliberately catering to tourists.

Destination portfolio

The coastal resorts of Languedoc-Roussillon are the boldest statement of image for most tourists to the region. Their architecture (designed by Jean Balladur) and environmental design dominate. They relate to the 'sun and sea' environment while it is the pyramid-shaped buildings that give La Grande Motte (one of the main centres) its distinctive character. The buildings are not universally liked but the general environment is harmonious. The ground floors of these pyramids are often occupied by shops and businesses. There are distinct 'quartiers' or neighbourhoods and a diversity in types and price of accommodation, including Villages Vacances Familiales (VVF) offering economical holidays for families on limited budgets.

Activities and attractions

Languedoc-Roussillon as a region has benefited greatly from tourism-led development and offers a diversity of scenery and activities. Walking, skiing, riding and climbing are available in the Pyrenees. Golf is available in many parts of the region. Beach activities are plentiful at the Mediterranean resorts and at Cap d'Agde there is one of the largest modern naturist resorts in Europe. The region is rich in cultural attractions – from Roman architecture to 20th-century modern. In the villages, buildings and traditions have been maintained or redeveloped, although enhanced with modern conveniences.

Monitoring and evaluation

Pearce (1989: 287, based on Courbis, 1984) evaluates the success of the Languedoc project. Courbis reports on a study involving the construction of a regional econometric model which enabled a simulation of the economy of Languedoc-Roussillon with and without the large-scale tourism project. The results of this analysis showed that by 1980 the regional output was from 10 to 14% greater than it would otherwise have been and that from 28,000 to 31,000 supplementary jobs had been created. Courbis considers that the creation of these jobs has been very cost effective. An investment of 1 million francs (at 1983 values) in tourism (including infrastructure and accommodation) was estimated to create 1.7 net jobs. In budgetary terms, a 1 million franc state subsidy led to the creation of from 11 to 12 net jobs which meant a cost to the state budget of from 80,000 to 90,000 francs per job. Unemployment for 1980 had been reduced by about 20 to 28%. Although the region continues to record one of the highest rates of unemployment in France, there can be little doubt that without the development of coastal tourism the economy of Languedoc-Roussillon would be far less healthy than it is today.

THE SCOTTISH HIGHLANDS AND ISLANDS AND LANGUEDOC-ROUSSILLON

Both regions have suffered from their 'peripherality'. Historically, they have been a long way from the metropolitan centres and this has resulted in comparative neglect by the 'centres'. In the case of the Scottish Highlands, that very remoteness is now a sought-after experience of many tourists, although the majority of these also expect modern conveniences. A sense of 'difference' is also sought – a difference that is expressed in lifestyles, in landscapes, in towns and villages. Languedoc-Roussillon's response to its isolation from the mainstream of French life has been dramatic and largely successful. Perhaps 'peripherality' as seen from a mainstream/metropolitan French view required such dramatic change – one that is less appropriate to the Scottish Highlands?

Exercise

Regional approaches

What are your views on the key differences between the two regional approaches discussed earlier in this chapter? For a region of your choice, which approach is more appropriate? Give your reasons.

The term 'provincial' implies a love–hate relationship. The French are not embarrassed by their rural roots, the expression, 'Scratch a Frenchman, find a peasant' implying that even the sophisticated, French businessperson or professional is only a generation or two removed from his/her peasant roots and is proud of that heritage. However, 'provincialism' is also almost an affront to the national image of sophistication.

Box 9.1   French provincialism

'French provinces are second to none in Europe for lethargy and bourgeois slowness.'

'How delightful to visit and how tedious to inhabit.'

'Le désert français.'

(Ardagh, 1990)

There is a need in both regions for a strategic plan which will set a framework within which:

- stimulated demand can be matched to the newly created supply of destination products, attractions and services

- cultural and natural diversity can be sustained, i.e. the character and ambience of the region – its 'spirit of place'

- quality with quantity can be achieved at an acceptable price.

Languedoc-Roussillon has to remain competitive with the nearby Spanish Costas, although even at the outset of the development – the early 1960s – the French government concluded that the Spanish Costas did not represent a model for tourism development that they wished to follow. The Scottish Highlands has to be competitive with established destinations and with emerging central and eastern European countries where there are regions that can offer a diversity of attractions and activities, for example nature-based tourism, at highly competitive prices, plus the 'novelty value' of being 'new' destinations.

Destination development approach

A significant element of the French approach was the direct and strong involvement of the public sector. For example, in Languedoc-Roussillon a number of key steps were taken by the government agencies:

- Land prices were frozen in order to limit speculation – land was purchased at the 'right' price, in the 'right' place to form coherent blocks suitable for the development envisaged.

- Rapid growth was achievable through direct involvement.

- 'Ribbon' development of coast was avoided (this landuse pattern is expensive to service and wasteful of land).

- Regional character/identity/communities/coherence was maintained.

An overall strategic plan facilitated achieving the key objectives:

- to match (stimulated) demand with (newly created) supply
- to maintain diversity (character/ambience)
- to achieve quality with quantity at an acceptable price.

The Languedoc-Roussillon development achieved its broad objectives and is generally regarded as a successful example of destination development. The Scottish Highlands have yet to make their 'great leap forward', although as discussed a series of smaller but integrated and no less significant 'leaps' may be more appropriate.

Bibliography

Aberdeen Transport Forum (2001) [Online] *www.scotiaweb.co.uk/transport/news.html* [17 February 2001].

Anon (1998) Languedoc Roussillon See Tourism WebGuide, France, Pyrenees, Mediterranee, Lodging, Sports ... *www.seek66.com/eng/homeeng.htm* [9 February 2001].

Ardagh, J. (1990) *France Today*. Penguin. London.

Boniface, P. (2000) Behind the scenes: tourism and heritage in the periphery to the French Mediterranean coast. *International Journal of Heritage Studies*, 6 (2), 129–44.

British Travel Authority (1997) in N. Morgan, A. Pritchard and R. Pride (2002) *Destination Branding: Creating the Unique Destination Proposition*. Butterworth-Heinemann. Oxford.

Burton, R. (1995) *Travel Geography* (2nd edn). Pitman Publishing. London.

Brydon, D. (1998) in Godde, P. (ed.) (1998) Community-based mountain tourism: practices for linking conservation with enterprise. Synthesis of an electronic conference of the Mountain Forum. 13 April–18 May. Harrisonburg, VA, USA. The Mountain Forum.

Crofts, R. (1995) The environment – who cares? Occasional Paper No 2. Scottish Natural Heritage. Redgorton, Perth.

Darling, F.F. and Boyd, J.M. (1964) *The Highlands and Islands*. Collins. London.

Davidson, R. (1992) European rural tourism in *Tourism in Europe*. Pitman. London.

European Commission (1992) *LIFE Programme*. EU initiative funding for implementation of 5th Environmental Action Programme. Brussels.

European Commission (undated) *Languedoc-Roussillon from Dialogue with Citizens, France*. *www.europa.eu.int/scadplus/citizens/en/fr/018216.htm*.

European Communities (2000) EU schemes in support of tourism, an internet roadmap for the tourism sector. European Commission. Brussels.

Fabre, G. and Richardot, P.A. (2000) The Salindrenque valley. *www.perso. wanadoo.fr/tourisme.cevennes.lasalle/text/english/*.

Herbert, S. (1997) Community involvement in small-scale tourism initiatives: new ideas in rural development, No 4. The Scottish Office Central Research Unit. Edinburgh.

Highlands and Islands Enterprise (1998) Inverness: The economic impacts of hillwalking, mountaineering and associated activities in the Highlands and Islands of Scotland; A strategy for enterprise development in the Highlands and Islands of Scotland; A tourism strategy for the Highlands and Islands; Sustainable Development in Scotland's Highlands (H&I LIFE Project).

Linklater, M. (1997) *People in a Landscape, The New Highlanders*. Mainstream Publishing Company Ltd. Edinburgh.

McCrone, D., Morris, A. and Kiely, R. (1995) *Scotland the Brand: The Making of Scottish Heritage*. Edinburgh University Press. Edinburgh.

Morgan, N. and Pritchard, A. (2002) Branding Scotland in N. Morgan, A. Pritchard, and R. Pride, *Destination Branding: Creating the Unique Destination Proposition*. Butterworth-Heinemann. Oxford.

Norberg-Schultz, C. (1980) *Genius Loci: Towards a Phenomenology of Architecture*. Academy Editions. London.

Rural Europe (1998a) Agricultural policy and rural development. *www.rural-europe.aeidl.be/rural-en/euro/p11.htm*.

Rural Europe (1998b) Highlands and Islands. *www.rural-europe.aeidl.be/rural-en/plr/uk/uk-hi.htm*.

Scott Wilson Resource Consultants (1997) *Scottish Visitor Attractions Review 1997*. Scott Wilson Resource Consultants. Edinburgh.

Scottish Tourist Board (1999) *Tourism in the Highlands and Islands 1998*. Scottish Tourist Board. Edinburgh.

Sirius Research (1990) Tourism in the Highlands. *www.eprc.strath.ac.uk/sirius*.

Slee, B. (1998) Tourism and rural development in Scotland in MacLellan and Smith (eds) (1998) *Tourism in Scotland*. International Thomson Business Press. London.

Smout, T.C. (1992) The Highlands and the roots of green consciousness 1750–1990. Occasional Paper No 1. Scottish Natural Heritage. Redgorton, Perth.

Smout, T.C. (2000) *Nature Contested, Environmental History in Scotland and Northern England since 1600*. Edinburgh University Press. Edinburgh.

CHAPTER 10

Protected areas

INTRODUCTION

In this chapter the 'transferable material', i.e. facts, ideas, experience etc. which may be applicable to other destinations in this 'protected areas' category, includes rural development, landuse conflicts, resort development, recreational impacts, wilderness values, wildlife and nature-based tourism.

PROTECTED AREAS

In most countries of the world protected areas are places which have been identified as being of special significance on account of their natural and/or cultural significance. Given their 'special' qualities, they are awarded a status intended to ensure their protection, their enjoyment by people and their appropriate use in perpetuity. They range from local nature reserves and urban neighbourhoods to national parks and world heritage sites. When their protection is given a formal status through a particular designation they are generally referred to as designated areas.

In this chapter several types of designated area are represented, notably national parks and world heritage sites. At December 2001 there were 721 properties which the World Heritage Committee had inscribed in the world heritage list. Of these 144 are natural, 554 are cultural and 23 are mixed. They are located in 124 countries or states and have as the overseeing body UNESCO, the United Nations Educational, Scientific and Cultural Organisation (*www.unesco.org/whc/heritage.htm*). The term 'world heritage site' is instantly recognised as designating something very special – in tourism terms a 'must see'. 'The designation of a new property, with the concomitant publicity, is virtually a guarantee that visitor numbers will increase [...] each has to solve the problems posed by the visitor management dilemma in its own way' (Shackley, 1998). The term 'national park' is probably more widely known internationally, perhaps the best known type of protected area, again implying a very special place. The conservation and management of these special natural places is monitored on behalf of the world community through the United Nations Environment Program World Conservation Monitoring Centre (*www.unep-wcmc.org*).

Given the growth in interest internationally in sustainable tourism, as well as in special interest tourism notably ecotourism based on natural and cultural resources, it is within these special areas that the challenges of sustainable development are greatest.

Conservation of their high scenic and ecological qualities is desired, yet these very qualities attract increasing numbers of visitors. Fortunately, since these areas have organisational structures and authorities charged with the dual responsibilities of conservation and visitor services, there is generally good availability of data on the changing circumstances.

THE CAIRNGORMS

The Cairngorms or the Cairngorm Mountains lie in the Central Highlands of Scotland. In the Cairngorms – as in the national parks of England and Wales – much of the land is in private ownership. This is in striking contrast to other countries where generally 'the nation' owns such 'special areas' and a public agency is the managing authority. The Cairngorms area is in part a 'national nature reserve' and a 'national scenic area', while smaller areas within it are 'sites of special scientific interest' or have other *local* conservation designations. Belatedly, the area will be designated a national park in 2003, under the National Parks (Scotland) Act (*www.scotland-legislation.hmso.gov.uk*) although the case for its designation goes back almost to the origins of the concept itself in the late 19th century. In the UK, none of these designations implies public ownership; rather, the areas they cover have been granted a limited range of legal protections against inappropriate development. In the Cairngorms, for example, public bodies such as the Forest Authority (*www.forestry.gov.uk/forestry*) own certain parts. Accordingly, public private agreements on management are the norm and often represent the compromise outcome of a lengthy process of negotiation.

Photograph 10.1 *The Cairngorm Mountains*

An example of private ownership in the areas is the 36,000 acre (14,569 hectare) Rothiemurchus Estate (*www.rothiemurchus.net/forest.html*), which includes some of the finest and largest remnants of the ancient Caledonian pine woodland and associated wildlife (*www.plant-talk.org/Pages/9scot.html*).

Half of the estate is within the national nature reserve and most of it is of special scientific importance. The estate employs some 40 people directly, while several other private businesses operate within it. Approximately 100 families are resident on the estate and it attracts over 300,000 visitors a year. For conservation reasons and to encourage and assist its owners to keep it generally open to public access it receives around a quarter of a million pounds a year from the public agencies, Scottish Natural Heritage (*www.snh.org.uk*) and the Forestry Commission. A concordat of public and private bodies exists to strike a balance between conservation and the need for social and economic development. Demonstrating the complexity of management of most 'British-style' national parks (as opposed to 'international-style' state-owned national parks) a number of bodies are represented on the concordat for the to-be-established Cairngorms National Park and include:

The Scottish Executive (*www.scotland.gov.uk*)

Highland Council (*www.highland.gov.uk*)

The Cairngorms Partnership (*www.cairngorms.co.uk*)

Moray, Badenoch and Strathspey Enterprise (*www.scottish-enterprise.com.uk/mbse*).

The Rothiemurchus Estate owner states that the broad objective is sustainable development that achieves real benefit for the local community and the visitors. This is hardly dissimilar to the stated objective of the public sector bodies represented. Theconcordat has, however, been criticised by several voluntary/not-for-profit sector organisations, the Mountaineering Council for Scotland (*www.mountaineering-scotland.org.uk*) and the Cairngorms Campaign (*www.cairngorms.demon.co.uk*), which were not invited to participate. They argue that it is a serious weakness that the concordat contains no non-governmental organisations (NGOs) such as themselves, although these bodies have a great interest in this area.

Destination portfolio

The Cairngorms contains the largest group of high mountains in Britain. Cairn Gorm, Cairn Toul, Braeriach, and Ben Macdhui are all over 4000 feet and many others closely approach that height. They form plateaux, eroded into granite mountains. [...] If the mountains be never entered or explored, but regarded merely as a scenic backdrop to the forests around their foot, these latter could still be delineated separately as three areas of outstanding beauty – the forests of Rothiemurchus, Upper Glen Feshie, and Mar.

(Murray, 1962)

A strictly ecological perspective would class the Cairngorms as: 'An arctic wilderness, displaced a few hundred miles south' (Adam Watson, mountain ecologist). This is certainly true of the Cairngorm plateau, which, while relatively low by European standards (Cairn Gorm has a height of 4,180 feet (1,245 metres)), gives the impression of greater height through the absence of foothills, adding to the distinctive character. However, despite frequent reference to the Cairngorms as 'wilderness' this is confined to the high plateaux and much of the area is a cultural/ natural landscape, the result of centuries of human exploitation – in places destructive and in others sustainable. The natural forest that remains (for example at Rothiemurchus) covers a comparatively small percentage of the area – precious remnants of the 'Great Wood of Caledon'.

Policies for landuse and development in the Cairngorms area have long been inadequate and no one set of priorities has been agreeable to all interested parties (as discussed in Chapter 5).

The multiplicity of long-established designations in the area – national nature reserve, national forest park, sites of special scientific interest – as well as the new national park designation – and the influential voluntary organisations with passionate commitment to the area, plus the powerful private and agency landowners in the area, has resulted in a highly complex management and development structure that must get the balance right.

Destination management/landuse

Red grouse shooting

Tourism use of the area includes the 'sport' of red grouse shooting. The red grouse (*Lagopus lagopus scoticus*) is unique to Scotland and 'iconic' – its image has been adopted for the label of a brand of whisky. The sport has been very important commercially since late Victorian times – on one estate of 200 square miles (52 sq km) shooting has been known to bring in some £5,000 in one week. Guests are drawn to the pursuit for the shoot itself, but also because it offers a chance to 'mingle with the aristocracy'. The owner traces his ancestry in the area back centuries and considers his approach to management appropriate. The grouse require heather to grow to 'mouth level' and this dictates the management of the moorland, and so 'Muir burn' (the burning of 'leggy' heather) is carried out in the spring to avoid 'leggy' heather. A broad ecological perspective on this traditional land management regime is that it is a questionable practice since it contributes to soil erosion and other problems in this harsh and often wet environment.

Deer stalking

Deer stalking is a unique experience in Scotland, due to the country's predominantly bare hills. As noted previously this is not a natural phenomenon – it was created largely by man through deforestation, although climate change has been a secondary factor. The red deer (*Cervus elephas*) of the open hill is unique to Scotland and the animals are selectively encouraged at the expense of a 'natural' balance of predators and prey in the area, although the natural predator, the wolf (*Canis lupus*), was in fact exterminated by man in the mid-18th century. However, the deer eat the young native pines, birch, rowan, alder and aspen trees as these species are attractive as soon as the young shoots emerge, notably in spring, when there is little else to eat. As a consequence there is no natural regeneration of the trees. The red deer – which were originally forest animals – have adapted over time to the resulting harsh, exposed environment and are notably smaller than their counterparts in forested parts of Europe. There can, however, be die-offs in severe winters, despite management which includes feeding the deer with hay. According to the UK Deer Commission (a government agency) (*www.dcs.gov.uk*) there are too many hinds (females). This is partly because hinds are not attractive to sporting shooters since they do not have antlers to take away as souvenirs/trophies. Additional 'control' of the herds only takes place if the deer cause damage to farmland. This is inadequate since excessive numbers are present – the ecological carrying capacity of the range is exceeded – but the more 'heads' the more profitable the shooting is for the estates.

Modern sporting deer stalking also requires roads to be built into the remote areas of the hills since many clients do not want to make the long walk into the hills. Since the estates own the land and have almost absolute power there is, arguably, inadequate control of hill road construction. The resulting landscape 'scars' are a controversial outcome.

Conservation groups and others argue that people need wild places more and more in contemporary society. 'Wild country' in Scotland is defined as areas which are more than two miles from the nearest road and new roads that penetrate the wild country remove this precious resource. The opportunities for this experience are declining in Scotland (and the world, generally).

It should also be noted that the opportunities for landuse conflict may be heightened by the fact that whereas in Scotland's first national park – Loch Lomond and the Trossachs – the park authority will have full planning powers, in the Cairngorms National Park the Scottish Executive proposes (July 2002) that three local authorities retain structure plan and development contol powers, with the park authority only having responsibility for local plan production. There is a view that this will result in a weak park authority unable to resist the pressures of property developers using the national park accolade to increase – for example – holiday and second home building and other forms of 'suburbanisation'. Turnbull (2002) also notes that in Badenoch and Strathspey, Highland region's part of the Cairngorms, the structure plan approved in 2001 allocates a 25% increase in house building by 2017 – in a district where deaths exceed births and woodlands sheltering endangered species such as the capercaillie and the red squirrel are already zoned for housing.

Exercise

Intra-recreational landuse conflicts (and the use of internet search engines)

How would you resolve this issue of conflict between differing recreational (and other) landuses in the Cairngorms? Landuse conflict is common and is a major issue in planning and policy making (see Chapter 5). For this or other upland areas with which you are familiar use the internet to find examples of solutions or compromises. Use a search engine such as *www.yahoo.com* or *www.yahoo.co.uk*; select 'Advanced search'; choose a 'search method' such as 'Matches on all words'; and key in appropriate search words. Use the websites you find (but bear in mind that some websites have a limited lifespan and 'disappear off-line').

Hill walking, rambling, mountaineering, wildlife watching

These tourists/recreationists seek the experience of wildness, isolation and quietness. Even footpaths can, for some, spoil the wilderness experience. Compared to the apparently 'obvious' economic contribution to an area of commercial hunting, such tourists have been alleged to make no contribution to local economy and this has been used as an argument against conservation-oriented management. However, recent studies have shown the opposite to be true in many parts of the Highland region where these activities are a major economic factor through the high spending on accommodation, food and drink and transport and the fact that return visits are common (Highland Regional Council, 1997).

Cycling

Cycling is an activity that has increased greatly in popularity in recent years. Technological developments have led to the evolution of the 'mountain bike' and enthusiasts can now reach areas of remote country accessible formerly only to the most dedicated hill walkers and climbers. While the activity has created some local problems of erosion, this is increasingly a manageable challenge often 'solved' through construction of simple trails which the majority of users are happy to follow. A variation of the activity is the 'extreme sport' of downhill mountain biking, formally recognised as an Olympic sport in 1986. Riders compete to complete the course in the shortest time. The 2002 Tissot Mountain Bike World Cup was held at the Nevis Range just outside Fort William on the specially constructed course (*www.nevis-range.co.uk*). The activity uses the gondola uplift facilities built for skiers, contributing to the economic viability of that development through all-year demand, an important consideration.

Skiing

Skiing contributed greatly to the wider public interest in the Cairngorms from the 1960s on. Aviemore became a major winter resort when skiing facilities were developed on Cairn Gorm. The facilities required for skiing are visible all year round over a great distance, while concentrations of skiers cause (local) physical/ecological impact damage to mountain vegetation which in turn leads to soil erosion creating a visual impact that many find to be in conflict with their expectations of this area.

Using fences to keep skiers/walkers confined to the immediate vicinity of the facilities is not seriously proposed, but some argue that getting to the ecologically fragile (and dangerous) mountain plateau is best managed by not making access to it 'easy'. This is the management principle of 'the long walk in'. Animal and plant species present confirm the special 'arctic' character of the area, in ecological terms, some species being common to Iceland, Spitzbergen and the Cairngorms. The landforms, wildlife and vegetation make this a genuinely special area.

Commercial skiing interests have sought to extend the area of development, with the resultant need for more ski lifts. In the mid-1990s, on days of good conditions, some 10,500 people per hour was common, while 6,000 people is a desirable maximum to avoid excessive queuing times and the generation of common complaints about high prices, too few runs and overcrowding – which is dangerous. In the mid-1990s the area was seven times busier than intended in the original plans and a common view has been that extra space for development would make no difference. The ecological reality is, however, that vegetation *is* being destroyed, leading to soil being washed out, followed by the formation of 'rills', while lower down the slope vegetation is smothered by the soil 'creeping' down hill. Progressively the surface becomes uneven and unskiable. Subsequent severe erosion could undermine facilities – e.g. buildings, pylons, etc. From an aesthetic point of view, when the snow disappears, the area is visually unattractive.

A focus of controversy in the early 1990s centred on development proposals for Lurcher's Gully. This area is scientifically and perceptually very important for its ecological and wilderness values. It has been protected under the Wildlife and Countryside Act 1981, but a 30–40% increase in skiing numbers was sought by the commercial skiing developers to reach the new, hoped for areas in Lurcher's Gully. The first proposal envisaged a two-way road for cars, with new parking; the revision accepted a bus-only, one-lane/single-track road. This proposal was finally refused planning permission and the decision was upheld following a lengthy public enquiry. Some years later, in 1999, new, alternative development proposal involving the construction of a funicular railway as the means of access to the plateau was given the go-ahead, again after a lengthy period of opposition.

Conservation interests, as represented at the top level by Scottish Natural Heritage, were by the late 1990s in direct conflict with those promoting the social and economic benefits to be derived from construction of the railway so providing upgraded ski facilities but also all-year visitor access to the plateau. While non-skiing visitors would be subject to a visitor management plan restricting unaccompanied access, some argued that this would be inadequate to protect conservation values in the context of the 100,000 visitors that are essential to make the development economically viable. They would have been transported to the fragile (and dangerous) plateau environment and arguably would not be too happy at not being allowed to visit it.

An alternative strategy accepted that upgrading of the skiing facilities was necessary but centred on a gondola scheme. This would have had the additional benefit (as some would see it) of removing existing high-altitude roads and parking since the gondola base station would have been located at a low level within the forested areas of Glenmore. This 'alternative strategy' for the northern Cairngorm area also envisaged a more dispersed pattern of lower key employment-generating tourism developments throughout the sub-region, including smaller scale upgrading of the existing skiing developments.

Conservation interests had long argued that skiing should not be concentrated in one (Scottish) area only i.e. Cairngorm. Rather, it should be developed elsewhere, where suitable, and so spread the economic benefits and minimise the ecological/perceptual disturbance. Aonach Mhor (*www.ski.scotland.net*) in the Fort William area was developed in the 1990s and Drumochter holds the potential for future development. However, it is becoming accepted that global warming is a reality and that this is likely to make skiing in Scotland an even more 'climatically marginal' activity.

In response, developers have argued that 'indefinite expansion' is not sought. The International Union for Conservation of Nature and Natural Resources (*www.iucn.org*) declared in 1981 that the Cairngorms are special and should be designated a world heritage site *if* appropriate management of the area could be implemented.

Conservationists have made the analogy – can an art gallery conserving the *cultural* heritage of an area agree to accept the loss of even 1% of its priceless and irreplaceable treasures? The loss of an area of *natural* heritage is even more critical in areas such as the Cairngorms where ecological integrity demands the whole core area must be conserved or at least maintained in a condition no worse than it is now where, historically, some development is already present.

From a perspective of management of the destination as a whole skiing has certainly had a significant and positive economic effect on the area and arguably it could be said that it 'put the Cairngorms on the map' for many people. However, it is clear that skiing in sensitive areas such as the Cairngorms can cause significant and irreversible damage to habitat and species. Much of the debate has been between those in favour of skiing development and those against. Holden (1998) concluded that the group representing the Cairngorms Partnership (*www.cairn-gorms.co.uk*) in the consultation exercise placed economic development over environmental protection, as clearly indicated in their statement of aim: 'Securing economic viability whilst limiting environmental impact to an acceptable level' (Cairngorms Partnership, 1996 in Holden, 1998: 249).

Holden (ibid.) sought the views of skiers themselves on the proposed development of the funicular railway and its environmental impact. He found that awareness of environmental damage as a result of skiing was low, although certain key groups (skiers aged 25 and over) did show appreciation and concern for the environment. It could be concluded from this that it is of great importance for the future viability of skiing in this area that awareness is raised of the importance of the environment. It is also desirable that skiers with a concern for the environment are attracted to the Cairngorms not only through promotion, but also through actual practice of sensitive management of the fragile environment, so their voices can be influential in directing future developments.

Other tourist/leisure activities in the Cairngorms

Water based activities

Loch Morlich lies between the principal northern access to the Cairngorm plateau and the more intensively developed area of Strathspey stretching from Aviemore to Grantown-on-Spey – the 'service community' of the destination (Gunn, 1989) (see the discussion of destination 'anatomy' in Chapter 3).

The loch is increasingly developed for recreation/tourism. Does the presence of sailing boats detract from the scenery? For some it does, but on balance it is considered acceptable. Powerboats, which create noise and pollution as well as waves which can cause bank erosion, are excluded from the area. Litter is minimised and moorings beyond the present numbers are not permitted. Cars are kept back from the beach, which is fragile and susceptible to erosion. A camping and caravan site is managed to high standards by Forest Enterprise, part of the Forestry Commission (*www.forestry.gov.uk*) and a network of nature trails and more demanding walks lead into the surrounding mountain and forest environment.

Wildlife based activities

Near the village of Boat of Garten is Loch Garten, some 7 miles (12 km) northeast of Aviemore. With the surrounding Abernethy Forest it offers a role model for a conservation-led management. Strict controls on development (facilitated by ownership of the area) have permitted the Royal Society for the Protection of Birds (*www.rspb.org.uk*) to encourage breeding of the osprey (once an endangered species due to 'predator control' in the interests of grouse shooting). Capercaillie, crested tit and dunlin are other characteristic birds of the area. Many visitors come to view the birds, especially at nesting time, without causing any disturbance and bring considerable income to the area. Other tourists and visitors come to enjoy the forest itself with its native species of Scots pine. These contrast with the blocks of 'exotic conifers' that characterise many other forests in Britain – i.e. non-native single-species tree plantations, generally Sitka spruce which were planted solely for timber production in the immediate post-World War I period. Forestry itself is not the problem in many rural destinations – it is the *type* of forestry that has been criticised – monocultures which are very low in biological diversity and visual appeal. Conservation-led management also creates more jobs than under previous 'traditional' patterns of landuse in the area.

Overall, however, there has been a lack of adequate landuse policy and subsequent destination management in this beautiful area. Some argue that landowners can do as they please, according to their (commercial) interests, rather than in the wider interest of ecological, recreational and aesthetic values or the local community. In turn, conservationists are criticised as encouraging 'preservation' rather than 'conservation' – forgetting that society 'needs timber as well as beauty' and, by implication, economic development and jobs.

Landscape management of the Cairngorms

Despite references to the area as wilderness, much of the area is a natural/cultural landscape – the nature/man interplay is the real attraction. The area has long deserved national park status. It has been Scotland's peculiar political structure that has precluded this internationally recognised designation from being introduced in the country – despite the fact that the inspiration of the international national park movement was a Scot (John Muir) (see Chapter 8).

Until recently there had been no successful challenge to the status quo – private landowners' opposition to anything other than the 'voluntary principle' approach to public access to open land. In the 1940s, a government committee firmly proposed this area (and others) as a national park. The government of the day turned this down, yet the land could have been purchased 'for the nation' for £200,000. A history of such proposals and refusals has led to critical reference to Scotland's continuing 'feudal' approach to land ownership although this has been changing since the late 1990s. Generally, landowners (and certain others) have viewed national parks as 'bureaucratic', characterised by interference from afar. They see the present system (i.e. the status quo) as 'flexible' and, by implication, better.

In the Cairngorms area in 1990, there were six major landowners and some 14 government/local government bodies – and no 'unified management policy'. The pattern has continued broadly the same until now, under the present government, the area will become Scotland's second national park (after Loch Lomond and the Trossachs) in 2003. Formerly, there has been no political will to set limits to development (as by considerations of carrying capacity). In a national park some 'restrictions' are unavoidable – on both landowners and agencies and on tourists and other visitors. This is a pattern established in almost every other country in the world and a rational approach to management has generally succeeded in achieving sustainable landuse and conservation and responsible access for increasing numbers of visitors.

The southern Cairngorms demonstrates a further approach to protected area destination management. The National Trust for Scotland acquired the Mar Lodge Estate in 1995, part of the core area of the Cairngorm Mountains (*www.nts.org. uk/mar.html*). A key objective of the new ownership is the integration of 'traditional' countryside activities – 'hunting, shooting and fishing' – with conservation, recreation and appropriate tourism development. While recreational use of the Mar Lodge Estate is currently at a much lower level than at Cairn Gorm mountain it is likely to rise. A number of issues in destination management arise, including the visitor experience. Management would benefit greatly from greater understanding of current visitor behaviour in the area. For example, what are visitors' motivations for making the visit and their expectations of 'consuming' it?

Visitors generally consider the area to be one of high quality and this underpins plans for the essential environmental rehabilitation of the area, identifying areas of conflict between the perceived 'wilderness values' of the area and essential environmental management and restoration. The sustainability of the estate – environmentally, socially and economically – is a central management theme.

Such management issues raise key questions. Is the design of sustainable 'products' in the natural resource field synonymous with the production of quality or are the two objectives in fact in conflict? Some potential visitors – perhaps the (allegedly) higher spending 'traditional field sport enthusiasts' – might measure a high-quality experience in terms of its supporting infrastructure such as sumptuous 'heritage' accommodation, superior service and convenient access. Ecotourists, a growing area of contemporary tourism, are likely to be drawn to this area on account of its regeneration as a near wilderness area. To this last group, 'quality' may be measured in terms of the *non*-introduction of 'facilities' and infrastructure, perhaps even their removal.

Interpretation of the natural and cultural heritage will play a key role in the evolving conservation and tourism-related use and management of this area. The current 'image' of the Scottish landscape is problematic, the more so in an area such as this which is considered the epitome of Scottish landscape. The promotion of Scotland as 'Europe's last wilderness' is in fact at odds with the ecological and social realities of its impoverished ecosystems (McVean and Lockie, 1969). Biodiversity is comparatively low, the area being devoid of much of the wildlife available to the tourist in rival, 'new' central and eastern European destinations such as Poland (*www.pl-info.net/en/tourism/active/ecology.shtml*; *www.poland. panparks.org/source/intro.html*). Further, an economically threatened local human population may be prepared to sacrifice sustainable development for the more rapid, if short-term gains available from 'unsustainable' developments.

Resorts and other settlements in the Cairngorms

It is unrealistic to discuss the Cairngorm Mountains without reference to the villages and other settlements in the area. Indeed, the national park plans include a zoning approach of core, peripheral and community zones, the latter embracing a number of small towns and villages. In the northern Cairngorms a number of these settlements lie in the district of Badenoch-Strathspey, notably Aviemore, which since the 1960s has been the main 'gateway' to the northern Cairngorms and where most tourism-related development has taken place (*www.aviemore.org.uk/*; *www.aviemore.org/chamber-news/news.htm*).

AVIEMORE

The first recorded reference to the settlement is as Avi Moir in 1654. Later, 'Aviemore' became known as an inn on General Wade's military road. When the Perth–Inverness railway was opened in 1863 it developed as a small tourist centre and there are today a number of stone-built villas of distinctive design dating from this period.

When ski developments began at Coire Cas on Cairn Gorm in the early 1960s, the vision for the village of Aviemore was a large year-round resort. The Aviemore Centre was opened in 1966 as the centrepiece – a complex of hotels, timeshare apartments, self-catering chalets, restaurants, shops, entertainment and sporting facilities 'which is unique in Britain, but many people feel that the centre is an eyesore in such a rural setting' (Whyte and Whyte, 1987). Others criticised the fact that the centre 'turned its back' on the existing village.

The first chairlift began operation at Cairn Gorm ski area in 1961, although it was not until 1966 that the £2.7 million was invested to build the 'Aviemore Centre' began to provide indoor activities for visitors. The Aviemore Centre soon became synonymous with Aviemore, indeed with Baddenoch-Strathspey the district and the 'Spey Valley', the tourist board name for the area at the time. The development was a bold experiment in its day and successful in creating a significant local tourism industry that brought skiing within reach of a wider range of the population while increasing local income and employment.

By the 1990s, however, three out of four visitors to Aviemore were disappointed with their stay. Part of the reason was that there could be no guarantee of snow. Despite the high plateau of the Cairngorms regularly experiencing subarctic conditions, Scotland has a maritime climate characterised by 'changeable' conditions. Global warming/climate change is a further significant factor in a region where skiing is already a 'marginal' activity. Perhaps, however, the main reason for decline in the popularity of the resort is a failure to recognise the changing tastes of an already specialist market for a more up-market product and experience.

Redevelopment proposals were drawn up in 1993 for the replacement and refurbishment of the main buildings, the expansion of conference provision and for diversification of the activities in the area, including throughout the year. A new visual image and a dramatic increase in visual quality were seen as essential to the regeneration of the resort.

Progress was slow. The year 1994 saw the reopening of 'Santa Claus Land', a small theme park near the Aviemore Centre. The mid-1990s also saw the rejection of the Cairngorms by the International Union for the Conservation of Nature and Natural Resources (IUCN, *www.iucn.org*) for world heritage site status. This was because of what was considered continuing inadequate management of, and protective arrangements for, this world-class natural heritage area. The most controversial proposal for the regeneration of the destination was for the construction of a funicular railway on Cairn Gorm. As noted, after a lengthy period of challenge to the proposal, work began on site in 1999. This has replaced the outdated and inadequate skilifts and is part of a general upgrading of the ski area which will continue to be seen as a major attraction in the area. A private company, the Cairngorm Chairlift Company (*www.cairngormmountain.com*), is the main developer but there is substantial public investment by key government agencies. Further development for Aviemore – a plan was prepared in 1996 – will complement this major work amidst continuing controversy. The Aviemore Partnership, established in 1994 and comprising public and private bodies, coordinates the interests of all and the local community in the economic regeneration of the village and the surrounding area – including HIE (*www.hie.co.uk*), Moray Badenoch and Strathspey Enterprise (*www.mbse.co.uk*), Highlands Council (*www.highland.gov.uk*), Scottish Natural Heritage (*www.snh.org.uk*), Highlands and Islands Tourist Board (*www.host.co.uk*), Scottish Tourist Board (*www.visitscotland.com*), Aviemore Community Council, and others who aim to see Aviemore fulfil its tourism and commercial potential. Aviemore and Badenoch-Strathspey district have received a boost through publicity emerging from the popular BBC television series 'Monarch of the Glen', based on the district (*www.monarchcountry.com; www.bbc.co.uk/scotland/entertainment/monarch*). The village also has its own website (*www. aviemore.org*) while the local tourist board (*aviemoretic@host.co.uk*) and the chamber of commerce for the area (*cairngorms-chamber@lineone.net*) are both online (see Figure 10.1).

Newspaper headlines reflect the aspirations and the subsequent decline in fortunes of the 'Aviemore Mountain Resort'.

From The Scotsman
'A Scottish mountain resort to rival Europe's best' (mid-1960s)
'Caught between beauty and the beast' (31 August 1992)
'The ugly skiing town that even Santa deserted' (1993)
'A soulless monument to uninspired design' (1993)
'Multi-million plan to turn the decaying Aviemore Centre into an ultra-modern mountain resort' (1993)

From 'Aviemore and Spey Valley 93' (*A&SV Tourist Board, 1993*)
'The internationally famous resort of Aviemore'

From 'Project Aviemore' Issue 1. Spring 1996. The Aviemore Partnership
'Vision to become reality'

From The Scotsman
'Ski resort halts slide downmarket' (3 March 1998)
'Selective but extensive demolition is recommended' (1999)

Figure 10.1 *How publicity can boost or blemish the fortunes of resorts*

The upturn in a sad trend of decline in the mid- to late 1990s was certainly influenced by the emergence of the Cairngorms Partnership: 'In 1994 the government set up a Partnership to prepare and implement a Management Strategy for the Cairngorms that would guarantee a sustainable future for this most special area of Scotland' (*www.cairngorms.co.uk*).

The proximity of – and, arguably, the dependence of Aviemore on – the Cairngorms is a key factor. The Cairngorms are set to become Scotland's second national park in 2003 (after Loch Lomond and the Trossachs in 2002). It is likely this would enable the designation of the area as a world heritage site since the management structure would then be considered appropriate. In this context of a natural environment of acknowledged superlative status are the developments at Aviemore and on Cairn Gorm of an appropriate 'world-class' level?

Exercise

Alternative perspectives on development

While the construction of a funicular railway on Cairngorm is now complete, at the core of the 'anti-'argument was the assertion that this would concentrate a great deal of public (and private) investment in a highly sensitive environment, where skiing is already a marginal activity. It has been argued that the safety of the increased number of visitors on the mountain plateau is unresolved. The developers' predicted figure is 225,000 summer visitors per year, although 100,000–120,000 is held to be more realistic by opponents, suggesting considerably less economic benefit. Even that smaller number of visitors could do great damage to the fragile mountain environment and to visitors themselves, as many will be unaware of the dangers of the plateau that most years kills a number of unprepared visitors when the weather changes suddenly. In response to the criticisms the developers agreed a visitor management plan. Non-skiing users of the railway would not be permitted onto the plateau. They could use the funicular railway and would then be directed into a visitor centre that would interpret the ecology of the mountain environment, while allowing views of the area from within the building. This could be seen as counter to a fundamental principle of environmental interpretation which is to encourage the visitor to experience the 'real thing' with an enhanced sense of awareness that good interpretation gives (see the discussion of interpretation in Chapter 2).

Doesn't everyone have a 'right' to enjoy his or her natural heritage? The funicular railway proposal will allow all visitors – including the young, aged and infirm – to reach the mountain plateau and enjoy an environment otherwise inaccessible to them.

Is this good practice in environmental interpretation? It is generally considered that interpretation should give people interest and understanding, but, importantly, also the motivation to experience directly the 'real thing' rather than a 'second-hand'/substitute experience.

Scottish Natural Heritage, the government body responsible for safeguarding the nation's natural heritage, accepted this approach and the agency withdrew its opposition to the scheme, which was then awarded planning consent.

The 'alternative strategy' for the northern Cairngorm area had envisaged a dispersed pattern of lower-key but (arguably) higher employment-generating tourism and other developments throughout the district. It would have included the upgrading of the existing skiing developments, primarily through construction of a gondola system for the transport of skiers and other visitors to the high tops. Construction impact would have been considerably less than that caused by construction of the funicular railway; moreover, the lower gondola station would have been located down the hill in Glenmore where there is an existing campsite/youth hostel/visitor centre and forest cover, which could have concealed much of the impact. This would also have allowed the current access road used by cars and coaches at present to be withdrawn from the higher level slopes down to the glen where it too could be concealed within the forest. Arguably, a better visitor experience would have resulted (Cairngorms Campaign: *www.cairngorms.demon. co.uk*).

The proposals for national park status for the Cairngorms include 'zoning'. The Aviemore-Strathspey area would be part of the *community zone* where visitor facilities, such as accommodation, would continue to be provided (although not exclusively there) as well as other recreational facilities appropriate to a *honeypot*. Between this community zone and the mountains is Glenmore, which would be part of the *buffer zone* where low intensity recreational provision such as low level walking, cross-country skiing, picnicking, nature trails and waterside activities would be provided (as at present). The high Cairngorms plateau and adjacent slopes would be the *core zone* (or wilderness zone) where conservation is the priority and access is on foot (and funicular?) only. The 'long walk in' would be the norm with no concessions to 'easy access' – a management approach generally used in Norwegian national parks. The current 'access debate' is likely to result in a general presumption in favour of 'responsible access' to wild countryside, replacing the erroneous assumption that there has been 'no law of trespass' in Scotland and elsewhere in the UK. While welcomed, this falls short of the long-established *Allemansrätt* in Sweden whereby everyone has the legal right to walk on uncultivated land while continuing to respect owners' property. 'Permits' to visit certain sensitive areas – comparable to the 'wilderness permits' in the US and Canadian national parks – are not envisaged.

The alternative strategy for development had a strong following. Proponents assert that declining employment in traditional rural activities has created a climate of laissez-faire towards development – 'so long as it brings in tourists'. They pointed out that every winter there is seasonal unemployment, despite the skiing; also, that most of the jobs created by skiing are not filled by *locals*, but by *incomers*. Many young locals do not want jobs in tourism, disliking its seasonality and low wages. They want 'ordinary' jobs – preferring, for example, path building – although this *is* indirectly a 'tourism' job, since the paths are built partly to encourage more tourists to the area. Other service jobs are, however, considered to be acceptable.

YOSEMITE NATIONAL PARK, CALIFORNIA

An alternative view of protected area development: 'the justified sacrifice'

John Muir is regarded today as the pioneer of modern environmental conservation. (see Chapter 8). In the 1890s he wrote:

Photograph 10.2 *Interpretation on wheels, Yosemite National Park*

Of all the mountain ranges I have climbed, I like the Sierra Nevada the best. Though extremely rugged, with its main features on the grandest scale in height and depth, it is nevertheless easy of access and hospitable; and its marvellous beauty, displayed in striking and alluring forms, woos the admiring wanderer on and on, higher and higher, charmed and enchanted. Well may the Sierra be called the Range of Light, not the Snowy Range; for only in winter is it white; while all the year it is bright.

He refers specifically to the central section of the range, some 36 miles (58 km) in length and 48 miles (72 km) in breadth, with Yosemite River at the centre and including the Tuolomne and Merced Rivers, 'innumerable lakes and waterfalls and smooth silky lawns; the noblest forests, the loftiest granite domes, the deepest ice-sculptured canons, the brightest crystalline pavements, and snowy mountains soaring into the sky twelve and thirteen thousand feet' (quoted in Engberg, 1980). The area was subsequently designated as Yosemite National Park. Even then Muir anticipated tourists flocking to the area and welcomed this, so they could enjoy the 'glad tidings of the mountains' but suggested that 'once arrived in the valley and made the choice of hotels, it is important to know what to do with one's self. I would advise sitting from morning till night under some willow bush on the river bank where there is a wide view. This will be "doing the valley" far more effectively than riding along trails in constant motion from point to point. The entire valley is made up of "points of interest".' Although rich in truth, it is was probably said rather whimsically. In practice most of Muir's ardent followers today are active tourists keen to walk both the valley and wilderness trails that Muir himself roamed.

Valuable lessons in the conservation versus development dilemma may be drawn from the more than a century of experience of Yosemite National Park (established 1890) (*www.nps.gov/yose*) and also a World Heritage Site since 1984 (*whc.unesco.org/sites/308.htm*). Yosemite Valley is the focus of the great majority of tourists visiting the park. From the valley floor at 4,000 feet (1,200 m) sheer walls of granite rise for half a mile, crowned by famous summits such as El Capitan and Half Dome.

The park has a total area of 1,189 square miles (3,080 sq km). Yosemite Valley is the 'sacrifice' necessary to encourage and maintain the 'constituency of support' of those visitors subsequently prepared to 'vote for conservation with their tax dollars' (personal communication, 1988, senior park staff). Expressed colloquially, this is the view of the US National Park Service. As a consequence, the valley is relatively intensively developed for tourism – several campsites, cabins, a hotel, an interpretive centre, shops, a network of hiking and cycling trails. The park is hugely popular – in the financial year 2001 there was a recorded total of 3,453,345 recreational visits. Impacts of visitors are managed, wear and tear is repaired, even crime is tackled by armed 'enforcement rangers'. Some argue that these visitors are not experiencing the 'true nature' of the park – they are confined to a 'tamed' area. In reality, they voluntarily confine themselves to this one part of the park. The management approach works – the goodwill generated is high and visitors consistently speak well of their experience. In fact, the rest of the park is 'open' – although 'wilderness permits' (available on a first come, first served basis) are required for certain areas, to maintain the environment and also the 'wilderness experience' of the users. In practice most visitors are content to leave the great majority of the park to the small percentage of wilderness users – backpackers and others – perhaps feeling that 'one day' they too will take to the high Sierras and maybe even join the Sierra Club (*www.sierraclub.org/john_muir_exhibit*), founded by John Muir and one of the earliest environmental organisations still in existence today.

Management challenges continue to arise. The Wawona is a hotel built in the valley in 1875 on the site of a lodging built in 1857 by Galen Clark, the first official guardian of what was to become the national park. It is arguably part of the cultural heritage of the park although some argue that it should be removed and reconstructed on the outskirts of the park, perhaps to serve as a welcoming 'gateway' to the destination. This is unlikely. Another 'challenge' is private car access to the valley. This is, however, being reduced on a voluntary basis in favour of a shuttle bus service phased in over a number of years to maintain public goodwill while achieving environmental objectives. There is also concern expressed by certain conservation groups that the increasing demands for the park to 'earn its keep' may come to dominate as a management philosophy, encouraging economic developments such as time-share accommodation and more retail outlets … wherever the market demands. This would require overturning the prevailing philosophy that like health and education, outdoor recreation and the enjoyment of national parks is part of the quality of life and the rights of the citizen (see Figure 10.2) (Yosemite National Park: *www.nps.gov/yose/planning/yvp*).

Reclaim natural beauty

Reduce traffic congestion

Allow natural processes to prevail

Reduce crowding

Promote visitor understanding and enjoyment

Restore, protect and enhance the natural and cultural resources of Yosemite Valley

Provide opportunities for high quality, resource-based visitor experience

Figure 10.2 *Yosemite National Park: general development and management objectives*

BANFF NATIONAL PARK, ALBERTA, CANADA

Banff National Park is part of the Rocky Mountain Parks World Heritage Site and faces similar development/conservation dilemmas to those of Yosemite. The township of Banff lies within the park and predates the designation of Banff National Park (1885) (*www.worldweb.com/ParksCanada-Banff*).

The early beginnings of Canadian tourism lie in Banff National Park and reflect the 'pragmatic' emphasis that lies behind much development, even in sensitive areas. In the 1870s, the expansion of Canada focused on enticing the western province of British Columbia to join the Canadian Federation. This it did, in return for the construction of the Canadian Pacific Railway. The enormous cost of construction was met by the Federal Government and the small, if well-developed tourism industry, through the foresight of the general manager of the CPR, William Cornelius Van Horne. He developed a philosophy of capitalising the scenery made accessible by the railroad: 'If we can't export the scenery, we'll import the tourists'.

The CPR's advertising 'delineated the view of Canada, both at home and around the world. Its view of Canada as a place of scenic wonders and cultural diversity prevails even to this day' (Hart, 1983: 7). It served to create a positive image of Canada, influencing immigration, trade and international political relations and helping to influence a major Canadian concern, national unity. This fact also conveys the wider implications of tourism.

The conservation philosophy of the late 20th century had encouraged speculation on the 'rightness' of having towns within national parks, but today it is not considered realistic to speculate on such irreversible errors. The contemporary approach is to accept such settlements, but to encourage further development only in a sustainable manner. In such important sites – where conservation and tourism are both important – there are differing interpretations of sustainable development and how it should proceed in the park. These range from a 'deep green' or 'eco centric' perspective to a 'technocentric' stance (see the discussion on perspectives on sustainability in Chapter 2). The former would advocate a progressive phasing down of the size of the township and its activities, ultimately to its removal – with appropriate compensation to the residents and businesses. The latter would be based on technological improvements leading to reductions in noise and waste and other forms of pollution created by the town as well as traffic management.

Exercise

'Inappropriate' development in protected areas

What is your (destination management) opinion on the removal (or not) of historical developments that have taken place in areas which are now 'protected' and which – from today's perspective – are considered inappropriate? Give examples of what you consider to be 'acceptable' development in a (countryside) protected area, commenting on any restrictions you consider necessary; also, give examples of what you consider unacceptable (with your reasons) that should be removed.

In Banff National Park there is a large visitor centre located on a mountain top and similar concerns have been raised about its continued presence in such a 'spectacular' location. In Britain similar questions have been raised – a new visitor centre for Glencoe, in the Scottish Highlands, has recently been completed in the village of Glencoe, replacing the centre constructed in 1972 on a prominent site within the famous glen (*www.nts.org.uk/glencoe.html*; *www.saveglencoe.org.uk/badideas/badideas.htm*)

Photograph 10.3 *Mountain-top visitor centre in Banff National Park*

OTHER CANADIAN PARKS: BRITISH COLUMBIA

Historically, economic pragmatism has been the favoured approach to development in parks. In British Columbia's earliest parks it was eagerly adopted. 'With

B.C.'s unparalleled scenery, Banff-style tourism could work here – all that was needed was parks'. In 1911, under that philosophy, Strathcona on central Vancouver Island (*www.gov.bc.ca/bcparks/explore/parkpgs/strathco.htm*) became BC's first provincial park and its first superintendent commented: 'The attracting of tourists will become a business on a commercial scale not now comprehended by our people'.

Mount Robson (*www.gov.bc.ca/bcparks/explore/parkpgs/mtrobson.htm*) followed in 1913 and Garibaldi Park (*www.gov.bc.ca/bcparks/explore/parkpgs/garibald.htm*) in 1930. The latter is now home to the world-class skiing resort of Whistler (*www.whistler-blackcomb.com*) where, among the challenges faced by destination managers, the largest population of black bears of any site in North America exists, attracted by the easy pickings of food from around the facilities and accommodation that are now of the scale of a small town.

A key challenge of destination management in protected areas is to respond appropriately to new trends in tourism and recreation without losing the best of the old and without disrupting the varied landscapes or the resident communities of an area which in comparatively recent times – for the very best of reasons – has become a protected area, generally long after it acquired its existing status as a 'residential' area.

THE TATRAS NATIONAL PARK, POLAND

In Poland, challenges to protected areas have arisen less through recreational or tourism trends than through fundamental political change. The Tatra Mountains (*hum.amu.edu.pl/~zbzw/ph/pnp/tatr.htm*) in the south of the country demonstrate the destination management challenges in that contemporary context – greater freedom of access for the population and pressing economic need to boost the economy of the country:

> People are always impressed by the distinct character of the vegetation and an abundance of species, colour intensity and a diversity of life.
>
> (Tatras National Park, 1993)

This hints at a significant contrast with the Cairngorms. The distinct characters of the Tatra landscapes are a consequence of 'zonation' of the natural vegetation. Natural plant communities – and related wildlife – change with altitude within the park. This truly 'natural' feature is generally lacking in Scotland as a result of human action over many centuries. The resultant 'man–nature' cultural landscape is undoubtedly beautiful, but to the trained observer (now including many tourists) soil erosion in many places and depleted wildlife diversity is a cause for regret. The great Scottish ecologist Fraser Darling said of his beloved Highlands that they were in many places 'a wet desert' – a landscape depleted of its flora and fauna and cleared of its native people.

This emphasises the great importance of conservation management and, in turn, the need to gain the support of tourists (and local people) for the efforts underway to restore and recreate vestiges of the 'natural' Cairngorm landscape and its wildlife. There is an 'economic imperative' here. Experienced travellers who have been drawn to Scotland by the (technically inaccurate) promotional slogan 'Scotland – Europe's last wilderness' are increasingly aware that it is in the emerging destinations of post-Soviet central and eastern Europe that authentic 'wilderness' is to be found. Even spectacular species long ago pushed into extinction by man in Scotland – the wolf and the bison – are still native to Poland and other countries which could begin to dominate the growing nature-based and special interest tourism markets.

Reintroduction of 'lost' species is a lengthy process, partly because of opposition from certain sectors of the population. Most farmers and gamekeepers, for example, instinctively oppose the return of the wolf or the lynx to their area, although evidence from other areas where such reintroductions have taken place suggests that a 'knee-jerk' reaction is at least questionable (see the discussion on the reintroduction of vultures to Cévennes in Chapter 10). Ecologically informed management could achieve a 'balance' between 'traditional' landuses and such 'new' – although, ironically, actually very old – ecological relationships (*www.myinternet.co.uk/wsgb/education/articles/reintroduction.htm*).

In Britain, serious consideration of wolf reintroduction is at a very early stage. Reintroduction of the European beaver to Scotland has already been the subject of public consultation by Scottish Natural Heritage and in 2002 experimental introductions were carried out (*www.snh.org.uk/news/pc-bea00.htm*).

Exercise

Reintroduction of extinct species

Visit this website and try out the exercises: *www.ltrr.arizona.edu/geos220/wolf/index.html.*

From a destination management perspective what is your view of the reintroduction of certain (now extinct) species, such as wolves, to an area such as the Cairngorms (or another destination of your choosing)?

CASE STUDY

Reintroduction of 'lost' wildlife

In the early 1990s the griffon vulture, which had been hunted to local extinction, was reintroduced to the Parc National des Cévennes (*www.les-cevennes-parc-national.fr/cevennes/default.htm*), at Gorge de la Jonte (*www.eurobirding.co.uk/cevennes_national_park.htm*). Now griffon and black vultures are resident species again, with Egyptian vultures as summer visitors. This is ecologically desirable – it helps restore earlier levels of 'bio-diversity' – and viewing the birds is popular with tourists, notably watching them rise on the morning 'thermals' or sun-heated updraughts.

As in the Cairngorms – and in the UK generally – the reintroduction of predators to the Cévennes was viewed with scepticism or even hostility by many local farmers, even though the vulture is not a predator, but a sca-venger, feeding on carcasses. A satisfactory management solution has been

> arrived at whereby local sheep farmers are paid to deliver the carcasses of sheep which have died through natural causes to certain points in the park where they are fed on by the vultures – providing a (managed) spectacle for tourists and also helping convince the sceptical locals that well-fed birds are less likely to attack live sheep.
>
> There are useful lessons for the Cairngorms to be derived from the Cévennes experience, since there are current proposals to reintroduce the European otter and – at some time in the future, if old prejudices can be overcome – the wolf. Only if economic concerns can be alleviated will species introductions be possible. The experience of central European countries such as Poland suggests that the opportunity to view such spectacular wildlife is likely to be a major tourist draw.

The Tatras National Park in Poland has a working relationship with the adjacent Slovakian National Park, although the two are separated by an international border. Since they are both located within the same geobotanical unit such collaboration is essential. Destination managers in each share similar conservation challenges:

> Mass tourism, concentrated in the most attractive and more easily accessible areas, causes pollution and intensification of erosion. Although some control of tourist pressure is possible, it is much harder to prevent the acidification of water; and the influence of the park management on air pollution is almost insignificant.
>
> (Tatras National Park, 1993)

Again a fundamental destination management principle is clear: tourism cannot be developed and managed successfully without reference to the wider context of the destination and a framework of sustainability – the 3Es of economic, environmental and equity considerations (Howie, 1996).

PARC NATIONAL DES CÉVENNES, FRANCE

The Cévennes has been referred to in the context of reintroduction of the Griffon and black vultures. Further lessons for appropriate destination management of the Cairngorms may be drawn from the Parc National des Cévennes, the fourth of France's National Parks, established in 1970.

The Cévennes occupy the southeastern edge of the Massif Central with its headquarters in Florac in the Lozère. This is a comparatively undiscovered area for non-French tourists; perhaps the best known connection being through the Scottish writer, Robert Louis Stevenson's book, *Travels with a Donkey in the Cévennes*. Stevenson could be regarded as an early (1870s') 'alternative tourist' to the region.

Designated area

The Cairngorms and the Cévennes have shared characteristics. In the Parc National des Cévennes, upland agriculture is in decline and 'green' tourism and countryside leisure activities are in increasing demand. Moreover, the Cévennes National Park is the only French national park in which there is a substantial resident human population, making it directly comparable with Scottish (and other UK) upland areas where the natural and the socio-cultural environments are intimately inter-related (see the discussion of protected landscapes in Chapter 5).

In certain respects French experience in sustainable rural tourism development is more advanced than in the UK, offering useful lessons. The management of change in the French countryside is heightened by the comparatively late urbanisation of the French population and the continuing higher ratio of rural to urban dwellers and there continue to be areas with severe problems, notably the remoter areas – the *communes du rural profond*.

In this context the French Regional Natural Park system is of considerable interest (*www.parcs-naturels-regionaux.tm.fr*). The slogan common to many of the French regional parks is 'Protection, Development and Welcome'. This philosophy is also embraced by the Cévennes National Park, which, while a *national* park, is the only one with a large resident population and it increasingly looks towards sustainable tourism development. Destination management integrating these three objectives is commendable, compared to the UK rural scene where each of these aims has often been promoted with inadequate regard for the other, often resulting in sectoral in-fighting. In the wider context, the Commission of the European Union (*europa.eu.int/comm/index.htm*) is committed to promoting rural tourism and regional development.

In 1993 the Federation of Nature and National Parks of Europe (*www.euro parc.org/international/europarc.html*) drew attention to the need for sustainable tourism in Europe's national parks and nature parks in the touchingly titled report, *Loving them to death?* (FNNPE, 1993). The Countryside Commission (1991) (*www.countryside.gov.uk*) initiated a debate on visitor management and tourist facilities in rural areas, highlighting the fact that traditional rural tourism/recreation has been largely resource-oriented to the neglect of visitor management, resulting in a less than satisfactory experience for the visitor, frequent adverse impacts on the local environment and host community, as well as lost opportunities for economic development through tourism.

CONCLUSIONS

These early initiatives provided a rationale and a context for destination management and for rural development generally, emphasising that 'sustainable' tourism is not solely 'green' tourism, but embraces socio-cultural and economic – as well as environmental – considerations.

The underpinning of destination management with a scientific base leads to identification of useful indicators for the monitoring of visitor impacts, biodiversity and other factors relevant to management of the destination. Studies of designated areas represent the 'sharp end' of sustainable tourism studies. Within a natural heritage area the objectives of natural and cultural resource conservation are of primary importance, yet, critically, must be integrated with the economic necessities of maintaining, or substituting for, local livelihoods. *Désertification* – the French term for loss of population through migration due to a decline in traditional employment opportunities – is a major political issue in the Cévennes, as in the wider region (Lozère). Significantly, there are 1,500 jobs in the parc and while population is decreasing elsewhere in the region, around the parc it is increasing. The contribution of the Cairngorms National Park to economic development in *its* region will be *one* measure of its success.

Bibliography

Ash Partnership and Cousins, Stephen (1992) *Development Opportunities in the Natural Environment*. Highland Regional Council. Inverness.

Commission of the European Communities (1990) Community action to promote rural tourism. October. CEC.

Countryside Commission (1991) *Visitors to the Countryside*. CC. Cheltenham.

Countryside Commission for Scotland (1990) *The Mountain Areas of Scotland: Conservation and Management*. CCS. Perth.

Darling, F.F. and Boyd, J.M. (1964) *The Highlands and Islands*. Collins New Naturalist. London.

Engberg, R. (ed.) (1984) *John Muir – Summering in the Sierra*. University of Wisconsin Press. Madison.

Engberg, R. and Wesling, D. (1986) *To Yosemite and Beyond*. University of Wisconsin Press. Madison.

English Tourist Board (1991) *Tourism and the Environment: Maintaining the Balance*. ETB. London.

Farming and Wildlife Advisory Group, Strathspey (1998) *NFUS Farmers Study Group – Cairngorms*. National Farmers Union Scotland.

Federation of Nature and National Parks of Europe (1993) *Loving them to death? The need for sustainable tourism in Europe's national parks and nature parks*. Sustainable Tourism Working Group. Grafenau.

Getz, D. (1986) Tourist-related population changes and their impacts in Badenoch-Strathspey, Scotland. *Tourism Management*, 3(4), 248–550

Hart, E.J. (1983) *The Making of Canadian Tourism*.

Highland Regional Council (1997) Economic Impact of Walking. HIE. Inverness.

Highlands and Islands Enterprise (1991) *A Strategy for Enterprise Development in the Highlands and Islands of Scotland*. HIE. Inverness.

Highland and Islands Enterprise (1992) *A Tourism Strategy for the Highlands and Islands. Consultation Paper*. HIE. Inverness.

Holden, A. (1988) *Cairngorms Partnership 1996*.

Howie, F. (1988) John Muir: Prophet of the Wilderness. *Heritage Interpretation*, 40 (4–5) and 41 (13–14).

Howie, F. (1996) Skills, Understanding and Knowledge for Sustainable Tourism, in Richards, G. (ed.) *Tourism in Central or Eastern Europe: Educating for Quality*. University of Tilbury. Tilbury, Netherlands.

Lew, A.A. (1987) *Tourist Attraction Research: Annals of Tourism Research*, 14 (4) 553–75.

McVean, D.N. and Lockie, J.D. (1969) *Ecology and Land Use in Upland Scotland*. Edinburgh University Press. Edinburgh.

Muir, J. (1901, 1981) *Our National Parks*. University of Wisconsin Press. Madison and London.

Murray, W.H. (1962) *Highland Landscape*. National Trust for Scotland. Edinburgh.

Parc National des Cévennes (1993) *Préparation du Programme d'Aménagement 1994–1998*. PNC. Florac.

Rural Development Commission (1992) *Tourism in the Countryside*. Policy Document. RDC. London.

Scottish Development Department (1990) *Scotland's Natural Heritage: The Way Ahead.* (Working together for sustainable development). SDD. Edinburgh.

Scottish Executive (2002) *Cairngorms National Park: Consultation on Draft Designation Order.* May. Scottish Executive. Edinburgh.

Scottish Natural Heritage (1992) *Enjoying the Outdoors: Consultation Paper in Access to the Countryside for Enjoyment and Understanding.* HMSO. Edinburgh.

Scottish Tourist Board (1992) *Tourism and the Scottish Environment: A Sustainable Partnership.* Scottish Tourism Co-ordinating Group. STB. Edinburgh.

Shackley, M. (1998) *Visitor Management: Case Studies from World Heritage Sites.* Butterworth-Heinemann. Oxford.

Stevenson, R.L. (reprint, 1989), *Travels with a Donkey in the Cévennes.* Chatto & Windus. London.

Tatras National Park (1993) *Tatras National Park Guide.* TNP. Zakopane, Poland.

Turnbull, R. (2002) Letters to the Editor, *The Scotsman*, 13 July.

Turner, R.K., Pearce, D. and Bateman, I. (1994) *Environmental Economics.* Wheatsheaf. London.

Whyte, I. and Whyte, K. (1987) *Exploring Scotland's Historic Landscapes.* John Donald Publishers Ltd. Edinburgh.

CHAPTER 11

Future destinations

Any predictions about the future are inevitably limited by a high degree of intelligent guesswork. 'Futures research' uses quasi-scientific means to provide a range of alternative scenarios, based largely on past trends that can be analysed and deductions drawn, but uncertainty prevails. The further ahead the predictions are made the higher the degree of uncertainty. Economic and political factors are strong determinants of future developments while these are intrinsically linked to social and environmental change.

At the global scale, urbanisation is likely to continue as populations migrate as a result of economic and political pressures and in response to environmental disasters such as desertification and other consequences of global warming. Wars will continue to place devastating pressures on many countries. An optimistic perspective assumes that increasing efforts will be made to tackle these global problems and the resulting human misery and that there will be no major setbacks to human progress such as catastrophes caused by asteroids striking the Earth or the outbreak of major wars. Even then, for the next few decades at least, tourism will remain an unattainable luxury for much of the world's population. Putting that aside, for the affluent countries tourism is likely to continue to grow as a major industry and as a preoccupation of their citizens.

EMERGING PRIORITIES IN DESTINATION DEVELOPMENT AND MANAGEMENT

Limiting or determining factors in tourism and in destination development have been widely discussed and Poon's 'new tourist' and the earlier predictions by Krippendorf and others of the characteristics of the 'turn of the century' tourist were addressed in Chapter 2. The motivations of this generation of tourist will influence the criteria determining the success of new destinations and sustainable development and management will be implicit in this. Lickorish (1991) offered a series of considerations for tourism developers:

- Is there a market?
- Is it viable economically?
- Is it socially compatible?

- Is it environmentally compatible?

All within a context of:

- means and motivations
- the changing consumer
- technological and other advances.

NEW DESTINATIONS

New destinations will emerge accordingly. They will be places to 'experience', rather than to visit passively, no less than a 'destination revolution' having occurred (*www.Locum-Destination.com*):

> A destination is worth leaving home for. Yesterday's destinations were buildings, cities and countries; tomorrow's successful destinations will be brands. In the past, tourism marketing was simply about 'somewhere to go'. Then tourism, leisure and cultural attractions began to offer visitors 'something to do'. Today's fierce competition for consumers' leisure spending is creating the destination as 'somewhere to experience'.

Locum Destinations argue that the leading 'destination makers' use strategies which merge retail, leisure, cultural and tourism interests – malls are given themes and theme parks incorporate retail outlets and accommodation – and for success the destination must be actively managed to encourage tourists/consumers to be active participants in creating their own experiences.

To many it seems crass to reduce a place and its totality of natural and cultural heritage to a 'brand', but this is the language of a particular discipline, marketing. How does that perspective relate to real-world examples? The case studies in this book give ideas; consider also the case of another emerging destination, China.

China was until recently closed to all but a few foreign tourists. As discussed in Chapter 5, changing political attitudes – although within the same political system – are progressively opening the country to tourism and it is predicted to be the world's top destination by the year 2020. Improvements in transport are likely to continue and this will be favourable for long-haul destinations, although perhaps constrained by environmental concern over the huge fuel consumption required. Unless this is accompanied by significant increases in fuel costs the nature of the contemporary consumer suggests there is not likely to be a drop in demand and improvements in efficiency of aircraft engines in the medium term may be a further factor. Again, for the affluent minority of the world's population who have leisure time and disposable income, tourism will continue to rank high in their list of priorities. Demographic trends support this. The future prospects favourable to tourism include:

- a wider awareness of the world through improved access to information and susceptibility to increasingly sophisticated promotional techniques
- greater interest in other cultures and genuine interest in knowing about host countries
- wider participation in further and higher education

- greater uptake of foreign language training

- a more peaceful world (at least in certain regions).

These factors will diminish the 'cultural distance' (McIntosh and Goeldner, 1990: 448) of previously remote destinations – i.e. they will 'seem closer'. Other social/cultural factors will continue to make travel more accessible than it was to previous generations:

- later marriage (and possibly lower divorce rates)

- smaller family size (giving more disposable income and earlier 'freedom' from childcare)

- earlier retirement (combined with good health) and increased longevity

- increased leisure time (although trends towards this predicted in the 1970s have failed to be realised)

- increasingly favourable cost of living to income ratios (more discretionary income to spend on 'non-essentials').

Alternatives to travel and tourism will also arise in this technologically enhanced, optimistic vision of the immediate future. Already for many, upgrading the 'in-home entertainment centre' takes precedence over the annual summer holiday some years; more dramatically, that same entertainment centre may soon be able to offer 'virtual reality' experiences that substitute for the 'real thing'. This has long been the realm of science fiction. The film *Total Recall* is based on a Philip K. Dick (1990) novel, *We Can Remember It for You Wholesale*, and envisages aspects of life in 2084 when it is possible to have vacations in the virtual destination of one's choice and with outcomes according to taste. When a man goes to the 'false memory transplant service' for an imaginary trip to Mars something goes wrong and memories of Mars and an unexpected and harrowing series of events force him to go the planet for real. An earlier novel, *The Feelies* (Farren, 1978), envisaged entire retirements lived in alternative realities of the customers' choices – albeit only 'in your head': 'Some time in the future [...] the ultimate goal has become to spend a lifetime in "The Feelies" – hooked up to sensory input machines, entombed in coffin-like structures, living out private fantasies manufactured to order'. Despite the alternative attractions that the near future will bring, it is clear that 'real' as opposed to 'virtual' travel retains its great appeal, although virtual 'samplers' may have a place, as may 'digital destinations', as discussed later in this chapter. One of the most spectacular examples of new incentives to travel – and new destinations – has already arrived with the long predicted dawn of space tourism.

Space tourism

Concorde, the supersonic passenger aircraft, dramatically reduced the times – if not the costs – of long haul travel in the 1970s, cutting flight times between London and New York to under three and a half hours, less than half the travelling time of a subsonic aircraft. Although grounded in 2001 after the first fatal crash the aircraft subsequently returned to transatlantic flights. This was hailed as a symbol of recovery of the airline industry generally after the 11 September 2001 atrocities, when the World Trade Centre 'Twin Towers' in New York were destroyed by terrorist activity (*www.worldtradecentre.com*), resulting in the international aviation industry being hit hard by the aftermath of the attacks which used four hijacked airliners (*www.news.airwise.com/stories*).

The general view has been that the next step would be suborbital flights just within the boundaries of space offering flights of less than one hour between, for example, New York and Tokyo. The subsequent step would be the dawn of true 'space tourism', taking passengers into Earth orbit and subsequently to the Moon and beyond:

> Space is the ultimate destination, a place beyond Earth where one can truly experience the vastness, beauty and true wonder of the universe. Through man's discovery of space, we can better understand ourselves, our potential for breaking all human barriers. As a space adventurer you will realize how small our planet is against the vastness of the universe (*www.spaceadventures.com*).

Space Adventures expect to make suborbital space flight possible by 2003–2005 by collaborating with independent corporations which are each developing their own version of a reusable launch vehicle (RLV). Space tourists on these suborbital flights will have to undergo a detailed four-day flight preparation and training programme. Then the rocket will be launched to beyond the normal limits of flight to regions above 62 miles (100 km), the beginning of 'space' as agreed by the Fédération Aéronautique Internationale (*www.fai.org*), a non-governmental and non-profit-making international organisation with the basic aim of furthering aeronautical and astronautical activities worldwide As the RLV nears maximum altitude, the rocket engines will be shut down and tourists 'will experience up to five minutes of continuous weightlessness and see the vast blackness of space set against the blue limits of Earth below'. To commemorate the space experience, tourists will be awarded Space Adventures astronaut wings and a lifetime membership in the Exeo-Atmosphere Club, an exclusive Space Adventures club for those who have experienced space flight first hand.

Demand for space tourism

In 2000, Patrick Collins of the company 'Spacefuture' (*www.spacefuture.com*) claimed that a report of the United States space agency NASA (*www.nasa.com*), 'General Public Space Travel and Tourism', which was not made available to the public, states that space tourism could start at any time and will become the largest business in space and that it gives a list of recommendations to help bring this about. He observed that 'NASA is required by law to help develop commercial space activities – yet it spends nothing on the activity which it has itself stated in print will be the largest business in space, while spending heavily on activities with no such potential'. He argued that passenger space travel will grow dramatically in the 21st century as aviation did in the 20th and that his research shows the idea is immensely popular, a majority of those surveyed wanting to take a trip into space and most of those saying they would pay several months' salary to do so. He argues further that given young people's longing for novelty and excitement the potential for marketing space travel services is great and that it is probable that passenger space travel will be immensely popular. Quantitatively, if just 10% of the rich countries' population were to take a single space flight at $20,000, this would represent a market of $2 trillion, yet more than 50% say they would like a flight and most say they would like to make several trips.

The 'next step' in space tourism actually occurred ahead of expectations and in advance of suborbital commercial flights when the Russian rocket *Soyuz* blasted off from central Asia shortly after 7.30am GMT on 28 April 2001 to dock with the International Space Station (ISS) the following day, carrying 'the world's first space tourist, Dennis Tito – straight into a row' (Stephen, 2001). NASA opposed the Russian plan to transport the American business consultant and former NASA engineer to the International Space Station, claiming the space amateur's presence might interfere with crucial work then being carried out by American astronauts on the ISS, although the head of Russia's RKK Energia space corporation disagreed. Denis Tito paid £13 million – equivalent to approximately one-seventh of the annual Russian space budget – to take part in the week-long mission and to realise his dream of more than 40 years and, at 61, became the oldest person to go into space. Ordinary Russians were delighted at the prospect that their nation, which had launched the first man, the first woman and the first dog into space, was launching the first tourist. NASA, which is an equal partner with Russia in the International Space Station but pays the greater part of costs, did not share this enthusiasm and was backed by the European Space Agency. They argued that tourists should not be allowed onto a station still under construction, while the Russians responded that after many hours of training Mr Tito was virtually a qualified cosmonaut, had passed every medical required, had promised not to touch any of the equipment and signed an agreement with NASA that he would pay for any breakages.

The first tourist into space returned safely to Earth.

In September 2001 it was reported that 'Travellers will be able to get to any point on Earth in two hours, if competing US and British studies of ultra high-speed, 5000 mph flight prove successful' (Hawkins, 2001, *www.spacefuture.com*). With similar programmes being pursued in Russia, the race for hypersonic flight – travel at over Mach 5, or five times the speed of sound – is underway. Concorde, currently the fastest passenger aircraft flying, travels at around Mach 2. This could pave the way for aircraft capable of travelling between London and New York in 40 minutes. NASA's real aim is, however, 'to make space travel cheap and safe enough for ordinary consumers and to bring down the cost of space flight for business from today's costs of $10,000 per pound for payload to be put into space to $100', so transforming the current market for satellite launches and tele-communications. Cheap space flight could be a reality in 25 years and hypersonic airliners could come even quicker (Hawkins, 2001).

It is likely that the International Space Station (*spaceflight.nasa.gov/station/index*) will now receive serious consideration as a tourism destination, given the commercial possibilities – albeit very much secondary to its scientific and other uses. This will pave the way for trips beyond the Earth – to the Moon initially, then to Mars – by professional astronauts followed eventually by tourists. Humanity will have become a 'spacefaring species' (Clarke, 1999) and the historical pattern will repeat: on Earth, travel to far-off lands was initially for conquest, for plunder, for trade and then for tourism; the same will happen in space – except 'tourism' may not be last in line.

EMERGING THEMES IN DESTINATION MANAGEMENT

Health and safety in the destination

Tourism grew rapidly in the second half of the 20th century and the trend continues into the 21st. It has been long accepted that tourism is capable of adding greatly to a country's or a region's wealth but the recognition that it is also capable of creating significant problems is more recent. The three broad categories of impacts are economic, socio-cultural and environmental, while tourism is also influenced by political circumstances and by health and safety considerations. The industry can be a causal agent of health problems in a destination (where tourists introduce 'exotic' diseases); conversely, its development can be limited by health and safety considerations. This is a further example of the need for contemporary tourism to be planned and developed with regard to a wide range of new considerations (see Figure 11.1).

Figure 11.1 *Travel and aspects of tourist health and safety*

Increasing travel + Growth of long haul tourism → **New destinations/New issues**

Unfamiliar environments

Cultural clashes

Political instability/terrorism

Poverty/envy/conspicuous wealth

'Irritation' (as discussed in Chapter 2)

More 'open' and less inhibited behaviour/sexual freedom

Disease

  Air- and water-borne infections:
    New bacteria, viruses, parasites
    Lower hygiene/sanitation standards

Crime/muggings

→ **New health and safety concerns** → **New tourism guidelines**

Health factors in destinations

Awareness of the medical arrangements available in a destination prior to a visit is a part of the normal considerations in holiday planning, although it has not been regarded as part of the mainstream concerns of destination professionals. Within the European Union, for example, reciprocal arrangements are available to a citizen of a member country within any other EU country. Advice on advisable immunisation prior to a visit to specific destinations has long been readily available through health centres and chemists, now including information on special and/or rare diseases such as AIDS/HIV. The risks from 'sun-sea-sand'-oriented activities are increasingly widely known – excessive exposure to the sun runs the risks of skin cancer and premature aging, while the risks from bathing in polluted seas have led many responsible authorities to clean their beaches and improve their sewage treatment facilities and to seek the status of 'Blue Flag' beach as a desirable 'selling point' of the destination (*www.seasideawards.org.uk*, see Chapter 8).

With the growth in popularity of adventure tourism more tourists are travelling to destinations where health standards are lower and the risk of falling ill is considerably higher than in their home countries. As long as many destinations have a major challenge in achieving reasonable standards of healthcare for their own populations, the onus is on the traveller to ensure adequate precautions against ill health prior to arrival in the destination.

On the positive side, health tourism is a distinctive tourism 'type'. Its origins lie in the dawn of tourism itself where 'health reasons' was a more acceptable reason for a holiday in an era when 'leisure' or 'doing nothing' was frowned on. It is now experiencing a revival that parallels a contemporary interest in diet, exercise and healthy, more natural lifestyles. Examples of health-oriented destinations are spa towns, places specialising in activity holidays and coastal resorts where sea bathing was once popular and which are now experiencing a revival as centres for 'thalassotherapy', notably in France. This is actually the reemergence of a historical motivation (*www.spamanagement.com*): for two centuries 'taking the waters' has been considered a revitalising treatment and for a long time the French healthcare system has covered expenses related to physical therapy in thalassotherapy centres, 50 or so along the Atlantic and Mediterranean coasts. Britanny and the Vendée are notable centres. Natural iodine, sea mineral salts, sea mud and seaweed are considered to be the contributors to health and well-being, while at a typical modern thalassotherapy centre, rather than bathing in the open sea, the sea is brought indoors where it is cleaned and slightly warmed and is free from excessive waves.

Medical/healthcare tourism

Medical/healthcare tourism – perhaps more akin to business tourism rather than leisure tourism – is also emerging within the European Union where, with the removal of political and trade barriers, patients may be flown from one country to another where they can be treated more cheaply, fare included. In Britain, certain private health insurers have offered this option of treatment while the government may allow the National Health Service to embrace the practice.

The existence of the International Society for Travel Medicine (*www.istm.org*), based in the USA, suggests the scale of the field in its many forms. The ISTM, with 1,200 members in 53 countries, is the largest organisation of professionals dedicated to the advancement of the specialty of travel medicine. It is committed to the promotion of healthy and safe travel in cooperation with national and international healthcare providers, academic centres, the travel industry and the media.

Safety factors in destinations

A clash of values and cultures may arise out of envy of a tourist's assumed wealth and lifestyle (see Doxey's 'Irridex' in Chapter 2). Conspicuously carried cameras or jewellery may represent a month's or a year's wages to a local. Concealing such items might be more realistic advice than advising the contemporary tourist to avoid certain 'seedy areas' for fear of 'muggings', since these may be the 'areas of local character' in the destination the tourist wants to experience. Since increasing numbers of tourists are seeking new destinations the incidence of such value clashes is likely to grow, some leading to violence. An 'enclave' approach to destination development (see Chapter 3) may be adopted in some places – separating tourists and locals – although this will not to appeal to the more 'allocentric' tourists. Ideally, the envy that can lead to violence against the tourist will decline as the increasing economic contribution of tourism enables disparities in wealth to be reduced, although clearly this would take time, even given destination development policies that embraced an active commitment to tackling social exclusion (see the Edinburgh case study in Chapter 6).

Inadequate attention to tourist safety affects tourists directly while media coverage of unpleasant experiences has an indirect and highly adverse impact on the destination generally, diminishing its reputation and image. In the 1990s certain US cities acquired a reputation as unsafe destinations due to a spate of widely reported personal attacks or 'muggings' of tourists. The media referred to a 'league table' of dangerous places for tourists (including New Orleans, Miami and Los Angeles) and this had a significant impact on visitor numbers. The 'league table' cities subsequently collaborated on their shared problem, one of the outcomes being more 'tourist police'. At the same time certain other international city destinations took advantage of the opportunity and proclaimed themselves 'safe cities'/'friendly cities'/'walkable cities'.

An extension of normal customer care to tackle some of these issues might need no more than a 'familiarisation' talk by a local representative of the travel companies in the destination or a short video en route on the aircraft/coach/boat. This might give sufficient prompts to the tourist to adjust certain behaviour patterns and so avoid causing unintended 'irritation' (Doxey's Irritation Index'). More radically, it may be reasonable to suggest that local people might also benefit from a greater appreciation of the true contribution of the tourist to their destination – informative talks given by tourism or destination staff in schools, community centres, shopping areas or other convenient places go a long way in improving 'tourist-host' relations.

Safety issues can have a long-term impact on destinations. Terrorism can destroy the tourism industry of a destination or dramatically reduce visitor numbers for a period of years. Examples of countries that have suffered from terrorism are Egypt, Peru and Northern Ireland. Two distinct types are recognised. Egypt and Peru's experience has been attacks unambiguously targeted on tourists. By damaging the tourist industry, a major contributor to the national economy, the perpetrators considered the ruling regime could be toppled. The second type, as in Northern Ireland, 'indirectly' damages tourism – commercial, government, military and police establishments and operations are the target – tourism is 'incidentally' damaged as tourists are unwilling to visit what they perceive as a 'war zone'.

Advice on countries and regions which are considered unsafe as destinations at a given time is available from the UK Foreign and Commonwealth Office (FCO) (*www.fco.gov.uk*):

> The FCO's country-specific Travel Advice notices aim to ensure that British travellers are well prepared before their departure. Select the country you are travelling to from the drop-down menu. If a particular country is not included in the list of Travel Advice notices this is because the FCO has no information on the country at the present time.

Advice is given on the precautions to exercise on visiting certain destinations and the inadvisability of visiting others destinations due to civil unrest, war etc.

Obviously, from the point of view of the tourism organisation of a destination, a listing here as 'inadvisable' is a serious blow to business.

There is a minority market for tourists who want to visit 'live' war zones – perhaps an extreme form of adventure tourism. Practical barriers – as opposed to moral questions that might be raised – focus on the difficulty of agreeing an 'acceptable' level of risk, critical to insurance issues. Related to this is the duration of the 'recovery period' of a former destination after a war ends. Obviously tourist (and other) infrastructure may be damaged or destroyed, but the major issue is one of safety – both actual and as perceived – as well as the 'sensitivity' of visiting such an area 'too soon'. Contrariwise, regenerating tourism may be a key element in the economic recovery of a war-damaged former destination.

DARK TOURISM

'Dark tourism' is a term coined by Lennon and Foley (2000) for tourism motivated by a desire to visit places associated with death and catastrophe such as famous assassination sites, for example that of President Kennedy in Dallas, Texas, or concentration camps and Holocaust memorials. As Reader (2001: *www.cult-media.com/issue2/Rreadee.htm*) notes, 'the process is often fraught with problems as governments and other agencies wrestle with the dilemma of how to depict and manage the often contentious past' (see the discussion of interpretation in Chapter 5). Visits to the sites of recent tragedies – for example the site of the World Trade Center/'Twin Towers' in New York destroyed by terrorist attack on '9/11' in 2001 (*www.worldtradecenter.com*) – raise issues of both genuine compassion and morbid fascination. Visits to World War II concentration/extermination camps are 'accepted' elements of tourism packages to Poland with controversy as regards the solemnity of such 'pilgrimages' (*motlc.wiesenthal.com/pages/t071/t07176.html*). In contrast, tourism development at locations of 'historically distant' past massacres or murders is generally considered acceptable and proper. Walking tours in Edinburgh, London and other 'historic cities on 'murder and mystery' themes are popular examples (*www.witcherytours.com; www.murder.com*).

In matters of tourist health and safety all sectors of the industry – accommodation providers, transport operators, the attractions sector and tourist boards and destination managers – have a part to play. Tourism professionals can offer advice on the development of 'new' destinations, for example the 'type' of development appropriate to both the destination and the target markets (as discussed in Chapter 3), considering the advisability of intermixing/integrating tourists and residents; or segregating them into 'enclaves'). They can also review the information available on risks to health and safety and incorporate this into brochures alongside 'traditional' tourist information. They can set up consortia to consider collective responses to destination image problems as exemplified by US cities in response to the widely reported 'muggings' of tourists in the 1990s – a more constructive and ethical approach than withholding information on the dangers/risks of a destination.

Tourists themselves have (or should have?) an obligation to observe codes of behaviour and be aware of cultural norms in the destination they are visiting. Behavioural change *does* take place on holiday. For example some people will take part in sex activities they would not try at home – they feel more 'liberated' away from the real or imagined constraints and norms of home. This may result in reluctance to adhere to destination codes of behaviour, even mild examples such as a 'no-go' area which tourists are *requested* not to enter since it is there to respect residents' right to privacy (*www.gocambodia.com/culture/behaviour_code.asp*).

Extreme reaction against tourists' behaviour may result in a call for alternative patterns of development in a destination. Sex tourism which exists alongside the 'mainstream' industry in various countries has been criticised by certain western religious groups and others such as Tourism Concern (*www.tourismconcern.org.uk*) on moral and human rights grounds and the continuing failure to control the spread of AIDS/HIV has heightened concern over health and safety issues. Finding an economically viable alternative to sex tourism – a significant aspect of the portfolio of certain destinations – raises international aid questions, while others question whether sex tourism is intrinsically a 'bad thing', arguing for better regulation and management as the way forward.

Exercise

Sex tourism

Is sex tourism a 'good' or a 'bad' thing? Research this topic, review the arguments for and against it and, for a destination of your choice, argue the case for its (responsible) development or for banning it.

COMMUNICATION AND INFORMATION TECHNOLOGY

'Computers' have taken centre stage in many people's perceptions of the modern world. Computers are 'changing the world' – for better or for worse – according to the individual's own perspective. Poon (1993) rightly places computers, or more accurately 'the microelectronics revolution', in context – 'computers', or 'new technology' or 'ICT' (information and communications technology), is one of several fundamental 'global imperatives'. This is not to downgrade its importance, rather to place it in the context of other major influences shaping 'tomorrow's world', specifically the tourism industry. These are: the environmental limits to growth; the birth of a new paradigm for tourism (a 'radical transformation of the prevailing common sense for the best productivity and most profitable practice at a given time'); and the microelectronics revolution.

Contrasting with the environmental limits to growth 'microelectronics can enhance the growth potential of the travel and tourism industry'. 'Microchips' are present in almost every modern device – they are even implanted under the skin of pets as identity tags. 'Microelectronics not only leads to the emergence of a new range of products, services, systems and industries in its own right, but affects directly or indirectly almost every other branch of the economy' (Freeman and Perez, 1988 in Poon, 1993).

DESTINATION INFORMATION

One of the ways potential tourists become actual tourists in a specific destination is through marketing. As discussed elsewhere in this book (see Chapter 3) people have images of places they would like to visit in their 'mind's eye', formed passively from conversations with friends or through the press and television or films, but purposeful marketing is a most powerful persuasive tool. The internet 'is an almost pure manifestation of marketing principles and practices ... (a) it levels playing fields, (b) it enables companies of different sizes to compete on more equal terms, and (c) it allows a company to open up a direct channel of communication with its customers (also) [...] the success of an Internet site is not always directly proportional to the amount of money spent on it' (Inkpen (1998). A limitation has been its disproportionate use by better off and younger potential customers but use is likely to widen, particularly as 'technologies converge' and the domestic television – located right at the centre of many homes – is able to offer full internet access. Booking can take place directly by means of e-mail and electronic payment (i.e. simply giving the number and type of the user's credit card). This *disintermediation* could mean the end of the 'traditional' travel agent who has been the intermediary between the customer and the travel (and often the accommodation) supplier, replaced by the global distribution system (GDS), linked by computers.

As well as travel to and from destinations, information *about* destinations has also been obtained through intermediaries, tourist offices – 'destination service organisations' – located in overseas 'tourist generating' countries funded by the national tourism organisations of the destination countries. Again, disintermediation may occur as potential tourists can communicate directly with the national tourism organisation of the country they are interested in by visiting their website.

It remains to be seen whether internet booking will fully replace the 'human touch'. Some will continue to prefer dealing with a person directly, especially in the expanding areas of special interest tourism where highly customised packages may be required, although it may become confined to 'up-market' customers willing to pay the necessarily higher prices. Meantime *www.travelocity.co.uk*, established in 1995 and *www.expedia.co.uk* in 1996 are early examples of what is available. Inkpen (1998) refers to these as 'new intermediaries' in that they offer a full range of travel and related services directly to the customer and – notably – not all these are provided by the site's main sponsor; in effect they are 'an electronic travel agent offering a wide range of travel services and travel-related information'. The increasing availability of 'broadband' connections which can be ten times faster than a standard 56.6k modem – 'internet in the fast lane' – will permit video to become a normal component of websites, greatly enhancing their content ... and selling power.

CASE STUDY

The very near future – a traveller's tale...

En route to the destination – interpretation in the sky:

> Excuse me sir, would you mind closing your blind – the other passengers are complaining you're disturbing their enjoyment of the in-flight movie....

My first reaction – tell them to get a life! We're at 30,000 feet, I'm enjoying the view, experiencing an ancient dream of humanity, yet all you think they want to do is stare at a movie! I struggle with my jacket over my head, allowing me to see out of the window, but finally give up, lower the blind, slump low in my seat and squint through a one-inch slot at the base of the window at the glorious ever-changing view. That 'pale blue dot' of Carl Sagan, the Earth, is spread out beneath us – and all they want to do is watch a movie – a movie they've probably seen a dozen times before.

Are airlines underestimating/insulting the 'new tourist' seeking REAL tourism – tourism that is Rewarding, Enriching, Adventuresome and a Learning experience – at *every* stage of the journey – including the flight?

An alternative view: let's not make assumptions about today's tourists – they just want to get the flight over and done with and get on with their holiday. Give them a movie – whatever you do don't remind them they're 30,000 feet up – give them something to take their minds off it.

The near future – in flight to a 'dream destination': interpretation is about first-hand experiences and here's the ultimate trip!

A video camera – a livecam – is giving real-time images of the view beneath us *right now*, on the small screen mounted on the rear of the seat in front. Other livecams are pointing forward, to the left and to the right and these images are available as inserts into the main screen. They give a view even better than the view out of the window, although those lucky enough to have window seats can have the best of both worlds.

There is a live audio *interpretation* of what the cameras are revealing, helping you to see and understand more. You can select an audio interpretation themed to your language and personal interests, e.g. natural history, geography, environmental issues – evidence of global warming, deforestation, marine pollution, rising sea levels, business opportunities – oil exploration etc., wonders of the world ... the sky is the limit!

When the viewing conditions are poor, recordings are shown taken under ideal conditions on a directly comparable flight. You're not seeing this live but what you see on the video *is* what's below you right now!

If you want the 'executive' view, you can select 'another channel' and rent a joystick to plug into the port beside the video screen allowing you to control additional cameras mounted on the plane putting you in charge of the camera – or cameras. You can be your own director/producer and can even record your movie and add your own soundtrack from an audio menu expressing what you're seeing, thinking, feeling ... at this moment.

If you like, the editing can be done for you – or you can do it. Soundtracks of your choice are available. Your basic video can be collected as you collect your luggage, the executive version 'may take a little longer . . . .

The technology necessary to support the basic form of this concept is already available. 'Vport: the future of in-journey entertainment' was launched by Virgin in May 2002, using flatscreen technology and videostreaming 'originally with 20 movies and a couple of hundred hours of TV programming. All the content is digitised, the viewer can "pause" the film they are watching, rewind a section, or fast forward through the dull bits'

(Anon., *Scotland on Sunday*, 19 May 2002).

DIGITAL DESTINATIONS – WHY NOT?

It is now possible to replace real actors in films with digital creations indistinguishable from the 'real thing'. If such 'synthespians' can be accepted, then why not 'syndestinations'?

The film *Total Recall* referred to the 'tourist' of the mid-21st century who could opt for a 'virtual vacation' rather than the 'real thing' according to how pressed for time he/she was or how much money they wanted to spend. Virtual reality in the early 21st century has not yet achieved that level of sophistication but it is not unreasonable to expect that it will. Already, however, 'digital destinations' exist in one form: it is readily possible to create still photographs which portray real places, although they have been 'manipulated' using digital technology to create an 'enhanced reality' – or a 'misrepresentation' – according to the viewer's reaction to that 'digital destination' (*www.digitaldestinations.co.uk*).

In an age of innocence and mass tourism, caricature and misrepresentation were the norm in tourism promotional photography. Scotland, for example, was identified by bagpipes/tartan/haggis and Hollywood's *Brigadoon*, a romantic village briefly emerging from the mists of time every century or so (Internet Movie Database – *www.imdb.com*). The tourism industry capitalised on the strong imagery but augmented it in promotional brochures and picture postcards with photographs of sun-kissed beaches and endless blue skies, regardless of climate statistics, in an attempt to compete with the booming '3S' destinations of Spain.

The contemporary phase of tourism takes 'authenticity' as the guideline in criticising cultural stereotyping as well as recognising that today's more experienced travellers are more 'litigation' ready if false expectations have been created of their chosen destination. Recent and current Scottish tourism promotional literature thus shows ample amounts of grey or 'atmospheric' skies and landscapes, while tartan and kilts have faded into the background. Even the evocative marketing slogan, 'Europe's last wilderness' is increasingly recognised as a misnomer for the beautiful, but ecologically and culturally impoverished Highland landscapes. Tourism has not suffered as a result of this more recent emphasis on 'reality'.

This phase may be ending as attention focuses on the *experiential* nature of tourism. Tourists seek places where activities can give rise to experiences. These experiences are influenced by the 'organic' and 'induced' images and other cultural baggage tourists carry with them and hence are influenced by both the tangible resources of the destination and the intangible attributes it offers to those receptive enough to it. Intangible attributes have long been recognised in 'literature about travel' as opposed to 'travel guides'. The latter have concentrated on the what, where and when; travel literature has placed emphasis on the spirit of place – the *genius loci*, very much influenced by the cultural lens through which the traveller 'views' the chosen destination. This 'lens' encourages tourists to interpret and consume tourism products beyond the purely visual experiences.

In this context, there can be no 'authentic' – in the sense of 'definitive' – portrayal of a destination (as discussed in Chapter 8). The conclusion arising out of this is that photographic and other imagery employed in tourism promotion need not be confined to 'truth', in the sense of the 'freedom from lies' once associated with photography itself and recently held to be obligatory. Digital imaging techniques offer 'controls' – and 'freedoms' – that can legitimately introduce potential tourists to the 'hyperrealities' of destinations that may correspond more closely to the experiences of the postmodern tourist.

Such *Photoshop Realities* are the cultural constructs of the contemporary travel photographer. While authenticity has become a benchmark for quality in recent tourism experience the arrival of digital imaging presents a challenge to what is meant and understood by authenticity.

Exercise

Consider your own reaction to the following scenarios:

1. Tourism promotion organisations must be careful not to misrepresent the rural tourism product by carefully selecting words and pictures that present a 'romantic gaze' (Urry, 2001) bearing little relation to reality. In much promotion of the British countryside, for example, 'nowhere is there the increasingly common sprawl of ribbon development, the clutter of signs, electricity pylons and telegraph wires, the bungalows on the hilltops, the roundabouts and the bypasses around the villages. Any sign of urbanisation of the countryside is simply carefully edited out' (Sharpley and Sharpley, 1997).

2. 'Many people are anxious when they're about to be photographed ... they fear the camera's disapproval. [...] they feel rebuked when the camera doesn't return an image of themselves as more attractive than they are.' But few are lucky enough to be 'photogenic', that is, to look better in photographs (even when not made up or flattered by the lighting) than in real life. 'The news that the camera could lie made getting photographed much more popular' (Sontag, 1978: 85–6). Relating this to places: 'Photographically, I don't believe the world is meant to be taken at face value. Unless you are a photojournalist, there is no reason not to use the world as raw material to make interpretive images that convey your personal reactions to a place' (Dennis, 1989: 133).

The role of destination managers and developers in the challenging and exciting world of the near future will be no less challenging than that of their colleagues who worked in the pioneering era of tourism in the 20th century.

Photograph 11.1a & 11.1b *No need for digital manipulation – just a change of viewpoint: Mont Saint Michel with and without cars*

Bibliography

Anonymous (2002) In-flight technology. *Scotland on Sunday*, 19 May.

Clarke, Arthur C. (1975) *Rendezvous with Rama*. Victor Gollancz. London.

Dennis, L. (1989) *The Essential Image: Techniques for Composing Successful Photographs*. Amphoto. New York.

Dick, P.K. (1993) *The Collected Stories of Philip K. Dick, Volume 2: We Can Remember It for You Wholesale*. Citadel Press. London.

Farren, M. (1978) *The Feelies*. Big O Publishing. London.

Inkpen, G. (1998) *Information Technology for Travel and Tourism* (2nd edn). Longman. London.

Lennon, J. and Foley, M. (2000) *Dark Tourism: the Attractions of Death and Disaster*. Continuum: London and New York.

Lickorish, J.L. (1991) Trends in tourism in Lickorish, J.L. *Developing Tourism Destinations*. Longman. Harlow.

McIntosh, R.W. and Goeldner, C.R. (1990) *Tourism: Principles and Philosophies*. John Wiley and Sons. Chichester,

Poon, A. (1993) *Tourism, Technology and Competitive Strategies*. CAB International. Oxford.

Sharpley, R. and Sharpley J. (1997) *Rural Tourism*. Routledge. London.

Sontag, S. (1978) *On Photography*. Penguin Books Ltd. Harmondsworth.

Stephen, C. (2001) *The Scotsman*, 2 April.

Urry, J. (2001) *The Tourist Gaze: Leisure and Travel in Contemporary Societies*. Sage Publications. London.

Verhowe'en, P. (director) (1990) *Total Recall*. USA.

INDEX